THE ARCHAEOLOGY
OF DEATH AND BURIAL

Mike Parker Pearson

SUTTON PUBLISHING

First published in 1999 by
Sutton Publishing Limited · Phoenix Mill
Thrupp · Stroud · Gloucestershire · GL5 2BU

Reprinted in 1999, 2000, 2001

British Library Cataloguing in Publication Data
A catalogue record for this book is available from the British Library

ISBN 0-7509-1777-6

Typeset in 10/12.5pt Sabon.
Typesetting and origination by
Sutton Publishing Limited.
Printed in Great Britain by
J.H. Haynes & Co. Ltd, Sparkford.

CONTENTS

LIST OF FIGURES

ACKNOWLEDGEMENTS

During the last decade I have learned much from colleagues and students in the Department of Archaeology and Prehistory at the University of Sheffield, especially from teaching undergraduate and Masters courses in funerary archaeology. Special thanks go above all to Andrew Chamberlain and also to Keith Branigan, Robin Dennell, Sarah Fowle, Rupert Harding, Ian Hodder, Paul Nicholson, Ellen Pader, Niall Sharples, Tim Taylor, and Roland Wessling. Karen Godden read and edited all the drafts.

Alex Norman drew Figures 1.1 (after McKinley 1997), 1.2 (after Jørgensen 1975, Champion *et al.* 1984, Whimster 1981, Girič 1971, Tasič 1972, Wesler 1997), 1.6 (after Woolley 1934), 3.3 (after Deetz and Dethlefsen 1967), 3.7 (after Rudenko 1970), 3.10 (after Rudenko 1970), 4.1 (after Shennan 1975), 4.2 (after Biel 1986), 4.3 (after Randsborg 1974), 4.5 (after Peebles and Kus 1977), 4.6 (after Steponaitis 1983 and Knight and Steponaitis 1998), 5.1 (after Joffroy 1954), 5.3 (after Thorsen 1980), 5.4 (after Randsborg 1984), 5.5 (after Rega 1997), 5.6 (after Binford 1972), 5.7 (after Green and Rollo-Smith 1984), 5.10 (after Higham and Bannanurag 1990), 5.11 (after Salamon and Lengyel 1980), 6.5 (after Renfrew 1976), 6.6 (after Renfrew 1973a and Hughes 1988), 6.7 (after Tilley 1993), 7.1 (after McCown 1937), 7.3 (after Klima 1987), 7.4 (after Arsuaga *et al.* 1997), 7.5 (after White 1992) and 7.8 (after Mellaart 1970). Figures 1.3, 1.4, 2.1, 2.2, 2.3, 2.4, 2.5, 3.1, 3.2, 7.9, 8.4, 9.1 and 9.2 were photographed by myself. Figures 6.1, 6.2 and 6.3 were drawn by myself and reproduced with permission of *Cambridge Archaeological Journal*. Figures 1.5 and 3.4 Stuart Piggott; by permission of HMSO. Figure 2.6 Mr Williams of Williams & Son, Cambridge. Figure 3.5 by permission of the British Museum. Figure 3.6 by permission of the Griffith Institute at the Ashmolean Museum. Figures 3.8 and 3.9 by permission of Orion Publishing Group. Figure 3.11 by permission of Moesgård Museum. Figure 4.4 by permission of Faber. Figure 5.2 by permission of *Acta Archaeologica* (Copenhagen) and Klavs Randsborg. Figures 5.8 and 5.9 by permission of *Analecta Praehistoria Leidensia* and Leendert Loouwe Kooijmans. Figure 6.4 Keith Branigan. Figure 7.2 by permission of the British Academy. Figures 7.6 and 7.7 by permission of the Palestine Exploration Fund and the Institute of Archaeology, University of London. Figure 8.1 Olivia Forge; supplied by Pete Stone. Figure 8.2 Michael Blakey and Mark Mack. Figure 10.1 Mark Brennand. Figure 10.2 Archaeological Research Consultancy University of Sheffield. John Owen of the Department of Geography, University of Sheffield, rephotographed Figures 1.5, 3.4, 3.5, 3.8, 3.9, 4.4, 5.2, 7.2, 7.6 and 7.7.

Permissions for quotations were given by: Macmillan, *Antiquity*, Lynne Goldstein, the *New Yorker*, Oxford University Press, Jonathan Cape, *World Archaeology*, and Cambridge University Press.

ONE

Learning from the Dead

Somewhere along the banks of the River Volga in Russia there is a large earthen mound underneath which are the burnt remains of a cremation funeral conducted over a thousand years ago. Although this mound has never been identified, we know of its existence thanks to a startling account of how it came to be built. We might question the reliability of aspects of this ancient story but it illustrates something of the richness and extraordinariness of those lived experiences which normally survive for archaeologists only as decayed bones, scraps and soil. Out of these unpromising materials we attempt to recover lost lives from the distant past.

The funeral of a Viking

Between AD 921 and 922 Ibn Fadlan was secretary of an embassy from the Kalif of Baghdad to the people of the middle Volga.[1] At the trading post of Bulgar he met people known as the Rus – Scandinavian merchants and military venturers living in Russia – and wrote a remarkable account of the funeral of one of their 'outstanding men'. The mourners placed the corpse in a wooden chamber for ten days while they cut and sewed garments for him. The man's wealth was divided into three: one part for his daughters and wives; one for garments to clothe the corpse; and the third for making *nabid*, an intoxicating drink, which the mourners consumed over the ten days in an orgy of drunkenness and sexual activity. His slave girls were asked who wished to die with him; one volunteered to be burned with him. '[I]n these ten days [she] drinks and indulges in pleasure; she decks her head and her person with all sorts of ornaments and fine dress and so arrayed gives herself to the men.'

On the day of the cremation, Ibn Fadlan went down to the river and saw that the man's longship had been brought ashore and placed on a scaffold supported by four wooden posts. A wooden canopy was put up in the middle of the ship and decked with fabrics. In the ship an old woman, called the Angel of Death, covered a couch with a mattress of Greek brocade. '[I]t is she who has charge of the clothes-making and arranging all things, and it is she who kills the girl slave. I saw that she was a strapping old woman, fat and louring.' The man's corpse was taken out of its temporary grave; it did not smell bad but 'had grown black from the cold of the country'. He was still wearing the clothes in which he had died and in the grave had been placed *nabid*, fruit and a pandora (a stringed musical instrument) which were all removed.

The corpse was reclothed in trousers, stockings, boots, a tunic, a kaftan of brocade with gold buttons, and a hat of brocade and fur. He was seated on the mattress and propped up with cushions, surrounded by *nabid*, fruit and fragrant plants; bread, meat and onions were placed before him. Many people gathered around, playing musical instruments. The dead man's kinsmen erected tents at a distance from the ship. The girl slave went to these tents to have sexual intercourse with each of the kinsmen, who announced in a loud voice, 'Tell your master that I have done the duty of love and friendship.' Animals were sacrificed and placed in the ship: a dog was cut in two, two horses were hacked into pieces with a sword, two cows were similarly cut up and a rooster and a hen were also killed and thrown in. The decapitated rooster was thrown, head and body, to the right and left of the ship. The man's weapons were placed by his side.

On the final afternoon the slave girl was led to a structure resembling a door frame. Standing on the palms of the men, she was lifted three times to overlook the frame. Ibn Fadlan asked the interpreter what she had said when looking over the frame. The first time she said 'Behold, I see my father and mother'; the second time 'I see all my dead relatives seated'; the third time 'I see my master seated in Paradise and Paradise is green; with him are men and boy servants. He calls me. Take me to him.' A hen was brought and she cut off the head, which she threw away while its body was put in the ship. She was then taken to the ship where she took off her two bracelets and gave them to the Angel of Death, and took off her two finger-rings and gave them to the Angel of Death's two daughters who had been waiting on her for the last ten days.

> Then men came with shields and sticks. She was given a cup of *nabid*; she sang at taking it and drank. The interpreter told me that she in this fashion bade farewell to all her girl companions. Then she was given another cup; she took it and sang for a long time while the old woman incited her to drink up and go into the pavilion where her master lay . . . [T]he old woman seized her head and made her enter the pavilion and entered with her. Thereupon the men began to strike with the sticks on the shields so that her cries could not be heard and the other slave-girls would not be frightened and seek to escape death with their masters. Then six men went into the pavilion and had intercourse with the girl. Then they laid her at the side of her master; two held her feet and two her hands; the old woman known as the Angel of Death re-entered and looped a cord around her neck and gave the crossed ends to the two men for them to pull. Then she approached her with a broad-bladed dagger, which she plunged between her ribs repeatedly, and the men strangled her with the cord until she was dead.

The closest relative of the dead man then took a piece of wood, lit it and, completely naked, walked backwards towards the boat, facing the crowd, holding the stick in one hand and using his other hand to cover his anus. The people each took a piece of tinder or firewood for him to light, which he then placed in the wood pile beneath the ship. The flames grew and engulfed the pyre and the ship. One of the Rus turned to the interpreter and said 'You Arabs are fools . . . You take the people who are most dear to you and you put them in the ground where insects and worms devour them. We burn him in a moment so that he enters paradise at once.'

> [A]n hour had not passed before the ship, the wood, the girl, and her master were nothing but cinders and ashes. Then they constructed in the place where had been the ship which they had drawn up out of the river something like a small round hill, in the middle of which they erected a great post of birch wood, on which they wrote the name of the man and the name of the Rus king and they departed.

One day we may be able to locate the actual mound and compare its contents with Ibn Fadlan's account. From the archaeologists' point of view it is a great shame that the ship was burnt. Had the ship been buried under the mound rather than incinerated, we might have a treasure house of information which could tell us much to complement the story and add to what was known by Ibn Fadlan. We would be able to study the construction of the boat, the life histories and possibly the genetic ancestries of the man and the slave, the full range, character and origin of the non-perishable grave goods, the local environment of the funeral and the quality of the sacrificed animals. Even with the cremated remains, a certain amount could be learned from the burnt bones and surviving artefacts, such as the age and sex of the deceased, the use of a boat and the provision in the ship of certain things such as the man's weapons. There are aspects of role and activity which the archaeological remains will never shed light upon, such as the part played by the Angel of Death or the size and duration of the funeral ceremonies.

HUMAN REMAINS: THE ARCHAEOLOGY OF DEATH OR THE ARCHAEOLOGY OF LIFE?

It is a strange paradox that the physical remains of the dead – the bones and any surviving tissues, hair, skin and so on – are most likely to reveal information about the life of an individual and not about their death. Bones and tissue provide a testament to people's past lives: how long they lived, what sex they were, what illnesses or diseases they suffered, how tall they grew, what genetic ancestry they had, what sorts of foods they ate, what injuries they sustained, how well built they were, and whether they were deliberately deformed, bound, tattooed, body-painted or scarified. Had the man and the slave girl been buried and not burnt, archaeologists might have learned more about their lives than Ibn Fadlan himself knew, such as their age, their injuries, pre-mortem state of health, their childhood growth, and whether the slave girl had ever had children.

This book is not so much about what can be learned from human skeletons concerning these issues of demography, diet, health and body modification *per se*, nor is it about the physical processes affecting human remains and their decay after their deposition.[2] Rather, it is about the archaeological study of the funerary practices that the living perform for the dead.[3] It is not so much about the dead themselves as the living who buried them. The dead do not bury themselves but are treated and disposed of by the living. Archaeologists seek not only to document ancient rituals by recovering the evidence of past funerary practices but also attempt to understand them within their historical contexts and to explain why they were enacted in the ways that they were. For example, we might ask why the Rus thought the way they did about cremation and the afterlife, why they destroyed a valuable item like the ship, and why sacrifice of the slave girl was a necessary act. As archaeologists, one of the main ways in which we interpret past societies is through recovering the material traces of those practices associated with the remains of the dead.

The Iceman

A good example of what this book is not about is the 5,000-year-old body known as 'Ötzi' or the 'Iceman', which was found by chance in the Ötztaler Alps of the South Tyrol.[4] All the evidence indicates that this man died while travelling in a high Alpine pass, a victim of the weather whose corpse was never retrieved. Funerary rites may have been performed for the absent body in the community from which he came, but there is nothing about the Iceman, his equipment or his circumstances which relates to the funerary practices of the period. His equipment and clothing, along with his tattooed body, are part of a time capsule from which we can try and make sense of what an individual's life was like.

Yet the Iceman's body and belongings can offer indirect evidence that might help us to understand the funerary practices that were carried out at that time. We may compare his remains, lost in the mountains, with those from burials from the region in which he probably lived around 3300–2900 BC. This contextual approach then enables the archaeologist to find out what has been selected for or omitted from the burials, given that the Iceman helps us to know something about how the living dressed and equipped themselves. Although this comparison can only be partial for the time being, graves of this period have been found at Remedello near Brescia in northern Italy, about 150km away.

The non-perishable artefacts from one of the Remedello burials, Grave 102, consist of a copper axe, a flint dagger and four flint arrowheads: a very close match to some of the Iceman's equipment.[5] Yet there were other durable items possessed by the Iceman which did not turn up in that burial: his drilled white marble bead, the multi-purpose flint scraper/blade, the small flint blade, the flint drill, the bone awl, the antler spike, the antler tip of the pressure flaking tool and the bundle of four antler fragments. In turn, the Iceman did not have the pots that are found in many of the Remedello burials as offerings or accompaniments for the deceased. Furthermore, the Iceman's dagger is smaller than the flint daggers in the Remedello cemetery and is most closely comparable to flint objects from Remedello identified as large arrowheads. The Iceman's dagger and arrowheads are also broken whereas those from Grave 102 are pristine, hinting that they were either not used much or were made specifically for the funeral.

Konrad Spindler considers that the man was dressed for the mountains, wearing items of clothing which he would not have worn at lower altitudes. He also speculates that the man's broken rib and his damaged and partial equipment, including his quiver of twelve untipped arrow-shafts and two arrows with damaged tips, may be evidence that the Iceman was fleeing from the scene of a violent conflict perhaps resulting from a harvest-time raid on his village. Whether or not Spindler is correct, his reconstruction of the man's last few days or hours helps us to understand that the funerary assemblages from cemeteries such as Remedello provide fixed representations of an individual's appearance and identity which were fluid and changing throughout his or her life.

This example of the Iceman gives us the way in to two sorts of representation. We know how he looked and how he presented himself, but we cannot compare him to how others presented themselves – his parents, his kin group and the people from the next valley for example. His funeral representation, had he been buried, would have told us about how others saw him as a corpse. Funerary practices serve to create an idealized representation – a 're-presenting' of the individual by others rather than by the man himself. We may all know of situations where viewing of a corpse has brought forth exclamations of how little the corpse resembles that person when alive, or conversely how closely it does. However, we could argue that the Iceman's own view of himself – what he wanted to wear, his tattoos, his equipment – is one version of reality, and the funerary treatment is another version of the same reality rather than an unreal, distorted, idealized and ritualized representation. Both representations – how he dressed in life and how his corpse, had it been retrieved, would have been dressed and equipped in death – are grounded in their own realities; it is just that the contexts are different.

INHUMATION

The term 'burial' is synonymous with the act of disposing of the corpse in western society, despite the fact that in some countries such as Britain cremation is the dominant rite. Archaeologists have often failed to remind themselves that burial ('inhumation' or 'interment') is simply one of the many means by which the dead are removed from the domain of the living or merely demarcated as dead. In fact archaeologists are able to locate only a small proportion of the total population likely to have lived in the past, given the numbers which can be calculated from settlement densities and other indicators of human presence. In two notable studies the total numbers of individuals whose bones were found in the communal Neolithic tombs and Bronze Age round barrows of Britain were calculated as deriving from populations far too small to have been demographically viable, thereby demonstrating that such monuments held only a small proportion of the Neolithic and Bronze Age dead.[6] Most ancient funerary rites seem to be archaeologically invisible, leaving no direct material trace.

The act of burial provides archaeologists with a wide variety of potential information about past funerary practices and their social contexts. The provision of a final resting place for someone's mortal remains is generally a carefully thought through procedure which may have taken days, months or even years to plan and execute. Burial is thus a deeply significant act imbued with meaning. It represents one of the most formal and carefully prepared deposits that archaeologists encounter even though the actual ceremony at the time may have been noisy, chaotic and disputed – we should not expect past cultures to have always buried their dead with the sombre *gravitas* that is so characteristic of most western funerals. The drinking, casual sex, playing of music and banging of sticks on shields at the Rus funeral are not unique; such behaviour would not be out of place in the funerary rites of many cultures around the world today.

The grave

The shape and depth of a grave may relate to the social status or gender of the person buried. It may also reflect the degree of formality in the burial rite. The hole or pit may serve not just as a repository for the corpse but its shape and dimensions may be constructed so that it echoes other contexts. There are many ethnographic examples of graves mimicking houses or storage pits. Batammaliba graves, in Togo and Benin, are constructed as underground miniature houses of the dead.[7] The graves of household heads are closed with a round flat stone, the *kubotan*, which in life is used to seal the hole which links the ground floor and first floor in the house. Funerary and birthing rites take place underneath this *tabote* hole, which embodies the house's life force and the continuum between birth, death and rebirth. Such examples teach the archaeologist to study funerary practices not in isolation but as a set of activities which link with other social practices such as building, dwelling and subsistence.

Rather than digging a grave specially for the corpse, the body may be placed in an existing hollow, scoop, ditch or pit dug for some other purpose, or in a natural feature such as a cave, fissure or rock shelter. The whole or partial human skeletons that are found in British Iron Age settlements are generally buried in abandoned grain storage pits or in silted-up ditches.[8] At Danebury hillfort there are many of these storage pit burials but the numbers must represent only a small proportion of the population; where everybody else went is unknown. They have been interpreted as the bodies of people sacrificed along with the animals and other offerings found in these pits.[9]

Grave orientation

Orientation of the grave, its occupant(s) and tomb structures built over the grave may all be significant. The orientation of graves is an important feature for those world religions in which burial is the main rite. Moslem burials are aligned so that the body is laid facing Mecca and the Qibla. In the medieval and early modern periods, Jewish burials were arranged either south–north, with heads to the south, or west–east. Alternatively, the head might be placed towards the exit from the cemetery.[10] Christian burials are laid west–east with their heads to the west so that they may arise on the Day of Judgement to face God in the east.[11] Within the pagan religions of post-Roman England and Viking Scandinavia, burials are orientated broadly east–west or north–south, copying the two orientations for longhouse dwellings of those periods. In the Viking Age these directions, towards the cardinal points, had cosmological significance.[12] Whether the arrangement of the pyre in the Rus funeral had such significance we do not know though Ibn Fadlan's references to the throwing of the dead rooster to the right and left of the ship suggest that something was going on. Indeed, the orientation of the dead is unlikely to be random.

Body arrangement

A dead body can be buried in one of many different positions: prone on its back, lying on one side, lying face down or even sitting up or standing. Bodies may be laid with their legs flexed or even tightly bent, perhaps tied so that the knees touch the chin. The discovery of skeletons in dramatic poses can suggest death occurred immediately prior to the body's being thrown into the grave pit, or even burial alive. At the pagan Anglo-Saxon cemetery of Sewerby in Yorkshire the skeleton of a woman, lying on her back, was placed below the skeleton of another woman, lying face down with arms and legs stretched out and spread.[13] It is through comparison and contrast that archaeologists discover what are the normal postures in order to recognize the anomalies.

Slight differences in how the arms and legs are placed may help to reveal differences between groups within the same cemetery. For example, Ellen Pader's study of pagan Anglo-Saxon (fifth to sixth centuries AD) cemeteries in East Anglia in eastern England combined body position with the placing of grave goods in a multivariate statistical analysis to show that variations across each cemetery defined the presence of smaller groups within the population of each cemetery.[14]

As in most aspects of archaeology, the bigger the sample the more there is to compare. We cannot say a great deal about one body on its own but we can infer much when it can be compared to hundreds of others. It is through statistical methods rather than empathy and intuition that we learn about the nature of past funerary practices. In archaeological terms Ibn Fadlan's ethnographic account is severely limited because it describes only one funeral; archaeologists would want to know how other Rus dead were disposed of, and whether there are comparable mounds in the area and how their contents differed chronologically and socially.

CREMATION

Cremation, the practice of burning the corpse on a pyre, generally leaves archaeological traces only when the fragments of burnt bone left after the fire are buried. Such deposits are termed cremation burials. Cremations can be outrageously extravagant affairs but they may leave few or even no archaeological traces. Very occasionally the site of the funeral pyre may be found but this tends to occur only when the pyre remains have been protected beneath later deposits (**Figure 1.1**). Pyre sites are sometimes found under cairns or mounds erected to cover the grave.

In order to bury the burnt bones left after a cremation, someone has to collect the pieces of bone from the extinguished pyre. The material selected for burial from the surface of the extinguished pyre normally forms only a proportion of the total debris, perhaps about 40–60 per cent of the original skeleton. Jacqui McKinley has noted that deposits of cremated bone from primary burials beneath Bronze Age barrows in England are generally heavier than those from Bronze Age open cemeteries, resulting from the more careful retrieval of bones for burial beneath a mound.[15] She suggests that such differences may have been due to the status or popularity of the deceased.

Scattered cremated bone can occasionally be found where it has become incorporated into ditches or pits. Identification of these burnt bones as human may be difficult. Where cremated remains are interred below ground, the collected bones are often buried within or underneath a pot or organic container. The deposit may contain not only the burnt bones but also pyre material such as charcoal, fuel ash slag, carbonized plant remains and the burnt residues of various pyre goods, while other unburnt items may be added to the collection. Additionally the bones may derive from more than one individual, as in about 5 per cent of British prehistoric cases. There may also be remains of animals;[16] for example, the discovery of bear claws in a number of Scandinavian Germanic Iron Age (AD 400–600) cremations may relate to the inclusion of a bearskin cloak on the funeral pyre.[17] Cremated bones may be kept for many years prior to burial, perhaps awaiting mingling with the bones of individuals still alive.

Generally, cremated bone will yield less information than unburnt bones on age, height, sex, health, injuries, facial characteristics and pathology. On the positive side, cremated bone often survives in soils that are too acid to preserve unburnt bone. We ought to be able to identify the remains of an adult man and a young woman in the Rus funeral's pyre deposit and perhaps also to recognize the cut marks of the Angel of Death's broad-bladed dagger on the woman's burnt ribs. Other things would also survive: the iron weapons placed by the man's side, boat fittings such as rivets, the burnt bones of the animals, the gold buttons of the man's costume, and the charcoal from the ship's timbers, the scaffold and the pyre wood. The degree of shrinkage and colour change in the bone will also provide clues to the temperature and duration of the pyre.

GRAVE GOODS

Grave goods may include items which were possessions of the deceased, or they might be mourners' gifts to the dead. They may serve to equip the dead for the world of the afterlife, or to prevent the dead coming back to haunt the living. Grave goods may be selected to serve as reminders of a person's deeds or character. The commonest grave goods are clothing and related equipment, containers and remains of food and drink.

Adornment of the body

[W]hen we dress we wear inscribed upon our bodies the often obscure relationship of art, personal psychology and the social order.[18]

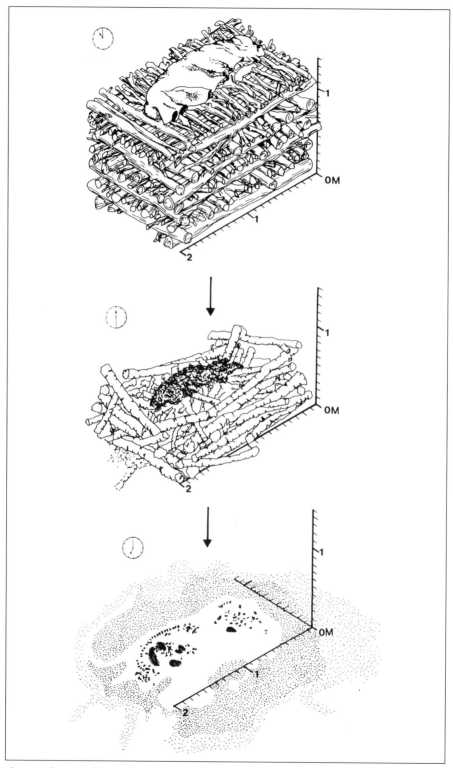

1.1 A schematic diagram of a cremation pyre and its collapse. This experiment, involving a pig not a person, illustrates how long cremation takes and what is left behind.

Though they cannot feel the cold and do not suffer pangs of modesty, we often like to dress up the dead.[19] They may wear clothes that they never did in life. They may wear their best, or those vestments that will be least missed. They may be dressed in apparel which is made specifically for the dead, a category that includes shrouds and winding cloths. They may be eviscerated and embalmed so that they do not decay. Alternatively they may be left for weeks to rot, with the smell all too apparent. All of these elaborate preparations are for that brief moment when the corpse is displayed for the living before disappearing for ever. It is in those final moments that the living's memories of the dead person are congealed.

As with other forms of material culture, it is easy to lie – to misrepresent ourselves – with clothes, to take on a personality and status which is other than our normal self. Clothes and ornamentation are strategic representations through which we project our personalities and values. But at a funeral, choosing what to wear for the big event is not a matter decided by the deceased. Even the decision to leave the corpse in the clothes the dead person wore in life is one taken by the living. The dressing of the dead is always carried out by the living and consequently the costume of the dead constitutes the mourners' reading or representation of the dead person's former self-representation through dress. The deceased may be provided with a whole wardrobe of clothing, furniture and even living accoutrements for use in the afterlife. As Ibn Fadlan recounts in detail, one of the main elements of the Rus funeral is the making of fine clothes so that the dead man may be dressed in items which he never wore in life.

In the category of dress can be included clothing, body modification (tattoos, painting, scarification, piercing), ornamentation (lip plugs, ear-rings), hair-style (including body hair), and even portable equipment. A spear or a water pot on, or even beside, a body constitutes their incorporation into the complex mass of symbols that is an individual's dress and appearance. The modern executive might feel somehow incomplete without briefcase, Filofax and mobile phone. A prehistoric warrior – or individual of warrior status – might have felt similarly diminished without spear and sword even though these need never have been used in combat.

As archaeologists, we should be wary of how we separate the material culture *on* the body (clothes) from the material culture *of* the body (posture and body modification) from the material culture *off* the body (weapons, furniture and other items). We need to be aware of how easily we impose our own categories on to the past, dividing up 'clothing', 'furniture', 'weaponry' and 'jewellery' out of assemblages whose totality relates to the entire representation of the deceased's appearance or 'dress'. The clothing of the dead thus constitutes a hall of mirrors, representations of representations, in which things may not be entirely what they seem at first glance.

In contemporary British culture, the outward appearance of the dead can be puzzling enough. A recently married woman might be decked out in her wedding dress, which was made for her grandmother. An old man may wear the suit that he almost never wore in life except to other people's funerals. And this is a culture where we believe we go naked before God. The coffin itself is a crucial part of the furnishing of the body; like the backless nylon smock worn by many of the dead, it cannot be used in life. The corpse may also have undergone some dramatic body modification: if we die in medically unsupervised circumstances (which about one-third of us do), the obligatory – and culturally sanctioned – post-mortem examination, performed on 22 per cent of the population in Britain, leaves us with the tops of our heads sawn off, our chests ripped open and our entrails messed about with.[20]

People in the past probably did not equip their dead for us to ponder over. Instead they provided them with items, posture and appearance which were considered appropriate to the context of death, to the mourners and to the individual deceased. The Rus on the Volga had his clothing made for the funeral, a tradition which may have been prevalent throughout the Viking world. In other cases items might be heirlooms that have been kept for decades. The choice of what should accompany the dead is one that changes and fluctuates. The fashion for dressing the dead in one era can be radically transformed in another. For the archaeologist, what is interesting is not just how the things were made but the comparisons with non-funerary contexts and with different periods in time to see how traditions of funerary garb changed.

Food and drink

Food is coercive. We have to follow its rhythm, and not vice versa. It has power over us. Food as identity, as our physical selves, as a way of thought, as sex, as power, as friendship, as a medium for magic and witchcraft, as our time-controller – in all these ways and more, food pervades our culture and gives meaning to our lives. It plays a central role in our societies, and provides us as much with intricate symbols and metaphors as with nutritional substance.[21]

Regular accompaniments for the dead in past cultures include animal bones (whole skeletons or merely portions), containers such as pots and bowls, trays and tableware. Archaeologists used to understand these items in very literal terms as mere accoutrements to feed the dead in the other world rather than as complex symbols which express the various values, aims and attitudes of the mourners in the face of death. The placing of food and drink in a grave is only part, and not necessarily the last part, of a whole sequence of feasts, fasts or food offerings which is triggered by a death.

Food marks the differential status of the living and the dead; on the Pacific island of Tikopia, mourners eat cooked food, symbolic of the social and domestic life disrupted by death, and raw food is placed on the grave as a symbol of the product of the deceased's labours.[22]

Food marks identity; the islanders of Dobu (off the south-east tip of Papua New Guinea) consider yams to be metamorphosized people and the cultivation of yams is perceived as a metaphorical representation of the kinship system.[23] Within the stone-set circular enclosure at the centre of each Dobu village are buried the women of the village's matriline and their brothers, ancestors who confer ownership of the soil and inheritance in the same way that seed yams generate yams for harvest.

Food marks social status; the cattle, horses and chickens in the Rus funeral may have been a measure of the man's standing. Alternatively these animals may have been highly symbolic of something else such as his gender or kinship, or the appropriate sacrifices required by divination.

Pots placed with the dead may contain liquids and foodstuffs. Yet funerary pots need not have contained sustenance: they may simply have stood for the symbolic meal partaken by the dead. In some cases the metaphorical association of pots at funerals is not as containers of food but as containers of souls. In the nineteenth century African Americans in the southern USA used to place broken pots on graves to prevent the dead from coming back.[24] In later years the pots were replaced by stopped clocks or watches, set to the time of death or to twelve, to wake the dead on Judgement Day.

Archaeological specialists in animal bones, palynology (pollen analysis), food residues and plant remains can, in the right conditions, identify the foods and drinks placed with the dead. For example, soil samples taken from an Early Bronze Age cist burial at Ashgrove in Scotland contained pollen which appears to have derived from a honeyed mead. This had probably spilled out of the Beaker pot found in the grave.[25] Using such analyses we compare different burial contexts, and make comparisons with non-funerary contexts. Were there a sufficient number of Rus cremations for comparison, we might be able to say more about the meaning and significance of the particular animals killed for the dead man.

Artefacts of separation and transition

Grave goods may prepare the dead for the other world but equally they may serve to prevent them from remaining in the world of the living or simply ensure a good send-off. In western culture cut flowers are a major feature of funerals, a tradition that may originate in the herbs, flowers and evergreens of sixteenth- and seventeenth-century England but which bloomed in Britain from the early eighteenth century onwards.[26] Although there is a growing tradition of planting living flowers at the grave, the symbolism of the short life of cut flowers is a significant feature of contemporary funerals. A recent dispute in 1998 in the Northamptonshire churchyard of Orlingbury highlights this quality. The Bishop of Peterborough has forbidden mourners to inscribe a gravestone with the term 'Nan' because the word is deemed unsuitable as a permanent and dignified marker for the dead woman. Yet he was perfectly happy for 'Nan' to be written in a floral tribute three feet high at the funeral, presumably because it was then a thing of transience.

The placing of a person's possessions on or in their grave may represent the dead's severance from the living. Among the Iban of Borneo a knife may be included in burials to symbolize the cutting of those ties. Conversely, the sacrifice of possessions, living and inanimate, may ensure communication with the other world. They may be viewed as gifts, tribute or even fines to be paid to the supernatural as expressions of a reciprocal relationship rather than a material exchange. Such gifts may not necessarily force a repayment from the supernatural but link the living to that realm. Animals such as horses and dogs, along with human sacrifices of slaves, spouses and entire entourages, have been regular sacrificial choices as 'companions' for the deceased. Equally, feasting animals – cattle, sheep, pigs and birds – are sacrificed for the dead but they are generally as much for the mourners as for the deceased and often only a portion of the animal may be placed in the grave, if buried at all.

The archaeologist has to be aware that grave goods are carefully selected and yet may have many different meanings. They may be ordinary items or they may be specially made for the occasion. They may be consumed or destroyed during the funeral or put in the grave. Equally, items destined for the dead may be left above ground or hung in the branches of a nearby tree, thereby condemned to almost certain invisibility to the archaeologist's eye. The study of variations in grave good provision is thus a difficult jigsaw puzzle with many pieces missing.

CEMETERY ORGANIZATION

Archaeologists have been interested in the location patterns of burials within cemeteries since the beginnings of the discipline because they may shed light on the relative dating of graves and the grave goods within them. According to the principles of horizontal stratigraphy, if a cemetery grows in size in one or more directions then the burials in one part of it will be of a different date to those in another. Early scholars such as Montelius and Déchelette were able to develop typologies of fast-changing artefact styles, such as brooch types in European Iron Age cemeteries, to build up chronological frameworks. Patterns of cemetery growth can, however, be very varied and complex. Few cemeteries grow randomly and there is normally some set of organizing principles in use.

Easily recognizable organized patterns are linear, hierarchical/concentric and segmented. Linear cemeteries, producing the horizontal stratigraphy described above, often develop from a focal point such as a founder's grave or a physical barrier such as a field ditch. The pre-Roman Iron Age cremation cemetery at Årupgård in Denmark is a good example, expanding southwards from around a burial mound of the Middle Bronze Age.[27] Concentric or hierarchical patterns grow out from and respect a central burial (**Figure 1.2**). At the large burial mound of the Magdalenenburg in Switzerland, dating to the sixth century BC in the Early Iron Age, the central chamber is surrounded by a cemetery of inhumations placed concentrically around this focal grave.[28]

Segmented cemeteries are divided into discrete sections or clusters and sometimes have open spaces between each group of graves.[29] Each segment may be arranged either in an unstructured group or in a row structure. Row-structured segments are arranged with the inhumations aligned either side by side or head to toe (**Figure 1.2**). An example of head-to-toe row structure is the Early Bronze Age cemetery of Mokrin in the former Yugoslavia.[30] Among Mississippian period cemeteries in the United States, Schild Knoll A was arranged into a series of side-by-side rows and unstructured clusters while Schild Knoll B had a more complex pattern of not only side-by-side rows and unstructured clusters, but also some graves arranged into a concentric pattern around the knoll and others arranged around a likely charnel house.[31] Lynne Goldstein interpreted these clusters as family or kin units and inferred that Mississippian society was organized on the basis of corporate or lineal descent groups. In cemeteries where discrete clusters are not apparent, it may be possible to identify spatial groupings on the basis of body positioning or other specific, localized treatment. Pader's study of body positioning, described above, was able to identify such groupings.

Social differences and cemetery organization

Cemeteries reveal much more than grave good variation and chronology, and may provide evidence about kinship, gender and other indicators of social status. Detailed analyses of these issues require the use of statistical methods on large samples of sometimes many hundreds of graves. The identification of intra-cemetery clusters often requires statistical techniques such as cluster analysis, principal co-ordinate and principal component analysis, and significance tests.[32] In some cases clusters may be gender-segregated, such as the first century BC–AD Iron Age cremation cemeteries of northern Germany and southern Jutland where brooches, needles and curved knives are found in the sector of female graves while swords, spears, shields and long knives are found in the area with male cremated bodies. In some medieval and later Jewish cemeteries in Europe it was the tradition to bury men and women in separate areas but the medieval Jewbury cemetery in York shows a more complex pattern in which male and female burials are intermixed yet with some evident clusters of male and female burials.[33]

Cemeteries may be status-segregated. In seventeenth- to eighteenth-century Manhattan African Americans were forbidden burial in the churchyards and had to use their own

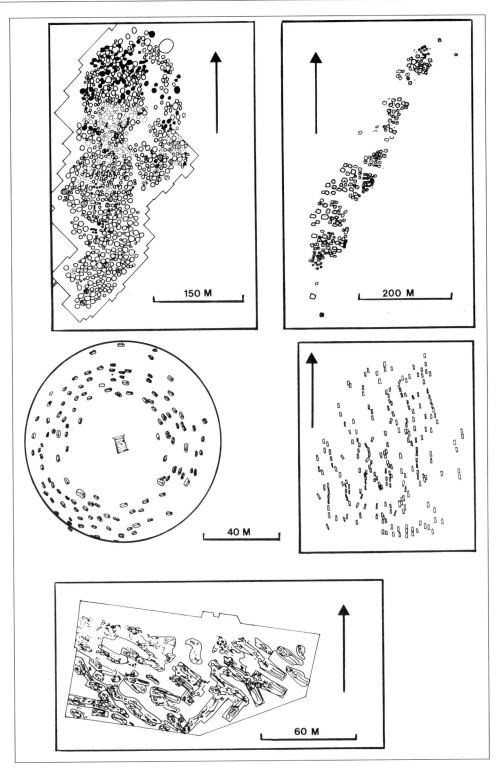

1.2 *Different forms of cemetery organization: (from left to right) linear (Årupgård), segmented (Carnaby, Iron Age East Yorkshire), concentric (Magdalenenburg), row segmented head-to-toe (Mokrin), row segmented side-by-side (Wickliffe Mound C, Mississippian period).*

burial ground.[34] At the Clift's Plantation in Virginia the burials were divided into two distinct groups. The northern group of burials was identified as those of the plantation owners – the high lead levels in the bones were caused by the use of pewter tableware (they had been slowly poisoning themselves!). The southern group, with much lower levels of lead, was identified as the burials of black slaves.[35]

Hierarchical patterns are often found in European churchyards; ecclesiastical codes specified burial plots according to social status. Post-medieval English churches and churchyards maintained a set of strong status distinctions in establishing a geography of holiness and inclusion.[36] The local lord of the manor and his family were normally interred within the church itself. The well-to-do were buried in the sunnier south side of the churchyard, vying for space in the prestigious section immediately outside the south door where their gravestones would be seen by every churchgoer. The poor were buried on the darker, north side of the churchyard, an area associated in folklore with evil and the devil (**Figure 1.3**).

In these medieval and later churchyards, burial plots were organized not only by status but also by family groupings based on descent and post-marital residence. Family plots can be clearly seen from the seventeenth- to twentieth-century gravestones in any churchyard. Archaeologically the distinction of churchyard burials into family groupings without the aid of gravestones can be near impossible owing to the degree of crowding and inter-cutting of graves. Urban churchyards became so crowded that, in the early nineteenth-century metropolises of Britain, gravediggers got drunk in order to cope with the appalling stench as they sawed through undecayed corpses and coffins. One gravedigger even had a corpse fall on top of him, out of the side of the grave he was digging.[37]

1.3 The traditional avoidance of the English churchyard's north side as a place of burial declined in the nineteenth century but was still so strong that the Magniac family, the lords of Colworth manor in Sharnbrook, Bedfordshire, deliberately placed their new burial vault on the parish church's north side during the 1860s to encourage others to abandon their superstition.

Distinction between normal and deviant individuals can also be expressed spatially.[38] From the late fifteenth century onwards in England there were traditions that suicides were staked down in burials at crossroads while women who died in childbirth were supposedly buried outside the wall around the consecrated ground of the churchyard.[39] At the early medieval cemetery at Sutton Hoo (early seventh century AD), a group of unusual burials lies to the east of the royal mound burials that include the famous treasure ship. This eastern group contains not one metal grave good. Some of the bodies appear to have been mutilated by decapitation or breaking of the limbs (**Figure 1.4**).[40] These individuals are most likely execution victims, either killed when the adjacent Middle Saxon royal burial ground was in use or brought here in later centuries for public execution. One of the earliest cemeteries in Europe, the Late Mesolithic cemetery of Vedbaek in Denmark, has been interpreted as a deviants' cemetery. Bryony Coles suggests that the age and sex profiles are not those of an ordinary population – there is a surprising number of individuals in mid-life, including childbirth deaths, and too few children or mature adults.[41] She suggests that most individuals from the Mesolithic Vedbaek community were disposed of elsewhere; they were not interred in this small cemetery set on a small hill behind the coastal settlement.

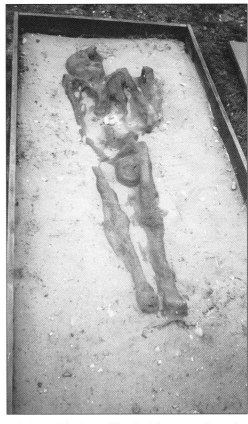

1.4 One of the Sutton Hoo burials preserved as stains in the sandy soil. Another of these burials, known as the 'ploughman', has his legs splayed astride a long wooden object initially identified as a plough though Martin Carver has suggested that it might be a collapsed gallows.

Segregation according to age is relatively easy to detect when the bones survive. It has been suggested as one of the structuring principles for the placing of skeletal remains in the distinct chambers of the stone-built Earlier Neolithic communal tombs in the Cotswold area of southern England, such as Burn Ground, Notgrove and West Kennet (**Figure 1.5**).[42] In the medieval Jewish cemeteries at Winchester and York child burials are grouped separately from those of adults.[43]

Finally, large urban cemeteries may be divided according to ethnic groupings or religious affiliations. In a modern British cemetery one will find special areas for burials of Moslems, Jews, Poles, Italians, Gypsies and showmen's families while Victorian cemeteries often demarcated areas for non-conformists separate from Church of England worshippers.[44] Such distinctions are often hard to detect archaeologically, though they may involve differences in grave orientation, grave preparation and grave goods. One example is the possible presence of East Europeans in the Roman cemetery of Lankhills at Winchester in southern England, which contains a small cluster of burials equipped with brooches of a type ordinarily found in that part of the Roman empire which is now Hungary.[45]

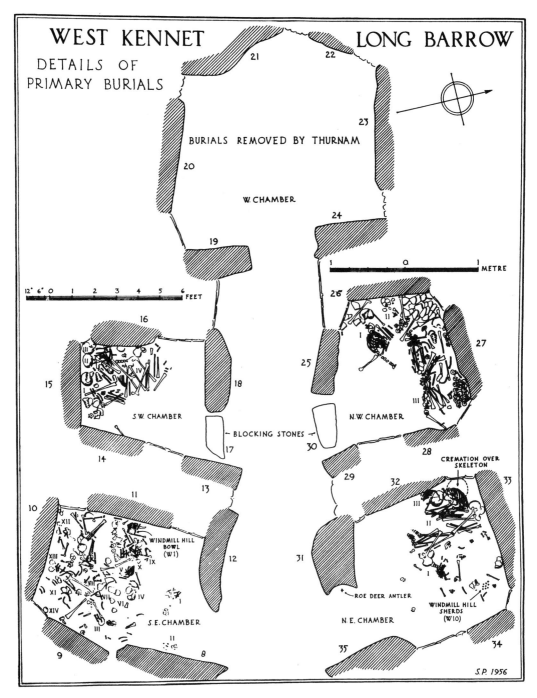

1.5 The distribution of bones in the Neolithic chambered tomb at West Kennet (c. 3400 BC). The abundance of foot and hand bones suggests that most corpses were brought whole into this tomb, with some skulls being removed in a secondary rite performed after the flesh had rotted from the body.

Changes over time

An important aspect of cemetery dynamics is that of founding and abandonment. Funerary archaeologists concentrate on the period when a cemetery was in use but may give less thought as to why it was begun or abandoned. It was probably for reasons other than perceived 'fullness' that most cemeteries in the past were abandoned or begun. Even when a community moves away from an area, people may return for many years to come in order to bury their dead in the same cemetery. The break with tradition that is marked by founding or abandonment can be a momentous event. A founder's grave may mark the fissioning of a lineage as one family group breaks away from the larger kin group. It may also be part of an expansion into new land as the decision is taken not to bring the dead back to the usual place of disposal. The act of burial itself also serves to physically 'plant' the dead into the land, making their remains an inalienable and fixed part of that land.

The moment of abandonment may scarcely be noticed, the last of a dwindling number of burials perhaps of the less notable members of the community, if a new cemetery or new rites have been adopted by the majority. The regional study of founding and abandonment sequences can yield information about significant social changes and watersheds. For example, during the period 600 BC–AD 600 in southern Jutland most cemeteries were founded or abandoned within certain short timespans, notably around 50 BC and AD 200, co-occurring with major changes in gender definition, household organization and political authority.[46]

HUMAN SACRIFICE

The killing of the slave girl by the Rus so that she might accompany her master in death is a classic example of human sacrifice. Other tenth-century burials which are probably human sacrifices are known from elsewhere in the Viking world. The Viking 'queen' buried in the exceptionally well-preserved Oseberg ship in Norway was accompanied by the body of an elderly woman, perhaps her personal slave.[47] In Denmark the cemetery at Stengade contains the burial of a man with a silver-inlaid spear in a wooden chamber grave on top of which is the decapitated body of a man wearing iron handcuffs. In the cemetery at Lejre a decapitated man in one of the burials appears to have had his hands bound, while a woman's burial appears to have been accompanied by a probable male.[48] Similar practices are also known in England between the sixth and seventh centuries AD.[49]

Human sacrifice has sometimes been discussed in terms of the sublimation of primitive aggression, designed to abolish uncontrolled violence by substituting violent rites which serve as a warning to the rest.[50] It can also be considered as the ultimate in reciprocal exchange or submission by the living to the supernatural, the gift or tribute which is the most precious that people can give to the gods – human life itself.[51] It has even been considered as the primary check against the animal in man.[52] Yet such a powerful concept may be surprisingly hard to define, especially since there can be a fine line dividing it from execution of war captives or criminals, or from altruistic self-sacrifice.[53]

Human sacrifice is generally considered to be directed at supernatural entities and carried out under the auspices of ritual specialists. Often the death is welcomed or even brought about by the victim who may be considered a scapegoat for society's ills and misfortunes. Thus, within the broad ambit of human sacrifice can be included the Rus slave girl and other sacrificial victims for funerals, the *kamikaze* pilots of Second World War Japan sacrificing themselves for the divine emperor, the killing of thousands of war captives by the Aztecs to ensure that the sun continued to rise, the South Asian practice of *suttee* in which the widow is cast alive into the flames of her dead husband's pyre, the death of the man-god Jesus Christ who sacrificed himself for others' sins, the self-sacrifice of cult members such as Jim Jones's followers in Jonestown, Guyana, and even the judicial executions of convicted criminals in America.[54]

As Gordon Childe noted in 1945, human sacrifice on a large scale has been a frequent characteristic of the funerals of autocratic rulers of emergent states, as exhibited by the Egyptian First Dynasty tombs at Abydos, *c.* 3100–2890 BC, the Mesopotamian royal tombs at Ur around 2500 BC (**Figure 1.6**) and the mid-second millennium BC Shang dynasty tombs at Anyang in China.[55] Since Childe's time there have been further discoveries. At Sipán in Peru the third century AD tomb of a Moche noble, 'the Lord of Sipán', also contained a tomb guardian and the bodies of another two men and three women; a similar tomb, that of 'the Old Lord of Sipán', also contained additional male and female burials.[56] At Palenque in Mexico the tomb of the seventh century AD Maya ruler Pacal lay hidden within the pyramid known as the Temple of the Inscriptions, accompanied by the skeletons of a group of young adults above the slab covering Pacal's sarcophagus.[57] Other examples are known from Kerma in the Sudan (*c.* 1800–1600 BC), Cahokia in the south-east USA (*c.* AD 1000), the first Chinese emperor's tomb at Mount Li in AD 210, and the early nineteenth-century Baganda kingdom in Uganda.[58] Why such mass sacrifices occurred at crucial moments in state formation is examined in detail in Chapter 7.

A second category of sacrificial victims is that of individuals who are killed and offered to the supernatural within special sacred places other than cemeteries. A spectacular case of mass sacrifice is indicated by the burials of over a hundred 'warriors' underneath the Temple of Quetzalcoatl at Teotihuacán in Mexico, around AD 150, possibly as supernatural guardians of the temple.[59] In well-preserved examples such as the Neolithic and Iron Age bog bodies of north-west Europe (which will be explained in detail in Chapter 3) and the mountain-top Inka period (1438–1532 AD) child sacrifices in Peru and Chile, the surviving skin and tissues often allow forensic study to determine the nature and cause of death.

The evidence from the Inka period in South America is incontrovertible. Spectacularly well-preserved corpses of children and young adults have been found 'freeze-dried' on mountain tops at extraordinary altitudes. Among the most stunning discoveries are a near-naked twenty-year-old man on the summit of Cerro del Toro in Argentina, who seems to have been drugged and left to freeze to death, a naked eighteen-year-old woman near the summit of Pichu Pichu in Peru, apparently killed by being hit on the head, and a young boy on Cerro el Plomo in Chile, wearing a tunic and accompanied by a silver human figurine and a gold llama figurine.[60] These and many others were offered by the Inka as *capacocha* sacrifices to the sun god, bestowing considerable prestige on the child's parents and on their local community. In death the victims became guardian spirits linked to the Inka ruler who derived his power from the ritual killings of these children.

In 1622, long after the Spanish had conquered the Inka empire and while they were destroying the Inka ancestor cult, Hernández Príncipe wrote about an earlier *capacocha* incident in which a local official from Ocros, named Caque Poma, was rewarded by the Inka authorities for building an irrigation canal by being given permission to sacrifice his own daughter to the sun deity. The father and daughter journeyed to Cuzco to pay homage to the Inka rulers and their gods and ancestors, subsequently returning home for the sacrifice. The girl went willingly to her death, walled up alive in a shaft tomb at the top of the mountain on which were located the storehouses for the crops from the newly irrigated fields. She

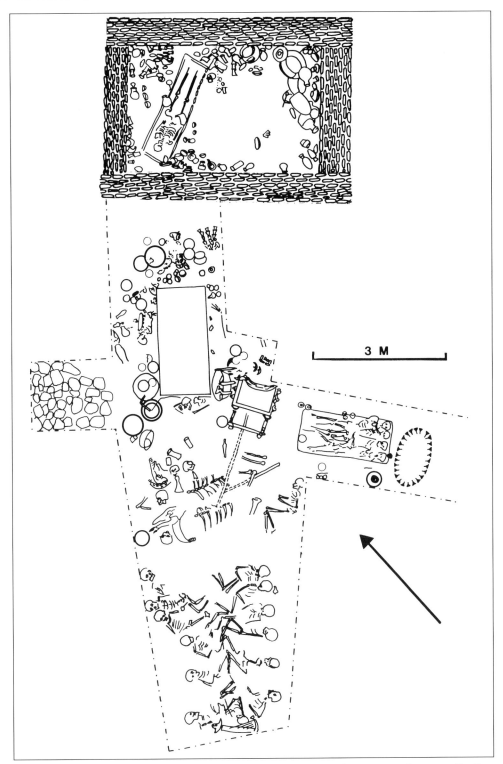

1.6 Grave 800, the tomb of Pu-abi (formerly identified as Shub-ad) among the sixteen royal graves at Ur. She was buried in a vault (at the top of the picture) with twenty-seven retainers including soldiers, handmaidens, a harpist and a 'keeper of the wardrobe'.

became an important local deity, embodying fertility, corn production and health, and Caque Poma became a successful man and subsequently an important ancestor.[61]

In a remarkable account of contemporary Chile and Peru, Patrick Tierney claims that the practice of human sacrifice did not die out after the coming of the conquistadores but is still practised by shamans for individuals seeking to avert natural disasters or to improve their wealth.[62] Tierney notes there are many stories in the region of cocaine traffickers allegedly sponsoring shamans to carry out human sacrifices so as to increase their wealth and success. Exactly where the line is drawn between gangster killings and local understandings of these events as human sacrifices is difficult to know.

CONCLUSION

It might seem that archaeology is a straightforward process of discovery followed by description, yet it is accompanied by interpretation at every step. Interpretation draws on theory – our rationalizations of our experiences in the world – in order to make sense of how and why people of the past treated their dead, disposed of their remains, and provided ways for the dead to co-exist with the living. The following chapters examine the theoretical themes which have guided approaches to the archaeology of death, such as the organizing frameworks provided by the human body and the inhabited landscape, the significance of power and gender relationships, the human awareness and experience of death and the political dimensions of funerary archaeology as a practice in the present.

First we must explore something of the extraordinary diversity of contemporary and recent treatments of the dead around the world in order to find out how different they may be and what aspects are commonly found. We will not be searching for what used to be called 'ethnographic parallels' – no single society has ever been the same as another. The aim of looking at the full range of known funerary practices is to ensure that we avoid imposing the rationalizations of our particular ethnocentric cultural logic on to the past. The analogies that inform our interpretations must be made explicit: they should be appropriately chosen, and not forced on to the archaeological context. As the next chapter will explain, analogies between ethnographic and archaeological data should be judged by the degree of congruence and compatibility between relevant aspects of those societies past and present.

Two

FROM NOW TO THEN: ETHNOARCHAEOLOGY AND ANALOGY

> The primary use of ethnographic parallels . . . is simple. It is to widen the horizons of the interpreter.[1]

The Tut'n'C'mon Motel was the setting for an archaeological fantasy, reflecting on the problems of interpreting ancient funerary rites.[2] An archaeologist of the distant future attempts to understand our present through the excavation of an American motel; a human skeleton lies on a bed and another lies in the *en suite* bath. The author suggests that future archaeologists would interpret this strange discovery as a wonderful tomb full of artefacts with sacred and ritual significance – the lavatory seat is confidently identified as an item of ceremonial headgear. The underlying message, however, is a serious one: how can archaeologists ever hope to gain even a partially accurate understanding of past societies from the material evidence alone? To find any sort of answer, we need to ask some rather more difficult questions – what do people think about death? What do people do about it, and why? An important approach to this sort of question is the use of ethnographic descriptions of funerary rites. By looking at the diversity of the human response to death, archaeologists trying to interpret the past can attempt to slough off ethnocentric presuppositions.

From the late 1960s there was a new interest in using ethnographic accounts of mortuary practices. Peter Ucko drew on a wide variety of studies of non-western societies to demonstrate that commonly held preconceptions among prehistorians could be challenged. The presence of grave goods does not necessarily imply belief in an afterlife; the orientation of a buried corpse might not reflect ideas about the direction of the other world; cremation need not imply any belief in the existence of a soul after death; and dynastic tombs need not indicate royalty.[3] Such is the extent of cultural diversity in dealing with death that any generalization is certain to founder because at least one society would be known to social anthropology to break the rules. Ucko concluded that if we want to draw a parallel between a particular practice in the present and an archaeologically recovered one, we need as numerous and varied a set of analogies as possible to check against the content and context of the archaeological material.

THE SOCIAL ANTHROPOLOGY OF DEATH

Ucko's cautionary tales for archaeologists on the use of ethnographic parallels were published at a time when detailed case studies of funerary practices were dramatically on the increase in social anthropology.[4] Many of these texts took as their starting points and themes certain classic ideas, developed by Arnold van Gennep and Robert Hertz, of liminality and transition, transformation and the importance of funerary rites in organizing the society of the living.[5]

Rites of passage

Van Gennep's universalist theory of the *rites de passage*, later elaborated by Turner and by Leach, sets out a tripartite process of transition from one social state to another. These moments of transition include events such as pregnancy, childbirth, initiation, marriage and death. The transition is effected through *preliminal* rites (rites of separation from the existing world), *liminal* or threshold rites (rites during the transitional stage), and *postliminal* rites (ceremonies of incorporation into the new world).[6] To van Gennep's surprise, in the societies he studied the rites of separation in funeral ceremonies were few and simple in contrast to the liminal rites and especially to the rites of incorporation of the deceased into the world of the dead.[7]

Hertz's work was similarly cross-cultural, derived especially from Borneo (although he never carried out any fieldwork) and also focused on the parallel transitions undergone by mourners, corpse and soul. Attempting to explain the fear that death engenders, Hertz analysed the process of double burial: in Borneo, as in many other past and present societies, the dead body undergoes more than one rite in the liminal period. He noted that death destroys the social being and strikes at society 'in the very principle of its life, in the faith it has in itself'.[8] '[T]he notion of death is linked with that of resurrection; exclusion is always followed by a new integration.'[9] The journey of the soul into the land of the dead is made visible to the living by the transformation of the putrescent corpse into clean bones and the readjustment and redefinition of the community of mourners.

It has been suggested that Hertz's theory of the passage of the corpse as a homology or model of the passage of the soul might be an invariate universal, but this theory requires modification when considering certain cases; rites of double burial in Madagascar, for example, lack the emphasis on beliefs about the afterworld and the journey of the soul which are prominent aspects of secondary burial in Borneo.[10] Huntington's analysis of mortuary practices among the Bara pastoralists of southern Madagascar emphasizes the progress of the double funeral as a mediation between order (associated with maleness, sterility, bone and the tomb) and vitality (associated with femaleness, fecundity, flesh and the womb), with vitality generated through funerary celebration to counter the excessive order of death: the notion of a journeying soul is absent.[11] Equally, Metcalf and Huntington point out that van Gennep's scheme is merely a vague truism which provides a framework of form to which the content of cultural values of each particular society must be attached to grasp the conceptual vitality of each ritual.[12]

Functionalism and after

In the first half of the twentieth century, in spite of the pioneering ideas of van Gennep and Hertz, anthropologists and archaeologists often tended to use *functionalist* explanations of human societies and behaviour. Functionalism emphasizes the pre-eminence of the social whole over its individual parts, the human subjects. Using a biological metaphor, societies are viewed as bounded social organisms with needs and operating as systems. Societies adapt to their environments in ways (and with consequences) of which their members may not be aware.[13] Functionalist interpretations of funeral ritual saw it as affirmation of the existence of social bonds among the mourners and as a strengthener of political authority in the face of the fear, fascination and repulsion caused by the presence of a corpse. Such themes were important in the work of the influential anthropologists Malinowski, Radcliffe-Brown and Evans-Pritchard.[14] 'The ceremonial of death, which ties the survivors to the body and rivets them to the place of death . . . counteracts the centrifugal forces of fear, dismay, demoralization, and provides the most powerful means of reintegration of the group's shaken solidarity and of the re-establishment of its morale.'[15]

Anthropological studies of more recent times explicitly moved away from this functionalist stance and developed more sophisticated notions of the relationships between funerary ritual and social structure, in which the arena of mortuary rites formed a nexus of conflict and power struggle.[16] As Goody noted for the transmission of property and the reallocation of rights and duties among the Lo Dagaa of West Africa: 'It is the funeral ceremonies that often reveal these tensions [between the haves and the have-nots] most clearly, for they cannot but enact the conflicts which exist within these intimate relationships.'[17] At Lo Dagaa funerals the corpse, whether of a man or woman, was always dressed as a man of authority in the finest clothes of chiefly status, thereby testifying not to the individual's own social role and identity (often called the *social persona*) but to the well-being of the social group as a whole.[18] The mode of burial of the corpse varied not only with status distinctions but also according to how the individual had conducted him/herself within a given role.[19] In his analyses of the relationship between corpse and soul among the Berewan of Borneo, Metcalf notes the occasional disconnection between mortuary treatment and social rank. Berewan mausolea are impressive wooden structures standing over 10m high; they are expressive of high status and their construction provides an opportunity for a new leader to consolidate his position. Since a tomb cannot be built for anyone living, these mausolea may contain the remains not of headmen but of people who often turn out to be nobodies, unimportant relatives whose deaths provided the opportunity for a leader to ennoble himself by constructing a grand mausoleum.[20]

Maurice Bloch's study of the relationship between kinship organization and the funerary rites of the Merina in highland Madagascar also highlighted certain contradictory tendencies between lived and idealized notions of social structure. People buried together in the communal stone tombs paradoxically probably never lived together since the reality of the kinship system of bilateral descent works against an idealized system of segmentary corporate groups which is expressed in the *famadihana* (ceremony of secondary burial), in the solidity and permanence of the collective tomb (**Figure 2.1**), and in the building of these tombs into the ancestral lands within Imerina.[21]

The value of such studies for archaeology is that they provide detailed contextual explorations of symbolism within funerary practices which archaeologists have learned to take into account. We have seen how funerals may be political events in which status is not simply reflected or represented but is actively constituted, and introduced the notion of funerary practices as idealized representations of social structure actualized in other everyday contexts. Other concepts can also be seen to have wide applicability, namely: pollution and purity, separation of living and dead, fertility and regeneration, rites of reversal, and conceptions of the dead as ancestors affecting the world of the living. These 'ways of thinking' are not universal in the sense that they lie outside time and space, existing everywhere, at all times; rather they need to be recognized as specific cultural logics and decoded from material remains and other evidence.

2.1 A Merina tomb in the highlands of central Madagascar. Bodies are arranged on stone benches inside the tomb and are taken out and rewrapped during secondary funerals (famadihana).

Pollution and purity

This binary concept was elaborated by Mary Douglas, and pollution or danger classically comes into play in those situations in which an entity is 'betwixt and between', falling between categories in our classification of the world.[22] Death is, of course, the situation *par excellence* where the living are confronted by the danger of a torn social fabric and the physical contamination of a putrescent corpse. Symbolic pollution of mourners, corpse and material goods overwhelms the living and, during the liminal stage of the rites of passage of death, must be contained by rites of purification and by acts of transference which attach the pollution on to specific people and items.

In the early 1980s Judith Okely's analysis of British Gypsies' concepts of purity and boundedness was one of the anthropological studies which had significant value for the emerging *structuralist* and *post-processualist* schools of thought in archaeology. Ian Hodder and others were centring their attention on the possibilities of studying material culture through these *cognitive* approaches, moving on from earlier methods which had tried examining ethnographic records in order to draw up hypothetical rules of behaviour to which ancient societies were expected to conform.[23]

Okely described Gypsy notions of symbolic boundaries which must be rigorously maintained to avoid pollution. She found a series of homologies linking inside/outside the body, inside/outside the home (the caravan or trailer), clean/unclean animals, and relations between Gypsies and Gorgios (non-Gypsies). Okely surmises that the corpse is considered polluting because boundaries have been broken; the inside has come outside and the turning inside-out of the corpse's clothes is an expression of this. The Gypsy traveller lives in opposition to many of the ways of the Gorgio, whereas the dying are brought to the Gorgio hospital and corpses must be sedentarized and pinned down by burial in a Gorgio cemetery. When dead, the Gypsy becomes like a Gorgio in this breaching of boundaries between Gypsy and Gorgio. The act of tidying the grave is an inverted identification with Gorgio emphasis on outer appearance. Expensive wreaths and an elaborate funeral are appeasements to the dead soul, whose home and personal belongings are polluted and must be destroyed or, in recent times, disposed of to Gorgios.[24] As exemplified by this example from Gypsy society, the pollution surrounding death relates to broader spheres of social interaction and boundedness.

Separation of the dead from the living

The fear of the dead is a regular feature of liminal time prior to the rites of incorporation. Whether we weep for the dead because we fear them or we fear the dead because we weep for them, the dead are universally a source of fear, especially during the corpse's putrefaction.[25] With the passing of time, the deceased may come to be venerated, and fear and veneration may go hand in hand. Places of the dead such as tombs and graveyards may also provide a material locus for feelings of dread and fear. The separation of the corpse from the living is one means by which fear of the dead is controlled. Many ethnographic studies allude to strategies designed to sever connections with the deceased, whether by disorienting the coffin on the way to the place of burial so that the dead cannot find their way back, by burying the dead across the running water of a stream, by the provision of blades among the possessions of the dead so that they may cut their ties with the living, or by the cutting of a thread tying the mourners to the tomb. The deliberate orientation of a tomb so that it does not correspond with the orientations of dwellings (such as the location of tomb entrances so that they face away from those of houses) is widespread.[26] Battaglia's study of the Sabarl Islanders of the South Pacific highlights the ritualized ways of forgetting that are employed in the funerary rites, so that the deceased makes the transition to the other world while bringing least pain to the living.[27]

Fertility and regeneration – rotting and fermenting

The themes of regeneration and growth, expressed by symbols of human and agricultural fertility, have been regularly noted since van Gennep's analysis of the symbolism of the rebirth of the god Osiris in ancient Egyptian funerals.[28] Victor Turner's elaboration of the concept of liminality similarly demonstrates the significance of regeneration within Ndembu funerary rituals, a point brought out in Hodder's interpretation of Sudanese Nuba burial, where graves cut in the shape of a grain storage pit have their floors covered with a scattering of grain.[29] Bloch and Parry have brought together a group of essays devoted to this theme of death and regeneration and it is worth quoting Bloch at some length. 'Merging birth and death in the funerary ceremonies is what creates a picture of fertility which transcends the biology of mere dirty mortality and birth. Funerary rituals act out, therefore, not only the victory over death but the victory over the physical, biological nature of man as a whole. Birth and death and often sexuality are declared to be a low illusion, located in the world of women, and true life, fertility, is therefore elsewhere. This is why funerary rituals are an occasion for fertility.'[30]

Several authors have criticized Bloch's contention that female sexuality and reproductivity is generally associated with death and discontinuity in funerary symbolism.[31] Dureau advises that while fertility symbolism does imply timeless social reproduction, it is based on a cyclical conception of time from womb to tomb rather than on an ideological manipulation of women by men. We should also view degenerative and regenerative symbolism as two sides of the same coin.[32] Metcalf and Huntington observe that corruption is a near universal symbol in funerary rites. They describe how the Berewan of Borneo store decomposing corpses in sealed jars in the kitchen, drawing off the liquids in a manner homologous to the preparation of wine from fermented rice.[33]

Rites of reversal and 'killing'

The carrying out of actions backwards, and things being inverted or turned inside out, are common ritual elements in funerary practices. Ucko considers the case of Zulu ceremonies in which the coffin bearers walk backwards, a hole in the house wall is used instead of the door and 'yes' is used to mean 'no' and *vice versa*.[34] The eschatology is that of a world of the dead inverted to that of the living. Turning inside-out the clothing on the corpse is a common practice in many societies; among the Lo Dagaa the smock worn by the corpse was turned inside-out. Reversal reinforces the normality and naturalness of everyday practices by defining their opposite in ritual time. It also serves to separate the dead and their realm from the living. The 'killing' of artefacts associated with the deceased can be linked to concerns with pollution and to the means by which possessions become 'dead' so that they may travel along the same supernatural channels as the spirit.[35] There are many ethnographic as well as archaeological examples of this activity associated with funerary practices.[36]

The power of the ancestors

In the 1960s grants for agricultural improvement were distributed throughout many areas of highland Madagascar. It is said that, to the surprise and concern of the agricultural advisors, many communities used the money to buy cement, either to repair old tombs or to build new ones. Thus cherished, the ancestors might then show their gratitude to the living. The beneficence of the ancestors would improve the fertility of the rice fields and rice production would increase. The role of the ancestors is very marked throughout the ethnic groups within Madagascar (**Figure 2.2**), and it is a phenomenon found in many other societies.[37] Formal worship of ancestors is a feature of many societies in East Asia.[38] Elsewhere, ancestors may not be worshipped as such but are treated with the respect due to elders.[39] Lehmann and Myers have claimed that a universal belief in the immortality of the dead exists in all cultures, while Steadman, Palmer and Tilley argue that ancestor worship is a universal aspect of religion. This contention is somewhat exaggerated since they include ghosts, spirits and ancestral totems as ancestors and define worship broadly as reverence or respect. Their work attempts to revise the conclusion of Swanson's early cross-cultural study which claimed that, in twenty-four out of the fifty societies analysed, dead ancestors do not influence the living.[40]

Although we must question the merits of defining ancestor worship so loosely and also retain a scepticism of not only the sample size but also of the ethnographic basis of such knowledge, Steadman, Palmer and Tilley's study highlights the power of tradition in kinship-based societies in which 'the way of the ancestors' provides an unquestioned authority and truth. We should not, however, ignore those societies where the dead are deliberately erased from memory, so thoroughly that individuals cannot remember names beyond those of great-grandparents. One example is that of the Achuar of the Ecuadorian rainforest, where funerary rites are designed to prevent the dead spirit from stimulating the memories of the living; the rituals deliberately lead to a collective amnesia which wipes out earlier generations. The break between life and death is total, with no bridge between the beyond and the here and now, nor any destiny as an ancestor or lineage founder.[41]

2.2 A Betsimisaraka community in eastern Madagascar address their ancestors in front of a stone tomb. Most Malagasy are Christian but still maintain deeply held beliefs about the importance and power of the ancestors.

Observations that ancestors are active in the affairs of the living have major implications for archaeologists whose focus is on the disposal of the dead, since contemporary western notions – of death being a binary opposite to life, and of the dead as unwanted matter akin to rubbish – are likely to colour our perspectives on the past as well as on other cultures. As noted above, funerary rites often serve to turn the newly deceased, a dangerous and polluting entity, into a benign ancestral spirit. The holding of a 'great feast' among the Berewan entails the summoning of the sacred ancestral dead to partake in a festival at which their presence is potentially rewarding and invigorating but also dangerous; it is during this feast that the danger passes.[42] Thus we might talk of the living dead or the powerful dead: a dead person is not simply inert and decomposing matter whence life or the soul has fled to a self-contained world of the dead such as an afterlife, but a spiritual entity which may be wrathful or benevolent, invoked to provide good things and placated with sacrificial offerings to ensure the termination of misfortune.[43]

CROSS-CULTURAL GENERALIZATIONS AND THE NEW ARCHAEOLOGY'S SEARCH FOR MIDDLE RANGE THEORY

In the 1970s attempts were made by archaeologists to draw on ethnographic studies of mortuary practices not for making parallels with specific archaeological contexts but for exploring cross-cultural regularities and generalizations.[44] The study of funerary practices was one component of *middle range theory*, the search for invariate relationships between the static remains of the archaeological record and the dynamic behaviours of the people of the past in creating that record.[45] If particular relationships could be demonstrated to occur in all observed cases, then middle range laws could be employed to make inferences about past societies.

So, some researchers began framing law-like axioms to define and describe the relationship between mortuary behaviour and its archaeological residues; the philosophical aim of this school of thought was to construct a general theory of human social dynamics. In the 1970s this approach was seen as so innovative that it became known as the *New Archaeology* and, even twenty years later, it is often still called that; it is also sometimes referred to as *processual* archaeology. Most of the early proponents of the New Archaeology were working in the United States. Among them was Lewis Binford, whose cross-cultural study of the relationship between mortuary variability (the degree of variation in funerary rites within one society) and social complexity (the complexity of that society) was a demonstration of one such theory of the middle range.[46]

Binford and mortuary variability

Binford proposed that one might expect:

* a direct correlation between the social rank of the deceased and the number of people with relationships to the deceased;
* the facets of the *social persona* ('a composite of the social identities maintained in life and recognized as appropriate for consideration at death'[47]) of the deceased as recognized in funerary rituals should vary directly with the relative rank of the social position which the deceased occupied in life.[48]

Binford's cross-cultural study involved some forty ethnographically documented societies recorded in an archive called the Human Relations Area Files. He knew that he could not obtain the level of detail that he really required about social status variation or socio-cultural complexity but reasoned that subsistence production broadly correlated with complexity: hunter-gatherers, shifting agriculturalists, settled agriculturalists and pastoralists were the four subsistence-based definitions of types of social group used by Binford, and he divided his sample into these broad categories.[49]

Binford then listed the possible classes or dimensions of the social persona commonly recognized: age, sex, social position, conditions of death (how death occurred), location of death (where the person died), and social affiliation (membership of a clan, sodality, etc.). He found that the societies classified as settled agriculturalists more often took these dimensions into account in symbolizing the social persona of the deceased in funerary rituals. The fewest dimensional distinctions were found among pastoralists, with slightly more among hunter-gatherers and shifting agriculturalists. Binford thus concluded:

1. The recognition of each of the social persona's dimensions of age, sex, social position, etc., varied significantly between settled farmers and the rest.
2. The number of these dimensions employed also differed; hunter-gatherers tended to employ fewer dimensions than settled farmers.

Effectively, the more complex societies (sedentary farmers) seem to have more complex funerary practices – they try to represent more information about the dead person and they emphasize different bits of the dead person's identity.

Finally, Binford analysed the relationships of these social persona dimensions with particular forms of funerary treatment. He examined the types of body preparation, treatment and disposition, grave forms, orientation and location, and grave good form and quantity which were reported for the societies in his sample.

3. The use of some of these particular funerary treatments varied with some of the social persona dimensions:
    a) sex was distinguished by grave orientation and grave good type only;
    b) age was distinguished by disposal of the body (grave, scaffold, river, etc.), type of grave and placing of the grave.

Summed up in more accessible language: 'who you are affects how you get buried and the separate bits that make up your identity get represented in different ways'.

Saxe and the social dimensions of mortuary practices

By the time Binford had published this work, Arthur Saxe had completed his PhD thesis on the social dimensions of mortuary practices.[50] Saxe used principles derived from role theory and from formal analysis (the study of the degree of 'redundancy' and 'entropy' in classificatory schemes). He proposed eight cross-cultural hypotheses which he tested on three societies: the Ashanti of West Africa, the Kapauku of New Guinea and the Bontoc Igorot of the Philippines. He didn't have to go to all these places – once again, the testing was done on data already collected and published by social anthropologists.

Saxe's hypotheses are an exercise in logic. I have summarized them into as simple a form as possible but, to do justice to Saxe's work, they take careful reading. The eight hypotheses are:

1. If we combine the various aspects of funerary treatment (for example, disposal above/under the ground vs. grave goods present/absent), we have a set of permutations in which the different combinations may represent different social personae. Saxe concludes that they might do but need not.
2. How social personae are decided and created is linked to the principles organizing social relations in that society. Saxe concludes that more complex societies have more dimensions (such as rank or social position) which cut across egalitarian principles of age, sex and personal achievement.
3. Lower status social personae would be marked by having fewer items than others, and conversely. Saxe finds that this is broadly the case in egalitarian societies, whereas in stratified societies it is true within each stratum or class.
4. The greater a person's status, the more likely that their most significant identities are represented at death, at the expense of their lesser identities, and conversely. Saxe finds only weak evidence for this.
5. The higher the degree of redundancy (degree of correlation) in burial attributes, the more complex and hierarchical the society, and conversely the more entropic (lack of correlation = paradigmatic) the less complex and more egalitarian the society. This hypothesis was untested.[51]
6. The simpler a society, the greater the likelihood of a relationship between the number of components in symbols, the number of contrast sets to define them, and the social significance of the symbols, and conversely. Saxe notes that this hypothesis needs to be refined.

7. The simpler a society, the less funerary variation there is in the treatment of deviants, and conversely. This was untested.
8. Formal disposal areas exclusively for burial of the dead (i.e., a cemetery) are maintained by corporate groups legitimizing through descent from the ancestors their rights over crucial but restricted resources, and conversely.

Given the data he was working with, there are no doubts about Saxe's scholarship. Yet there are difficulties in testing through cross-cultural surveys. Primarily, the researcher today can never be entirely certain how accurate the ethnographic records are. I can't imagine any researcher having the time or the ability to revisit every society ever described by an anthropologist. It is more than just a matter of whether the anthropologist got everything 'right' first time – there are always questions to be raised about objectivity, impartiality and understanding. Such cross-cultural surveys from written data have to be taken on trust to some extent, which leaves a rather large hole in attempts to apply the methods of experimental science to an observational science such as archaeology or anthropology.

Goldstein and Hypothesis 8

The most interesting of Saxe's hypotheses is Hypothesis 8, which was developed from Meggitt's observations in Papua New Guinea of affirmations of title to land by the living members of a group claiming links to a founding ancestor.[52] Where land was scarce, the dead were buried in cemeteries, but elsewhere, where land was not a crucial resource, disposal practices were less formal. The hypothesis posits a functional relationship: that this particular social response is a function of the social system's interaction with ecological factors. It assumes that, while the individuals may be entirely unaware of the latent functional purpose of their actions, their social system deals with the problem of resource scarcity by developing these ties between people, ancestors and the dead.

We are fortunate that Hypothesis 8 has been re-tested, again through the use of ethnographic records. Lynne Goldstein followed it up with a study of thirty ethnographic examples.[53] She found that part of the hypothesis was sustainable: that the maintenance of a permanent, specialized and bounded disposal area was one means by which a corporate group, seeking to legitimize its rights over scarce resources, might ritualize this relationship. The existence of such a disposal area is likely to represent a corporate group which has rights over the use and/or control of crucial but restricted resources.[54] In other words, the absence of a formal disposal area does not necessarily inform us about social structure whereas its presence does say something about the existence of corporate groups and ancestor veneration.[55]

Of all of Saxe's hypotheses, Hypothesis 8 is the one which has continued to be used and discussed. It was criticized by Ian Hodder on the basis of his ethnoarchaeological work on cemetery organization among the Nuba of the Sudan and has been recently reviewed by Ian Morris in a study of Classical Greek and Roman funerary rites, and by Christopher Carr.[56] Hypothesis 8 may take us some way towards understanding why cemeteries are constructed but it fails to help us understand when and why formal disposal areas, rather than other forms of legitimation, are employed by groups to assert title to scarce resources. Furthermore, relationships with ancestors go considerably further than simply establishing functional relationships to land, as surmised by Saxe and Goldstein.

Tainter and energy expenditure

Despite Ucko's caution about social inferences from mortuary practices, several of his examples show that wealth and/or status may be reflected in the contents, form, size or location of a tomb and he concludes that 'in the vast majority of cases known ethnographically, a culture or society is not characterized by one type of burial only, but . . . on the contrary, one society will undertake several different forms of burial and . . . these forms will often be correlated with the status of the deceased'.[57] A cross-cultural study on this theme was carried out by Joseph Tainter in an ethnographic analysis of 103 societies, to explore the relationship of social status and differential treatment of the dead.[58]

Tainter found that certain funerary practices were consistently associated with social rank, namely complexity of body treatment, construction and placement of the interment facility (i.e. grave or tomb), the extent and duration of mortuary ritual, material contributions to the ritual, and human sacrifice. He devised an abstract notion of *energy expenditure* and found that the social rank of individuals correlated with the degree of energy expenditure in their mortuary rites in 90 per cent of cases. In contrast, social rank was marked by grave goods in less than 5 per cent of cases.[59]

Christopher Carr's recent cross-cultural study of thirty-one non-state societies supports Tainter's findings on energy expenditure but also finds that in as many as thirteen of the thirty-one case studies (i.e. 42 per cent), differences in grave good provision are linked with differences in *vertical social position* (i.e. rank in a hierarchical social system). He also concludes that the quality of grave goods or offerings placed in the grave (but probably not their quantity) is also indicative of the status of the deceased.[60]

Carr's approach is critical of Binford's sampling of societies and limited numbers of variables, as well as his assumption that subsistence mode would relate to degree of social complexity.[61] Carr's most important, if obvious, conclusion is that mortuary practices are determined by a complex mix of primarily philosophical-religious and social factors and secondarily, physical and circumstantial ones. Further, social organization and social personae are often portrayed indirectly in funerary practices through the filter of beliefs and world view which themselves often affect funerary practices independently of social, physical and circumstantial courses. Beliefs determining mortuary practices and the treatment of remains are often primarily beliefs about the soul and its journey to the afterlife and beliefs about universal orders, including structural oppositions. The only factors which vary with social complexity are the expression of personal identity – which decreases with increasing complexity – and the indication of *horizontal social position* (i.e. age, sex or membership of a clan or sodality) which increases with complexity.[62]

While Carr realizes that this and other middle range statistical generalizations do not constitute middle range theories expressing invariate relationships between social behaviour and mortuary ritual, he seems keen to develop such an approach, suggesting Hertz's theory that the fate of the body is used as a metaphor for the fate of the soul might be one such universal, a proposition that I have questioned earlier.[63]

Criticisms of the New Archaeology

The processual approach of the New Archaeology, proposing positivist-derived universals for relationships between material remains and their social correlates, has failed to yield anything more than a few generalizations to which there are sometimes many exceptions. Tainter's energy expenditure model and the Saxe/Goldstein hypothesis are the two that have survived though these, along with the evolutionist, cultural ecological, functionalist and materialist frameworks within which they were generated, have been criticized from various directions.[64] Within social or cultural anthropology, in the late 1970s and after, there was a move away from such functionalist and materialist outlooks. Terms such as 'simple' and 'complex' carry connotations of previous racist schemes of 'savage' and 'civilized' and have been judged to be no longer morally acceptable for distinguishing between contemporary societies.[65] A further ramification is that 'simple' societies are equated with 'egalitarian' and 'complex' with 'hierarchical', implying that hierarchical societies are at the apex of human achievement and evolution. Yet societies with 'simple' social organization and technology may have very complex cosmologies. Within archaeology, the processual concerns with universal generalization and social evolution have been challenged by new approaches which consider their views, especially of non-industrial societies, to be mechanistic, reductionist and de-humanizing.[66]

The concerns of the New Archaeology, in looking for middle range rules of human behaviour, had led to a focus on what people did, to the extent of ignoring the ways of thinking which are reflexively linked to social practice. The proponents of New Archaeology's middle range theory have been looking for the wrong rules, focusing on *what* people did rather than *why* they did it.

FUNERARY PRACTICES: AGENCY, POWER AND IDEOLOGY

Many anthropological writers of recent years emphasize that funerals are political events at which the status of the deceased as well as that of the mourners is actively negotiated and re-evaluated. Geertz's analysis of the turmoil of a particular Javanese funeral provides a clear account of the way in which the ideological and political conflicts waged over the deceased were out of all proportion to the importance of the dead ten-year-old boy.[67] Metcalf and Huntington devote a substantial part of their book to the discussion of the transition of kingship during royal deaths, for example among the Shilluk kings and the Dinka politico-religious leaders of the Sudan, emphasizing how royal rituals and their funerary constructions serve in turn to build the institution of kingship.[68]

The New Archaeology of the 1970s tended to see funerary practices, and the roles or social personae of the dead, as reflections of behaviour providing a record of rank and status. Archaeologists of today's *post-processual* school are more likely to doubt the clarity of that reflected image – funerals are lively, contested events where social roles are manipulated, acquired and discarded. The deceased as he/she was in life may be thoroughly misrepresented in death – the living have more to do than just express their grief and go home. Thus the material culture retrieved by archaeologists as the remains of funerary rites is not the passive 'statics' resulting from active behavioural 'dynamics' but is itself part of the active manipulation of people's perceptions, beliefs and allegiances.

As a specific realm of human activity, funerary rituals are incorporations and revelations of worlds and entities often very different from those invoked in other circumstances. In many cases they are concerned with idealized roles, spirits, communities and relationships which may refer more to the imagined past than the experienced present. As we have seen, Bloch's identification of a disjuncture between Merina social representations portrayed through funerals and tombs and the social and economic actualities of everyday life is one such case. 'The presence of the past in the present is . . . one of the components of that other system of cognition which is characteristic of ritual communication, another world which unlike that manifested in the cognitive system of everyday communication does not directly link up with empirical experiences. It is therefore a world peopled by invisible entities. On the one hand roles and corporate groups . . . and on the other gods and ancestors, both types of manifestations fusing into each other.'[69]

One of the problems with Bloch's formulation is that it postulates an ideological realm of representation which is separated from the everyday experiencing of economic and political reality. Rather, we should think of human experience as developing within a myriad representations, whether they be the gender and status relationships played out in domestic activities, or the roles reconstituted in funerary ritual. Thus funerary rituals are not simply an ideological 'mask' of an everyday reality but simply one arena of representations among many.[70] In addition, human experience is not compartmentalized between the ritualized and the everyday but draws on knowledge of each to interpret and act in the world.[71]

Social practice and agency

Social theory that emphasizes role and social persona has been largely superseded by theories of *practice* in which roles are not pre-defined but are created through social practice.[72] Roles should be considered as fluid and amorphous, open to manipulation in very subtle ways; institutionalized roles may constrain or enable behaviour but people's adherence to them may be variable.[73] Thus identities symbolized in death are the results of many different forces acting upon the mourners and on the deceased.

Whereas archaeologists have searched for generalizations and universals, anthropologists in recent years have explored variation and difference within the uniqueness of each culture. 'Much like the concept of culture, approaches to death in anthropology have undergone a process of parochialization. Parochialization has had the effect of eliminating a transcendental and universal conception of the problem.'[74] This development of what Fabian calls a 'folklore' approach to how others die has led him to infer that such studies place funerary-related behaviour at a safe distance from the core of our own society, turning it into a study of the 'other' which avoids rather than faces the 'supreme dilemma' of death.[75]

While we will come back to this issue in Chapter 7, such approaches towards the particular and contingent have been important for establishing people, their beliefs and their *agency* (what people do as knowledgeable actors, the intentions behind their actions) as the subject of study, rather than the systems and structures of functionalist approaches. The usefulness of the anthropological conception of an *emic* view (the subjective perceptions and beliefs of people within a society) and an *etic* view (the objective analysis of the behaviour of those people from the outside), of which the distanced etic view is seen as the properly scientific approach, also comes to grief.

In funerary practices, as in all aspects of lived experience, thought and action form an inextricable duality which must be understood in terms of people's beliefs and agency rather than simply rationalized on our own terms from the outside. Such views are now firmly established within recent social theory.[76] Instead of sifting through the particulars of ethnographic observations to find latent functions and rationalities of which the subjects may be blissfully unaware, and which can be posited as cultural universals, we need to be aware of the quasi-universals and general themes which provide a framework for cultural variation but alone and taken from their cultural contexts tell only a small part of the story. Metcalf and Huntington summarize this relationship between the universal and particular:

Placed in the context of a particular ideological, social and economic system, rituals of death begin to make sense in a way that they cannot if we pursue elusive cultural universals . . . Caution is doubly necessary in connection with death rites because of an odd paradox. Contrary to what one might expect, conceptions of death are not only elusive, but also highly variable . . . Meanwhile, concepts of life . . . have a certain universal familiarity about them . . . the same symbols occurring in rites designed to promote fertility and the preservation of life . . . Death is more intangible.[77]

ETHNOARCHAEOLOGY AND THE RECONSIDERATION OF ANALOGY

Ethnoarchaeology, a word which came into general use in the late 1960s, describes the use of field observations in the ethnographic present gathered by archaeologists addressing particular questions posed by archaeological data. Much ethnoarchaeology, nearly all of it on subjects not related to mortuary practices, developed in relation to the New Archaeology's call to develop middle range theory. The New Archaeology aimed to gather ethnographic data and frame questions within the hypothetico-deductive reasoning of a positivist philosophy of science.[78] Ethnoarchaeology was also the central method of Ian Hodder's *cognitive* school between 1979 and 1985, in the early stages of what was to become known as post-processual archaeology. Here, the aim was to understand the contextual workings of material culture symbolism within particular societies to understand how that material culture might fit into or be used to constitute ideological strategies of power and domination/resistance.

Forms of ethnographic analogy

Ethnoarchaeology relies on the use of *analogy*, the equivalence or correspondence of one thing to another. My examples throughout this chapter of funerary practices from diverse societies can be useful as analogies to the archaeologist studying an ancient culture. Such ethnographic analogies must be used with caution and archaeologists are very clear about their validity. Yellen defined four types of analogy: general, buckshot, spoiler and laboratory.[79] General analogies are limited to a few basic premises such as the observation that all human societies employ symbolism. Buckshot analogies are specific, tested hypotheses that might be developed from one specific ethnographic context and applied in a 'scatter-gun' fashion to any particular archaeological context which might fit those specific circumstances. Spoiler analogies are those specific instances when we might use an ethnographic case to dismiss an archaeological generalization or an inadequate archaeological interpretation. Finally, laboratory analogies are derived from experimental archaeology and do not require interpretation of an ethnographic 'other'.

Hodder reformulated analogies as formal, probability and relational.[80] *Formal*, or piecemeal, analogy is a basic building block of archaeological interpretation; through initial interpretation we come to recognize 'a hole with a human skeleton in it' as 'a grave' on the basis of resemblance of form or appearance. However, formal analogy is severely limited when moving beyond identification into more complex interpretations and understandings.

Probability analogies are made through the use of quasi-universal cross-cultural generalizations. Tainter's rule that social status is indicated by the degree of energy expenditure in 90 per cent of societies is an example of this. A problem with probability analogies (other than that we must hope that we will not encounter cases that fit into the other 10 per cent!) is that the reasons *why* the relationship holds are not necessarily explicated. What matters is that the rule holds, not that its linkages can be necessarily explained or understood.

Invariant naturalistic inferences of this kind should not be considered as unassailable truth. As Alison Wylie has argued, there is no one set of standards or reference points, a 'transcendental grid', to which all hypotheses about the past can be referred.[81] Instead she considers universalizing inferences as simply part of a continuum of different kinds of inference which must be applied locally according to knowledge of the context under investigation. She proposes drawing on linking principles which establish diverse and independent lines of evidence, a kind of triangulation of inferences from different directions.

The *relational* analogy is an indirect analogy between an ethnographic context and an archaeological case study, based on the structuring of social relations. We may consider a relational analogy as that which links different manifestations through a common structuring principle. Hodder's work on the notion of pollution and purity in structuring relationships between men and women shows how different material outcomes stem from the same underlying ideas in Nuba society, and in British Gypsy society.[82] Hodder is never clear as to whether his structuring principles have cross-cultural universal validity; if so, then it is hard to see exactly how his notion of relational analogy differs from the laws of human behaviour presupposed by the probability analogy. It is better to assume that structuring principles are not universal and to work on the assumption that we require a certain level of inter-contextual analysis (Wylie's 'triangulation') in order to establish whether they are relevant for the purposes of analogy. A recent example of relational analogy interprets Stonehenge and other stone monuments of the British Neolithic as places built for the ancestors by comparison with the meanings of stone in Madagascar. The strength of the analogy lies not in the logic of the bridging argument, as with a probability analogy, but in the degree of corroboration and goodness of fit with the evidence of the archaeological case study, its ability to open up previously unforeseen avenues of study, and to reveal new insights into evidence which previously had not been understood.[83]

Ethnoarchaeologies of death

By the 1980s it was clear that archaeologists themselves would have to gather the specific ethnographic data that they were interested in, rather than continuing to pillage anthropologists' case studies in the hope of finding a few morsels of relevant interpretation. This applied as much to the specifically death-focused contextual studies as to the Human Relations Area Files. Furthermore, the anthropologist's frozen moment was wholly inadequate for drawing comparisons with sequences of change in past societies. Towards the end of Hodder's African ethnoarchaeology he became increasingly concerned with the study of time and change, a marked departure from the notion of observing an ethnographic 'snapshot' of a static or synchronic moment in the present in order to make inferences about past societies in dynamic or diachronic perspective.[84] While many anthropologists were now becoming increasingly interested in developing historical perspectives to their studies of the present, only archaeologists were capable of using archaeology with history in their studies of contemporary societies. As Hodder's Baringo studies had shown, ethnoarchaeology also required a regional setting in which the spatial and temporal could be combined, in contrast to the standard anthropological approach of staying within one village community.[85] Good ethnoarchaeology also requires a society-wide awareness of social practices beyond those being specifically investigated.

Curiously, in contrast to Fabian's criticisms of anthropologists' evasion of tackling how we die in the west, funerary ethnoarchaeologists have concentrated their researches on British and American practices. A summary of this work is given below.

Some work by archaeologists has been done with the ethnographic 'other'.[86] The following case study of funerary practices among the Tandroy of southern Madagascar shows just how dynamic funerary ritual and architecture can be and how the correlation between social status and funerary expenditure has varied over the last two hundred years. By focusing on the development of monumentality in tomb building, the study demonstrates that the long-term time dimension is essential for ethnoarchaeological inquiry, in contrast to static ethnographic representations used in cross-cultural analyses or the brief historical sequences (fifty to a hundred years) which are occasionally addressed in social anthropological research.

TANDROY FUNERARY PRACTICES AND THE RISE OF MONUMENTALITY

Androy, the 'land of thorns' inhabited by the Tandroy, is a region in the semi-arid south of Madagascar where pastoralism is the dominant form of subsistence in contrast to the rice cultivation of much of the rest of the island.[87] The dead are buried singly below ground, and tombs in the form of stone-walled enclosures filled in with boulders are erected over them so that the dead are not disturbed again. The bodies of dependent kin may later be inserted into the top of the tomb.[88] These sacred monuments are found throughout the region of the Tandroy and Mahafaly people. They are often huge, over 12 metres square and 1.2 metres high, with large standing stones – 'man stones' – at either end and a central monument in the centre (**Figure 2.3**). This monumentality is a tradition of relatively recent origin, and just one of a number of different types of burial forms used by the Tandroy in the last few centuries.[89]

The Tandroy emerged as a political and ethnic entity in the sixteenth century, with clan groups ruled by leaders known as *roandria* engaged in endemic warfare and feuding. One lineage, the Zafimanara, was paramount and, despite a highly fragmentary political situation, maintained its power until the late nineteenth century. We do not know whether there were important distinctions between Zafimanara, commoner and slave burials in the seventeenth and eighteenth centuries except that Zafimanara *roandria* have been traditionally laid to rest in caves, probably since the late seventeenth century. This variant style of interment is further distinguished by the placing of the body above ground. During the early eighteenth century the standard funerary rite involved burial within wooden enclosures hidden in forest.[90] This practice continues today and has connotations of poverty and low status in many areas, contrasting with stone tomb construction. During the early eighteenth century male circumcision rituals, rather than funerals, appear to have been the focus of consumption and for mediating social relationships, in contrast to today.

Tomb types and placing of graves

The use of stone in burials dates to the late eighteenth century, commencing with paired standing stones ('man stones') and with kerb stones around the grave. The earliest stone tombs were small rectangular cairns with standing stones at the east and west ends, probably beginning around 1820. By 1880 large tombs with low drystone walls were being built (**Figure 2.4**), while concrete and stone tombs with high walls, central tomb 'houses' and tall 'man stones' appeared in the 1930s. Finally, in recent years some tombs have been constructed with walls comprised of carefully chiselled stones with closely

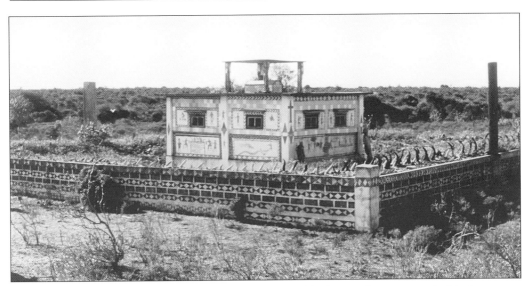

2.3 A modern Tandroy tomb. As well as depicting aeroplanes and bush taxis, the structures raised in the centres of tombs often take the form of colonial administrative buildings, but the tomb is modelled not on the house but on the cattle pen.

fitting joints. The change in fashions is such that ancient or old forms may often not go out of use but continue to be constructed alongside innovative styles.

The building of stone tombs in prominent positions in the landscape is largely replacing the forest cemeteries where burials are enclosed within rectangular timber palisades. These palisade burials are similar in size to modern stone tombs but their earlier forms, in the nineteenth century, were much smaller with dimensions similar to the early stone tombs. Today the difference between palisade burial in forests and burial in a large and highly visible stone tomb is regarded as a distinction solely between rich and poor. In the sand areas of Androy, stone is today either carted in quantity from many kilometres away or the tomb is constructed with a mixture of stone and wood to simulate stone tombs. In this latter case, the minimal use of stone is in the provision of tall 'man stones' and a small cairn over the grave.

There are social conventions governing the placing of graves and tombs in relation to one other.[91] Burials of senior individuals are always to the south of juniors while women's burials (which are not graced with 'man stones') are to the west of men's. Thus these warp and weft principles are employed in the complex spatial ordering of successive interments in relation to each other, whether the tombs are single or contain several graves. The classification of tombs is further elaborated by the division of stone tombs with multiple burials into three types: *mirampy* (where one tomb is built up against another, sharing a party wall); *miharo* (where a new grave is dug next to another tomb whose wall is subsequently demolished so that the two graves may be incorporated into a single tomb); and *mijo* (where a second burial is inserted through the fill of an existing tomb).

Tombs, cattle and houses

Tombs today are modelled on the cattle pen. Their size is comparable to the wooden-fenced rectangular cattle pens which are built traditionally in the north-east part of the village. These pens are constructed of uprights and cross-pieces and have their entrance in the south-west; in

2.4 An early Tandroy stone tomb, built for Mahasese, a king who died c. 1905–1910. This large style, first originating in about 1880, represents a metaphorical cattle pen in stone. Smaller earlier tombs, the same sizes as wooden houses, were first constructed in the earlier nineteenth century in remote areas.

houses the south-west doorway is traditionally reserved for slaves and women. This comparison between stone tombs and cattle pens is made explicit in the term 'stone cattle pen', one of the several words for stone tomb. The metaphor is further strengthened by the placing of cattle bucrania (the upper part of the skull with the horns attached) all over the tomb.

Cattle are the economic and symbolic driving force of Tandroy society. Their killing at an interment, the draining of their blood into the ground prior to the act of burial, and the marking-out of the grave's edges with blood are all central aspects of funerary ritual (**Figure 2.5**).[92] The exchange of cattle in relationships of obligation between wife-giver and wife-taker groups at funerals is a further indicator of their ideological significance.[93] Cattle are traditionally not killed at times other than funerals. The animals chosen for sacrifice must be castrates, since a bull's potency might challenge the sacredness inherent in the tomb site. The consumption of meat from the animals sacrificed at the tomb is restricted to strangers and non-kin attending the funeral and to the funerary priest who assuages the pollution of death.

Cow's milk also has sacred connotations. Boys and men are the milkers of cows; it is forbidden to women though it is said that they have the right to drink directly from the udder. The milk must be taken in a calabash, cow by cow, to the house and enters the house only through the south-west door. Only then may all the milk be poured together into a calabash or wooden bowl (no other material is used). Wooden vessels are similarly the only containers used in ceremonies conducted by ritual specialists. The cattle pen is the focus for specific ceremonies, protective and fertility-related. Shoes must be removed, as is required on tombs at burials, at clan gathering places, when entering the house and at ceremonies in other locations.

2.5 The stampeding and display of cattle in a village prior to and on the route of a funeral procession, and the driving of the host village's herd in front of the coffin to the place of burial, reveal the ideological importance of cattle in Tandroy culture.

The small stone tombs of the nineteenth and early twentieth centuries are not considered to be 'stone cattle pens' nor have they been in living memory. It thus seems likely that the metaphorical link between cattle pens and tombs is a recent one. We do not know if these ancient tombs had cattle bucrania placed on them since these survive for no longer than thirty years. If there is a metaphorical model for the early stone tomb then it is most likely to have been the house, with its same proportions (always slightly longer than it is wide) and size (about 3m wide and 4m long). Also, the 'man stones' of the east and west ends of the tomb echo the roof posts at the north and south ends of the house (known as the 'skull post' and the 'head post' respectively). It may be that the early stone tombs are modelled more specifically on the collapsed house, with their low walls and end posts still standing. The house of the deceased is left to collapse and this is the condition reached by houses immediately prior to their ritual burning once the deceased is installed in the tomb. The 'man stones' of some nineteenth-century tombs are trimmed at the top in a similar way to the end posts' tenon to which the ridge pole is mortised. However, the size and shape of the standing stones, and the name 'man stone', are also very evocative of the human form. The latter seems most likely to have been a powerful symbolic association but this is not to deny the possible association with house end posts.

The origins of monumental tombs

The story of the origin and development of stone tombs involves a number of changes and transformations, notably their increase in size, the increased height of 'man stones', the change from 'semi-detached' tombs (*mirampy*) to singular tombs, and even the probable reversal in the direction of seniority (initially descending from north to south and changing to south to north). This series of transformations must also be set in its context of kinship relationships, landscape setting, clan migration, and changes in other forms of burial, among both the Tandroy and neighbouring groups such as the Bara and Mahafaly.

Stone tombs originated when certain clans moved from the southern sand region to the rocky outcrops of central and northern Androy. From archaeological fieldwork and research on oral histories of migration, we are able to date this northward movement of the Afomarolahy clan to between about 1800 and 1880.[94] It was during this period that they settled adjacent to the rock massif of central Androy. In this rocky area we discovered a number of ancient Tandroy stone tombs. The names of some of the individuals buried in these tombs are still known, and can be found in the genealogical lists compiled for each lineage of the Afomarolahy and related clans.[95] By reckoning the date of death from these individuals' placing within the genealogies, the earliest rectangular cairn burials with 'man stones' are estimated to date to between 1860 and 1880. While there are small cairns of the early eighteenth century in northern Androy, these are different in shape and were probably constructed by Bara pastoralists who now live well to the north. Burials marked only by 'man stones' began earlier, in the eighteenth or even seventeenth century.

Those buried in the first monumental stone tombs were members of clans which were subordinate to the ruling Zafimanara, now known as the Andriamañare clan, but were ranked above other clans. The tombs were constructed in regions previously deserted and forested, and in grazing areas; these early monumental tombs were hidden deep in the forest, but away from the communal cemeteries of wooden fenced tombs. In simple terms the tombs were built because stone was now available. However, they appear at a time of considerable upheaval and many factors are probably involved. The Afomarolahy were moving into new territory, away from the constraints of traditional authority. They were encountering hostile Bara cattle herders in competition over grazing areas. They may also have been influenced by the Bara's styles of stone tomb but, as far as is known from oral histories, they did not intermarry.

The numbers of the Afomarolahy clan were expanding rapidly and, around this time, new group identities of lineage and sub-lineage may have been created partly through monument construction. The first men to be honoured with this style of burial were rich in cattle but had neither political office nor marriage connections with the royal clan. The centralized power of the royal clan waned around 1888, when Androy split into five small polities. The stone tomb tradition was not widely adopted by other clans until the twentieth century, but today these tombs are found throughout Androy. While forest burial within wooden enclosures continues, the construction of prominently placed stone tombs is an overt demonstration of wealth and status through which social and exchange relationships are mediated.

A number of quasi-universal themes emerge: that funerary monumentality is linked to moments of political uncertainty both personal and institutional, that the innovations are begun by a (relatively) high-status group, and that their example is later emulated. Yet there are many other dimensions such as the significance of the marginal grazing areas, the early tombs' associations with male burials within male domains, the relationship between the ruling clan and the Afomarolahy, and the political dynamics within the Afomarolahy clan.

THE ETHNOARCHAEOLOGY OF US: FUNERARY PRACTICES IN BRITAIN AND THE US

There is nothing more dismal than an English funeral. The unnatural quietness, the unspoken sorrow, the grotesque pomp of watching the coffin disappear behind an electric curtain in the knowledge that it will only later be committed to the regulated gas jets of a crematorium furnace are all features which stand in stark contrast to the lively celebration of Tandroy death. In Britain the remains of the dead, whether cremated or inhumed, are marginalized and made to disappear, buried in suburban cemeteries or scattered in gardens of remembrance (**Figure 2.6**).[96] As Nigel Barley puts it, 'we do not just dispose of our dead, we throw them away and have no continuing relationship with them'.[97] He notes that the provision of cut flowers and the returning of ashes to nature are the only expression of decay linking to growth, whilst there is a tension in the need for ritual and, at the same time, a deep distrust of it.[98]

Archaeologists turned their attention to contemporary British and American funerary rites from the early 1980s, adding to a growing literature by sociologists and historians.[99] In addition, there is a growing corpus of manuals and excavation reports on graveyards, crypts and cemeteries of the last few centuries.[100] The contribution of the ethnoarchaeologists among this mound of literature can be largely summed up as a focus on the material culture of death, exploring trends in the ways that it is used to separate the dead from the living, to define identities and status. As Finch puts it, 'funeral monuments can be seen to be active, operating in many simultaneous contexts and discourses'.[101] We shall look at three themes: the rise of cremation in Britain, the mismatch between individual status and energy expenditure, and the relationship between religious creed and funerary practices.

The rise of cremation

In Britain today cremation is the normal rite; it is the destination of 72 per cent of the population, having reached what may be an upper limit after a century of rapid acceptance.[102] Cremation was legalized in 1884 after a fifteen-year campaign. Opponents considered it

2.6 British crematoria are situated at the margins of society, in areas which are ambivalent in their landscape associations and meaning. Unlike churches which are often visited for aesthetic pleasure or spiritual contemplation, the interior of the architecturally undistinguished crematorium is seen only at funeral services.

irreligious, pagan and a major obstacle to the resurrection of the body on the Day of Judgement. Its vaunted benefits included greater hygiene and sanitary precautions against disease, lower costs of funerals, protection of human remains from vandalism, funerary services held indoors and prevention of premature burial.[103] The campaign for cremation took place at a time of changing attitudes to hygiene which influenced perceptions of dead bodies as spreading 'miasmas' and diseases. Additionally, tastes in funerary pomp and ostentation were already beginning to change towards moderation and simplicity by the 1870s.[104] For some, the beauty and simplicity of urn burial, with its classical associations, invoked an aesthetic ideal of the garden. It is also possible that the once-abhorrent notion of cremation may have become more acceptable and familiar through the colonial encounter with the cremation religions of India. More recent justifications of cremation include the saving of land from becoming worthlessly cluttered by graves, its simplicity and lack of fuss and the creation of greater choice in depositing the remains. Such 'pragmatic' concerns belie complex changes in attitudes to the corpse, to the significance of the dead, and to religious beliefs.

As Sarah Tarlow points out, the rise in cremation signalled not only a shift from preserving the body (in lead coffins and using embalming techniques) to destroying it but also the individual identity of the deceased was rapidly broken down as well. The uniformity of urns, niches and plaques, the scattering of ashes into the anonymous gardens of remembrance, and commemoration by a collective monument and a line in the Book of Remembrance all contributed to the dislocation and anonymity of the dead. Cremation also accompanied and embodied a growing sense of privacy in bereavement, in which the immediate family and friends were not to be intruded upon in their grief.

Peter Jupp's study of choices between cremation and inhumation in 1980s Leicestershire identifies three main themes: religious beliefs, circumstances of death and social context. Firstly, funeral choices tend to be more elaborate, involving burial and memorialization, when the bereaved and/or the deceased were actively but traditionally religious, or perceived a religious or spiritual risk in death. Secondly, abnormal deaths (mass, sudden or premature) which are seen to be 'meaningless' and especially upsetting are similarly likely to mobilize the elaborate procedures of burial, perhaps since these deaths involve major social readjustments which are aided by 'funeral rituals deliberately designed to act as a vehicle for abnormal grief and to do justice to the lives cut short'.[105]

Finally, as previously documented for 1970s Cambridge, Jupp demonstrates that the economic and class position of the next-of-kin is also a significant factor. The observation that cremation has spread to a large extent as a class-associated phenomenon is supported by a distinction between rural dwellers and urban/suburban populations and rural incomers.[106] Rural working class with long-term local roots and close family relationships are more likely to be buried than cremated. This links to other aspects of preference for burial, of which positioning in the British class system is simply one factor. The degree of rootedness within close communities may well be a significant element in choosing burial. For certain social and/or regional groups such as the travelling show families, Gypsies, immigrant Catholics and many rural communities, cremation is still largely unacceptable and will probably remain so in the foreseeable future.

Status and expenditure

In costing less, the rite of cremation is an important aspect of the degree to which families in Britain choose to express their status in the scale and elaboration of funerary practices. The Victorian way of death is well known for its lavish displays of wealth consumption and its close grading of expenditure according to social position, prior to the advent of growing funerary simplicity as early as the mid-nineteenth century. As the 1977 Cambridge study indicated, there was almost an inversion in this relationship within a century. The Gypsies and show people were among the most ostentatious in all aspects of funerary display while the majority of those who lived in expensive residential property had simple and cheap funerals.[107]

Aubrey Cannon's survey of nineteenth-century Cambridgeshire gravestones led him to propose that this move towards simplicity by the higher status social groups was part of a long-term cycle in display, in which the wealthy initiate a tradition of modest funerals, considered to be 'good taste', in contrast to the existing funerary elaboration. He invoked a 'law of expressive redundancy' to explain such long-term cycles in funerary display in the context of Victorian England (and north-east Iroquoia in the contact period).[108]

The cycle is initiated by a first phase of high expenditure in funerary rites conducted by the rich – a moment of expressive elaboration. Later, as other groups or classes adopt similar lavish funerary displays, the élite adopt modest funerals to mark their difference from everyone else – expressive restraint. The reason for this, Cannon claims, is that after a while continued elaboration and expense just fail to impress. In the meantime, the lower social groups continue to emulate the now outmoded and vulgar ostentatious fashions once employed by the élite. Gradually this new practice of 'expressive restraint' spreads down the social ladder.

The concern for social status to be matched in funerary expenditure can be found in late fifteenth- and sixteenth-century sumptuary laws, in attempts to limit the emulatory expenditure of the *nouveaux riches* in competition with the traditional landed aristocratic classes, and a few decades later in the writings of the monarchist and churchman John Weever: 'sepulchres should be made according to the qualitie and degree of the person deceased, that by the Tombe every one might bee discerned of what rank hee was living.'[109] Finch describes how Weever proposed that the nobility should be marked by raised tombs with full-sized effigies and 'the meaner sort of gentrie' by ledger slabs, thereby restoring a social order threatened by the provision of the most lavish memorials to the 'tradesman, or griping usurer'.[110] Finch's study of seventeenth-century Norfolk church memorials, however, shows how these artefacts were actively used in the social strategies of élite families, particularly in creating the identity of a wider county élite.[111]

Religious difference and community identity

One rural community in Britain where inhumation is still universal is that of the Gaelic speakers of the Outer Hebrides or Western Isles of Scotland. The southern islands of the group are predominantly Catholic while the northern are strongly Presbyterian, yet funerary practices in this century are broadly similar in both communities, in contrast to much of the rest of Scotland and Britain generally.[112] The graveyard is located far from the church and settlement, often close to the sea, and traditionally the coffin was carried jointly by all the male mourners from the church. On the predominantly Catholic island of Barra the funeral procession's long journey between the two, with the coffin in the middle, the men at the front and the women behind, served to emphasize the separation of the dead from the living, the segregation of the world of men from women, and the interdependence of the male community. 'With each step the dead person is farther removed from this world' so that the deceased comes to occupy a ritual status 'not as an "actor", to be sure, but as an "object".'[113] The moment of physical separation comes when the coffin is lowered into the ground and the tassels attached to the coffin – the front one previously held on the procession by the male chief mourner and the rear one by the female – are removed.[114] While it has been traditional in other parts of Scotland for women not to make the journey to the grave, all attended the graveside and there was 'a great profusion of meat and drink brought to the place of interment'.[115] Vallee concludes that social status played a comparatively minor part in the ordering of social relations at funerals, and sees a structuring of solidarity and difference according to kinship, age and sex, religious affiliation and locality of residence.[116]

CONCLUSION

Some processual archaeologists have wondered whether this mismatch of social status and funerary expenditure will be found only in industrial societies and not in traditional societies where duties and obligations are defined by tradition and ritual. As Cannon's work on the Iroquois and the above study of the Tandroy indicate, this mismatch is also an element of non-industrial societies and it is contextually and historically specific. The social and ideological factors influencing funerary practices, and those practices' reflexive influence in return, can be shown to be important and complex. The extent to which we might expect a coherent relationship between ideology and funerary practice is far from plain. There been a tendency to treat traditional societies as if they do not have a history which includes fast-changing funerary practices, and there is also a problem of failing to appreciate the sometimes enormous impact of the colonial world on the societies in question. For example, we might envisage the establishment of a hierarchy of funerary elaboration consonant with status precisely as a result of external interference and domination.

As Cannadine has remarked, 'the history of death is at least as complicated as the history of life'.[117] The simple equation of practice with belief, and the existence of cross-cultural regularities or of stable and conservative rituals and traditions cannot be taken at face value. The archaeologist's task is, as a result, made more difficult. Extrapolations and interpretations must be derived, as far as possible, from contextual study rather than assumed regularities between the observed and the imagined. Yet material culture is not simply a reflection or result of human behaviour as it was envisaged by middle range theory. Material culture may be seen as partly constituting beliefs, ideology and practices. The role of ethnoarchaeology is thus not to fill the ancient and prehistoric past with possibilities derived from other people's present but to open up our imaginations to the extraordinary range of human approaches to death and life. As Bryony Coles says, 'the greatest contribution of anthropology is not the identification of odd artefacts nor the provision of information about any single aspect of human activity, but the provision of a framework for human action that shows us when the past has not been satisfactorily explained'.[118]

THREE

READING THE BODY

The body represents our primary and most fundamental source of contact with death. In a sense, the only portrait of death which we have is that which is inscribed on the livid corpse. The corpse is therefore not merely an object over which people vent their emotions but also one which is utilized to convey a representation of death and the hereafter.[1]

How we deal with a corpse says much about our attitudes to the human body generally, as well as to the dead and, specifically, to particular deceased individuals. The human body is not only a surface through which we categorize the world and give it meaning but it is also the basis for human experience and engagement with the world.[2] In the face of the universal fact of death, attitudes to the corpse are various and changeable. These attitudes are formed through the practices of treatment of the dead and are embodied in various ways. What is done to the corpse, where it (or its residues) are placed, and how that person is remembered or forgotten are all means by which we attempt to establish an understanding of a person's life and death, and of our own lives and deaths. Whether we embrace death or distance it, our attitudes speak volumes about our quest for ontological security (coming to terms with the finitude of being) as well as about society's values and conceptions.

Variations in treatments of the corpse, coupled with the paradox of bodily health regimes in the face of the body's certain demise, may have contributed to a contemporary set of concerns about the human body, its limits and its role in the construction of self-identity. The body is 'a product of the theories and practices which surround it and as those theories and practices are multiple then so too is the body multifaceted'.[3] Shilling defines the human body as 'an unfinished biological and social phenomenon which is transformed, within certain limits, as a result of its entry into, and participation in, society'.[4]

Such notions are not entirely new. Van Gennep, discussing rites of initiation, works from the other direction: 'Finally, if one also considers excision of the clitoris, perforation of the hymen, section of the perineum, and sub-incision, it becomes apparent that the human body has been treated like a simple piece of wood which each has cut and trimmed to suit him: that which projected has been cut off, partitions have been broken through, flat surfaces have been carved – sometimes, as among the Australians, with great imagination.'[5] For Mary Douglas the body is the natural system of symbols *par excellence*, through which the physical experience of the body orders the social world, modifying and being modified by the social categories through which it is known.[6] Foucault conceives of the body as a socially constructed product of power/knowledge, contingent on the myriad social practices in which it is enveloped.[7]

Reworkings of the body, and thus of self-identity, are common features of funerary mutilation among mourners, such as the practice of removing female relatives' fingers with a stone axe among certain New Guinea societies, or the self-laceration, battering and deliberate self-immobilisation by cutting thigh muscles performed by Australian

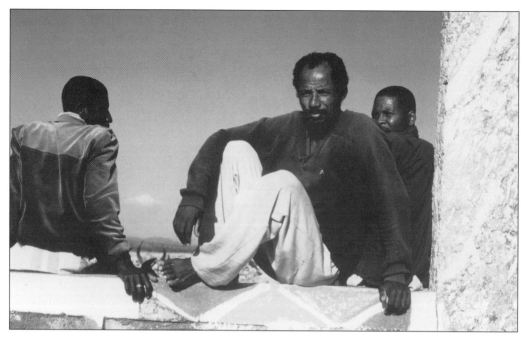

3.1 Retsihisatse, a Tandroy archaeologist, at his mother's funeral. None of the male relatives cut their hair or beards during the period between her death and the interment which took place three months later. Immediately after the interment was completed, all the men in the family – down to the smallest boys – shaved their heads.

Aboriginal mourners of the Warramunga group earlier this century.[8] Other less drastic bodily changes include the mourners' cutting of hair or deliberately letting it grow long and unkempt (**Figure 3.1**).[9] Very occasionally this may be accessible archaeologically, as in the discovery of eyebrow hair from several individuals, surviving in association with a razor and a cremation burial under a Bronze Age barrow (G3) at Winterslow in southern England.[10] However, it is the corpse which is the setting for the most important and radical bodily transformations. The treatment of the dead body represents the 'finishing' of the human form and, as such, can inform us of long-gone attitudes to the body.

Crossing boundaries

In 1977 the outspoken structuralist anthropologist Edmund Leach explained to a sceptical audience of archaeologists that they should reflect on the category distinction between 'living' and 'dead' and the fuzzy area in between.[11] He attempted to set forth a structuralist interpretation of how Palaeolithic mammoth-hunters may have conceptualized death. One of his basic premises was that all humans are interested in what distinguishes the inside from the outside of their own bodies,[12] especially with the orifices which connect the two (anus, urethra, penis, vagina, nipples, mouth, eyes, nose, ears). He claimed that, in all known religions, such orifices have major symbolic significance even though we may not fully understand their meaning.[13] His ideas echo Mary Douglas's suggestion that 'interest in [the body's] apertures depends on the preoccupation with social exits and entrances, escape routes and invasion'.[14] Julia Kristeva's use of the term 'abjection' to describe the horror and disgust of neat body boundaries undone is another nod to structuralism within feminist psychoanalysis.[15] Her notion of boundary transgressions – corpses, menstrual blood – as sites of power and danger is an important one with archaeological applications.

Leach's condensed structural triad of *culture* (This World) : *betwixt and between* : *nature* (The Other World) incorporated these principles to establish a series of boundary categories. The corpse was to be burnt, eaten or buried in the 'betwixt and between' which lay at the boundary to the other world, the inaccessible Other, which may be located either below the ground, above the sky, beyond the walls, or in the temple shrine's holy of holies.[16] These simple but important principles laid out by Leach were largely forgotten or ignored, even by the cognitive archaeologists,[17] although similar concerns illuminated early post-processualist approaches to the physical body[18] and rethinking of the placing of the dead in the landscape.[19]

DISTANCING DEATH IN RECENT AND CONTEMPORARY BRITAIN

Attitudes to the corpse have changed considerably in Britain with the growing popularity of cremation. The act of disintegration symbolized by cremation may be contrasted with the undertakers' (funeral directors') efforts to secure the preservation of an inhumed body and the mourners' sentiments that the dead are only 'asleep'. Earlier notions are revealed by the imagery used on carved tombstones. Whereas sixteenth-century memorials in England and Scotland display primarily aristocratic heraldic motifs, those of the later seventeenth century portray skulls, crossbones, snuffed candles, felled trees, bells, hourglasses and other *memento mori* (**Figure 3.2**).[20] The portrayal of the demise of the mortal and corrupt body at the bottom of the tombstone is often juxtaposed to the fate of the heavenly, pure soul at the top. This down-to-earth seventeenth-century attitude to the corpse's ultimate fate of becoming dry bones, and the eighteenth-century transition away from it, can be seen in many churchyards: tombstone motifs such as death's heads and blunt references to the manner of death change to euphemisms of loved ones only sleeping, at rest, or waiting in heaven (**Figure 3.3**).[21] From the end of the eighteenth century to the mid-twentieth century, inscriptions relate less to ancestral kin and more to spouses and immediate family, stressing the emotional nature of their relationships. Death was no longer a duality between the body's transformation into food for the worms and the soul's eternal spiritual life, but a sunset, a voyage over the sea, or a harvest, followed by the meeting of loved ones in the hereafter.

This 'prettification' is not confined to the memorial stones. The winding sheet was replaced by the shroud, often decorated, and by the coffin largely by the eighteenth century. Those who could afford it were often buried in lead-sealed coffins to enhance the body's preservation. During this period the undertaking profession also emerged, thereby ensuring that the mourners were separated further from their confrontation with the corpse. The corpse was only presented to the living after rouging, wiring of the mouth and other techniques to make it seemly and dignified. Coffins might be packed with bran and corpses' legs tied together to prevent any knocking and clunking while the coffin was being carried. Throughout Britain, changes are also evident in the manner of burial. From excavation of churchyards such as Barton-on-Humber, in eastern England,[22] it seems that the medieval and early post-medieval tradition of burying in relatively shallow and irregularly placed graves without permanent markers was abandoned in favour of 6ft deep graves set on regular grids and clearly marked so that the intercutting so common with earlier burials would be less likely to occur. Other material changes include the increasing popularity of coffin plates.[23] By the eighteenth century individual identities were emphasized more than before, indicating an increasing framing of the self.[24] Instead of distancing the dead as a separate entity, the central emotion associated with death was

3.2 A skull and crossbones on a later seventeenth-century tomb in Eyam churchyard, Derbyshire. There is a representation of an hourglass on the other side.

grief for individuals who were out of contact but with whom one would be later reunited.

As Sarah Tarlow points out, this transition in attitudes to the corpse, to the individual and to mourning took many decades. These oppositional views were polarized and also subject to modification within the same society. In the same way that the adoption of cremation in the nineteenth century was class-related, so the 'euphemistic' approach to death grew as an emulatory process of 'lead and lag', as Aubrey Cannon has documented for nineteenth-century Cambridgeshire gravestone styles, where changes are initiated by the independent farmers and later taken up by their agricultural workers.[25] Cremation may be seen as similarly oppositional to the 'euphemistic' death, an abrupt ending to the loved one's corporeal existence. The changing attitudes to the corpse are thus sequential yet incompatible; attitudes do not evolve gradually but are radical reactions against existing orders. Today in Britain, the idea of 'green' funerals, linked to contemporary concerns for environment and landscape, is gaining popularity as are 'do it yourself' humanist or non-religious funerals.[26] 'Green' burial is seen as a way of not only protecting endangered wildlife sites but of rekindling the 'awe, fascination, magic, mystery and wonder which wild nature has always offered us' in contrast to the hollow and mechanical commodification, alienation and destruction which are embodied by dominant philosophical approaches.[27] This new movement evidently sets itself apart from the practice of cremation in oppositional terms and, in the coming century, may rise in popularity at the expense of cremation, led by a growing number of middle-class and upper middle-class environmental radicals, visionaries, New Agers and others, as once cremation used to be promoted.

There are, of course, many different treatments of the corpse in contemporary western society. We may burn, bury or dump,[28] although sea burial is rare. Alternatively our corpses may be 'exposed' to medical practitioners' incisions to provide spare parts for transplant into the bodies of the living. At the same time, the medicalization of death[29] requires the carrying out of post-mortems on a substantial proportion of the dead; the skull is sawn in two and the chest cavity is broken open in the search for medical causes of death. It may not be long before the American practice of cryonics is adopted in Britain, involving the freezing of the corpse (or for a more modest fee, just the head) in the hope that superior medical technologies of the future will be able to restore life and to cure the fatal illnesses of which these people died. Such refusal to accept the inevitability of death shows an attitude to the body's mortality somewhat contrary to other contemporary concerns, such as the psychotherapeutic emphasis on coming to terms with death.

	DEATH'S HEAD	CHERUB	URN + WILLOW
1820			▨
1810			▨
1800		▨	▨
1790		▨	▨
1780	▨	▨	
1770	▨	▨	▨
1760	▨	▨	
1750	▨		
1740	▨		
1730	▨		
1720	▨		

3.3 Deetz and Dethlefsen's studies of New England gravestones identified a change similar to that in Britain. They found that death's heads were replaced by cherubs and urn and willow motifs in the period 1760–1790.

DESTROYING THE BODY

Archaeologists cannot dig up funerals, only the deposits resulting from their terminating practices. Very often, and perhaps for the larger part of prehistoric populations, we have no physical remains or traces of funerals or of the dead at all. Exposure of bodies in trees, or on platforms, or on the ground surface, or even shallow burial may lead to the complete destruction of any remaining bones. In many cultures the funerary practices contribute actively to the removal of all traces of the material remains of the dead, as in the case of cremation where the ashes are scattered.

Cremation

There is little that is purely functional in people's treatment of the corpse. A graphic example of this is the practice of cremation carried out in the Northern Isles of Scotland in the Bronze Age (c. 2400–1100 BC). Most of the woodland on these islands had disappeared earlier, during the Neolithic, and the only available combustible materials were dried peat and driftwood. The successful cremation of a human body normally requires the burning of about a ton of dry timber. Bearing in mind that these scarce timbers were also essential to house construction, the building and firing of peat and driftwood pyres must have been a remarkably difficult undertaking. Since cremation seems to have become the dominant funerary rite throughout the entire British Isles during the Bronze Age, these islanders were not so much being perverse as acting out a set of beliefs about the nature of the corpse and its transformation which were of great importance to them. Death cannot have been simply a disposal problem but a mythic and symbolic discourse of considerable complexity.[30]

This is illustrated by the beliefs behind Hindu cremation practices in India, in which the dead may be taken to the city of Varanisi (Banaras or Benares) and cremated on the terraces which line the Ganges, with their ashes then scattered in this sacred river. Maintenance of the cosmic and social order and achieving liberation from it are central themes of Hindu religion. Ritual sacrifices sustain order and gain merit for future reincarnations, and since the fourteenth century BC funerals have followed the formula of cremation set out in the Vedic texts. The corpse is a sacrificial offering to Agni, god of sacrificial fire, who disperses its elements. The body becomes ashes, the eyes are directed to the sun and the breath is scattered to the winds. Through fire the new body is reborn into the afterlife. The ancestors living in this other world themselves have to die in order to be reborn as people.[31]

The funerary practices of the Yanomamö of Amazonia present us with another archaeologically invisible rite. The dead are cremated and the ashes are ground to powder in a hollowed-out log. They are then placed in gourds which are stored in the roof of the kin group's house. The log is burnt after it is rinsed in plantain soup, which is drunk. At a second ceremony the gourds' contents are mixed with plantain soup and drunk by the close kin and friends of the deceased. This act of endocannibalism is followed by a celebratory feast.[32] The dead are both feared and valued. Their memory is not cultivated and they should be forgotten, yet at the same time their vital essence must not be lost to the living and is incorporated and recycled in the living bodies of the kin group.

Secondary rites

Hertz's essay on collective representation focused on secondary rites.[33] We may define these rites as involving a long intermediary period after which the remains of a dead body are recovered from their original place of deposition and moved to a new location. Technically all cremation practices (except where the ashes remain at the pyre site) involve secondary rites though the term is normally reserved for practices which involve the transformation from corpse to clean bones which are laid to rest in a second ceremony. Working from written accounts of various 'Dayak' societies in Borneo, Hertz recognized that the physical progression of the dead individual's remains, from fleshed to rotting corpse to clean bones, mirrored the spiritual journey of the dead person's soul from the land of the living through limbo to the land of the ancestral dead. The mourners similarly passed through three stages of primary rites, mourning and secondary rites.

Although we think of Christianity as associated with single-rite practices of cremation or inhumation, including ideas that the skeleton must stay intact until the Day of Judgement, there are many Christian cultures where secondary burial is the norm. Orthodox communities in northern Greece,[34] Anglican and Catholic communities in central and eastern Madagascar[35] and Roman Catholic Neapolitans[36] all practise rites of secondary burial, removing the body from its place of decomposition to an ossuary or individual vault. With secondary burial, the ultimate destination of the disaggregated human remains is likely to be well removed from the contexts of earlier funerary stages.

Patterns resulting from partial removal of human bones can be looked for archaeologically.[37] Secondary rites appear to have been a major part of funerary practices in the British Neolithic, between 4200 and 3000 BC; bone bundles and disaggregated skeletal remains were placed in tombs, caves or other burial deposits. Certain parts of the skeleton

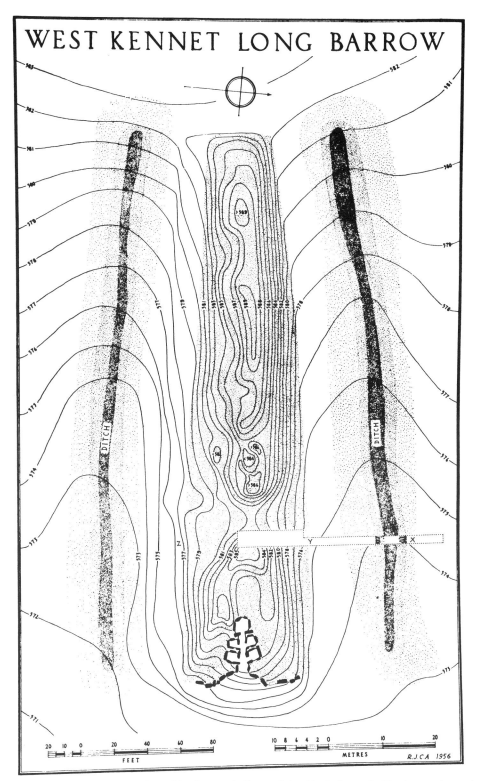

3.4 West Kennet long barrow was formed by digging chalk out of the side ditches and piling it up to form a long mound. The burial chambers at the east end of the mound contained human bones.

were moved from one context to another. For example, skulls are under-represented in the chambered tomb at West Kennet in southern England (**Figures 1.5 and 3.4**), but are found in profusion in the nearby ceremonial causewayed enclosure of Windmill Hill.[38]

The disaggregation of the body may be an ideological imperative by which the individual is denied and the collective asserted; the physical body acts as a metaphor of social organization, as Shanks and Tilley have argued for collective burial in British and European Neolithic chambered tombs and long barrows.[39] Yet meanings and metaphors vary considerably. The same rite of destruction in one culture may have very different significance and consequences in another cultural context. The archaeologist's interpretive problems may be further compounded by later movement of those remains or destruction of their final resting places.[40]

EATING THE BODY

Cannibalism is one of the most sensational topics in both archaeology and social anthropology and yet incontestable claims for its existence have proved elusive.[41] The case has even been made for its non-existence except as a mythic construct of the colonial mind in defining 'otherness', while the colonized have also accused Europeans of cannibalism.[42] Indeed, one of the clearest cases is the sixteenth- to eighteenth-century English and European practice of consuming as medicine powdered human bones, pieces of mummy (*mumia*), human bone marrow and blood; most extraordinarily, in Sweden and Denmark the warm blood of beheaded criminals was drunk as a cure for a variety of disorders. It is also recorded as being ingested by epileptics in parts of nineteenth-century Denmark.[43] One of the indirect pieces of evidence has come from the investigation of the transmission of a viral disease, *kuru*, among women and children of the Fore of Papua New Guinea, which appears to be associated with removal of the brain and, supposedly, cannibalism of the dead.[44]

Anthropological explanations of cannibalism

As Sahlins notes, cannibalism is always symbolic even when it is real.[45] Other than those situations of disaster and starvation,[46] cannibalism is rarely just gastronomic. The case of the Miyanmin of Papua New Guinea may be one exception, where blood feuding is thought to have turned into a quest for human meat.[47] We can dismiss as unsubstantiated Lévi-Strauss's claim that cannibalism formed part of a symbolic gastronomic opposition in which kin were boiled and outsiders were roasted.[48] Cultural ecological research in the 1960s and 1970s focused on the nutritional value, and adaptive potential, of eating human flesh.[49] Aztec nobles' eating of limbs from human sacrifices, observed by the conquistadores, has been interpreted by Harner and Harris as an adaptive means of acquiring protein in an environmentally exhausted ecosystem even though most sacrifices were carried out at the time of the harvest when food was plentiful.[50] For Harner and Harris, the symbolic motivations of rebirth for the eaten and the divine nature of human flesh were simply rationalizations of a latent ecological materialism – symbolism and culture 'covering up' for meat protein hunger – a position rejected as patently absurd and ethnocentric by others.[51]

Most social anthropologists prefer to explain the phenomenon in terms of notions such as symbolic communion, acquisition of the deceased's prowess, release of the soul, revenge or punishment of the deceased's ghost.[52] It is never just to do with eating but is primarily a medium for the maintenance, regeneration and even the foundation of the social order.[53] Endocannibalism (eating of kin) may constitute funerary rites and form part of the transmission of ancestral essence across the generations.[54] Traditionally Gimi women in Papua New Guinea ate the flesh of their dead menfolk to prevent it from rotting in the ground, to free the deceased's spirit so that it might rejoin the ancestral forest spirits, and to exact revenge for a mythic scenario when women's penis-like flutes were stolen by men who, in the process, caused women to bleed menstrually.[55] Exocannibalism (eating of strangers) is rarely an aspect of funerary rites other than after a revenge killing in response to a death.[56] Both practices are documented for Amazonian Indian groups such as the Ache or Guayakí, though the knowledge and practice of cannibalism is hidden as far as possible from the probings of anthropologists and other outsiders.[57] Finally, the essential ritual of Christianity is charged with symbolic cannibalism. Transubstantiation is the doctrine whereby the wine and the bread which Catholic worshippers take during communion are considered to become the blood and flesh of Christ after their blessing.

Archaeological evidence of cannibalism

Like ethnography, archaeology is one of those fields in which the otherness of the savage and primitive is reified through claims of cannibalism, thereby serving to reinforce self-identities of civilized superiority. The popular imagination, as reflected by newspaper interest, is always ready to devour stories on archaeological discoveries of cannibalism.

There has been something of a recent revival in cannibalistic interpretations from archaeological evidence.[58] At the cave site of Fontbregoua in south-eastern France, human bones among Neolithic deposits of butchered animal bones exhibit the same cut marks, while longbones are broken as if to extract marrow, all in the absence of carnivore toothmarks.[59] Modifications of human bones found in deposits of the Pueblo II/III period (AD 1000–1300) at Chaco Canyon and Mancos – sites belonging to the Anasazi culture of the south-western USA – have been considered as revealing probable cases of violent death followed by cannibalism.[60] Criteria that archaeologists have used in identifying cannibalism from the study of human remains include:

1. brain exposure
2. facial mutilation
3. burnt bone
4. dismemberment
5. a pattern of missing elements
6. greenstick-splintering of longbone shafts exposing marrow cavities
7. cut marks
8. bone breakage
9. anvil or hammerstone abrasions
10. many missing vertebrae
11. fragment end-polishing (deriving from cooking in a coarse ceramic pot).

No single instance is judged sufficient to provide evidence of cannibalism and all criteria have to be met.[61] For example, detailed taphonomic studies of Neanderthal bones previously thought to be indicative of cannibalism, especially the burnt and split bones from Krapina and the damaged skull from Guattari Cave on Monte Circeo, do not support the cannibalism hypothesis.[62] Those archaeological cases that do qualify all appear to involve aggressive cannibalism, inflicted on defeated outsiders, which is perhaps not surprising since compassionate cannibalism, of the sort practised by kin during funerary rites, may be considered less likely to result in such extensive bone modification.

Cannibalism is, therefore, extremely difficult to demonstrate archaeologically beyond doubt; absolute proof requires the identification of human tissue or bone in human coprolites.[63] The difficulty of proving the existence of cannibalism from archaeological remains is, on one level, methodological. But there is also an ideological problem, outlined above, in that the cultural baggage of chauvinist and racist attitudes to the 'primitive' is so strong in popular perceptions that archaeologists are often at pains to refute such claims because they are deeply reluctant to bolster unquestioned attitudes of discrimination which, in the west, are centuries old. Until cannibalism can be understood as simply one means among many of transforming the dead corpse, rather than the monstrous bogey so repellent to the civilized mind, such sensationalizing stereotyping will continue to be reinforced.

LAYING OUT AND ADORNING THE BODY

Bodily positioning in the grave is an important feature of the body's manipulation. *Rigor mortis* sets in within twelve hours of death and the dead body is normally arranged in some way while it is still flexible. Eyes are often closed and other orifices may be blocked up. The bowels generally move once after death. After rigor mortis the body will loosen up and may be further rearranged. 'The dead and the sleeping, how they resemble one another' is a quotation from the world's earliest text, *The Epic of Gilgamesh*, a hero's quest for immortality dating probably to around 2000 BC and later written down on Babylonian cuneiform tablets.[64] It is not surprising that in so many cultures the corpse is laid out in the grave in an attitude of repose. It may be curled in the foetal position, laid on its side, or laid out with its head on a pillow or headrest. Among the Andean Inka the mummified corpse was tightly bound in the foetal position. Both sleeping and foetal positions may be the prelude to rebirth or arrival in the land of the ancestors.

Body positioning may be a means of marking differences between and within social groups. In the Early Bronze Age cemeteries of south-east Europe (*c.* 2400–1700 BC) all burials were crouched and faced east but males were laid on their right sides and females on their left sides.[65] Orientation is often an important aspect of positioning. Sometimes the east, the direction of sunrise and rebirth, is the direction faced by the corpse. However, the immense variation of orientations even within the same society prevents the drawing of universal conclusions and each context must be considered individually. Ethnographically, often the orientation of the dead must be opposite or at least different from that of the living in sleep. For the Tandroy of southern Madagascar, the corpse lies in state within its house with head to the west and feet to the east while the living sleep with heads to the east.

Dressing and containing the body

The requirement to prepare the corpse, including some form of purification, is almost universal among contemporary cultures. It is often detectable archaeologically in the posture of the corpse, its placing in a special container or its treatment with substances which leave identifiable residues.

Containing the corpse is a preoccupation for many. The dead may be placed in jars, hollowed-out tree trunks, cattle hides, textile wrappings and even Cadillacs. The notion of containment in a coffin is so deeply engrained in western society that we take it for granted that bodies should be boxed in some way or another. Gittings has shown how the coffin's increasing popularity in early modern England was linked to changes in attitudes towards individualism and Tarlow has linked it to changing perceptions of the corpse. Such containers may be rationalized as hygienic and sanitary, yet their major role is to hide and remove the corpse from view so that the physical aspects of its decomposition do not attract attention. Indeed, attention may be focused on the coffin itself as in the case of the remarkable modern Ghanaian coffins in forms of animals, cars, tools, boats and vegetables, generally expressing the deceased's profession or position in life. Such brightly coloured and irreverent coffins may be considered antagonistic to conventional Christian attitudes and thus as elements of a lively resistance to religious orthodoxy.[66]

Schneider and Weiner have similarly discussed the many roles of cloth in funerary practices, including its use in dressing or wrapping the corpse.[67] Feeley-Harnik's study of the *lamba mena*, the funerary shawl for wrapping corpses and enclosing with the corpse in Madagascar, explores the symbolism of how kin relations are represented through these fine cloths.[68]

THE ABSENT AND ANONYMOUS BODY

In his semi-humorous examination of the bizarre rituals of the English, Nigel Barley observes that one particular English obsession is with retrieving the body after disaster or accident. In contrast to other cultures, '[i]f there is no body, it is impossible to hold a funeral that allows you to move on'.[69] The Whitehall cenotaph in London, in memory of all those missing and unknown warriors of the First World War, is one of the few 'burials without bodies' in British culture. This national focus for the outpouring of grief for the war dead remains the location at which the main Remembrance Day parade takes place. The American Tomb of the Unknown Soldier stands in Arlington Cemetery and, as Ingersoll and Nickell have pointed out, its importance derives from its symbolism of sacrifice for one's country involving the annihilation of self. '[I]t is the monument to the greatest western sacrifice, the sacrifice of self beyond hope for transcendence in a moment of history. The Tomb is the white *tabula rasa* of erased individual and social existence, the lonely statement to those living that but for the grace of God, so go you or I.'[70]

Much has been written about the war memorials of the two world wars.[71] The First World War ended with over half a million British soldiers' bodies unidentified or missing. The trauma of so many deaths was exacerbated by the inability to recover so many corpses and also by the failure to return the identified dead to their homeland. Alongside the building of the cenotaph monuments to the supreme sacrifice – loss of individual identity – the British and American governments went to considerable trouble after both world wars to reinstate the dead as individuals, although the massed dead of most previous wars had been buried in communal and unidentified grave pits.

In a curious reverse of those secondary rites in which the individual dead are rendered anonymous by collective burial, the funerary practices of both world wars attempted to commemorate the individuals who died in the mass slaughter. That commemoration extended to the erection of some 25,000 war memorials in the towns and villages of Britain alone. Most were raised as local monuments on which were inscribed the names of the dead from that parish or town. Their ordering was hierarchical and not collective, with officers distinguished from other ranks and specific military statuses set down. In the rigidly class-structured society of early twentieth-century Britain, those who had died in a common struggle were set apart in death according to their military rank which tended to conform to their social class.

Yet the concept of the cenotaph is more widespread than puzzled archaeologists might be aware. Cenotaphs are regular features of the Tandroy funerary landscape, in the form of standing stones which are ceremonially erected for those who are buried away from Androy, their homeland. Archaeological examples include certain British Bronze Age round barrows, such as two from Irthlingborough, in the English Midlands, which contained no primary burials even though one had a central burial pit. The enigmatic Anglo-Saxon ship burial in Mound I at Sutton Hoo contained no trace of a body.[72] Perhaps the firmest evidence for identifying this mound as a cenotaph is the placing of a pair of shoes over 3m from the likely position of the head, suggesting that the central wooden burial chamber was set out as though it contained a body rather than actually containing one.[73]

KEEPING THE BODY

One of the best known techniques of keeping the corpse is by means of its transformation into a mummy. The term 'mummy' is curiously erroneous since it derives from an Arabic word of Persian origin for wax or bitumen, and yet these substances were not normally used in mummification; this was probably due to ancient misidentifications of the black discoloration of Egyptian mummies.[74] The process of mummification is especially associated with ancient Egypt but has been far more widespread culturally and geographically. Early archaeological inferences by Elliot Smith of hyper-diffusion from Egypt to South America, the Canaries, Madagascar and other parts of the world arose from an inability to understand that the desire to keep the body as intact as possible can arise from very different cultural and ideological roots.[75] This failure of comprehension crops up frequently in 'fringe' archaeology which often claims supposed connections between cultures distant in time and space in a manner very different from the constrained use of analogy by more thoughtful writers. Such bogus theories tend to present cultural innovation as possible only under the influence of contact with a 'higher civilization', a worrying indication that the western mind-set is still fixated on racist ideas of domination and cultural superiority.

Other means of keeping the body include embalming, as in the case of Lenin and Eva Peron, preservation through freezing, as is pursued in cryonics, or by removal of flesh and entrails, or through the keeping of holy relics, such as the saintly relics of the early medieval period, described below. Examples of the removal of entrails and flesh are known from the Siberian Iron Age, as in the case of the Pazyryk tombs examined later in this chapter.

PHARAOHS OF THE NEW KINGDOM AND THE CORPSE AS COSMOS

The body was the focus of funerary rituals in ancient Egypt, most graphically illustrated by the mummification of pharaohs of the New Kingdom's 18th–20th Dynasties (c. 1570–1070 BC). Burial in the dry sand of Egypt leads to a natural process of mummification, as has been observed for burials of the Predynastic Period (before 3150 BC) and some authors have sought to explain this later treatment of the body as the straightforward employment of these natural processes, especially with the pharaohs' bodies located in the environments of pyramids and tombs where they might decay without such treatment.[76] This explanation is unlikely because the earliest pharaonic burials were placed within mortuary structures where they did decompose, something the Egyptians could have avoided if they were really imitating the sand's natural properties of desiccation.

Another rationalization is that of sanitation: the length of pre-interment funerary practices for early pharaohs may have led to the need for preservation of the corpse. At this period there may have been only practical concerns in play, with no conceptions of an afterlife or ideas about immortality being expressed in the mortuary rituals.[77] It is indeed possible that bodily preservation began as a short-term strategy to meet immediate political ends of displaying the corpse in ever-lengthening funerary rituals but there is every likelihood that the concern with bodily preservation was associated right from the beginning with hopes for obtaining immortality beyond death.[78] Long pre-interment rituals do not necessitate artificial modes of preservation and, in any case, early mummification did not achieve good preservation. The ancient Egyptians were undoubtedly aware of the desiccating properties of sand but that does not explain why a rite whereby the corpse was preserved artificially was restricted initially to the dominant classes. Mummification can only be explained as a complex cultural practice which encompassed a variety of changing attitudes to the body, death and the cosmos.

Mummification: methods and myths

The process of mummification involved different techniques which were available at the same time and also changed through time. Herodotus, writing in the fifth century BC, describes three methods varying in price.[79] The most expensive involved the drawing of the brain through the nostrils with an iron hook, followed by removal of internal organs through an abdominal incision. The corpse was cleansed with palm wine, purified with incense and stuffed with perfumes, and then soaked in a bath of natron (a hydrated carbonate of sodium) for seventy days before it was finally washed and bandaged. We know that the natron 'bath' had to be a dry one and a recent experiment using these methods, on a human body donated to science, has successfully replicated the desiccated appearance of a mummy. Earlier methods of mummification changed between the 18th and 21st Dynasties (between c. 1570–1293 and 1070–945 BC); later techniques included the placing of hands by the hips instead of crossed over the chest, the use of artificial eyes, the packing of sawdust and resin into the mouth to preserve the face's shape, the replacement of the treated internal organs back in the body and the packing of mud or straw under the skin to fill out the desiccated limbs.

The myths related to mummification can be recovered from the Pyramid Texts (inscribed on the walls of the burial chambers of the pyramids from the 5th Dynasty onwards) of the Old Kingdom (2686–2181 BC), the Coffin Texts of the Middle Kingdom (c. 2040–1780 BC) and later the Book of the Dead (papyri placed in tombs) of the New Kingdom; the main themes of judgement of the dead and a subsequent afterlife seem to have run throughout (**Figure 3.5**). Myths are narratives which continue to be recalled and enacted so that people understand their own destinies in universal terms of a once and current tale of morality and fate. In the Egyptian case these mythic themes may have been embroidered and modified for over three thousand years; Plutarch recorded their most common version in the Christian era.

The myth of Osiris's resurrection starts with the story of his death at the hands of his treacherous brother Seth, his body shut into a chest and thrown into the Nile. His sister Isis retrieved his body but Seth cut it into pieces and scattered them throughout Egypt. Isis gathered up all the pieces except his penis which was swallowed by an oxyrhynchus (a sharp-nosed fish sacred to the goddess Hathor). The body was put together and wrapped in its own skin by Anubis, sent by the sun god Re, and was given new life by Isis and her sister Nephthys who fanned it with their winged arms. Henceforth Osiris reigned in the afterlife as god of the dead. At every death, that person changed into an Osiris.

The theme of resurrection depended on the recognition of a multifaceted mind-body entity, consisting of a *ka* (the life-force – a fragment of divine essence from the universal spirit – represented as a pair of arms), an *aakhu* or *akh* (the blessed spirit – represented as a bird) and a *ba* (the 'personality', soul and moral conscience – represented as a bird with a human head) as well as the body *kha-t*.[80] Additionally, the individual had a *name* (the act of naming created the person) and a *shadow* which remained with the body even in death but could wander about. Since both *ba* and *aakhu* left the body at death, they had to be reincarnated in it and thus the body had to be ready to receive them. The *ka* resided in the tomb and all three might enter into communion with the body and be reunited with it.[81]

Tutankhamen

While at least forty-four royal mummies survive from the New Kingdom (1570–1070 BC), only three of them have survived without being robbed. They are, of course, the body of Tutankhamen and the two foetuses from his tomb.[82] The latter were each bandaged and placed in two nested wooden body-shaped coffins without any elaboration other than the gilding and plasterwork on the coffins. Tutankhamen's body, in contrast, was treated with considerable elaboration (**Figure 3.6**). We know from impressions and marks on the bodies and bandages of other pharaohs that their corpses were wrapped with an array of artefacts enclosed in the bandages. In some cases the gold or, in non-pharaonic burials, copper alloy or resin plugs that covered the abdominal embalming incision have survived. While Tutankhamen's treasures provide a probable scale against which we may consider the treatment of other pharaonic bodies, the ideological and political context of his reign may have marked his body out for special treatment. The apostasy of his predecessor Akhenaten's monotheistic worship of Aten was abandoned in favour of the traditional gods during Tutankhamen's lifetime. Tutankhamen's death in 1325 BC precipitated a crisis since he left no

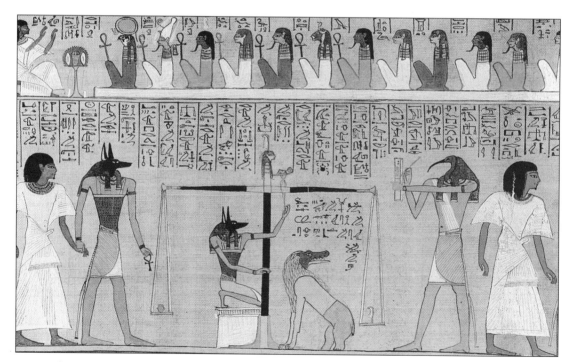

3.5 The Egyptian judgement of the dead. In the scales of a large balance, the feather of Ma'at (Truth) is weighed against the heart of the deceased. Should the heart be heavy, indicative of an impure and wicked conscience, it will be fed to Am-mut, the eater of the dead.

heir.[83] Thus the burial must have been the focus for significant legitimatory statements about supernatural order and succession and consequently the symbolism and grandeur of the funeral may not have been exactly representative of the rites for other pharaohs.

The route to the tomb taken by the dead pharaoh's body symbolized a pilgrimage between the ancient sacred cities of Lower Egypt. It was transported on a boat-shaped bier drawn by red oxen, symbolizing the colour of Lower Egypt, and then on a boat to the funerary temple. Red was also the colour of the shroud which covered the coffin, of the sandstone sarcophagus and its painted granite lid, and of the pottery which was broken at the moment of entombment. In the burial chamber within the tomb, the body lay with head to the west and feet to the east so that it would face the rising sun on revival, within an extraordinary series of containers. The sarcophagus lay within four nested golden shrines and enclosed three mummiform coffins. The innermost of these was of solid gold while the outer two were of gilded wood. All were decorated with images of the winged Isis and Nephthys and the sacred vulture and cobra, the symbols of Upper and Lower Egypt respectively.

The adjoining room contained the large canopic chest in which the viscera removed from Tutankhamen's body were enclosed in alabaster jars; the liver, lungs, stomach and intestines were each entrusted to a particular deity and enclosed within miniature mummiform coffins with magical inscriptions carved on their inner surfaces. The brain had been extracted through the nostrils and seems not to have been kept; the heart remained in the body and the abdominal incision was closed by a golden plate.[84] His skull cap was decorated with gold and glazed terracotta beads to form four cobras inscribed with names of the sun god Aten. Surmounting these were a gold vulture and serpent. Similar motifs were placed by his thighs. Fine linen bandages wrapped each finger and toe, then each limb and finally the whole body. His penis was bandaged in the erect position. At the same time unguents were poured on to the corpse (unfortunately in such quantities that they ultimately and paradoxically destroyed much of the body) and items of glass, cornelian, lapis lazuli, feldspar, iron and especially gold were incorporated within the bandages. This incorruptible and everlasting metal thus served to protect the dead pharaoh during his transformation.

Tutankhamen's extremities were protected by gold finger-stalls, rings, toe sheaths and sandals, and his forearms were covered in gold bracelets. His chest was covered with gold necklaces, ornaments and a collar and the head was covered by the unsurpassed gold mask. A gold dagger and sheath and a gold-handled dagger with an iron blade were placed at his waist. His neck, the vital juncture of head and body uniting the two parts of the social and the eternal worlds, was adorned by an amulet of iron (at that time a rare and novel material) and was especially protected by gold necklaces, beads, vultures, cobras, a papyrus with names of deities, a gorget, and two *djed* pillars (emblems of Osiris), on either side. As represented on the coffins, Tutankhamen's crossed arms held the shepherd's crook in his left hand and the farmer's flail in his right.

Written on Tutankhamen's body and its containers, in the form of a staggering range of largely gold ornaments, was a series of dualities which represented a complex series of references to the worlds of the living and dead, the lands of Upper and Lower Egypt, and the joining of head and body and of body and soul. His corpse embodied not only a kingdom but a whole cosmos.

SAINTS' BONES: HUMAN RELICS AS MAGICAL SUBSTANCE

The early medieval European obsession with saintly relics marked a somewhat contradictory attitude to the purity and pollution surrounding the corpse.[85] The body, in Christian dogma,

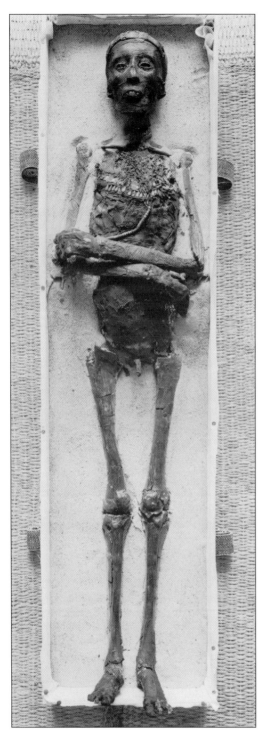

3.6 *The unwrapped mummy of Tutankhamen. It was originally bandaged in a linen sheet and covered by the gold mask which was the innermost of four nested royal visages that may portray a progression, from outside to inside, of increasing god-like serenity.*

was separated from the soul in death but would be reunited thereto on the Day of Judgement when the living would rise from the dead. This theme of ultimate and universal resurrection was tied to the notion of the man-god Jesus Christ's return from the dead, subsequent to his sacrifice on the cross. Remains supposedly of this artefact and of Jesus, his disciples and other saints were infused with purity and sacred power. In contrast, ordinary bodies were contaminated and abhorrent. We are told that the bodies of saints were so pure and incorruptible that they did not rot in the tomb. The grave of St Etheldreda, Abbess of Ely, who died in AD 674, was opened many years later and, according to Bede, her body was found to be remarkably well preserved. For most people 'relics *were* the saints, continuing to live among men. They were immediate sources of supernatural power for good or for ill, and close contact with them or possession of them was a means of participating in that power.'[86]

In the two main periods of interest in saintly relics, AD 750–850 and the eleventh century, the bones of saints were prized for their thaumaturgic power and 'their ability to substitute for public authority, protect and secure the community, determine the relative status of individuals and churches, and provide for the community's economic prosperity'.[87] These relics were exhumed, sold, exchanged as gifts and even stolen in the struggles to obtain their sacred power. Jewel-encrusted reliquaries were constructed to hold a single saint's relics and these containers of sacredness were installed securely in the chancels of the richest monasteries and cathedrals of Europe. During the Merovingian period (AD 480–700), saints' remains were even strapped to the bodies of Frankish kings and nobles inside belt-buckle reliquaries. Their heightened demand in the later eighth century was linked to the expansion of Carolingian authority and especially Christianity's triumph over other religious ideologies in western Europe, while the eleventh-century resurgence may have been linked to the growing popularity of pilgrimage and the establishment of new churches. As Brown summarizes, 'high prestige objects such as relics can play an important role in deeply divided communities. Disagreements and conflicts within society may be expressed, even conducted through disputes over the identity and value of such objects.'[88]

THE FROZEN TOMBS OF PAZYRYK: THE BODY'S SKIN AS SACRED BOUNDARY

Some of the most remarkable prehistoric bodies ever found are those buried between about 500 BC and 300 BC in the foothills of the Altai mountains in the former Soviet Union, close to the frontiers of China and Mongolia.[89] Of a group of twenty-five circular cairns, one (Barrow 1) was excavated in 1929 and another five in 1947–9 to reveal bodies and a wealth of organic and other materials which had been preserved in the permafrost. Even though the tombs had been robbed, the quality of surviving remains stunned archaeologists throughout the world. The survival of skin tattoos and of a small tent for inhaling *Cannabis sativa* were just two of the extraordinary kinds of evidence recovered.

At the centre of each barrow was a large rectangular tomb shaft. The corpse was placed, with its head to the east, in the south side of a wooden chamber which itself lay in the southern part of the grave shaft. The outer skin of this chamber was constructed from roughly hewn logs while the inner was made of dressed timbers (**Figure 3.7**). The body, or bodies, lay within a tree trunk coffin which, in the case of Barrow 5, was held closed by logs driven into the side of the chamber (**Figure 3.8**). The chamber roof was covered with birch bark, moss and sometimes larch bark and shrubs. Horses were then buried in the northern third of the tomb shaft (along with a wagon in Barrow 5) with their heads generally towards the east. Of the five larger cairns (36–46m diameter) excavated, the dendrochronology (dating by tree rings) of the chamber timbers indicates that two (Barrows 1 and 2) were built in the same year, Barrow 4 was built seven years later, Barrow 3 thirty years after that, and Barrow 5 eleven years after that.

Rudenko considered that the tombs were constructed either in spring or in autumn on the basis of later written sources for the Scythians who lived on the steppes to the west in the fifth to third centuries BC.[90] Like the Scythians, the Iron Age society known as the Pazyryk culture which built these tombs is thought to have been nomadic and pastoralist, roaming their territory on horseback with their herds.

The preserved bodies

The corpses in the large barrows had all been embalmed. Entrails and musculature were removed whilst the brain was extracted through a hole trepanned in the skull. Patterns of long slits were made along the arms and legs, on the back, on the thorax and across the stomach. These were sewn up with horsehair or sinew thread (**Figure 3.9**). Curiously, some of these slits continued as far as the fingers and toes, or to the nipples and groin. One man (in Barrow 2) had his skin pierced with small deep holes in the buttocks, legs and shoulders, possibly for insertion of a preservative such as salt. The man in Barrow 5 had the middle finger of his right hand bound at the nail with a thread which was attached to the skin of his groin. The women's bodies in Barrows 5 and 2 had been padded with horse-hair and plant material.

The man in Barrow 2 had been bludgeoned on the head with a battle-axe and scalped, with the skin from ear to ear torn backwards as far as the neck. Yet what was left of his hair had been shaved. The Barrow 2 woman's head was entirely shaven, with her plaits placed by the

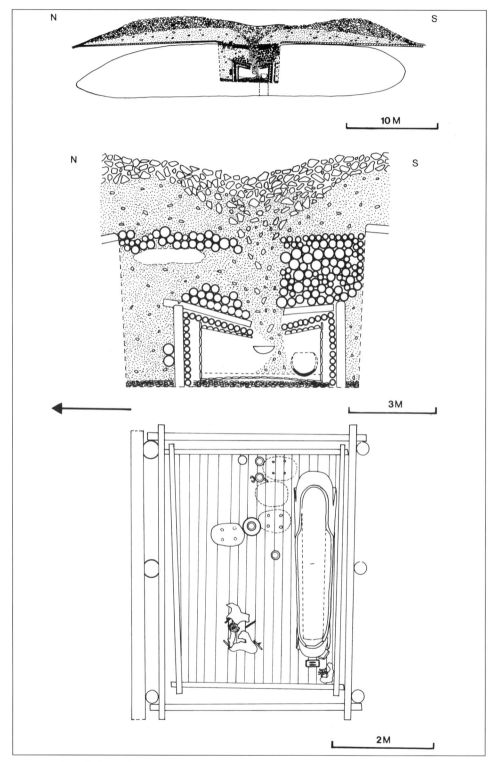

3.7 A section through the robbed-out mound of Barrow 2 at Pazyryk (top) and a section (middle) and plan
(bottom) of the burial chamber. The tomb shaft was covered by a cairn of logs (mainly uprooted trees), soil and
stones. In the tomb were the coffin (right), four-legged tables, a pot, other containers and many grave goods.

3.8 The coffin in Barrow 5 contained the body of a man. On top of his coffin lay the corpse of a woman. The large logs wedging the coffin shut can be seen protruding from the side of the chamber.

head, whereas the heads of the woman and man in Barrow 5 had some hair remaining, the former's divided into two plaits and drawn through a hat. The men had no facial hair – it was presumably shaven or plucked – but the man in Barrow 2 was provided with an artificial beard of human hair. In Barrows 1 and 2 locks of human hair were found sewn into pieces of leather and felt. At the head end of the coffin in Barrow 2 a leather bag contained a lock of hair. In the same tomb a miniature leather purse contained human fingernail clippings.

The orifices by which the skin 'boundary' is penetrated are not particularly marked, except that a wooden peg was found in the nasal area of the man's skull in Barrow 4 and the eye sockets of a young man buried in another cemetery of similar date at Shibe were sewn up. Otherwise, there are only vague hints that nipples, groin and navel were points of concern in the corpse's preparation. We should remember Kristeva's observations about the transgression of neat body boundaries at death as sites of power and danger.[91] The symbolism of bodily transgression at death is also hinted at in Rudenko's reference to Herodotus's description of the royal Scyths who 'make cuts in their hands as a sign of mourning for the dead, slit a part of their ears and thrust an arrow through the left hand'.[92] The only other visible bodily transgression on the Pazyryk bodies was that of ears punctured for earrings; a single one on the left earlobe for men and one on either side for women. The Barrow 2 man's head wound and scalping were probably the result of death in combat.

We might interpret these elaborate procedures as evidence of somewhat over-enthusiastic attempts – at least in the number and extent of the incisions – to preserve the body for eternity. The shaving of head hair might be explained as preparation for

3.9 *The body of the man in Barrow 5, showing the stitching of his skin up his back and across his shoulders after soft tissues had been removed.*

trepanning, while the keeping of hair and nails could be interpreted as the keeping of these extremities of the body to avoid the danger of their being used for magic or by evil spirits. Each of these rationalizations may be true to some extent but we need to bear in mind the whole picture if we hope to understand these bizarre rites. Collectively these practices appear to relate to a set of strong attitudes about the body and its boundaries, notably the skin and the extremities of hair and nails. It is not the substance of these corpses which was of importance (i.e. the musculature and entrails) but the covering or surface. This had to be trimmed of hair and preserved like a tent stretched over the skeletal frame.

Tattoos and animal symbolism

This interpretation might be satisfactory as a link between theory and data but it requires further corroboration from other forms of evidence. This is provided most spectacularly in the tattooing of the man in Barrow 2 (**Figure 3.10**). His right leg, arms, back and torso bear tattooed designs of animals and other motifs. The tattoos were applied probably by needle pricks rather than by sewing and would have appeared as blue marks on a white skin. The discoloration of the underlying muscle but not of the fat layer between indicates that the tattoos were applied when the man was young, prior to his putting on weight in middle age. We might surmise that the man's body tattoo was applied during his youth, perhaps at a formative stage in his life, during initiation into adulthood. Rudenko draws on written accounts of groups such as the Scythians to suggest that tattooing was a mark of manhood and courage among groups of noble birth though it is more likely a mark of high status given the survival of similar tattoos on the body of the 'ice maiden' found nearby in 1993.[93]

How do we interpret these tattoos? It is likely that the tattoos were rarely exposed in public; the dead were accompanied with close-fitting shirts, kaftans, trousers, stockings and shoes, suggesting that they were normally fully clothed when alive. The meanings of tattooing vary from culture to culture, being medicinal 'vaccinations' against diseases among the Shan of the Thai/Burmese border,[94] or marking oppositional identities, group identities or distinctions among prisoners, soldiers, sailors and others in European societies.[95] In historical Polynesian societies tattooing reinforced the social skin with a barrier between the self and unmediated divinity to form a character armour which protected and also constituted the person, a stigma of humanity which was not shared by those untattooed individuals who were close to the gods.[96] As Alfred Gell points out in his study of Polynesian tattooing, its meaning derives wholly from context and it is through contextual analysis that we might hope to unwrap the meaning of the tattoos on the man in Barrow 2.

Other indications of this emphasis on the outward appearance of the body come from the finds of mirrors (two in Barrow 2 and one in Barrow 6) and combs. Analogous concerns with skin come from the treatment of animal hides. In most of the graves there is not only a perhaps unsurprising number of leather receptacles (given the significance of leather goods among pastoralists) and fur garments but also a remarkable quantity of cut-out leather designs especially of particular animals. Even the coffin in Barrow 1 is decorated with leather cut-out silhouettes in the shape of cocks. The construction of these beautifully shaped coffins from brittle larch wood was no easy matter and we might interpret their use, along with the wooden chamber (rough-hewn on the outside and dressed on the inside), as metaphorical representations of the skin. Even the horse gear included leather face-masks to provide the animals themselves with a second skin.

We can pursue a related line of enquiry through analysis of the symbolism of the tattoos on the man's body. Apart from a few spotted designs on the lower back and on the lower right leg, the motifs are of various animals. At least seven out of sixteen of these animals are mythical beasts which incorporate elements from different species to form what we might call griffins or chimeras. There is a fantastic monster (perhaps a lion-griffin) on his left breast and back, and a smaller one on his right breast. His right arm is decorated with a winged monster apparently attacking a donkey with twisted crupper, a ram with twisted crupper, a deer in the same attitude with an eagle's beak and birds' heads on its antlers, a fanged carnivore, and a deer with twisted crupper and birds' heads on antlers and tail. The left arm is decorated with two deer and a mountain goat; although poorly preserved, two of the animals can be seen to have twisted cruppers, one has a bird's head and tail, and another has an eagle's head. There are a fanged and horned monster, a fish and four rams on his right leg.

A dominant theme of these body tattoos is the juxtaposition of the chimerical creatures and other carnivores with herbivores whose twisted bodies are suggestive of their being attacked. The meaning of chimerical designs has recently been addressed in studies of Iron Age Greece and western Europe, focusing on the mixing up of different parts as a disordered denial of difference linking with a perception of chaotic violence to produce an imagery of danger and risk generated by boundary-crossing and polarity.[97] These interpretations strike a chord with the associations of chimerical beasts and animal violence depicted on human skin in far-away Pazyryk. However, we need to explore the context of these representations if we are to understand them in localized terms as well as globalized understandings within the Iron Age world.

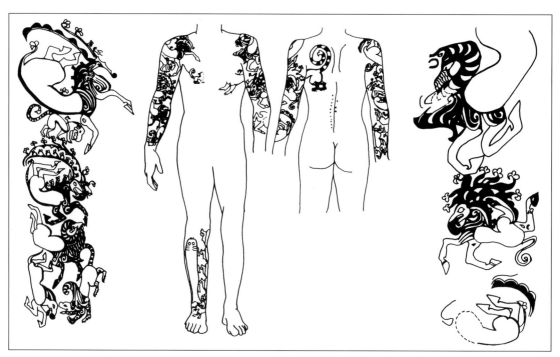

3.10 Tattoos on the man in Barrow 2. Those on his right and left arms are shown in greater detail. There are no tattoos recorded on his left leg because the skin was not preserved.

Material culture and animal symbolism

The contexts in which these animals are represented on other forms of material culture from the tombs reveal particular patterns, especially when comparing the outer grave shaft area which contains horses and horse gear with the inner burial chamber where the body is placed. Although many animals are represented in the Pazyryk art, their numbers and their associations vary. The rarest species are humans (only represented as bearded heads), horses, fish, boar, wolves, and eagles or predatory birds. Herbivorous elks, deer and rams are largely confined to bridle fittings. Carnivorous felines are also found on bridles but are equally found on saddle decorations. The most common animal motif on saddle decorations, however, is of predator and prey: the carnivore attacking a herbivore, the latter often with a twisted crupper, as on the body tattoos. A variety of birds, notably swan, cock, woodcock and grouse, are found less frequently on bridles and saddles and more often as cut-outs appearing on a woman's head-dress, on a coffin, on clay bottles, on a felt canopy and as mane covers. Chimeras/griffins (or monsters) adorn saddle fittings, bridles and other items of horse gear but they are more common than other animals on the fittings within the inner burial chamber (as opposed to the outer grave shaft area), such as those which appear on the torque (neck ring) in Barrow 2.

Thus the chimeras/griffins (both on the human skin and in contexts in close association to the human body) and, to a lesser extent the birds, are most directly associated with the human realm inside the inner burial chamber. The monstrous chimera/griffin creatures, however, may be perceived not only as 'imaginary' but also as liminal 'betwixt and between' creatures of danger, power and chaotic violence. Their adornment of the human skin thus serves to draw attention to and to reinforce the central significance of this boundary between the individual and the chaos beyond, transgressed by the tattooing but thereafter protected by these powerful and dangerous entities. Similarly the predator/prey pairs of carnivores attacking herbivores occur especially on the saddle, the interface between person and horse. It is interesting that horses, like humans, are generally not represented in the art. They are also adorned, as people are, and are incorporated into the tombs of people. Horses were thus symbolically close to humans though they were treated not as equals but as companions to the dead.

The tattooed man in Barrow 2 was not only scalped but his head was pierced by three holes made by an oval battle-axe, in addition to his skin being methodically sliced open across his body.[98] Although he was probably about sixty years old when he died, his wounds indicate a violent death for this old warrior. Tattoos were probably indicators of high status and noble birth, but they might also be read as the garb of the warrior.[99] Treherne, drawing on Vernant's analysis of Homeric Greek warrior bodies, suggests that 'in the fray, the body of the individual warrior served as an "heraldic device" on which were emblazoned the values which proclaimed his honour'.[100] Even though the tattoos may have been entirely hidden under his clothes during battle, the Pazyryk warrior's skin was protected by its motifs of power and danger from its rupture and the resultant moral danger of the body's permeability, disfigurement and death.

BOG BODIES: HUMAN SACRIFICES OR SOCIAL OUTCASTS?

At the same time that the hollow corpses of Pazyryk were being buried, a small group of people in north-western Europe were meeting their ends in unusual ways that would bring later attention to their bodies. The preserved corpses of over 1,800 individuals, from many different periods, have been recovered in the last few centuries from peat bogs in Denmark, Germany, Britain, Ireland and Holland. Sixteen of the 418 bog bodies or bog skeletons found in Denmark have been dated by radiocarbon to between *c.* 840 BC and *c.* 95 AD, that is, from the Late Bronze Age, through the pre-Roman Iron Age and into the first half of the Early Roman Iron Age.[101] In contrast to the Pazyryk bodies, these corpses were probably disposed of without any intention that they might be illustriously preserved in both memory and materiality. Their story is magnificently told by Wijnand van der Sanden in a masterly review of bog bodies, their contexts and conditions of discovery in north-west Europe.[102] The Danish bog bodies were made famous by P.V. Glob, who drew extensively on Tacitus's *Germania*, written in AD 98, to interpret them largely as sacrifices to the earth goddess of fertility, Nerthus.[103] Glob was not the first to draw on Tacitus's references to '*ignavos, imbelles et corpore infames* [cowards, deserters and 'sodomites']' who were drowned under wicker hurdles in bogs and swamps; this explanation was first published in 1824 but Heinrich Himmler later used it in a speech to Waffen-SS officers in 1937, explaining that this was not a punishment of these 'degenerates', 'but simply the termination of such an abnormal life'.[104]

A few examples can illustrate some of the ways in which these bog bodies were treated. Tollund Man was discovered lying crouched on his right side with his head to the west and looking south. His eyes had been closed and he was entirely naked save for a leather cap, a leather belt and the leather thong noose, secured tightly around his neck, with which he seems to have been hanged. His hair was cropped short and there was stubble on his jaw. Grauballe Man lay naked on his back, with his body twisted, legs flexed and his head to the north (**Figure 3.11**). He suffered from tooth decay and also incipient spinal arthritis. Unlike Tollund Man, his hands survived in good condition and their fineness demonstrated that he had not performed manual work.[105] Among his stomach and intestine contents were whipworm eggs and grasses infected with ergot, a fungus which may cause fits, mental disorders and gangrene and from which LSD is derived.[106] Ergot poisoning, known as St Anthony's Fire because of the burning sensation it causes in mouth, hands and feet, sometimes reached epidemic proportions in the historical period after wet summers affected rye harvests.[107] Grauballe Man had swallowed a dose sufficient to render him comatose or dead, after suffering convulsions and hallucinations.

Borremose I was an adult man deposited sitting with crossed and bent legs and with his head twisted round. His eyes had probably been closed, and his thick stubble indicated that he was not shaved on the day of his death. Again, his fine hands suggest that he was a stranger to manual work. His right leg had been broken above the knee (either pre- or post-mortem) and his brains were visible through a hole bashed in the back of his skull. In addition, a slip-knotted hemp rope was attached around his neck. Although naked, he was laid with a small scrap of cloth under his head and two sheepskin capes rolled up at his feet. Borremose II was probably a woman; she lay face down with her head to the north and feet to the south. Her hair was only one inch long and she was naked except for a leather neck thong threaded with an amber bead and a bronze disk, and pieces of cloth laid over her legs. Three short sticks, the bones of an infant and half a clay pot lay with the upper part of her body. Her right leg was fractured below the knee, probably pre-mortem. The amber bead is an artefact normally associated with the graves of high-status individuals in the region at this date (first to second centuries AD). Borremose III was a plump woman laid face downward with her head to the east, with one leg drawn up to her waist. Although her hair was of medium length, the back of her head had been scalped and her face was crushed, probably by a heavy blow. Her body was laid on a bed of tiny white cottongrass flowers which the marsh ecology indicates were probably picked from another part of the bog.

Death and diet

Although there are no consistent orientations or formal arrangements of the body and limbs, there are a number of interesting features which are common to these Iron Age bog bodies. About fourteen individuals provide clear evidence of how they died – by hanging or strangling, throat cutting, battery with a blunt instrument, decapitation, stabbing and possibly pegging down and drowning.[108] A number were killed using several of these methods and some were badly beaten. For example, before his throat was cut, Grauballe Man was wounded on his right temple and his fractured tibia indicates that his leg was deliberately broken. The violence meted out was excessive, both post-mortem as well as pre-mortem. Lindow II, the best preserved of three bodies from this English bog, had been garrotted and stabbed in the throat in such a way that, had these been effected simultaneously, then a small fountain of blood would have issued from the incision. In addition he was twice hit on the head, probably with an axe, so hard that bone chips from his skull entered his brain and one of his molars cracked.[109]

Although the identification of Harris lines (lines on the skeleton caused by nutritional stress) in the lower leg of a girl from Windeby led Glob to suggest that her winter diet was inadequate, the fine hands and feet of certain other bog corpses and the quality of associated items suggest that many of these people who ended up in bogs had been of an unusual social status.[110] For example, the quality of the textiles accompanying the Huldremose and Haraldskjaer women is comparable to that of those found in contemporary graves of high-status individuals in the Early Roman Iron Age.[111] Also, although some of the individuals were short, the bog corpses and bog skeletons tend to be in the taller range of the Iron Age

3.11 The young man from Grauballe bog. His twisted head had been almost severed by a slit across the throat from ear to ear. His stubbly face, with open eyes, was shaved but his hair was of ordinary length.

population – a factor that they share with the ruling élites of the first to fourth centuries AD in Denmark – possibly because their diet was superior to that of others.[112] Such conclusions are at odds with the three instances where stomach contents indicate a last meal of gruel made from barley, linseed, knotweed and gold-of-pleasure. This simple food, presumed by some to be a special meal for the condemned, is just as likely to have been standard fare.

Leather and nakedness

Many Iron Age bog bodies were apparently deposited in the bog naked or near-naked.[113] Their only clothing is normally of animal skin, especially the short skin cape which reaches to just above the waist; woven clothing is normally found separate from the body or lying over or under it.[114] The most fully dressed example, the woman from Huldremose, was wrapped in one skin cape and covered with another while a woollen scarf was draped around her neck and a woollen skirt was wrapped around her waist; a woollen *peplos* (an outer robe) was found nearby. The injuries to her right leg and foot and right arm show that she had been hacked at repeatedly. In many cases we cannot be sure whether clothing has survived or not, or whether earlier researchers missed textile remains associated with the bodies, but there is the possibility that the close association of leather items (capes, armbands, shoes, hats, belts) with these bodies may have been deliberate. If they are found wearing any garment, then these are nearly always of leather and also inadequate to hide much of the body, especially the genitals and lower regions.

We do not know whether leather clothing was a regular component of dress during the Iron Age since cremation was the dominant funerary rite in Denmark and Germany during these centuries, and there are few burials against which we might compare dressing of the corpse. There are, however, Middle Bronze Age mound burials which contain clothes and garments mostly made of woollen textiles but without leather capes whereas a single bog body known to be of this earlier date, from Emmer-Erfscheidenveen in Holland, was wrapped in a skin cape and his woollen and other leather clothes lay around him.[115] At the other end of the chronological range, the 'girl in blue' from a first century AD (Early Roman Iron Age) high-status inhumation at Lønne in Jutland was buried in a blue woollen dress without any trace of leather clothing.[116] Traces of clothing surviving as oxidized imprints on copper alloy and iron dress fittings in Early Roman Iron Age burials also attest to the common use of textiles rather than leather.[117] This potential emphasis on leather garments on the Iron Age bog bodies may be out of place for the styles of the period and their restricted and immodest use suggests that they were tokens of a 'second skin', drawing attention to the body and possibly accentuating notions of a body clothed but immodest. The partially shaved heads of some of the victims may similarly have served to emphasize a state of impropriety and shame. The nature of the associations with leather is not easy to gauge but, as the clothing of animals, these skins, leathers and furs may also have served ritually to separate the victims from the world of humans.[118]

Sacrifice or execution?

As mentioned above, cremation was the dominant archaeologically visible funerary rite during the period in which the bog bodies were deposited. In the final stage of the rites, the cremated bones were placed in a pot along with no more than a single metal dress fitting and buried under a small round mound. These final resting places were on high and dry land generally about half a kilometre from water, in contrast to the close proximity of settlements to water sources.[119] The symbolic geography of the Iron Age dead was divided into three: the worthy dead above, fully transformed by fire into dry burnt bones and associated with things made through fire; the middle world of the living; and the wet underworld of the sacrificial and executed dead who were entirely untransformed and returned to an animal-like state. The bogs were also final resting places for a wide range of offerings which include pots containing grain, wooden figurines, ploughs, imported metal cauldrons such as the Gundestrup cauldron, human hair, clothing, bronze neck-rings and weaponry.[120]

Some of these items might be redolent of fertility and reproduction but others may have been removed from circulation for reasons of maintaining social equalities. The settlement evidence prior to c. 150 BC, from sites such as Grøntoft, indicates broadly egalitarian village communities with slight but growing differences in economic resources between certain farmsteads.[121] This evidence of communities in which all households were involved in farming is at odds with the evidence of the Borremose, Grauballe and Haraldskjaer bodies which indicate the existence of people who did not participate in manual labour. Large and dominant farms, such as those excavated at Hodde and Kraghede, along with élite funerary rites, appeared on the margins of these Iron Age societies after c. 150 BC.

There is no doubt that the circumstances behind each death and deposition preclude their interpretation as being due to a single set of causes.[122] However, serial killing and clandestine murder, followed by secretive disposal of the body, do seem to be unfounded and inappropriate explanations.[123] Suggestions that many bog burials might be the unfortunate results of failed attempts at rescue or retrieval involving injudicious use of ropes can also be discounted.[124]

We might interpret the 'work-shy' bog people as victims of human sacrifice or executions of war captives, social scapegoats or outcasts such as witches. Many may have come from the upper echelons of society and may have been witches, shamans or priests.[125] Their apparent life of leisure, however, coupled with their degrading deaths is perhaps a leitmotif for a society in transition from local, relatively egalitarian communities to one composed of warring and unequal social divisions.

A group of perhaps three bog bodies from the early first millennium AD were found in Lindow Moss in England. One of these, Lindow III, has a vestigial thumb, and John Magilton has raised the possibility that this rendered this individual imperfect in a society in which physical perfection was a requirement of kingship and the morally imperfect were preferred for sacrifices according to Caesar.[126] There are continental Iron Age bog bodies also with physical abnormalities such as the Dutch cases of the Yde girl suffering from mild scoliosis (deformation of the spine), the Zweeloo woman's skeleton with exceptionally short forearms and legs, the two male skeletons from Dojringe, one with his right arm shorter than the other, spina bifida and two trepanation holes, and the other man with a short left arm and a perforated but healed skull, the boy from Kayhausen in Germany whose damaged hip would have prevented him from walking normally, and the thirty-year-old woman from Elling in Denmark with osteoporosis.[127] Given that so few of the Iron Age bog bodies have been thoroughly examined, a remarkable proportion have physical abnormalities. This raises the possibility that many of them may have been considered to have been 'touched by the gods' and were somehow imperfect (either physically or mentally) yet special, set apart from ordinary people. They may have been raised specially for sacrifice, leading lives of leisure until the moment of their deaths. Tacitus's 'shirkers' may, in fact, have been a special category of people, honoured by their eventual sacrifice to the world of the supernatural.

CONCLUSION

The body is not simply a biological entity but is a carefully crafted artefact, further worked and transformed after the moment of death. It is used to convey representations of death and the afterlife, of society's boundaries, of the nature of humanness, and of the ordering of the social world. The treatment of the corpse embodies complex concepts not only about the living body (what it is to be human, how to follow codes of conduct) and society at large (how the social order is represented) but also about the nature of death. The archaeological remains of the body are the culmination of rites of passage which serve to separate the dead from the living and install them within another dimension of human understanding. In certain cases, such as collective burial after secondary rites, we find only the terminal actions of those ritual processes. In others, such as the Pazyryk graves, aspects of the rites prior to entombment are recoverable, such as the cutting open and sewing up of the corpse's skin. The ruler's physical body was often a metaphor of the body social (society at large), as we have seen with Tutankhamen's mummified body, and the treatment of that corpse might reflect either the dangerous liminal period of interregnum or the institutional overcoming of such temporary rending of the social fabric. There are no universal interpretations of how the corpse is used in different societies by different people – each investigation must work contextually at recovering past attitudes and understandings.

FOUR

STATUS, RANK AND POWER

The boast of heraldry, the pomp of pow'r,
And all that beauty, all that wealth e'er gave,
Await alike th'inevitable hour:
The paths of glory lead but to the grave.[1]

Before the late 1960s and 1970s, when the ideas of the New Archaeology became influential, *culture history* approaches to social interpretation had emphasized the need for an empiricist caution when making inferences about the symbolic, ritual and social aspects of human behaviour from archaeological remains. This was most explicit in Hawkes' and Smith's 'ladder of inference', in which the most accessible aspects of the past were considered to be technology and economy.[2] With the New Archaeology's rejection of culture history's inductive modes of reasoning in favour of hypothetico-deductive methods, there was a new optimism about investigating the upper rungs of the inferential ladder. If the right hypotheses could be formulated then propositions about ritual and social organization could be tested.

SOCIAL EVOLUTIONARY THEORY

At the root of the New Archaeology's approach to the social dimensions of mortuary practices was the acceptance of the concept of *social evolution*. Archaeologists and anthropologists have conceptualized stages in evolutionary advancement since the earliest days of the discipline. In the nineteenth century John Lubbock wrote of a threefold division of savagery, barbarism and civilization, and this 'evolutionary' thinking was still a major feature of Gordon Childe's Marxist-derived schemes of the 1930s and 1940s.[3] The New Archaeological perspective on social evolution developed from the unilinear and multilinear evolutionary approaches of cultural anthropologists Steward, White, Fried, Service and Sahlins.[4] These approaches derived not so much from Darwin's biological theory of descent with modification but from his nineteenth-century contemporary Herbert Spencer, who proposed a model of social evolution in which societies evolved from simple to complex according to the 'survival of the fittest'.[5] Service and Sahlins's fourfold scheme of band, tribe, chiefdom and state and Fried's scheme of egalitarian, rank, stratified and state societies have haunted archaeological thinking ever since the 1960s even though archaeologists have disputed the pathways by which past societies developed complexity or have split certain categories into smaller units, such as 'group-oriented' and 'individualizing' chiefdoms and 'simple' and 'complex' chiefdoms.[6]

Many New Archaeological mortuary studies were thus specifically geared to identifying the level of complexity of early societies: were they relatively egalitarian bands and tribes, ranked chiefdoms, or class-stratified early states? Not only did this approach contain an implicit notion that complexity, and thus adaptive fitness, were directly associated with social inequality and exploitation but the range of variation in human societies was reduced to these four categories. The social anthropologist Edmund Leach retorted that he knew of over fifty types of chiefdom; to reduce them to a single category was absurd and reductionist.[7] More sustained attacks on the social evolutionary theories of the New Archaeology have come from post-processual archaeologists and others.[8]

Broadly there are two general problems with the application of this form of socio-political analogy. Firstly, as Leach noted, the use of catch-all concepts such as 'chiefdom' may be initially useful in making sense of diverse cases and materials but it masks the global variation and thereby restricts our understanding of differences between particular societies which might be characterized as chiefdoms. For example, British prehistory from the Neolithic to the Iron Age, a period of more than three thousand years, might be characterized as a period of chiefdoms but this does not particularly help in understanding the changes and diversity of that long timespan. As Whittle notes, '[o]nce the imperatives are broken to reduce societal arrangements to a manageable number of types and to arrange these in evolutionary paths . . . there seems less and less reason to retain the general model'.

Secondly, the model requires the matching of particular archaeologically visible traits with a checklist of anthropological features which collectively constitute chiefdoms. Not only are the archaeologically visible traits a small proportion of the total checklist but their identification is often riddled with ambiguities and contestable inferences. For example, monument building and redistribution of tribute characterize some but certainly not all chiefdoms, yet such archaeologically visible practices are often given necessary prominence in archaeological identifications of chiefdom societies.[9]

MORTUARY VARIABILITY AND SOCIAL ORGANIZATION

Lewis Binford and other American New Archaeologists argued for the analysis of *variability* within the mortuary practices of a single 'culture', for the purposes of reconstructing social organization. The New Archaeologists wanted to explore the different roles and identities that might be used in the funeral symbolism of each individual and attacked the validity of the sort of ethnographers' descriptions that claim 'the So-and-so tribe do this' and 'the Such-and-such tribe does that'. As Saxe observed, each individual was 'a coherent social personality who not only engaged in relationships with other social personalities but did so according to rules and structural slots dictated by the larger social system'.[10] This concept of mortuary variability introduced by Binford and others was intended to break down the normative characterization of funerary rites as products of mental templates or social norms of behaviour.[11] Chris Peebles considered that the archaeologist might infer the principles behind social differentiation from the range and frequency of different disposal treatments, since each individual might be assumed to have been buried in accordance with their social standing in life.[12]

Defining status

Goodenough's *role theory* offered New Archaeologists a means of dividing the composite social persona of the individual into a series of roles or social identities which might be identified archaeologically.[13] A woman might hold the social identities of leader, mother, farmer, married woman; any or all of these multiple identities might be symbolized in non-material or material form during her funerary rites. Saxe suggested that, in the case of disposal of the dead, decisions by the living about the social identities symbolized would be determined by the rights and duties of the relationships between the deceased, in their various identities, and the living.[14]

For funerary archaeologists a central tenet has been to distinguish between status (standing, position or rank) achieved in life and ascribed status. In sociological theory, *ascribed status* is constituted of attributes over which we have no control (age, gender and race) whereas *achieved status* is that position attained by us in life through education and personal advancement, a feature which sociologists considered to have a greater role in contemporary society than in past societies.[15] However, archaeologists have used the terms rather differently, to differentiate between societies in which high status is achieved (i.e. broadly egalitarian) and societies in which it is ascribed through heredity (i.e. hierarchical ordering of status by birth).

Vertical and horizontal differentiation

Societies in which each status grade is classed in an unequal relation to others may exhibit *vertical differentiation* or ranking – in which there is differential individual access to wealth and status – and *stratification* in which social classes or 'strata' are organized in unequal access to the basic resources that sustain life. For Fried, a ranked society is 'one in which positions of valued status are somehow limited so that not all those of sufficient talent to occupy such statuses actually achieve them'.[16] Fried is effectively describing what others have called chiefdoms,[17] though his scheme allows for societies being both ranked and stratified or being stratified without being states.

Chris Peebles and Susan Kus proposed a theoretical scheme which used interpretation of the aspects of the social persona represented in funerary contexts as a basis for distinguishing social inequalities characteristic of ranked societies.[18] Their scheme divides the social persona into two parts: the *subordinate* and the *superordinate*. Subordinate aspects are age, sex and achievement while alive. Superordinate dimensions are indicated by energy expenditure, grave goods or other symbolism which are not attributable to age, sex or achieved status.[19] In other words, social differences at the superordinate level might be indicative of inequality. Any society in which burials included both subordinate and superordinate social personae could be interpreted as a ranked society.

In considering such an interpretation, the archaeologist might distinguish between *vertical differentiation* (e.g. king, commoner, slave) and *horizontal differentiation* (membership of a sodality or moiety). Peebles and Kus suggested that vertical differentiation could be distinguished from horizontal in two ways:

- symbols indicative of vertical differentiation would be distributed in a pyramidal model of social strata (few in the top stratum and many in the bottom),
- the amount of energy expended in the mortuary practices might also be taken into account.

In his earlier work, Peebles had already established another distinction, between local and supralocal symbols. The former differentiate individuals within a given locality and the latter would be likely to cross-cut various geographical and ethnic boundaries. Peebles and Kus employed these principles in deriving a hierarchical structure for burials of the Mississippian period (AD 1050–1550) in the monumental complex in Alabama known today as Moundville, which is examined in detail at the end of this chapter.

Tainter and measures of complexity

Tainter's approach to measuring social complexity included the interpretation of mortuary ritual as a type of communication system in which certain symbols convey information about the deceased. Tainter explored the concept of *redundancy* in funerary attributes:[20]

- Situations of high redundancy (duplication of sets, referred to as 'organization') occur when attributes are closely and consistently correlated with specific groups. In a hypothetical example, bear claws, knives and pots might be found only in association with each other, while beaver teeth, scrapers and beads might similarly co-occur as a separate group.
- Situations of low redundancy (or 'entropy', a term borrowed from mathematics) are marked by few associations of attributes to particular groups.

Since high redundancy is expected in heterogeneous, complex information systems, Tainter inferred that the social correlate of a mortuary system with high redundancy would be a hierarchical and complex society. Conversely, low redundancy was indicative of simple, egalitarian societies.

By measuring the degree of structural differentiation in horizontal (age- and sex-based) and vertical (ascribed or achieved rank) dimensions of status, Tainter hoped to measure the degree of overall organization (or redundancy) by studying differences in energy expenditure between different graves.[21] He chose to measure vertical differentiation, in contrast to horizontal, since he considered it less ambiguous and reckoned that the number of rank levels marked the degree of structural differentiation. He quantified his results to claim that Middle Woodland societies in Illinois had a structural differentiation of 13.671 and a degree of organization of 0.7496, dropping in the early Late Woodland and then increasing in structural complexity in the later Late Woodland and Mississippian.

Tainter's approach has not been without its critics, both from within New Archaeology and later post-processual approaches. Problems include the degree of completeness required to measure with any accuracy a system's internal differentiation, the ability to determine distinct levels of status marked by energy expenditure, and the inability to deal with the interdependency of vertical and horizontal differentiation.[22] Perhaps most glaring is the reductionist and scientistic fallacy of representing a society as a number!

NEW ARCHAEOLOGY CASE STUDIES OF STATUS

James Brown worked with Mississippian mortuary practices from a ceremonial centre at Spiro in eastern Oklahoma. His methodology drew on techniques of formal semantic analysis. By constructing a key diagram based on funerary behaviours Brown was able to identify different groups of burial types in terms of pathways within a dendritic or tree pattern. From this he identified, for example, those burial types where adulthood was a precondition for inclusion. He also established a means of ranking the burial types in terms of the scale of 'custodial care' (the extent and quality of post-mortem treatment) and the different proportions of the total population that they involved. Finally, he compared the Spiro pattern to those from ethnographically documented chiefdoms of the Natchez and Choctaw in the south-eastern USA.[23]

John O'Shea's analysis of Arikara, Pawnee and Omaha burial practices in the North American Great Plains during the historical period is the New Archaeology's most detailed and rigorous study of mortuary variability. These three neighbouring groups all practised single grave inhumation and O'Shea was able to study the excavation results from a number of different cemeteries dated to the period c. 1675–1860. While he could draw on a certain amount of ethnographic description of kinship, social structure and funerary rites, O'Shea was particularly interested in developing an explicitly archaeological methodology that took into account the filtering processes which intervene between the amount and type of information observable in a living society and that which is left for archaeological recovery.[24] From his study of the ethnohistoric data, O'Shea observed that vertical social position was symbolized by the degree of elaboration in grave construction and by the types and quantities of grave goods, while horizontal social positions (e.g. membership of clan, moiety, sodality, etc.) were expressed through channels of neutral value.[25] In other words, horizontal dimensions were marked by perishable material culture such as coiffure, clothing and totemic grave goods, whereas vertical status distinctions were marked by non-perishable artefacts.

Mortuary variability on the Great Plains

O'Shea's analysis was directed principally at the co-associations of grave good artefacts and their occurrence in individual graves. His artefact typology drew on function, raw material composition and native/Euroamerican manufacture to identify eighty-six artefact types divided into three major classes: trade-derived body ornaments, clothing ornaments and implements; native-derived ornaments and implements; and 'sociotechnic' objects (bird or small mammal bones, stone pipes or pipestone ornaments, stone spear points and animal effigies). O'Shea's methododology was composed of four stages:

1. Statistical pattern searching for associations of sets of artefacts and of sets of graves;
2. Statistical sorting according to age, sex, frequency and spatial distribution;
3. Classification of each sub-set according to status differences (vertical, horizontal and a third category, special status differentiation);
4. Interpretation of each group or sub-set and inference of its social significance.

His statistical methods of analysis included a measure of association (Kendall's tau), principal component analysis and cluster analysis. The first was used to establish how well artefacts correlated with each other and with burial types, age and sex. PCA was used to identify the main groupings of associations between artefacts (R-mode analysis), and cluster analysis was used to identify similarities of structure between graves (Q-mode analysis). Rank differences, correlating with many of the ethnographic observations, were found in each of the three tribal groups with vertical distinctions expressed through artefact variety and the presence of expensive trade goods. Among the Pawnee, chiefly rank was recognizable by the presence of pipes and high wealth levels; ritual offices by associations with pipes and bird beaks; and special prestige positions by carved catlinite, spear points, bird beaks and other items.

Horizontal distinctions were also recovered: differences between adults and sub-adults (i.e. children and adolescents) were marked by grave size and age-specific artefacts; male/female distinctions were similarly apparent in sex-specific artefacts; and membership of intra-tribal societies (secret societies, sodalities or moieties) might be marked by the presence of a mussel shell. Special status distinctions were identified as being due to the circumstances of death (mass graves and unusual body positioning), missing body (cenotaph burial), and 'adversarial execution' (decapitation).

O'Shea found very little distinction between the three tribal groups but his analysis of long-term trends among the Arikara and Pawnee demonstrated very fast changes. These included a shift from single to multiple cemeteries, perhaps in efforts to maintain autonomous identities when villages were merging and there was friction over status positions. The increasing importance of female activities symbolized in the burials was interpreted as due to the decline in the male-controlled fur trade and the growing importance of maize and other agricultural production in trade with the whites, even though the tools now found in women's graves were for processing and manufacturing rather than agriculture. O'Shea suggests that these changes might have also resulted from the demise of long-distance exchange links between men for Euroamerican goods, a decline caused by the arrival of white traders within the villages.

Among the Arikara, the reduction of small-scale status distinctions might also have happened in response to village mergers, so that a set of unambiguous status grades was established within the enlarged communities. In contrast, the Pawnee retained and consolidated their system of vertical differentiation, causing increasing wealth differences and making the age-based distinctions (between sub-adult and adult) harder to maintain.[26] During the whole period under study, these societies were being decimated by disease and warfare and affected by acculturation. O'Shea noticed that cemeteries had a short span of use, about sixty years, and that funerary fashions, including grave orientation, were apt to change quickly and episodically.

Social differentiation in the Mesolithic

Marek Zvelebil worked with O'Shea to investigate the large Mesolithic cemetery of Oleni'ostrov in Karelia, employing a similar 'dimensional' approach.[27] They noted that there were several differences in grave good association other than those based on age or on sex. 'Wealth' of grave goods (the number of grave goods in a grave) tended to correspond with the presence of tooth pendants: bear with the 'wealthiest' (mostly with adult men), then elk or beaver (mostly with mature men and women of all ages), and finally those burials with no pendants (mostly old men). They interpreted these differences as markers of physical prowess perhaps linked to food procurement. There were also special status positions. Four interments, including both men and women, may have been shamans' burials; these people were buried vertically and facing west, the opposite of the horizontal east-facing graves of the others. Three of this group had 'wealthy' grave good assemblages. Another group were buried with carved effigies, perhaps other ritual specialists whose various ages (including adolescents) led O'Shea and Zvelebil to suggest that this position was ascriptive or hereditary. Another special status group, suggested as connected with hunting responsibilities, was identified from the interments of eleven adult males each buried only with bone projectile points. Thus O'Shea and Zvelebil concluded that this was a society with considerable social differentiation, some of it hereditary. The number and variety of grave goods led them to infer further that these Mesolithic people had a complex economy, centred on trade in stone tools, linked to an incipient system of institutionalized social inequality.[28]

Jacobs's subsequent re-analysis questioned these conclusions, noting that the local origins of even the 'prestige' artefacts such as slate knives did not correspond to O'Shea and Zvelebil's interpretation. Their hypothesis led them to 'unnecessarily complexify the site'.[29] Jacobs concluded that the inverse variance of meat consumption (based on stable isotope results from the skeletons) with artefactual 'wealth', the non-correlation of increased meat consumption with skeletal strength, and the age/sex homogeneity of the artefact clusters and wealth classes all mitigated against O'Shea and Zvelebil's reading of the burial organization as a mirror of a complex society.[30]

Jacobs hit upon a problem not with O'Shea and Zvelebil's methodology but with their interpretation of the different clusters. Associations with certain and copious grave goods may have less to do with wealth and more to do with the mourners over-compensating for an untimely death with abnormal expressions of grief and loss.[31] In establishing whether social status might be ascriptive or hereditary as opposed to achieved during life, archaeologists have suggested that the appearance of occasional child graves containing wealth commensurate with wealthier adult graves should demonstrate the presence of hereditary status distinctions and thus vertical differentiation. However, the issue is not as straightforward as we might assume. Ethnographically documented instances of providing dead children with adults' grave gifts are known, for example, for the Tiwi hunter-gatherers of the islands off northern Australia.[32] Jupp's study of contemporary English funerary practices (see Chapter 2) also highlights the trauma of untimely death and the associated elaboration of funerary rites. The death of a child or young adult may be a tightly contained family tragedy but it may also put in motion an escalation of mourning and funerary offering by the social group at large.

For the Oleni'ostrov cemetery, everything hinges on the *meaning* of the grave goods. Zvelebil has since identified the elk figurines found at Oleni'ostrov as important signifiers of the cosmic elk of circumpolar symbolism. A figurine's presence in a grave announces that individual's relationship with the realm of supernatural power, though its presence in a youngster's grave need not be indicative of hereditary status. It all depends on what significance we give to grave goods, in their varying quantities and forms.

GRAVE GOODS AND STATUS

Bob Chapman's analysis of Iberian Chalcolithic (Copper Age) communal tombs at Los Milliares (*c.* 3000–2200 BC) identified a central cluster of what he called 'prestige' tombs on the basis of their contents, which included ivory and copper objects, ostrich eggshell beads, jet and amber beads, stone vessels and alabaster figurines.[33] He argued that the difference between these tombs and those without 'prestige' goods, or with only a few such goods, was indicative not of an egalitarian society, as proposed by Almagro and Arribas, but of a ranked society.[34] The funerary practices of the preceding Neolithic period were interpreted by Chapman as showing low-density corporate groups based on kinship and descent (on the basis of small tomb sizes and the few, locally made grave goods), evolving into non-hereditary ranked groups in the Chalcolithic, and then into a stratified society with hereditary leadership in the Early Bronze Age. The burials of this latter period (also known as the Argaric period) were individual rather than collective and were placed within the settlements. The distribution of prestigious grave goods (such as gold and silver ornaments) cross-cut age and sex differences; among the five different status grades identified by Chapman, there are burials of infants and children in the uppermost, suggestive to Chapman of hereditary leadership and ascriptive status.

Sue Shennan's analysis of the Early Bronze Age (2400–1700 BC) cemetery at Branč in Slovakia was similarly focused on grave goods.[35] Her research also addressed the important conundrum of the wealthy child burial and asserted that the young children buried in finery – presumably girls, given the items' other associations with adult women – were evidence of ascribed status.

As well as looking at co-associations, Shennan devised a scale of value for each artefact type in terms of its labour investment (**Figure 4.1**). Thus non-local artefacts embodied not only the labour involved in their manufacture but also that required for their transport. The elaborate head-dresses and other ornaments worn by women and girls were generally of higher value than the artefacts associated with males. At the same time, male and female burials were strongly differentiated not only in sex-specific costumes but also in the manner in which the corpse was laid in the grave. Shennan concluded that there are two possible, and contrasting, interpretations of this funerary evidence. Either the social position of women was higher than that of men, or women were dressed in the wealth accumulated by their immediate male kin.[36]

Frankenstein and Rowlands' interpretation of prestige-goods systems controlled by paramount and lesser chiefdoms in the Late Hallstatt Iron Age of central Europe (*c.* 650–450 BC) relied similarly on a hierarchy of grave goods in the various mounded single chamber-graves which seemed to mark those individuals of high status. Paramount graves were identified by the presence of gold items, drinking equipment, a cart and other luxury accoutrements, best exemplified by the more recent discovery of an exceptional grave of this period at Hochdorf (**Figure 4.2**).[37] Lesser chiefs' chamber-burials might contain a vehicle and drinking kit but not the gold and other precious items. Frankenstein and Rowlands considered that the ownership of such prestige goods was achieved by control at the highest levels of these long-distance trade goods and their redistribution down the developing social hierarchy. This redistributive prestige-goods model can, however, be criticized on several counts. Firstly, prestige goods should have filtered down the hierarchy yet there is no real evidence for this 'trickle-down'. It is also likely that there was not actually a roaring trade in items such as drinking equipment; once acquired, these drinking sets were most likely used for local beverages rather than imported wine. They were probably symbolic of a courtly style of feasting and drinking in which political authority was linked to the dispensing of hospitality rather than the control of long-distance exchange links.[38]

In an analysis of social differentiation in Bronze Age Denmark, Klavs Randsborg tried to measure wealth by reducing the 'values' of bronze and gold artefacts to weights of each metal.[39] Graves containing gold were generally richer in bronze than those without. Male graves generally contained more bronze and gold than women's. Thus he concluded that the amount of metal reflected social status, indicating inequalities between men and women as well as within each sex (**Figure 4.3**). There was also a correlation between population density and the degree of inequality, suggesting that denser populations generated greater social complexity. The status of women also seems to have risen during the Bronze Age, perhaps a consequence, Randsborg suggests, of the intensification and expansion of agriculture.

The extent to which we might fix the value cross-culturally of different metals was later pursued by Colin Renfrew in his study of the gold-ornamented burials in the Chalcolithic (*c.* 4000–3500 BC) cemetery at Varna on the Black Sea coast of Bulgaria.[40] Renfrew proposed five criteria for establishing that gold was imbued with a 'prime value', that it was symbolically constructed as a conspicuous, rare item of high value in Chalcolithic society:

1. Gold was used as personal adornment over key parts of the body, such as the face and genitals – it occurs on clay masks and as a gold penis cover.
2. Gold was a regular component of symbols of power, such as 'maces' and 'sceptres'.
3. Certain artefacts were made to appear as if made from gold, such as a stone axe which had been coated in gold leaf.
4. Gold was used more sparingly than copper, so that sheet gold provided a maximum surface area in relation to its weight.
5. Gold is reflective, shiny, untarnishable and durable.

We might quibble with some of Renfrew's assumptions – for example, that items placed over face and genitals have high value – but his framework offers a useful approach to establishing the relative values of grave goods and their materials. Where it is more problematic is in the interpretation of the meanings behind that value: were the gold-rich burials celebrating chiefs, as Renfrew believed, or was the gold a sacred and magical material associated with religious specialists, shamans or even deities? In other words, are the 'sceptres' actually wands?

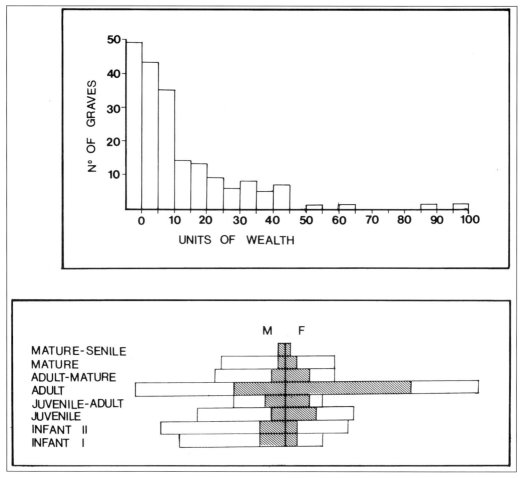

4.1 The top bar chart shows the distribution of 'wealth' scores for the graves at Brancě. In the lower bar chart the age and sex distributions of the skeletons are matched against their 'wealth'; those individuals with more than 10 units of wealth (shaded) are distinguished as 'rich'.

DIET, HEALTH AND STATUS

Cultural ecology has been another key concept for New Archaeology, presenting human society as a system adapting to the wider ecological system through the interaction of various sub-systems within the social whole. The concept of *adaptation*, derived from cultural ecology, has been associated with New Archaeology since Binford's statement that 'material culture is man's extrasomatic means of adaptation'.[41] One aspect which has been applied to funerary contexts is that of identifying a society's adaptational efficiency through the fitness of its population as evidenced by the level of health indicated from stress indicators in bones and teeth.[42] Conversely, it may be argued that stress-related traumas and lesions denote an increased ability to survive illness and stress and are thus evidence for population fitness and effective adaptive strategies; the absence of stress indicators might be a feature of those persons who died without ever recovering from the initial onslaught to the body.[43] Of course, there remains a major philosophical problem with the functionalist portrayal of societies as primarily adaptive entities selecting themselves for long-term survival through adaptive fitness.[44]

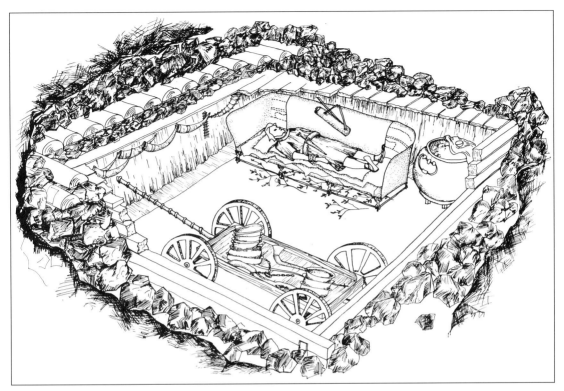

4.2 A reconstruction of the burial chamber in the Hallstatt D period Iron Age tumulus at Hochdorf in Germany.

Dietary and health studies from human remains have significant potential for opening up new avenues of research into differential social status, when conducted hand-in-hand with other methods of analysis. It was largely in the 1970s that osteological studies of nutritional stress markers, trace element analysis and stable isotope analysis illustrated the potential for identifying inequalities in the health and diet of past societies. More recent reassessments of diagenesis (the decomposition of bones, tissue, etc.), sampling methods and interpretation have highlighted the indirectness of the dietary evidence and the caution and care required to produce reliable results.[45]

Nutritional stress markers

Traces of specific nutritional stress on human bones may be caused by scurvy and rickets, deriving from vitamin C and D deficiencies respectively. Rickets was a common complaint among the poor in eighteenth- and nineteenth-century Britain but otherwise there seem to be few applications for archaeological studies of status based on the presence or absence of specific nutritional stress-related diseases.[46] Non-specific nutritional stress markers include enamel hypoplasia, anaemia (iron deficiency manifested on the skeleton as porotic hyperostosis), cribra orbitalia, Harris lines, osteoporosis in juveniles and stunted growth.[47] One example of how studies of such stress markers can contribute to research on social status is Cook's study of first-molar enamel defects in Middle Woodland populations of the first millennium AD in Illinois. She identified a consistent pattern consonant with the differences in status inferred from grave goods, grave type and location. Not only did low-status individuals suffer from a higher frequency of

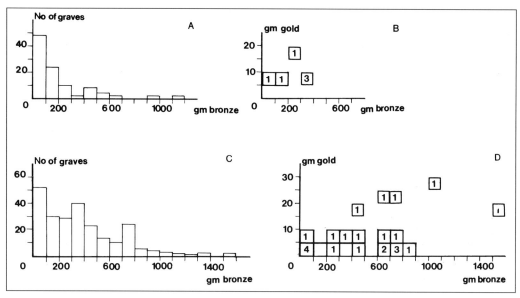

4.3 Bar charts of 'wealth' scores for Danish Middle Bronze Age (Period II) female and male burials. A: Female graves without gold; B: Female graves with gold; C: Male graves without gold; D: Male graves with gold.

enamel defects but this was true for children as well as adults, interpreted as evidence for hereditary or ascribed status.[48] However, definitive diagnosis of single dietary deficiencies in a particular skeletal population can be difficult from these non-specific stress markers.[49]

Trace elements and stable isotopes

Along with the dozen trace elements necessary for maintaining health, strontium and barium are non-essential trace elements which serve as dietary markers.[50] While strontium, like other trace elements, is susceptible to diagenesis, it does seem to be useful in differentiating meat-dominant and maize-dominant diets although there is no simple proportional relationship between bone strontium and dietary ratios of plants to meat.[51] Comparisons of strontium levels in 'élite' and 'commoner' burials from the Mississippian period of south-eastern North America showed that there were no significant differences, suggesting a similar diet for the entire sample regardless of differences in grave goods and grave location.[52] In contrast, strontium levels in bones from Olmec burials (1150–550 BC) at Chalcatzingo in Mexico differed with grave good provision, suggesting that the better provisioned in death had consumed more meat in life.[53] Barium behaves similarly to strontium in bone but is more likely to be affected by diagenesis.[54] It is an indicator of diets reliant on marine resources and has applications for investigating issues of dietary change.[55] Differences in bone lead levels in the historic period may be useful for recognizing social inequalities, such as access to pewter vessels or to water from lead pipes, and possibly different occupations.[56]

Stable isotope analyses of carbon and nitrogen in human bones have been used to answer questions about the introduction of maize, millet and sorghum (especially maize into different parts of North America), the variable reliance on animal or vegetable protein and the reliance on marine as opposed to terrestrial food resources.[57] Hastorf and Johannessen's study of nitrogen and carbon stable isotope variations in Andean Inka-period human bones and residues in cooking pots shows interesting changes over time which can be compared to other changes in house layout and ceramic forms.[58] Between Wanka II (AD 1300–1460) and Wanka III (the Inka period; AD 1460–1532) there was an increase in maize in the diet (indicated by Carbon[4]), interpreted by Hastorf and Johannessen as resulting from consumption of maize beer. They suggest that the emergent élites of Wanka II (indicated by differences in house sizes and burials) were distributing maize beer to foment political allegiances and alliances, creating indebtedness and a growing rift between emergent classes of élites and commoners.

The optimism of the 1970s in using these techniques was tempered by more cautious considerations of methodology and diagenesis yet there are very good indications that such methods will contribute considerably to identifications of dietary differences within ancient populations. As yet, the research in stable isotope and trace element analyses is primarily coming from North America but new studies of British Neolithic populations have identified surprisingly high nitrogen values indicative of heavy reliance on animal proteins (meat or milk or blood), raising possibilities that they were either pastoralists or that the individuals sampled were differentiated from others by their predominantly carnivorous diet.[59]

RETHINKING GRAVE GOODS AND STATUS

The theoretical perspectives on status employed by the New Archaeologists derived largely from structural functionalist theories of society such as those of Talcott Parsons and, as such, they encapsulate post-war North American concerns which differ from European perspectives on class, inter-group conflict, social closure (as opposed to mobility), and the nature of social status.[60] In more recent work on this subject, status is considered as formed out of three dimensions: one's political, kinship and gender entitlements, one's lifestyle (as a totality of cultural practices such as dress, speech, outlook, bodily dispositions and tastes that organize our perceptions of the social), and one's economic class (in the Marxist sense of people's relationship to the ownership or control of the means of production).[61] Bryan Turner defines status as based on a specific style of life, maintained and expressed through shared living and eating arrangements, privileged access to power, wealth and scarce resources, and the maintenance of intra-group marriage alliances and other customary conventions.

Status thus involves struggle over scarce resources but is not directly equivalent to class since status groups are communal collectivities requiring reproduction of a typical lifestyle whereas economic classes do not necessarily participate in self-identifying lifestyles. For contemporary market-based societies both aspects, along with citizenship entitlements, form the three dimensions of status. Turner suggests that we should recognize different factors in pre-capitalist non-market societies. Such societies were not composed of 'classes' but social orders ('estates') in which economic, political and religious elements were so inextricably interwoven as to be inseparable.[62] Social stratification (the nexus of status, class and power) in traditional societies tends towards closed social orders or castes in which concepts of honour (displayed through possession of heraldic devices, formal costumes and insignia of social prestige) and religious beliefs such as pollution and sacredness are essential in organizing and legitimating the social order at large.[63]

From role to practice

During the 1980s there arose a series of criticisms of the New Archaeology. Role theory and its concepts of role and social persona were reviewed and critiqued. Emphasis was now placed not on the constraints and inescapable conformity of individuals' roles but on the social practices that created a person's identity.[64] Society was now considered to be constituted by agency rather than roles.[65] People were seen to be knowledgeable, improvizing actors rather than automatons acting out pre-ordained social roles in which they were prisoners of a grand design. Another weakness of the processual approach was archaeologists' uncritical use of ethnographic data, often secondhand or based on few observations and not fully documenting possible variability, potentially resulting in misleading generalizations.[66] For any generalization, there were invariably exceptions to the rule. The ethnographic record was treated as a timeless present or recent past whereas in truth it often records periods of radical and often disastrous change; thus the imputation of a synchronic social order was a false one. By implication, the frozen picture of a community in snapshot becomes a model for past societies, rendering them cartoon-like sequences of static frames – a series of superimposed presents which fail to illuminate a historical context of contingency and change.

Mortuary practices have been treated as a passive reflection of abstract concepts of society and social structure, whereas they should be treated as the arena of activity in which are moulded the institutions through which social relationships are actively brought into being, transformed and terminated through exchanges and alliances.[67] In many societies, funerals are not simply reaffirmations of social structure and social roles but a central moment in life, inheritance and economy. The dead do not bury themselves: '[I]f graves are in any way an index of social status it is the social status of the funeral organizers as much as the social status of the deceased that is involved.'[68]

The implications of this more recent conception of social status are several. We should recognize that identities forged through funerary rites are composed not of roles but of cultural practices.[69] For example, grave goods are not just elements of an identity kit but are the culmination of a series of actions by the mourners to express something of their relationship to the deceased as well as to portray the identity of the deceased. Status is thus not so much a role to be reflected in mode of burial and associated grave goods but a panoply of practices which are historically situated and open to manipulation. Secondly, concepts of honour and sacredness may be far more important than wealth and ownership in organizing society's values.

Beyond rank and status: from form to content

Criticisms of studies in the New Archaeology vein focus on underlying interpretive assumptions and preconceptions. For example, the energy expenditure model assumes a congruency of expenditure in the ritual as a whole with the expenditure calculated from the archaeologically observed remains.[70] The New Archaeological approach placed emphasis on form rather than content. The meaning and symbolism of particular grave goods or the mortuary rites themselves were played down; why a chiefly burial was associated with particular items was not treated as particularly important whereas the association of those artefacts and their indication of 'wealth' were central to the analysis.

Early post-processual critiques reasserted the significance of meaning in interpreting mortuary practices. Pader observed that the quantity and quality of artefacts deposited with male and with female corpses among the Amazonian Barasana represented neither differential wealth nor a simple division of labour but women's identities bound up with households and men's with ritual and communal activities by which they achieved control and domination over women.[71]

Rank and status are not givens at moments such as funerals but are actively contested. For example, expressions of status through funerary ostentation were a facet of power struggles in sixteenth-century Elizabethan England. The queen closely controlled the aristocracy's funerals through sumptuary laws in order to restrain displays of ruling class strength and stability and to maintain the gradations of society in the face of growing discrepancies between wealth/power and rank/status.[72] A case like this reveals something of the tensions and discontinuities in the maintenance of hereditary power. The presence of hereditary succession to high office has been taken by New Archaeologists to be a marker of developed or complex chiefdoms along with early states, and implies the existence of a dynastic ruling élite who are separate from commoners. Of course, if we look at any hereditary ruling dynasty in documented history we find that there are inevitable breaks in the bloodline.[73] What is significant, and needs to be remembered by archaeologists, is that the institutional nature of the position – whether pharaoh, queen or emperor – as well as the means whereby an individual succeeds to it – by inheritance, election or usurpation – are equally important for examining power relationships and political structure.

Gifts or possessions?

Grave goods should be seen not simply as personal trappings, whether or not polluted by association with the corpse, but as items bound up in gift exchanges with the dead, as in the case of personal equipment definitely never used but apparently made specifically for the deceased. Under an Early Bronze Age round barrow at Irthlingborough in eastern England, an adult male had been provided with a flint dagger and other flint tools which microwear analysis confirms had never been used and which might, therefore, have been made for the funeral.[74] The Middle Bronze Age burial mound at Borum Eshøj in Denmark contains a young man's burial which is a reminder that grave goods are not straightforward reflections of status but are caught up in the power-play and agency of funerary pomp (**Figure 4.4**). Within the well-preserved tree trunk coffin what was apparently a sword had been laid on the corpse. Closer inspection revealed that the wooden sword scabbard actually contained a bronze dagger far too short for the scabbard.[75] We might be charitable and suggest that the group of mourners staging the funeral made a mistake or that the placing of a dagger in a sword scabbard was an accepted ritual act; neither of these possibilities, however, is likely given the evidence from other burials of the period, in which swords and not daggers accompany the corpse. This was a deliberate deception.

There are enough ethnographic examples of funerary dress forming a skewed representation of that which is worn in life to make the archaeologist wary of interpreting the adornment of the corpse as representative of the person's possessions and dress style in life. Patricia Rubertone has interpreted the increased deposition of wampum (shell beads) in seventeenth-century Native American graves not as an increase in ornamentation of the corpse but as ritualized consumption embodying political resistance, by ensuring that wampum did not go as tribute to the whites.[76] In any case, personal objects are often disposed of in ways other than burial with the corpse. For example, in southern Madagascar the Tandroy burn the polluted possessions of the dead within his/her house, which is set on fire at the end of the mortuary rites.

Richard Bradley has also drawn attention to the decline through time in the value attached to innovations. Using O'Shea's study of the Pawnee and Arikara, he illustrates this loss of value in native goods against traded imports and suggests that a 'rich' grave fifty years later than a 'not so rich' one may have had less social significance in its contemporary society.[77] We should also be aware of the possibility that certain grave goods may have accompanied the corpse only because there was no appropriate living successor to inherit such items.[78] A possible example of the deposition of heirlooms may be the placing of jet necklaces in British Early Bronze Age burials (c. 2500–1500 BC); from the wear on the beads and the evidence for multiple repairs and replacements of beads, many of these necklaces were clearly very old by the time they went into the grave.[79]

Paul Halstead and John O'Shea, however, apply a 'risk buffering' perspective to grave goods in their theory of social storage.[80] The exchange of foodstuffs for personal valuables in times of plenty may enable the valuables' re-conversion to food during times of scarcity and famine, as O'Shea suggests for Navajo silver jewellery. Equally, the deposition of valuables in funerary contexts might be a means of preventing those valuables retained by the living from losing their value. By keeping just enough in circulation, the potential for an inflationary spiral is controlled. Even if the motive for such adaptive behaviour is attributed to particular individuals' perception of the situation rather than to 'society at large', such a functionalist approach reduces all social action to its adaptive value.

While the functionalist approach has been valuable in showing that societies previously considered as 'primitive' were in fact well adapted to their environments, it presents human agency, and especially ritual action, as driven by ecological concerns rather than social relationships. The interesting issues surrounding agency, tradition and power are simply side-stepped in reducing explanation of social phenomena to the realm of society's latent adaptation to its environment.

RELATIONSHIPS BETWEEN RANK AND POWER

Post-processual archaeological perspectives brought two critical reformulations to funerary archaeology. These were the recognition that mortuary practices might embody and reveal the workings of power and ideology, and the identification of funerary rites as legitimatory events when rank and power might be disassociated.[81] As Bloch argued in his study of Merina ritual symbolism in Madagascar, society might be divided into many different social ranks and yet political and economic power could be exercised by a small ruling class over the rest of the population regardless of people's respective rank. Functionalism presents ideology as mere 'feather-waving', as part of the epiphenomenal 'projective' or 'cognitive' system which functions to maintain the social and economic system. Classical Marxist notions of ideology present it as 'false consciousness' or as legitimation of inequality in relations of production. In contrast to both these approaches, ideology could be redefined in a post-processual approach as people's lived relation to the symbolically constructed conditions of their existence.

To understand funerary practices, archaeologists have now to consider that such events are representations of the perceived reality of social relations and are also open to conflict, negotiation and misrepresentation. Funerals are moments when the structure of power may be radically reordered; they are not simply reflections of the social order. People's understandings of social relationships and the very meaning of existence are also expressed in material and non-material form. Funerary rites are just one medium, albeit a powerful one, among the many ways of representing and forming lived experience, both ritual and mundane.

Legitimation, time and change

Gordon Childe pioneered several directions which were later followed up as key concepts in post-processual approaches, notably the relationship between power and status in funerary rites and the awareness that funerary material culture does not always reveal to the archaeologist a direct reflection of social status. In his largely forgotten 1945 paper on long-term trends in funerary rites, Childe made some important observations about timing.[82] He noted that, as a general rule within prehistoric Europe, tomb permanence was replaced by elaboration of dwellings, and that, latterly, less wealth was expended on tombs and their furnishings, and that royal tombs often appeared at moments of legitimatory crisis and affirmation during transformations from kin-based societies to territorial states. He defined royal tombs as marked by: magnificence and magnitude; extravagant wealth of grave furniture; the presence of human sacrificial victims (**Figure 1.6**); and use of a significantly different rite from everyone else (in contrast, he considered that chieftains were buried similarly to commoners but with more pomp and expense). In ancient Egypt, Minoan Crete and the central European Iron Age of Hallstatt D, 'civilization was preceded by the rise of chiefs to the status of divine kings who concentrate the social surplus'. The appearance of royal tombs was due to either internal economic forces, notably long-distance trade, or to contact with 'higher civilizations'.

Childe was criticized by Stuart Piggott who was suspicious of this sociological approach and pointed out that royal tombs did not always appear at moments of state emergence. He was certainly correct that Childe was overstating his case, but he failed to understand Childe's more subtle point that big funerals often went with politically unstable

4.4 The Bronze Age tree trunk burial from Borum Eshøj, with its sword scabbard (in the coffin and left) containing a dagger (top right). The organizers of the funeral may have been attempting to pull the wool over the eyes of others attending the funeral. By cheating in this way, they were perhaps misleading others about their collective social and economic standing.

and formative situations, that élite funerary ostentation contributed to political legitimation.[83]

During the 1980s a number of studies identified and elaborated on Childe's notion of long-term trends by identifying cycles of ostentation, characterized by wealth deposition and/or labour investment, associated with phases of simplicity in funerary rites. Cycles of legitimation are noticeable in the burial practices of Victorian England and the Danish Iron Age, where rich funerals heralding the emergence of an élite were followed by anti-ostentatious élite burial rites in succeeding centuries.[84] Bradley similarly recognized a succession of periods in British prehistory when the funerary domain was taken up as an arena for conspicuous display and consumption and then dropped in favour of other contexts such as votive deposition in water, settlement defence and ceremonial monument construction.[85] Morris has identified a similar monument cycle in Classical Athenian funerary rites.[86]

MOUNDVILLE: FUNERARY RITUALS OF A PREHISTORIC 'CHIEFDOM'

It is without doubt in the understanding of emergent social inequality that studies of status from prehistoric funerary practices have made their biggest impact. The analyses have tended to concentrate on extinct societies in which wide varieties and large numbers of grave goods were interred with the dead. The cosmologies which might have related to grave good provision are rarely examined. Secondly, largely because of problems of chronological definition, large sweeps of time are taken as single moments. Thirdly, however systematic, rigorous and objective the methods of pattern sorting and cluster recognition, the interpretation of these results is forever ambiguous and open to question.

The Mississippian culture complex

Between *c.* AD 1050 and 1550 a large part of south-eastern North America was inhabited by Amerindian communities engaged in a series of related cultural practices involving the demarcation of sacred plazas, the construction of flat-topped rectangular mounds within them, the growing of maize, and participation in a shared symbolism of ceremonial weaponry, copper gorgets, marine shell ornaments, and particular motifs such as winged serpents, skulls, raptors and eyes within hands. This culture complex is known as the Mississippian and is best known from a number of regional centres, the largest of which is Cahokia in Illinois.[87] Despite the evident similarities with contemporary Mesoamerican civilizations, there is no evidence for any major discontinuities of population at the end of the preceding Late Woodland phase nor for migration from across the Gulf of Mexico. None the less substantial elements of a Mesoamerican ideological and cosmological package seem to have been adopted, notably cosmological orientation, flat-topped ceremonial 'pyramids', ceremonial plazas, certain styles of representation, and the cultivation and eating of maize.

Moundville in Alabama is the second largest ceremonial complex, formed by a group of twenty-nine mounds surrounding a plaza in the middle of which there are three of these large mounds.[88] In the first half of the twentieth century, 3,051 burials were excavated at Moundville, mostly from cemeteries around the outside of the plaza but a small proportion of these burials were excavated from within mounds. Houses were also located in the outer zone. At some point the plaza was surrounded by a buttressed timber palisade on its south, east and west sides while the north was open to the Black Warrior River. The plaza, like the mounds, is orientated on the cardinal points. The central mound (Mound A) has a slightly different orientation, NNE–SSW.

Human remains were buried as supine inhumations, normally north–south but also east–west, south–north and west–east, and as bone bundles. There were also certain special deposits such as infant burials and adult skulls in post-holes, mound fills and as accompaniments within certain graves. These special deposits have been interpreted as associated with foundation and closing rituals. In addition, other special deposits included decapitated and otherwise mutilated burials, and a group of three achondroplastic dwarfs buried face down.

Grave goods and status

Peebles and Kus's study[89] of grave good associations in 2,053 graves identified eleven funerary 'clusters' in addition to the special deposits:

- The largest groups were burials with no grave goods (1,256 cases) and burials with ceramics only (Clusters V–X; 341 cases).

Another two clusters contained a small variety of grave goods:

- Cluster III comprised 211 burials with pots in the shape of animals (beaver, bat, frog, fish, duck, marine shell), animal portions (deer, bird claws and turtle shells), shell gorgets, freshwater shells (with children) and stone axes (with adult men);
- Cluster IV was made up of fifty burials with projectile points, possible gaming counters and bone awls.

Peebles and Kus considered that all these groups might represent statuses which had been achieved in life and which included people of both sexes and all ages. They termed this group of clusters the 'subordinate' dimension, in contrast to the three 'superordinate' clusters Ia, Ib and II:

- Cluster II consisted of sixty-seven burials (more than 15 per cent of them in mounds) of all ages and both sexes with oblong copper gorgets, cubes of galena (lead ore) and shell beads.
- Cluster Ib (forty-three graves, about a quarter of them buried in mounds) contained only adult males and children, buried with copper ear spools, stone pallets (possibly used for paints), various minerals (red and white paints?), bear tooth pendants and oblong copper gorgets.
- Cluster Ia (seven individuals all buried in mounds) were probably all adult males and were equipped with copper axes, copper-covered shell beads, pearl beads and, in most instances, infant skeletons and skulls in their grave fill.

This superordinate group (Clusters Ia, Ib and II) was considered to represent the upper echelons of a ranked society, marked apart not only by their special grave goods but also by their frequent occurrence in mounds (although a further six of the eleven cluster groups also had some burials in mounds) (**Figure 4.5**).

Peebles and Kus found five other indications of what they took as more evidence of a ranked society.

1. One settlement area had larger houses, fragments of artefacts similar to those in the 'high-status' burials, and infant burials under hearths. These buildings were interpreted as élite residences.
2. The settlements in the Moundville region exhibited a hierarchy of site sizes in relation to their hypothesized catchment areas.
3. Settlements were located on the rich soils and areas with greatest ecological diversity, thereby ensuring potential local autonomy.
4. There was evidence of productive activities which transcended the household, notably monument building and specialist craft production of beads, pottery and shell objects in areas away from the residential sectors.
5. There were social mechanisms of buffering environmental unpredictability, in the form of a possible public granary, long-distance trade goods and a large palisade to protect the community from endemic warfare.[90]

Twenty years later many of these arguments can be seen in retrospect to have required special pleading. There is no necessary inference from the second, third, fourth and fifth points of the existence of a ranked society. The first point, however, does link inequalities in grave good provision with inequalities in households but the 'élite residences' may simply have been ceremonial buildings. While there are clearly inequalities in grave provision and placing, Peebles

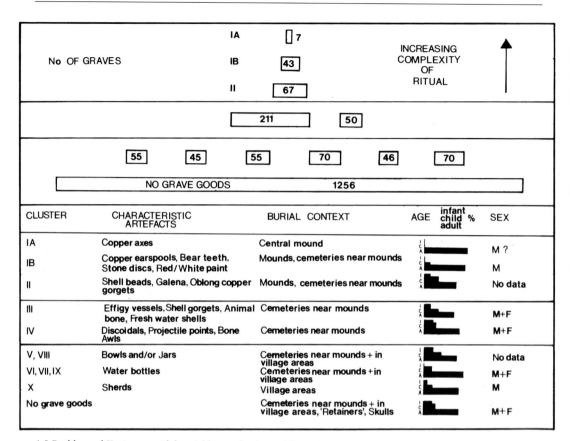

4.5 Peebles and Kus's pyramidal social hierarchy derived from the burials at Moundville.

and Kus's identification of ascriptive ranking can also be challenged. The top group (Cluster Ia) are all adults and probably male and the second (Cluster Ib) are male with a handful of children. The status items used to define these clusters might mark positions which could have been achieved in the main. The few children in Cluster Ib (and there is no indication from Peebles and Kus's analysis whether these were buried in mounds) might have had these items bestowed by mourners of high office.[91] The same might be said for the mixed group in Cluster II.

The chronology of the burials

The Moundville material spans some 600 years and thus Peebles and Kus subsumed all temporal variation within their static hierarchical model. Steponaitis and Knight's chronological phasing of the ceramics identifies four broad periods, Moundville I (AD 1050–1250), II (AD 1250–1400), III (AD 1400–1550) and IV (AD 1550–1650).[92]

During the phase of initial centralization at Moundville (c. AD 1050–1200) only two mounds are known to have been built. Between AD 1200 and 1250, the beginning of a phase of regional consolidation (AD 1200–1300), the sacred space of the plaza was defined by the building of most of the mounds, the arrangement of graves around it, and construction of a palisade. In the cemetery on the west side there were high-status burials with copper gorgets, shell beads and carved stone disks (Peebles and Kus's Clusters II and possibly Ib). The burials were concentrated in the western part of the site. During this period, the plaza was also a settlement area but, in later centuries, Moundville turned into a place of the dead.

Between AD 1250 and AD 1450 burials extended along the west side of the plaza and covered both east and west sides with particular concentrations on the northeast side (**Figure 4.6**). The period between AD 1300 and AD 1450 has been described as 'an entrenched paramountcy' and probably all of the lavish burials (Cluster Ia and Ib) date to this period.[93] Thus the 'élite' burials were restricted almost entirely to a brief period of at most 200 years between AD 1250 and 1450. The palisade was no longer repaired after *c.* AD 1300 and the place was largely abandoned by the living, becoming a necropolis for outlying communities, but perhaps used as a chiefly residence and ceremonial centre. Between AD 1450 and AD 1650 only three mounds seem to have remained in use. Whether Moundville's significance was ancestral and historical at this time or whether it was now merely a minor élite centre is debatable. Moundville and other centres may have been visited by the Spanish conquistador De Soto and his army in AD 1540 when they encountered a political grouping in the region named Apafalaya, ruled by a chief of that name.[94]

Grave goods: meaning and value

Not only are there problems with chronological phasing and the temporal diminution of value as highlighted by Bradley, but the routes to élite power and the contingent circumstances of Moundville's rise and decline should be understood in terms of structure and agency rather than social evolution.[95] Not only might the copper of the 'élite' burials have become more easily available in the later Mississippian but it may have served rather different purposes than those which today we might initially expect. Steponaitis has pointed to the symbolism of non-functional weaponry in 'élite' contexts and compared it with an ethnohistorically recorded Natchez ceremony of placing a calumet (arrow- or spear-thrower) on the bier of a dead chief in commemoration of ceremonies in which he participated during his life.[96] Secondly, the 'élite' burial goods appear to emphasize 'shininess' and perhaps body painting (the minerals could have produced red and white pigments). Such aspects may have linked these individuals, predominantly adult males, to central ideological symbols such as the sun and fertility; they may have been ritual as well as political leaders.

Another possible avenue for future research is to examine the totemic nature of animal items and representations. The richer burials are marked by bear tooth pendants whereas other animals are represented in the plainer graves. These are broadly of species not eaten in the Mississippian period and might be representative of ambiguous categories.[97] Taboo animals which were largely not eaten as food may have held totemic significance in which certain species of animals were equated with different categories of people.[98]

Maize: economy and cosmology

Archaeologists often refer to the Mississippian culture as a prime example of a complex chiefdom with ascriptive ranking of élites and commoners but this identification is questionable. Osteological studies suggest that there were no dietary differences between 'élites' and 'commoners', while John Blitz's study of the Lubbub Creek complex and its locale argues that the dispersed distribution of 'prestige goods' is indicative of their widespread availability and exchange among small farmsteads.[99] Saitta's recent re-analysis of Mississippian society proposes a variable, unstable communal social order with differential ceremonial positions rather than class-based chiefdoms with tributary or prestige-good economies.[100]

What are the reasons for this way of life coming into being around AD 1050? Late Woodland burials from the preceding centuries in the Moundville region show nothing of the distinctions found at Moundville. These communities were organized into large villages and small hamlets; they exploited largely wild food resources and seem to have been essentially egalitarian.[101] In contrast, Mississippian settlement patterns show dispersal of the population into farmsteads and small hamlets with the two earliest Moundville mounds forming a small ceremonial centre during Moundville I. It was only later, in AD 1200–1300, that Moundville came to truly dominate the region at the top of a tripartite hierarchy comprised of Moundville, other small local centres, and dispersed farms.

While maize was available but rare in the Late Woodland period, it became a staple crop by Moundville I. It has been regarded as the agent of economic intensification which made possible the complex social organization of Mississippian society. Yet food is good to think as well as good to eat.[102] We should also consider maize as a symbolic item which was acquired not simply as a subsistence product but as part of a wider ideology with revolutionary implications for people's beliefs about the world.

The sacred power of maize and its ritual significance are well documented among the Inka of South America.[103] In Mesoamerica, maize was even personified as a god among the Maya at this time.[104] Ethnohistorical records for south-eastern North American societies indicate that this sacred corn possessed a soul, that burnt corn was gathered to feed the souls of the dead, and that symbolic deposits were added to platform mounds in the context of the 'green corn dance'.[105] The adoption of maize was the most revolutionary change between AD 800 and 1000 (accompanying mound construction, rectangular wall-trench houses, shell-tempered pottery and elaborate funerary goods and other artefacts), apparent in the abundance of charred maize retrieved from archaeological excavations and in dietary intake revealed by analysis of skeletal remains.[106]

It was almost certainly significant as a complex symbolic food with elaborated political meanings. The use of mound platforms for feasting and the employment of large pots covered in cultic symbolism may be aspects of corn's importance at that time.[107] Emerson points out that maize or its preparation are often portrayed by the small stone figurines interpreted as the Earth-Mother, a fertility deity controlling life and death.[108] Prentice argues that humans were equated with plants, so that the seeds which bring forth new life can be equated to the souls of the dead reborn in children.[109] What maize provided was not simply a foodstuff but an entire cosmological reorientation through which the dead were 'planted' in the ground like rows of corn in order to be regenerated.

Cosmology and power: archaeology and ethnohistory

At the heart of the matter of Mississippian emergence there is a problem relating to social theory. Cultural ecological and adaptationist theories explain the rise of a complex social hierarchy and the adoption of maize in terms of adaptation to the stress of warfare or to the risks of crop failure. Even if such theories are rejected in favour of approaches which stress the role of human agency, tradition and innovation, ideology is sometimes still regarded as simply a mechanism by which social inequality is legitimated.[110] Yet ideology does not perform simply a secondary function to justify social ranking. It involves people's efforts to make sense of their world, their continuous attempts to understand and interpret it. Maize was at the heart of an entirely new perspective which probably involved complex notions of a hierarchy (literally a sacred order) and of the planting and harvesting of maize as a metaphor for the cycle of life and death. The arrival of maize in south-eastern North America provided a

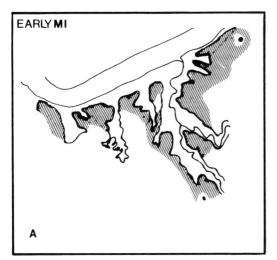
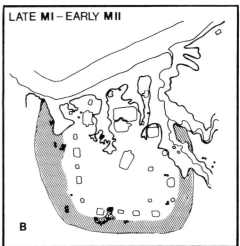
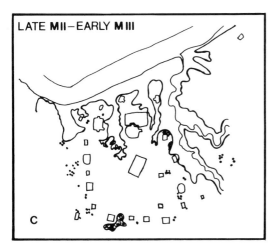
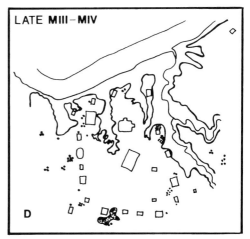

4.6 *The successive phases of ceremonial mounds and cemeteries at Moundville, south of the Black Warrior River. A: Area of settlement (shaded) and just two mounds. B: Settlement (shaded) within a palisade and some burials (dots), with most of the mounds built. C: Burials and some use of the mounds. D: Burials and little use of the mounds.*

hitherto unknown way of conceptualizing the world. Just why this ideological and cultural package was picked up throughout the region at this time – and in a myriad of local permutations – is a matter of historical contingency, long-term tradition and human agency. But the cosmological message and its attendant features such as feasting, an explicable and ordered universe, and an understood afterlife would have been of fundamental importance.

There have been some exciting advances in exploring the cosmogony and cosmology of Mississippian as well as Mesoamerican societies.[111] The Mississippian world was ordered in quadripartite form, expressed in ceramic motifs, house form, mound shape and rectangular plazas, and arranged according to the four cardinal orientations. There was probably a further division, mediated by the male sacred order, between an underworld linked to earth, fertility, disorder, redness and perhaps feminine forces, and an upper world of sky, the sun, warfare, politics, whiteness, purity and male forces.[112] Knight has also proposed a triad of cults and their symbols: a warfare/cosmogony complex manifested by items such as symbolic weaponry and motifs; a native earth/autochthony symbolism represented by the mounds and their periodic burial under new soil as a means of purification; and an ancestor cult represented by temple figurines.[113] He emphasizes that political organization and religious organization are normally so closely intertwined and congruent that there is little sense in attempting to separate them.[114]

We can find interesting comparisons for these interpretations in sixteenth- to nineteenth-century ethnohistoric accounts of the hierarchical Natchez and Choctaw who lived in this region and considered their ancestors to have come from Mexico.[115] In a culture which worshiped the sun, the chiefs of the Natchez were called the Sun or Great Sun and were absolute rulers with semi-divine status. The paramount chief, the Great Sun, is described as living in a house, built like a temple, on top of an artificial mound. Chiefs were dressed with copper headdresses and necklaces, and their spouses, servants and subjects were sometimes sacrificed at their funerals. There is even an account of a commoner strangling his infant for the dead chief. The upper torso of the Sun's corpse was painted red and the thighs were covered with alternate rows of red and white feathers, prior to burial in a temple mound. Although the Suns were men, descent was matrilineal. The workings of the system of class exogamy ensured that fourth to seventh generation descendants of the Suns were classified as commoners. Yet at the same time, individuals born as commoners could achieve noble status through prowess in battle.

We have thus recovered the true meaning of 'hierarchy' as a sacred ordering. The placing in mounds of certain male burials, decked out in their shiny sun-reflecting symbols, and of others with their red and white paints and copper gorgets takes on a more satisfying meaning with new possibilities, in contrast to the sterile enquiry into status differences and complexity, in which form and content are sundered and content is rejected. The Natchez case study also highlights the futility of attempting to differentiate between achieved and ascriptive rank since both processes were operating at the same time. Indeed, the quest for ranking as a measure of social organization becomes almost irrelevant within a more integrated study of ideology and power.

CONCLUSION

The investigation of social complexity and degrees of status differentiation has been the principal concern of funerary archaeology in the last thirty years. The idea that burials provide an insight into the manifold aspects of an individual's social persona has been especially applied in the study of grave goods, though the complexity of their interpretations has to be recognized. Are the grave accompaniments possessions of the deceased or gifts from mourners? Or are they heirlooms buried with the last of the line? Their inclusion might also vary according to changing rules of inheritance or broader political and ideological currents in society. Equally, the meaning as well as the form of funerary symbolism has to be interpreted: are the 'high-status' burials at Moundville or Varna political leaders, religious specialists or both?[116] Perhaps there is an important theme to be explored in the route to absolute power when leaders assume political and religious power simultaneously.

Funerary studies have also seen changes in approach from role theory and evolutionary social complexity to theories of practice and concerns with the historical and political situatedness of funerary events, from static frames of ranking and measures of complexity at any one moment to historical trajectories of successive political acts in which the living use the dead as resource, vision and representation.

FIVE

GENDER AND KINSHIP

Gender centres on the social construction of masculinity and femininity: the social values invested in the social differences between men and women. In this respect gender archaeology is part of the study of social structure, as significant as rank in the social stratification and the evolution of past societies.[1]

The study of the archaeology of gender has been a phenomenon largely of the 1980s and 1990s, with many of its themes developed along lines found in post-processual approaches.[2] The archaeological study of kinship has a rather different recent history, emerging briefly within the early optimism of the New Archaeology in the 1960s and early 1970s and now, after years of neglect, set to make a reappearance hand-in-hand with advances in biomolecular studies of ancient DNA and other analyses of osteological remains.

The concept of gender and its relationship to biological sex have been widely debated and defined. In 1975 the anthropologist Gayle Rubin stated: 'Gender is a socially imposed division of the sexes. It is a product of the social relations of sexuality.'[3] Its most recent archaeological definition is simply that it is the cultural construction of sexuality.[4] For Alison Wylie, gender is not a given nor a property of individuals but a construct with a clear political dimension, a dynamic historical process.[5] Marie-Louise Sørensen adds that this social construct, of central importance in the structure of past societies, is negotiated and maintained through material culture.[6]

Our preconception of predetermined categories of males and females makes problematic the understanding of sex and gender outside our own cultural milieu. Archaeologists must work with an awareness of the dichotomy between natural, biological sex and constructed, cultural gender.[7] As Tim Taylor and Tim Yates have pointed out, we should be prepared to expect considerable complexity and fluidity of sexual identities not only within the assigned primacy of the masculine-feminine pairing but also within non-heterosexual categorizations.[8]

THE OSTEOLOGICAL IDENTIFICATION OF SEX

The possession of male or female genitalia is usually a certain guide to an individual's biological sex, whereas the identification of male or female characteristics from skeletal remains is less clear cut. The average adult female skeleton has a broader pelvis, a less prominent chin and smoother brow ridges than the male.[9] There is also an average difference in height. Osteologists may be able confidently to assign sex to adult human skeletons in up to 95 per cent of cases but the sexing of child skeletons is much more problematic. Sexual dimorphism in the skeletons of children can be detected in the permanent teeth and the sciatic notch on the pelvis though these tests are not conclusive.[10] Even with adult remains, assignment of biological sex may be biased towards males and may explain why so many cemetery groups often appear to contain more males than females; Weiss estimates that this systematic bias in sexing adult skeletons is of the order of 12 per cent in favour of males.[11] A further factor affecting sexual dimorphism in skeletal remains is caused by hormonal abnormalities: an insufficiency of oestrogen in females may lead to dwarfism while an insufficiency of androgen in males (resulting from castration when young, for example) may affect the growth of joints and ends of bones, leading to thin-boned long-leggedness and an elongated mandible.[12] It has been claimed that a girl's body can maintain high levels of androgens by strenuous exercise, leading to narrow, male-like pelves.[13] Recovery of ancient DNA (described at the end of this chapter) provides new methods of sex determination which are proving their worth in difficult areas such as the sexing of child skeletons.

There are certain categories of individual who may be biologically indeterminate, either from a congenital syndrome or as a result of culturally induced bodily transformations. The former group of inter-sexuals are rare, numbering around 1 or 2 per 1000 of the population, and result from conditions such as foetal androgenation (andreno-genital syndrome [AGS] in genetically female foetuses), gonadal dysgenesis, Kleinfelter's syndrome (three or more sex chromosomes resulting in female hormones and male genitalia) and testicular feminization syndrome.[14] As Beth Rega points out, such individuals often occupy important social positions in many cultures, yet are too rare ever to constitute a major axis of sex identification.[15] Cultural transformations of bodily sex are, of course, well known in the modern world. Trans-sexualism or the creation of additional sexual categories may be achieved by altering hormones or through surgery. One specific hormonal method possibly used in prehistoric societies is the ingestion of pregnant mares' urine.[16]

FEMINIST THEORY AND THE RISE OF A 'GENDERED' ARCHAEOLOGY

There is no consensus on the definition of feminism and feminist theory, and images of a homogeneous, ideologically coherent frame of reference are largely resisted.[17] As a movement of resistance and struggle against male oppression for women's empowerment, feminism's theoretical goals include a critique of male supremacy and the definition of sexual difference for women. Initial rethinkings of the new women's history, anthropology and archaeology focused on the countering of androcentric narratives, the recognition of powerful individual women in the past, the search for matriarchies in past societies, and the redressing of the balance through recognition of realms of women's power hitherto ignored. Sørensen has outlined two categories of archaeological sources most useful for pursuing archaeologies of gender.[18] Those realms commonly involved in communicating gender categories are burial activities, individual appearance through costume (much of it from funerary contexts), and some types of art (some of it funerary). More problematic are archaeological remains from domestic units and behaviour which may produce information on food production, labour division, rubbish categories and spatial order. It is very clear that funerary archaeology is a crucial element of any research into past gender categorizations.

Androcentric narratives within funerary archaeology

Archaeology is a continuous struggle to excavate our own preconceptions and unacknowledged assumptions. This is perhaps clearest in our attributions of meaning to grave goods, as Meg Conkey and Janet Spector have highlighted in their critique of Winters's double-standards in his analysis of Late Archaic burials from the American

Midwest.[19] When trade goods were found in a male grave Winter considered that they indicated the man's involvement in long-distance exchange systems, whereas in a woman's burial such items were assumed to be gifts from male relatives. Quernstones in the graves indicated, in the case of women, that their tasks included seed-grinding and, in the case of men, that they were involved in making the querns! Many of our unacknowledged assumptions permeate our interpretations – about the universality of a sexual division of labour, gender dimorphism (the ways that men and women's bodies look different), the commodification of sexuality, the associations of women with the private, domestic, minor, peripheral and the natural, the definition of women by their reproductive capacity and men by their social role, the exclusion of women from hunting, and the perception of certain activities (notably hunting) as intrinsically more important than others such as gathering.[20]

Ian Hodder has recently remarked on his own double-standards and reappraised his differential treatment of the representation of men and of women. The elaborate female symbolism in the Near Eastern Early Neolithic, embodied especially in figurines, could be treated as demonstrative either of their power or their powerlessness whereas the elaborate symbolism of men in the Late Neolithic, largely from burials, was accepted without question as indicative of their power.[21] We may also include feminist critiques of Lévi-Strauss and others' models of kinship; such models rest on an initial premise of the exchange of women, in which women are considered as powerless chattels swapped by their fathers and brothers.[22]

Within funerary archaeology, the principal methodological issue concerned with unexamined assumptions has probably been the ascription of biological sex on the basis of associated grave goods and dress. With the increasingly systematic application of rigorous osteological analyses, this ought to have been largely consigned to archaeology's own dustbin but it is still a problem in certain quarters, reinforcing contemporary gender stereotypes and furthering the invisibility of potential additional or transvestite gender categories.

An interesting case is the identity of the individual buried with a range of extraordinary grave goods within a mound at Vix, in eastern France, around 500–480 BC during the Hallstatt D period of the Early Iron Age (**Figure 5.1**).[23] The surviving skull and other bones were initially identified as belonging to a 30 to 35-year-old woman, henceforth known as 'the princess of Vix', but a subsequent study suggested that the sex of this person was not only indeterminate but might even be male.[24] This led to a reinterpretation of the Vix princess as a transvestite male priest.[25] Spindler's reassessment fitted with Pauli's previous identifications of male transvestites in two élite burials of the same period from Stuttgart-Bad Cannstatt in Germany, in which spearheads were found with female ornaments.[26] Subsequently, a third osteological study has confirmed that the Vix princess was most probably a woman and Bettina Arnold has argued that the Stuttgart-Bad Cannstatt individuals are also actually women, as are remains from other important Hallstatt D/La Tène A burials that Spindler and other (male) archaeologists have considered to be men, indicative of male status within a male power structure.[27]

Sam Lucy's reassessment of sex and gender in East Yorkshire Anglo-Saxon burials finds that, instead of the expected binary split between women with jewellery and men with weapons, there is a large proportion of 'neutral' graves or unaccompanied graves. Although the osteological analyses were hampered by poor bone preservation, three women (two certain, one possible) were buried with weapons at West Heslerton cemetery and three of the burials with jewellery from Sewerby are possibly male.[28] Brush had previously come up with similar conclusions from the mainly cremation cemetery at Spong Hill in Norfolk,[29] and Lucy argues that the absence of sex-linked artefacts in a third of the graves suggests that gender may not have been an important structuring principle in pagan Anglo-Saxon society.[30]

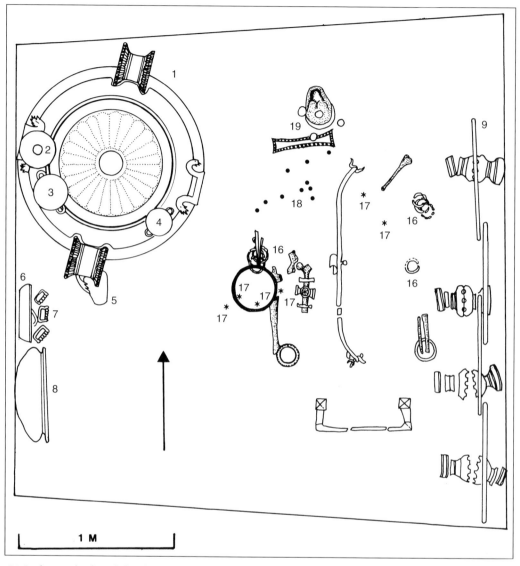

1 M

5.1 *In the wooden burial chamber at Vix lay partially preserved human remains on a wagon box (its wheels 9 to the right of the picture), together with an enormous bronze krater (a Greek vessel for serving wine, 1 in the picture), imported ceramics (3, 4), bronze and silver containers (2, 5–8), a gold 'diadem' on the skull (19) and other personal grave goods such as beads (18), fibulae (brooches; 17) and bracelets (16).*

Of course, in both the Yorkshire and Spong Hill cases, the observations we can make on the non-perishable material culture are only a partial view of the full costume worn in death. Conclusions on the absence of a binary male/female gender distinction in dress must thus remain tentative given that the clothing does not survive. A recent reappraisal of certain supposedly female Anglo-Saxon burials from different parts of England has also led to the identification of a possible third gender of men-women, akin to the North American *berdache*.[31]

Women's power, women's wealth

A second theme of gender studies in archaeology has been to explore the evidence for women's power in past societies. Paula Webster cites both Simone de Beauvoir and Shulamith Firestone as considering that women have been universally oppressed, with the root cause of this oppression being women's restriction to a maintaining and nurturing role, owing to reproductive labour and associated childcare burdens.[32] Can archaeology shed light on the claims of such programmatic statements?

In her book *Women in Prehistory*, Margaret Ehrenberg highlights certain outstanding women's burials, among them the Vix princess and the woman in an Iron Age chariot burial at Wetwang Slack in East Yorkshire.[33] Given their unquestionably high-status grave goods, the latter two burials must be those of members of the most powerful groups within their communities. Liv Helga Dommasnes points out that the identity, power and significance of the Norwegian Viking Age queen buried in the Oseberg ship is often played down in favour of the men's activities of carving, shipbuilding and sailing embodied in the boat and other associated artefacts.[34] In all these cases, other archaeological and documentary sources indicate that these women held positions mostly occupied by men and can be presumed to have possessed some power. Their existence demonstrates that women were not excluded from these positions.

The problems of interpreting women's power from their grave goods and funerary costumes were addressed by Hodder in his ethnoarchaeological observations on women's jewellery among pastoralists in the Lake Baringo region of Kenya.[35] In this patrilineal, virilocal and polygamous society, the low status of women is at odds with the quantities and quality of the ear-rings and necklaces worn. Young women might wear up to forty necklaces but those aged over fifty might have only twenty-five or so. Were women to be buried in the costumes they wore in life, Hodder argued, then their status might appear to be greater than it actually was.

Another example of women as bearers of men's wealth can be found in Marilyn Strathern's study of the Mount Hagen area of Papua New Guinea. Although women 'become like men' at important ceremonies their decoration is distinctly different, signifying their role as intermediaries (bearing items of exchange) rather than negotiators (enacting the exchanges). A woman's formal dance dress for *moka* ceremonies symbolizes this intermediary status, the bailer shell on her front perhaps loaned by her brothers to her husband and the pearl shell on her back intended as a gift from her husband to her brothers. In the past, wives used to display their husbands' wealth at *moka*, swathed in long ropes of cowrie shells and wearing shell aprons. Similarly, brides also used to wear some of the bridewealth valuables.[36]

Many archaeologists have failed to notice their pervasive double-standard of subjecting male burials and female burials to differing interpretations of whose wealth and goods they contain.[37] As these two ethnographic examples show, the ownership and use in life of grave good wealth is one of the most challenging questions for any archaeologist attempting to understand funerary material culture in terms of status, power and gender roles.

Matriarchs and Amazons

The interest in prehistoric matriarchy stems largely from claims by J.J. Bachofen in 1861 and Frederick Engels in 1884 that it formed a universal stage in human culture after an initial stage of promiscuity and prior to what Engels termed 'the world historic defeat of the female sex'. Engels suggested an early stage in human development characterized by group marriage with descent traced through women and matrilocality. Women had supremacy in the household and their high status derived from their central position within the social relations of production.

These conclusions were based not on archaeological evidence but on ancient myths and ethnographic cases. It is probable that Engels' vision of matriarchal society was heavily influenced by Lewis Henry Morgan's nineteenth-century ethnographic account of the matrilineal and matrilocal Iroquois, among whom the women controlled food production and distribution, and life in the longhouse, and had a major influence on male council elders, ritual specialists and war parties.[38] There are many other examples of matrilineal and matrilocal societies known today from other parts of the world, such as the islanders of Dobu in Melanesia,[39] but none of these, including the Iroquois, would be considered matriarchal, with women as a group having absolute power and authority over men.

Marija Gimbutas's interpretation of Early Neolithic (10000–5000 BC) farming communities as matrifocal and probably matrilinear, agricultural and sedentary, egalitarian and peaceful and worshipping a supreme female goddess, stems from her research into the symbolism of female figurines and statuary from household contexts in south-east Europe and the Near East.[40] Although unsupported by most archaeologists, her views have become unassailable for certain ecofeminist groups and New Agers.[41] Recent contextual studies of figurine symbolism demonstrate very satisfactorily that, despite Gimbutas's best attempts, there are no easy equations to be made between female figurines and matriarchal societies or mother-goddess cults.[42] In fact, there are some very good reasons, discussed in Chapter 7, why the interpretation of mother-goddess worship from these clay figurines is wholly bogus.

There is somewhat fuller funerary evidence for the position of women in Early Neolithic farming communities from central and western Europe around 5500–5000 BC, in the form of cemeteries associated with longhouse communities of the Linearbandkeramik culture (referred to as the LBK). On the basis of cross-cultural generalizations about house floor areas, Ehrenberg suggests that these communities in their large longhouses may have been matrilineal and matrilocal.[43] In societies with matrilocal residence and matrilineal descent, such as the Iroquois, communities of sisters tend to stay together under one roof after marriage and thus large floor areas above 35 sq m for a single house are mostly recorded in such societies. As with any cross-cultural generalization there are always exceptions. For example, the LBK longhouses are generally thought to have had a single main hearth rather than a string of hearths as found in the Iroquois houses; in this respect they may be more similar to the longhouses of patrilineal, virilocal groups such as the Barasana of Amazonia.[44] Curiously, the LBK funerary evidence has also been interpreted as similarly resulting from a matrilineal kinship system, although the inferences made in that study are highly questionable.[45]

Whereas Neolithic matriarchies are hard to pin down, Iron Age Amazons are much easier to identify in the funerary record. The ancient Greeks gave a special place in their cosmological beliefs to stories about societies of warlike and fierce women; Hippocrates and Herodotus wrote extensively about them, locating them in the region of Scythia and Sauromatia to the east of the River Don. From the Ukraine and the Caucasus, dating from the fifth century BC and later, we now have a substantial number of warrior burials that are considered to be females.[46] Their weaponry variously includes armour, spears, arrows and shields. In many cases, the osteological analyses of burials of this period are not to modern standards and some of the 'male' skeletons may also conceivably be female given the likely alterations to the pelves of active, mounted women warriors.[47] Taylor estimates that about forty female warrior burials are known from Scythia and reports that about 20 per cent of the warrior graves from Sauromatia are thought to be female.[48] Given the problems of methodology, in which osteological analyses are not always done in isolation from prior inferences about gender made on the basis of artefact assemblages, there are many potential flaws, biases and problems in the study of gender from funerary contexts.

GENDER IDENTITY AND CONTEXTUAL MEANINGS

We have to recognize that in trying to interpret a gendered past all the assumptions and methodologies built into earlier accounts have to be re-examined, nothing can be taken for granted.[49]

Apart from the difficulties of osteological determinations of biological sex and the problems of identifying examples of culturally constructed sex, the interpretation of genders is fraught with difficulty. Ethnographic case studies from communities such as the Hua of the eastern Highlands of Papua New Guinea illustrate the ambiguities, variability, permeability, and changeability of gender construction and negotiation.[50] The Hua classify individuals not only by genital characteristics but also by their amount of *nu* – a female and male vital essence (which has a liquid form, and resides in bodily substances such as blood, urine, fat, mucus or semen). *Nu* content defines such categories as *figapa* ('uninitiated' or 'like women') and *kakora* ('young male initiates' free of all female *nu*). Children and women of child-bearing age are full of female *nu*, while young men who have abstained from heterosexual sex and women's food have male *nu* but no female *nu*. Post-menopausal women who have produced several children (and thus used up their female *nu*, becoming drier and harder) become masculinized whereas old men (who have gained female *nu* from years of sexual intercourse, casual contact with women and eating food prepared by women) are reclassified with advancing years as *figapa*. Thus, on a sliding scale of degrees of maleness and femaleness, genitally female persons may be categorized as masculinized and *vice versa*.

The example of the Hua not only undermines the notion of man and woman as unchanging essences, but it also raises the possibility that gender transformations need have no material correlates and that clothing may signify a gender role at odds with that adopted by the wearer. We can find similar examples from our own era: in the nineteenth century trousers were considered to have a clear gender-associated value so that women's 'transvestite' adoption of them was seen as ambiguous and challenging.[51] Today in the western world, trousers no longer affect the gender identity of the wearer though – *pace* the Scots – skirts still do.

Within the Marxist framework of Engels' interpretation of women's changing status, it is through their place within the social relations of production that their gender status is defined. Similar ideas can be found in Ehrenberg's discussion of the impact of the Later Neolithic 'secondary products revolution', when power was supposedly wrested from the hoe-and-spade women cultivators by the ploughmen, and in John Barrett's model of changing gender roles in the British Late Bronze Age.[52] Barrett argues that changes in domestic space, in food preparation and serving, and in inheritance systems (marked by the end of cremation burial) led to new emphases on the control of agricultural and probably human fertility. Metals and the new iron technology played an increasingly subsidiary role so that new gender roles and age sets were established outside and independent of the sphere of metal production and exchange. However, Henrietta Moore suggests that the cultural valuations given to women and men in society arise from something more than just their respective positions in the relations of production.[53] In other words, what men and women respectively do has less significance than the meanings that those activities acquire.

This brings us into a problematic area since we need to assess not only the cultural valuations of those activities in the past but also to struggle to identify our own value schemes. Linda Hurcombe points out the need for such clarity in explaining to her students her assumption that men were more likely hunters and women gatherers: 'To say that such ideas are sexist is to miss the point of sexual dimorphism as an evolutionary strategy and to be biased by our own cultural experience of the *status* of activities. The female students wanted women to be seen as hunters because this was the task *they* valued more.'[54]

Viking women

Something of this problem comes across in archaeologists' searches for women in high-status burials such as those at Vix and Wetwang discussed above. Anne Stalsberg's analysis of Viking tradeswomen in northern Europe provides an interesting comparison.[55] Previous androcentric interpretations of weighing scales in female graves took them to represent farewell gifts from husbands, tokens of high rank or evidence that the woman died while her husband was away and she was temporarily in charge – effectively anything other than the possibility that the woman herself was a trader.[56] In any case, there are many medieval Scandinavian references to women active in trade at a slightly later date and, of course, women are often the principal traders in many societies in West Africa and elsewhere. Stalsberg suggests that this problem of recognition of women's trading roles is due to the shackles of tradition within archaeological scholarship.

In the earliest explicit study of gender roles and funerary remains (and probably the earliest publication on the archaeology of gender), Dommasnes examined the different statuses of women and men in Viking Norway.[57] As well as enjoying power and authority in the growing economic arena of foreign trade, women also held considerable power in the household. From the tenth century onwards, 'rich' and elaborately constructed women's graves appeared, during a period of social unrest when men were away from the farms and women had to take full responsibility at home.[58] Yet women appear generally to have had influence rather than direct power except within the household.

The large grave mounds of western Norway contain multiple burials but women are, with one exception, never found in primary positions within them. Secondary burials (that is, the person is buried as the second or subsequent one in the mound) are also twice as common for women as they are for men. If the burial mounds were established for farm founders then these features are consonant with a gender-based hierarchical society.[59] Dommasnes also points out that, although in their graves women were provided with a wide range of tools (with the exception of smithing equipment), the only items which were reserved for women were textile implements. This might suggest that Viking women not only specialized in cloth production but maintained an independent trade-derived income from its sale. Finally, she suggests that women's status was more dependent on associations with a fertility cult than on their economic position within the relations of production and that, as the position of women declined during the Iron Age, so the fertility cult lost its dominant position and was relegated from public life.

LITTLE PERISHERS: THE ARCHAEOLOGY OF CHILDREN

In rendering the invisible visible, there has been a recent growth of interest in the archaeological study of children and their gender development.[60] As Sofaer Derevenski and others point out, 'childhood' is a concept which is highly culture-specific, implying sentimental western notions of learning, play and indulgence, in contrast to those many societies where the young work in adult projects from an early age. One of the areas of interest is the fact that children were almost certainly major contributors to all past societies yet their remains are so often under-represented in cemeteries and other funerary contexts.[61] This is all the more extraordinary when considered against Andrew Chamberlain's estimate that most prehistoric populations had childhood mortality rates of at least 50 per cent and Rega's estimate of 15–30 per cent mortality for children under one year of age.[62] It certainly focuses attention on the unusualness of those children who are buried in the same way as adults. Rega's analysis of the Early Bronze Age cemetery at Mokrin (in the former Yugoslavia), for example, highlights the significantly greater mortality of girls to boys but, instead of leaping to the conclusion that young girls were neglected in favour of boys, she argues the opposite. Given that young children and infants were normally buried under the houses and settlements, the inclusion of these children in the cemetery distinguishes them from other children. The small proportion of children's graves at Mokrin (far fewer than would be expected from the likely mortality rate) suggests that the particular children buried here were fairly special and it therefore indicates that girls were more important than boys.

Ellen Pader's analysis of age-sex relations in pagan Anglo-Saxon cemeteries in eastern England highlights the ways that age-based relations linked children and women: both shared significantly more attributes with each other than either shared with men – male children were rarely found with male sex-linked artefacts whereas many children, both male and female, were treated as female in terms of their associated grave goods.[63] It was only at sub-adulthood that the relationship between the sexes became apparent in the consistent associations with sex-correlated artefacts.[64] At Early Bronze Age Mokrin, in contrast, the primary axis of differentiation was by sex and even the smallest children were buried according to a strongly demarcated categorization of gender.[65] Malcolm Lillie comes to rather different conclusions for cemetery populations from the Ukrainian Mesolithic and Neolithic where specific gender determinations had not been achieved by the children prior to death even though the wide variety of artefacts placed with them suggests that they were recognized as significant social actors.[66]

Perhaps one of the most salient points about child burials, noted by Lucy, is that they bring home to us the gap between those being buried and those doing the burying; as funerary archaeologists we only ever see children as manipulated entities within an adult world – they are buried by adults.[67] Thus we never experience the world of children, only the experiences of adults coming to terms with and attempting to ascribe meaning to their foreshortened lives and premature deaths.

Some critiques of post-processual archaeologists' concerns with power, domination and resistance stress the omission of phenomenological aspects of individuals' lived experiences. *Phenomenology*, in the tradition of the philosopher Husserl, is the attempt to understand experience 'from within the flow of life, rather than from the outside, looking at the things we take for granted and bringing to attention things that have been forgotten or made to seem trivial by the theoretical tradition'.[68] Recent approaches have stressed how 'bodies can be addressed by social and historical processes without ceasing to be individual and material'.[69] Lynn Meskell attempts a phenomenological approach in reconstructing the experience of burying young children within the Eastern Necropolis of the New Kingdom (1570–1070 BC) site of Deir el Medina in Egypt.[70] In one of her examples, a severely disabled boy suffered from scoliosis of the pelvis, had an abnormal left hip, one leg shorter than the other and his legs were swollen. The body was wrapped and placed in a wicker basket which was too short: his feet protruded through a hole in the side. Meskell points out that the burial was neither expensive nor ostentatious but did illustrate care and concern in the placing of the necessary food offerings within the grave pit before the vault was covered with large stones. She concludes that the boy's untimely death warranted care and personal responses since he was already considered an embodied person.

Her observations on the personal and immediate nature of the mourners' grief and the pathos of the troubling sight of the sticking-out feet, however, exemplify the problems of perception and interpretation of an alien culture. What is presented here is an interpretive view of what we, in western society, ought to feel as a result of our attitudes towards the disabled. The evidence could be interpreted in other ways; the disabled boy may have been neither loved nor mourned – his death may even have been welcomed. The carefully arranged offerings and the large roof stones may have been primarily to ensure that he did not come back to trouble the living.

As others studying the anthropology of emotion and the archaeology of compassion have noted,[71] the evidence is often ambiguous. This is not simply a problem of lack of evidence but of reading and understanding the complexity of contrasting emotions and the interplay of inner feelings manipulated and orchestrated through the expectations of the ritual routine. While Meskell is entirely right to pursue archaeologies of emotive and embodied experience, we tread a thin line between enquiry and empathy. Empathetic approaches are, unfortunately, more than likely to lead us back into imposing our own unacknowledged preconceptions.

No survey of child burial studies would be complete without considering child sacrifice, infanticide and death through exposure or neglect. There are now a number of studies of Roman Britain, ancient Carthage, the Inka empire, and Late Roman–Early Byzantine Israel where very different kinds of infanticide have been claimed from archaeological evidence.[72] Unsurprisingly, the quality of the evidence and the strength of the claims varies between cases. The different contexts range from the public and highly ritualized sacrifices of the *capacocha* ritual among the Inka to the apparently clandestine disposal of unwanted babies at Askalon in Israel.[73]

WOMEN, MEN AND CHILDREN IN DANISH PREHISTORY

In his provocative book *The Prehistory of Sex*, Tim Taylor suggests that the emergence of strictly gendered clothing aided the entrenchment of social inequality.[74] By naturalizing difference in sex through gendered dress, the existence of social hierarchy can also be made to appear natural and unquestioned through sleight-of-hand. The Danish sequence from the Mesolithic to the Iron Age provides an opportunity to examine this intriguing claim as well as to follow the changing gender relations within one part of the world over a period of five thousand years between *c.* 5600 BC and AD 400. It is also an opportunity to examine critically Michael Mann's sweeping statement that gender relations remained broadly constant, in the form of patriarchy, from earliest recorded history (*c.* 3000 BC in the Near East) to the eighteenth century.[75]

The origins of gender's cultural construction have been estimated as dating back to archaic *Homo sapiens*, about 200,000 years ago, but are not archaeologically visible until the last 100,000 years with the first appearance of burials and artistic representations.[76] A suspiciously large proportion of the Eurasian Middle and Upper Palaeolithic burials are sexed as male, leading Whelan to question earlier conclusions such as Harrold's inference that Upper Palaeolithic 'males and females do not differ significantly in regard to the distribution of grave goods or features of any category' – women may just not have been buried by and large.[77] Thus our search for gender categorization is limited, for the moment, to later periods and the quality of research into the Danish later Mesolithic and its cemeteries (c. 5600–4200 BC) provides an ideal starting point for study.

There is a large body of literature on gender in Danish prehistory.[78] Much of the material on the Bronze Age has been extensively reviewed by Sørensen in a detailed critique of the different approaches and the varying nature of their androcentric, empirical and theoretical difficulties so I shall present here a brief summary of trends interpreted largely from the funerary evidence.[79]

The Mesolithic period

The evidence from the later Mesolithic burial groups such as Vedbaek, Nederst, Strøby Egede and Tybrind Vig indicates gender-related burial associations between males and females and specific types of grave goods.[80] Although numbers are small and graves occasionally have no grave goods, some burials exhibit a marked gender distinction defined by the costume of the deceased or attendant artefacts placed with the body.[81] For example, women's burials are characterized by collections of pendant tooth beads which the excavators interpreted as originally sewn into clothing. In only one instance at Vedbaek is a single pendant tooth bead found with an adult male, behind the back of his head. Male burials often include a flint blade placed in the pelvic area and stone and antler axeheads around the upper part of the body. Some female burials have attendant artefacts in the form of a bone awl and flint transverse arrowhead above the head; one has a bone dagger over the pelvis. The association of axes with males and quantities of tooth beads with females is found in the other Mesolithic cemeteries of Denmark and the Skatteholm cemeteries of southern Sweden.

Yet there may have been a third gender. Within a triple grave at Vedbaek were the corpse of a year-old child with a 25 to 30-year-old adult of indeterminate sex to its right, probably killed by the bone arrowhead lodged between its neck vertebrae (**Figure 5.2**). To the infant's left lay a 35 to 40-year-old, also of indeterminate sex, with a small flint blade below the lower jaw and a collection of animal and human tooth pendants, unperforated red deer teeth, a pine marten's lower jaw and bones of roe deer. This latter individual stands out as something of an anomaly and might indicate the presence of a third gender, a ritual specialist or both. To a lesser extent, some of the grave goods may have been related to age differences; the tooth bead assemblages found with adults are larger and have more species variety (not just red deer but also wild pig, aurochs, ox and elk).

The Neolithic and Early Bronze Age

In the earthen barrows and stone dolmens of the subsequent period, the Earlier Neolithic (c. 4200–2800 BC), skeletons are rarely preserved.[82] Although grave goods often survive, little can be said about gender relations, except that a single burial from Dragsholm contained the skeleton of a twenty-year-old man with a pot, amber beads and a stone battleaxe. The same is broadly true of the stone passage-grave burials of the Middle Neolithic although bones have survived in a few cases. Charlotte Damm argues that although men, women and children are present in these deposits, their often disarticulated remains are not differentiated.[83] In other words, individual identities of the dead in the Middle Neolithic were wholly dissolved into an anonymous collectivity of ancestors (**Figure 5.3**). Of course, we have no knowledge of how gender was constructed within the

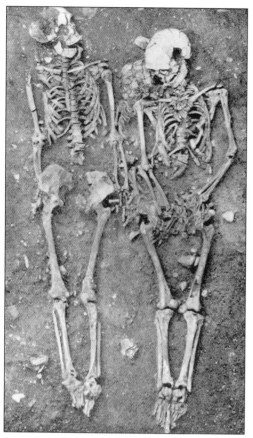

5.2 The child buried between the two adults of indeterminate sex in the Mesolithic cemetery at Vedbaek. The combination of tooth beads and a flint blade with the right-hand body does not fall within the gender categories exhibited by other burials and hints at the possibility that this individual was of a third gender.

sequences of funerary rites prior to final and collective deposition, let alone in the other aspects of everyday life, but Damm suggests that the ideological representations articulated by communal megalithic burials are those of differences and inequalities between territorial or kin-based groups.[84] An interesting feature of megalithic tombs on Zeeland is that many are paired. One chamber is always smaller and less well constructed than the other. Unfortunately none has preserved any human bones so we do not know if this pairing served to distinguish people by age, gender or kinship.

The mound burials of the Late Neolithic Single Grave Culture (2800–2400 BC) and Early Bronze Age Dagger period (2400–1800 BC) present us with a rigid classification of gender conformity, just as we see in eastern Europe at that time (**Figure 5.4**).[85] Some women's burials are accompanied by small polished stone axes, flint blades, bone tools, ceramic pots and ornaments of copper and amber. The flexed skeletons lie facing south but the majority of males lie on their right sides with heads to the west and females lie on their left sides with their heads to the east. The pattern applies to children as well as adults, though there is evidence of a lack of fit between sex and gender in that 15 per cent of males are buried in the female gendered position.[86] Of course, such pronouncements are problematic because most of the burials survive as body stains with bones rarely surviving and thus cannot be osteologically sexed.

The Middle Bronze Age

The preserved coffin burials of the Middle Bronze Age (1800–1300 BC) have attracted considerable interest with respect to gender since not only are certain burials exceptionally well preserved, but there appears to have been a very strong categorization of male and female gendered objects and costume attributes.[87] Men's and women's dress was different in many ways, notably in headpieces and coiffure and the wearing of cloth.[88] Randsborg's analysis of metal wealth in Bronze Age graves (**Figure 4.3**) demonstrates that both women and men were buried with often substantial quantities of bronze and gold (the generally heavier average weight of metal in male graves is due to the presence of swords, which are not found in female burials).[89] The increasing quantity of female-gendered bronze dress items deposited in votive hoards towards the later part of the Bronze Age is in inverse proportion to male-gendered artefacts and has caused much discussion as to its meaning.[90]

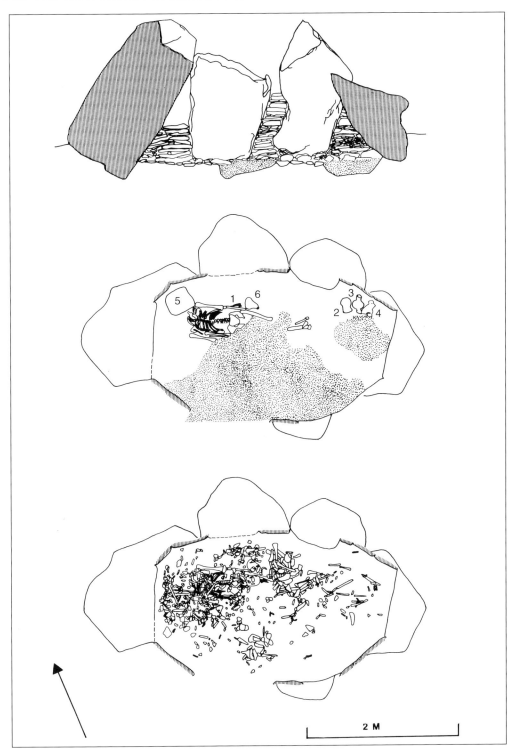

5.3 A section and plan of 'Klokkehøj', a megalithic tomb of the Funnel Beaker period in Denmark. It initially contained (c. 3300 BC) the headless skeleton of a 20–35-year-old man (middle) with a stone 'pillow' (5), a child's skull (6), a bone strip (1) and three pots (2–4). Around 2800 BC the disarticulated bones (bottom) of nine children and thirteen adults were added.

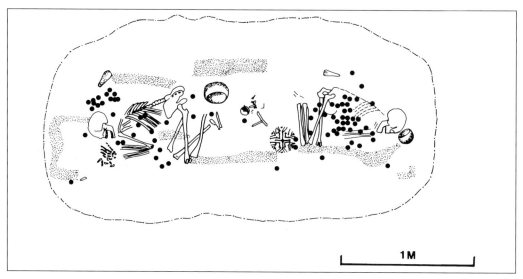

5.4 *A burial of two young women of the Single Grave Culture from Bedinge, southern Sweden, associated with an unusually lavish assemblage of two flint carpentry axes, four pots, four flint blades, a copper ear-ornament, over a hundred amber beads, three bone bodkins, a pot-decorating tool and sheep bones.*

The Iron Age

The Late Bronze Age and Early Iron Age funerary tradition is almost universally cremation (other than the bog bodies; see Chapter 3). For the Early Iron Age the gender associations of metal dress fittings are not clear, owing to a sad lack of osteological analysis on large cemeteries such as Årupgård. Randsborg speculates that women's labour would have been important in this agricultural economy marked by the appearance of field systems but that their power would have been curtailed by the establishment of closed households, in the form of longhouses with byres. There is no way of knowing, and the disappearance of women's bronze jewellery as offerings in bogs may signify merely the collapse of an élite or of an exchange system rather than a significant change in gender relations. The highly egalitarian picture gained from Early Iron Age burials and longhouses is contradicted only by the evidence that some of the bog bodies performed no manual work. There seems to have been no gender distinction in selecting these individuals for the dubious honour of dying in a peat bog.

From the late first century BC, shortly after the appearance of élite farmsteads and cremations, most cremation cemeteries were divided into male and female zones or were entirely single sex. Although burials from the Roman Iron Age in eastern Denmark often do not have skeletal material preserved, enough osteological studies from other parts of Scandinavia and northern Germany indicate that gender associations of the material culture largely conformed to sex differences but that there were substantial areas of overlap.[91] For example, over 10 per cent of burials with spindle-whorls were males while almost 15 per cent of weapon burials were females.[92]

This broad picture obscures chronological changes within the Roman Iron Age; by the second century AD the relatively autonomous categories of male and female equipment were becoming intermingled within individual graves. This erosion of gender representations was also occurring in the increasingly mixed cemeteries. Around AD 200 there was a major reordering of funerary practices, in line with changes in household organization, military structure and industry.[93] Cemeteries were re-established as gender-segregated spaces and women's elaborate costumes and finery marked them apart from male dress styles. Yet by AD 400 the spatial segregation in cemeteries was once again breaking down.

Taylor's claim that gender distinctions in clothing became apparent in Europe only with the emergence of other forms of status differentiation in the Late Neolithic and Early Bronze Age cannot be sustained.[94] The evidence shows that in the Mesolithic period gender differentiation was probably greater than the marking of age differences. Mann's proposition of stable gender relations is similarly without foundation. The Danish prehistoric sequence provides us with a remarkable view of the dynamic and changing relationship between men and women and the ways that genders were constructed, dissolved and reformulated over time. These changes coincided with significant economic, cultural and political transformations, indicating that the politics of gender were inseparable from other social processes and practices.

DRESS, GENDER AND KINSHIP

As discussed in Chapter 4, Sue Shennan's analysis of the Early Bronze Age cemetery at Braně (c. 2400–1700 BC) concludes with two opposing hypotheses about social organization.[95] She suggests that if the high status of certain women was ascribed (inherited), they were more likely to survive infancy than boys, raising the possibility that descent may have been calculated through the female line and that female children were therefore vital to group continuity. Given the small size of the community represented by the cemetery (about forty people at any one time), men may have been brought in as marriage partners from outside. Alternatively, she suggests that a different picture results from interpreting women's wealth as achieved (essentially as awarded at marriage). The few 'rich' men, in contrast to the many 'rich' women, are explained as polygamous husbands and the women's wealth derives from bridewealth payments or the use of wives as vehicles for displaying their husbands' wealth. In this scenario, descent might be patrilineal and residence uxorilocal. Shennan was unable to decide between these two possibilities.

Subsequently, Stephen Shennan and John O'Shea have interpreted the larger quantities of metal goods in women's graves (as opposed to men's) from Early Bronze Age cemeteries in the region as indicative of male wealth and prestige, thereby supporting the second alternative.[96] Their virocentric position is attacked by Rega who states, 'While the metal wealth in female graves may indeed represent a male contribution, the mortuary data alone do not allow determination of "ownership", whether symbolic or actual.'[97]

Mokrin: status and gender

Studies of gender and kinship are closely tied to studies of status and all need to be understood together. O'Shea develops the notion of *associative* status, in addition to achieved and ascriptive status, where an individual holds or obtains a social position by virtue of a relationship (of kinship, marriage or adoption) to another individual or group.[98] He gives as an example the burial of certain women in head-dresses in the Early Bronze Age cemetery at Mokrin;[99] head ornaments are regularly found with adult and mature women but are rare among old women, leading O'Shea to suggest that the wearing of head-dresses was relinquished in later life. From this he suggests that they may have had an associative character and that this might reflect consanguineal or affinal ties to the holders of male offices.[100] Thus he perceives that the women wearing head ornaments owed that right to their relationships with particular men.

At the same time O'Shea argues that the general poverty of old people's dress accoutrements and grave goods is an indicator that this was a society in which status was accumulated by giving away wealth and possessions; the lack of such items among the elderly may have related inversely to their status.[101] The situation may also have been complicated by the different responses of mourners to untimely deaths and to those dying in old age. At the end of a long life, personal possessions might be recycled, handed down or disposed of in other ways but, for the life cut short, the use of these items other than as grave goods might be deemed inappropriate. In either case, we need not accept O'Shea's interpretation of women's head ornaments as associative status markers.

Regardless of these interpretive problems, the costumes of the deceased and the manner of their burial reveal a very strong dichotomy in the presentation of male and female regardless of age or other social factors. Rega found that 94 per cent of the adults at Mokrin were buried in a form accordant with their sex, and the same was probable for the children. While everyone faced east, females lay on their right sides with the head to the south or south-east and males lay on their left sides with the head to the north or north-west (**Figure 5.5**). The anomalous 6 per cent are considered by Rega to be due to inaccuracies in standard sexing techniques, as those results fall within the expected range of sex determination error.[102] Although costume and grave goods relate to some extent to age and other factors, ten of the nineteen non-ceramic artefact types relate exclusively or predominantly to either males (three types) or females (seven types).[103] Males and females were presented as engaged in separate but equal lives with both difference and complementarity highlighted.

The most interesting burial at Mokrin is that of an elderly male (large and robust) buried with dress ornaments normally associated with adult females: a pair of pins, a neck-ring, four bracelets and two gold hair-rings.[104] This individual's ambiguous status is further highlighted in two ways. Firstly, there is a striking contrast between the poverty of most old people's burials and the fact that this was one of the most splendidly equipped graves of the whole region. Its ambiguousness is also expressed by its position within the central overlap between the distinct clusters which sub-divide the Mokrin cemetery into four groups. It thus embodies the fundamental significance of gender in structuring Early Bronze Age social relationships. In such a society, ambiguity of this kind might be considered powerful and/or dangerous. Rather than viewing this individual as a one-off curiosity, we might consider that his/hers was the most important burial within the whole cemetery.

KINSHIP AND THE NEW ARCHAEOLOGY

One of the earliest applications of a New Archaeological approach to archaeological data was Binford's analysis of funerary deposits in Galley Pond Mound, a Late Woodland-Mississippian mortuary site in Illinois.[105] His approach required acceptance of a nested series of assumptions or inferences. As a piece of creative thinking, it illustrates clearly Binford's early optimism that all aspects of past societies were accessible through the archaeological record and could be addressed by framing the appropriate hypotheses. However, Binford's logic is, in this case, tortuous and hard to follow and his inferences are speculative in the extreme.

On the floor of the mortuary structure at Galley Pond (**Figure 5.6**), there were bone bundles (groups of disarticulated bones, especially skulls and long bones). Binford divided the bone groups into different categories:

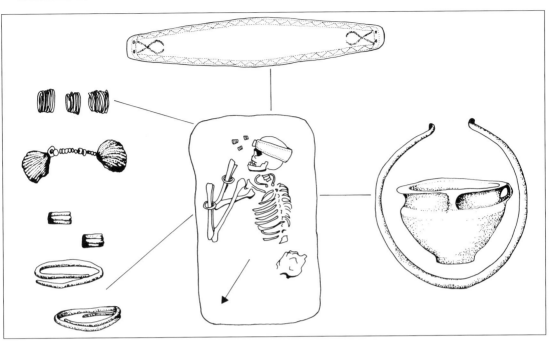

5.5 *At the Early Bronze Age cemetery of Mokrin in the former Yugoslavia, the arrangement of male and female burials shows that gender was a central structuring element of funerary representation. This body of an adult female faces east with her head to the south. She wears a gold-foil crown, gold hair-rings, and bracelets and a neck-ring of copper.*

A. Bundles consisting of a skull and long bones and rearticulated extended burials. These were complete individuals who shared the same undifferentiated treatment of skull and body proper.
B. Burials in which the skull faces one way and the rearticulated legs another.[106] These were complete individuals whose skull and leg bones were differentiated at burial.
C. Incomplete individuals – either just skulls or just long bone bundles.

He found that eight out of the ten Category A bone groups were oriented north–south, as were all the individual skulls (part of Category C). In contrast, all the long bone bundles (part of Category C) were aligned east–west. His first inference was that the east–west and north–south orientations of the bundles, skulls and bones related to a dual social division. Binford's second inference was that the north–south orientation was symbolic of the local community and therefore the east–west orientation must be symbolism used by another community or by a minor segment of this one. He supported this inference by pointing out that the mortuary structure, domestic structures and all 'high-status' burials (apparently burials from nearby sites which were given elaborate treatment) were aligned north–south.

From the fact that the skulls had not been nibbled but the long bones had, Binford surmised that the two categories of bones (skulls and long bones) had different pre-interment histories and thus may have had two separate custodians or groups of custodians. Inference 3 was that orientation was determined by the moiety affiliation of each custodian, the person responsible for bringing already disarticulated bones for burial in the mound. Inference 4 was that interment of bodies in the mortuary structure was

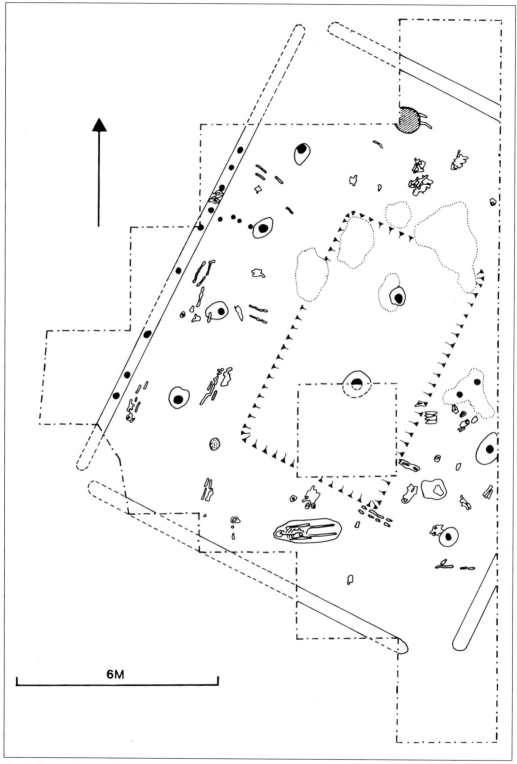

6M

5.6 Galley Pond Mound contained a rectangular mortuary structure with an outer wall trench, three rows of post holes and a sunken central area. The bone bundles were scattered around its interior.

done only by the local community. If a non-local custodian retained either the skull or the long bones, that element would not be placed in the mortuary structure. Four combinations of bone groups could be recognized:

1. A complete skeleton of skull and bones (both custodians were local residents).
2. Just a skull or just bones (the other portion retained by a non-resident custodian).
3. Skull and bones from different bodies but on the same orientation (the resident custodians were both members of the same moiety).
4. The bones one way and the skull the other (the resident custodians were members of opposing moieties).

Since all the remains identified as female were represented by complete skeletons (bone group combination 1), Binford's Inference 5 was that residence and descent were matrilocal and matrilinear. Through this ingenious but tortuous logic Binford tried to reconstruct the major aspects of this Late Woodland community's kinship; from a series of inferences he claimed to identify this community as a dual organization of matrilineal and matrilocal moieties.

Binford's breathtaking leaps of faith at each stage in his study are no greater than those in certain post-processual case studies, and perhaps such soaring optimism is a feature of many of the earliest case studies within the grip of a new archaeological paradigm. Binford's study may also have relied on unacknowledged similarities with ethnographic material. As Allen and Richardson point out, it is difficult to conceive of such an elaborate reconstruction without recourse to ethnographic data, in this case probably historic south-east North American burial practices and kinship patterns.[107] If we were to begin again on the Galley Pond Mound material, we might pursue the appropriateness and applicability of those ethnographic cases more explicitly. It is also most probable that the north–south symbolism is a feature not just of the Galley Pond community but of many Late Woodland communities in that region, and we would need to reconsider the meanings of the different orientations. It is doubtful that we could support Binford's conclusions today.

In 1971 Saxe published his analysis of Mesolithic burials at Wadi Halfa in Egypt. The lack of major differences in grave good provision and grave construction led Saxe to infer that this had been an egalitarian society. His best evidence for potential social differences was in the degree of flex of the corpses' legs, in other words the variations in the angle between the vertebral column and the femur. The bodies were laid mostly on their left sides, with their hands in the area of the chest or face and with their knees bent into a tight flex of sometimes less than 45 degrees to the vertebral column. Saxe noted that females were treated more variably than males and included:

a) the only right-sided burial
b) the only burial facing north and extended on its back
c) greater variation than males in hand positioning
d) a wider angle of leg flex between 45 and 180 degrees (average 80 degrees) whereas male flexion was less than 45 degrees.

Saxe considered that these variations were due to differences in pre-interment and interment rituals. He hypothesized that post-marital residence was patrilocal, that the women were wives who were incomers. Male corpses were treated uniformly, presumably by the local population adhering to the same traditional methods, whereas women were interred by their own non-local kin with their separate and various traditions of laying out and burial.[108]

Again, this case makes a number of dubious assumptions but not to the extent of Binford's study. We may speculate just as plausibly that the differences resulted from men burying the males and women burying the females, each with their own cultural traditions of interment. Less speculatively, these differences may be most simply explained as the means by which the corpses' genders were categorized and communicated. Other New Archaeological approaches to reconstructing prehistoric kinship patterns can be found in studies of Natufian society,[109] and of Californian Native American societies.[110]

Problems with archaeological reconstructions of kinship

Social anthropologists Allen and Richardson have criticized archaeologists' outmoded conceptions of kinship classifications and realities, pointing out that residence and descent within particular societies are often not clearly patterned exclusively or even predominantly into single forms such as virilocal or matrilineal.[111] There is a distinction to be made between kinship rules and reality and there need not be any correlation between types of residence patterning and types of descent (i.e. matrilocal does not presuppose matrilineal). Their criticisms are, however, largely aimed at non-funerary studies which were attempting to extrapolate kinship from ceramic design variation.

Pader reiterates the criticisms of Allen and Richardson and specifically criticizes the 'purity argument' that proposes that insiders can be distinguished from outsiders by funerary treatment.[112] Her other main criticism, relevant for Shennan's notions about community size and the need for exogamy (out-marriage), is that the populations within a single cemetery may well derive from a variety of different settlements: the community of the dead may well be very different from the communities of the living.

As we have seen, attempts to use mortuary remains to infer kinship and other related aspects of social organization studied by social and cultural anthropologists have been largely unsuccessful; descent, residence and notions such as matriarchy not only elude our search but have been, in any case, demonstrated to be far more complex and problematic entities than archaeologists have been prepared to accept. However, there are two areas where at least a crude understanding of such elements of social organization may be possible. The first is in those instances where stratigraphic sequences of burials may allow us to draw certain conclusions about gender and kinship. The second is through the use of human biological data, in conjunction with funerary analyses of archaeological context and association.

STRATIGRAPHIC SEQUENCES AND KINSHIP

Stratigraphy is the study of sequences of deposits, normally vertically, where one layer lies on top of the other. In undisturbed sequences the lower layer always pre-dates the higher. In such situations archaeologists can establish not only relative dating but also sequences of deposition. By studying such sequences of burials it is possible to make inferences about social precedence and succession from the vertical ordering of the dead.

The large Viking Age (tenth to twelfth centuries AD) grave mounds of western Norway contain large numbers of bodies. Dommasnes has shown that although more women's graves than men's are found in the larger mounds, they are all, with one exception, secondary burials. For all sizes of mound, secondary burials are twice as common among women as among men. She concludes that the relative lack of women's primary burials may be due to their social position within families. The mounds, often built close to the farmhouses, are interpreted as family tombs constructed over the grave of the 'founding father' of each farm.[113]

A similar set of stratigraphic patterns is found among the Early Bronze Age round barrows of Wessex in southern England during the Beaker period. Inferences about the social structure can be made from grave goods and from the relative placing of human remains in burial mounds. Some of the grave goods can be divided on gender lines, suggesting a certain division of labour between men and women, symbolized in death. While male graves contain arrowheads, daggers, wristguards, belt rings, amber buttons, stone axes and fire-making tools, female graves are associated with shale and jet beads and the majority of awls and antler picks; certain items (flint blades, ear-rings and pebble hammers) are shared equally.[114] Whereas daggers, ornaments and small tools were regularly placed in graves, other items were generally deposited elsewhere. Metal axes, spearheads and halberds are found invariably in boggy contexts as hoards or single finds. These are often in rocky and impressive locations which were evidentially special places. It seems clear that such deposits were votive offerings, occasionally broken and, for certain unknown reasons, inappropriate accompaniments to buried individuals.[115]

Further insights into Bronze Age gender and age distinctions can be gained from the relationship between primary and secondary burials within barrows (**Figure 5.7**). Where adult males are buried first, later burials may be of other adults or children, yet where adult females are buried first they are rarely followed by adult males.[116] This pattern can be found in the excavated barrows within linear barrow cemeteries such as Shrewton in Wessex or more dispersed groups such as Irthlingborough-West Cotton in eastern England.[117]

These patterns, in which adult women as primary burials are followed only by children, other women or adolescents while adult male primaries are followed by any combination, closely match the interment sequences in Tandroy tombs in southern Madagascar.[118] Within this strongly patrilineal society, women's corpses are often returned to their father's community for burial. When an adult married woman dies before her husband she will be buried in a single grave which is then covered by a walled cairn. If she dies after he does, she will be buried either as a secondary within his tomb or as a secondary within her father's tomb. A man will normally have his own tomb if he has married and established a family, otherwise his body will be interred as a secondary burial within his father's tomb. Other secondary burials inserted into the tomb covering the primary grave of either a man or a woman are their dependants – young women and men, children and adolescents (although children below about six are buried separately in children's cemeteries).

The striking similarity of these two sequential orderings of burial is very suggestive of a shared emphasis on the male line, which we might interpret as symbolizing patrilineal descent. In the Tandroy case, the tombs may be many miles from the villages of their occupants and those buried in the same tomb may be either blood relatives or kin by marriage, and may have spent relatively little time in the same community. None the less the tombs fix patrilineal ancestry into the landscape. In both cases the relationship between primary and secondary burials sets forth an idealized representation of how kinship and family should be organized, thereby fixing in ritual the ways that everyday life should be led. Thus we can infer that the funerary rites of the Wessex Bronze Age embodied and represented a patrilineal notion of succession.

Mass graves and stratigraphy

An intriguing postscript on Early Bronze Age burial and kinship in north-west Europe can be constructed from a coastal site at Wassenaar in the Netherlands.[119] Here a mass grave dating to *c.* 1700 BC contained twelve individuals (**Figure 5.8**). Unlike the jumbled chaos

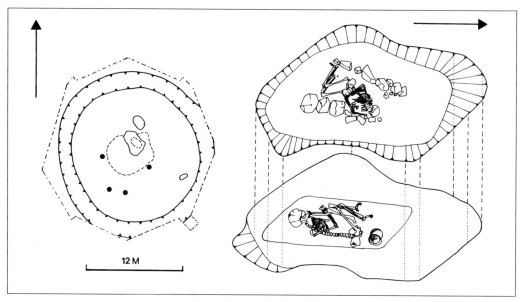

5.7 A plan of multiple interments within an Early Bronze Age round barrow at Shrewton, Wiltshire, showing cremation burials (dots), two off-centre inhumations, and a central burial pit. A secondary burial (Interment 2) has been dug into the top of the primary central burial (Interment 1).

of a mass grave of the Early Neolithic discovered at Talheim in Germany,[120] the Wassenaar bodies were carefully laid out in two opposing rows, one to the east and one to the west, with their legs overlapping. The excavators were able to ascertain from the arrangement of limbs that the corpses were laid out in sequence from the north end to the south (**Figure 5.9**). The arrangement of the bodies exhibited a symmetrical structure in which the adult males were placed centrally while the two women (one certain and one probable) and the very young children were laid at the edges. Additionally, the two women were laid on their fronts and children under twelve were laid on their sides; the rest were laid on their backs. This grotesque tableau presents a remarkable insight into Bronze Age classifications of gender and possibly kinship, presenting a horizontal framing of relationships not dissimilar to the vertical differentiation found in the British round barrows.

INTEGRATING FUNERARY AND BIOLOGICAL APPROACHES

There are three major biological techniques available to archaeologists studying kinship. The first is the analysis of the form and shape of bones and teeth, either as measured elements (metric traits) or as recorded minor anomalies (non-metric traits). There are more than 400 non-metric variants (as opposed to metric or measured variance) described for the human skeleton. They are not caused by disease but their development may be affected by nutrition and factors operating during the growth period. The causes of most non-metric traits are still unknown but some have been found to be genetically inherited to varying degrees, notably cranial features.[121] Non-metric traits have been used to study potential genetic relationships within cemetery populations to test whether pre-identified sub-groups or spatial clusters might have corresponded to kin groupings.[122] Certain epigenetic traits are sometimes associated with physical attributes through the mechanism

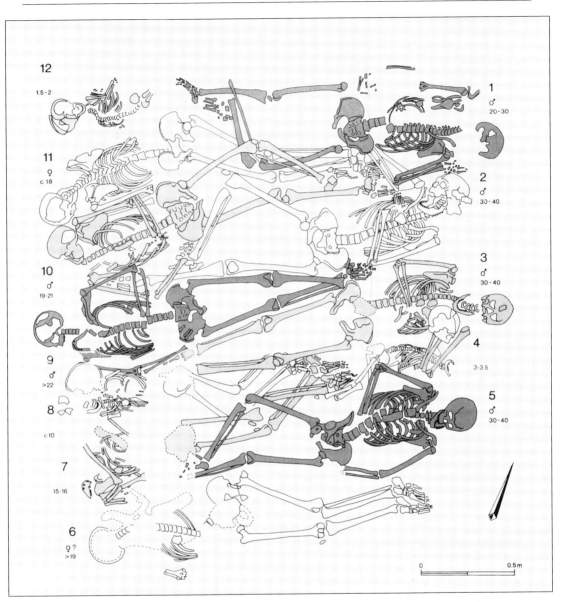

5.8 The Early Bronze Age mass grave at Wassenaar, the Netherlands. Skeleton 10, a young man, had a flint arrowhead between his ribs, whilst the skeletons of three other men showed evidence of blows. The skull of Child 4 had apparently been separated from the body at burial.

of pleiotropism (the phenomenon whereby the same genes code for different aspects of the phenotype). There is little certain evidence that many non-metric traits are necessarily the result of genetic inheritance. Also problematic for the archaeological study of kinship is the consensus that certain traits are widely dispersed within large populations of hundreds and thousands of people and are rarely limited to a particular descent line.

The identification of blood groups from ancient human remains – palaeoserology – is possible from blood cells surviving in bone as well as in preserved soft tissue but determining an individual's blood group from surviving bone alone is difficult, given

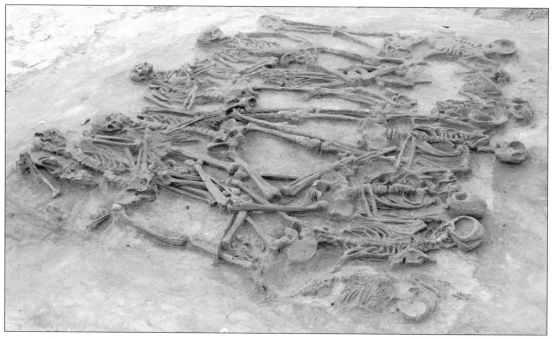

5.9 The skeletons at Wassenaar under excavation, seen from the north.

problems of non-specific absorbtion, contamination and possible technical error.[123] One study of blood types has confirmed the likely kinship between Tutankhamen and the mummy identified as Smenkhkare.[124]

DNA (deoxyribonucleic acid) is a molecule which contains inherited genetic information and is mostly located in the chromosomes. Humans have 23 pairs of chromosomes bearing 50,000 genes. DNA is also located in the mitochondria, outside the nucleus – mitochondrial DNA is inherited solely from the mother whereas chromosomal DNA is inherited equally from both parents. Mitochondrial DNA is more useful for studying ancient remains since it is a small and well-characterized molecule, it is more readily amplified in the PCR technique (polymerase chain reaction) than single-copy chromosomal DNA, and it is highly variable allowing easy identification of differences between individuals unless closely related.[125] It now appears that the survival of ancient DNA is not correlated with the age of the remains but is more dependent on factors of histological preservation.[126] Although ancient DNA is invariably partial and fragmented, frozen and mummified bodies may produce the best results. The major problem still remains that of contamination by modern DNA and convincing results must involve adequate controls, should be repeatable (ideally in independent laboratories), and must be statistically verifiable phylogenetically or by comparison with DNA-independent controls.[127]

Matrilineal kinship in prehistoric Thailand

Evidence for matrilineal succession has been found in Bronze Age Thailand at Khok Phanom Di.[128] Burials were superimposed in tight clusters (**Figure 5.10**) within a large mound of ash and food debris which probably derived from funerary feasts and gradually accumulated during the cemetery's use, providing a well-defined vertical sequence. Analysis of non-metric traits in skulls, teeth and limb bones showed that people buried within a cluster were more likely to share certain abnormalities. Stress marks on the pelves of women buried near infants were interpreted as showing that the women could have carried at least that number of children (though there is now considerable doubt whether parturition can be detected from so-called 'parturition scars' on the pelvis). Pots in adjacent graves sometimes had similar decorative styles. Finally, what was probably a ritual of tooth removal had been practised on a different set of teeth for people in one cluster as opposed to another. If these clusters were genetically related kin groups then their vertical sequences could provide genealogical histories over five hundred years.

Until about the twelfth generation (out of twenty) there was little difference in grave goods distributed between men and women but this changed with the appearance of elaborate female graves containing thousands of beads, beautiful pots, red ochre, a purple substance possibly used as a nipple ornament, clay anvils and cylinders of potting clay. There is an evident association here between women and pottery: perhaps these women were celebrated in death as potters whose skills had brought them esteem and wealth. Charles Higham and Rachanie Bannanurag consider that the value of these individuals to the community was so great that they would have remained in the village of their birth and thus would have participated in a matrilocal pattern of residence (though of course they could have moved on marriage and been returned after death for burial).

In addition, these richly endowed women were often accompanied by elaborate infant graves though they were also succeeded by poorer descendants, presumably daughters and granddaughters. The 'rich' infant burials might hint at inherited status but the plain graves of immediate descendants indicate that high status was attained through achievement and was not inherited; we might describe this as the female version of a 'Big Man' society. The 'rich' infant burials were thus not reflections of these children's inherited personal standing in life but were perhaps expressions of their mothers' standing and esteem and of maternal grief at their deaths.

Britons and Germans in pagan Anglo-Saxon England

One of the main questions for archaeologists working on the Anglo-Saxon period in England focuses on the relationship between the indigenous Romano-Britons and the Germanic incomers who arrived from the Continent during this period (c. AD 400–600). Did the two populations live side by side and if so, how did they integrate? Did the Britons largely move west? Were many of them wiped out by disease? How many immigrants came from Germany and Denmark? Recently Heinrich Härke has produced evidence, gathered from forty-seven pagan Anglo-Saxon cemeteries, that men buried with weapons were, on average, taller and stronger than those men buried without.[129] The armed men were taller and stronger, he supposed, because they were better fed and looked after. By correlating the dates of these weapon burials with armed conflicts recorded in the *Anglo-Saxon Chronicle*, Härke concludes that the periods when these spears, swords and shields were placed in men's graves were largely times of peace; what was being signalled was not men's status as warriors but the construction of their masculinity.[130]

Looking at cemeteries such as Berinsfield in Oxfordshire, Härke further wondered whether these armed men might have been of Germanic descent while those without weapons were of British descent.[131] An analysis of the distribution of non-metric traits on the skeletons from Berinsfield produced clusters of certain traits among the armed men

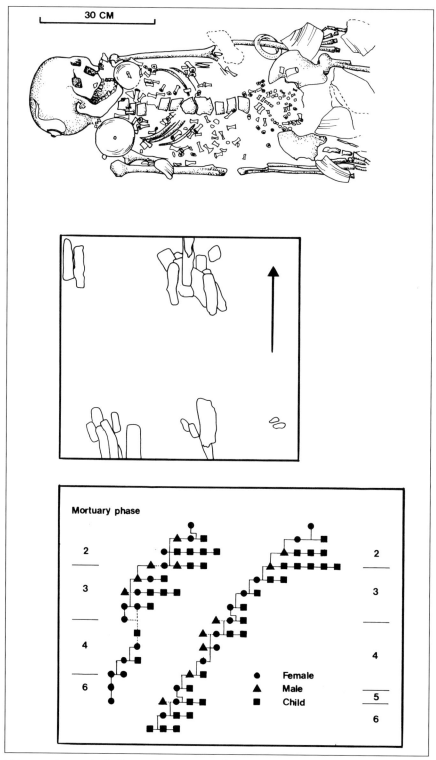

5.10 A 'rich' woman's grave in the Bronze Age cemetery of Khok Phanom Di, Thailand. The graves were arranged spatially into clusters (middle) and kinship links within the clusters could be reconstructed as family trees (bottom).

and others among the unarmed ones, with very little overlap.[132] Here was evidence to suggest that the two groups were of different descent.

There are, however, some problems with the interpretations based on the osteological observations. The average difference in height between armed and unarmed males is more than 2cm, but this difference is small when compared to the variation in stature *within* each of the groups with and without weapons. Even where the weapon burials show less variation in height than those without, as at Berinsfield, tall stature may just have been an important criterion for bearing arms. Furthermore, the distributions of non-metric traits were considered only for males, yet the female burials show different associations of traits to the males. Two females possess pairs of traits which are associated with males both with and without weapons, posing difficulties for Härke's model of co-residential non-interbreeding families.

A programme of DNA extraction was attempted on these groups so that comparisons might be made with modern German and British populations. Unfortunately, extracting ancient DNA is extremely difficult and the failure to find remains of ancient DNA in the skeletal material led to the project's abandonment.[133]

Non-metric traits and kin groups in the Neolithic: La Chaussée-Tirancourt

Neolithic long barrows and chambered tombs occasionally survive with the human bones undisturbed, though in most cases these survivals probably represent only the final phase of deposition after one or more periods of clearing out. At the remarkably well-preserved megalithic tomb of La Chaussée-Tirancourt in the Somme region of northern France, excavations recovered over 360 burials, accumulated between its construction around 2800 BC and its closure and alluvial inundation around 2100 BC.[134] Burials have survived mostly from the second and third of the three main phases of the tomb's use and alteration. During the second phase, earlier burials were cleared away and some sixty burials were added, deposited in three spatial groupings which could be further distinguished by associated non-metric traits. The western group within this east–west oriented tomb had high frequencies of hypotrochanteric fossae (a feature on the proximal end of the femur) and low frequencies of a third trochanter on the femur; this latter trait was found in the other two bone clusters. The bone group on the south side of the chamber was characterized by a high incidence of incrustation on the humeral trochlea.

In the third phase of the tomb's use, these deposits were not cleared out but became covered by a soil layer on top of which another three hundred bodies were deposited in what had been a series of eight wooden cases arranged around the chamber. The presence of non-metric traits was spatially restricted to four of the cases. There was a high incidence of incrustation on the humeral trochlea in the case on the south side – immediately above the earlier bone deposits with similar traits. This and two other cases in the south-west of the tomb contained bones where the female arm bones lacked olecranon fossa perforations and, as in the deposits below, the femurs had a high incidence of hypotrochanteric fossae. In contrast, many of the tibiae in the case in the north-west of the tomb had an additional articular facet.

Owing to these fortuitously high incidences of non-metric traits, Chris Scarre has suggested that we may identify distinct kin groups sharing a communal tomb, an idea that has long been considered for such chambered tombs.[135] More extraordinarily, the longevity of deposition is suggestive of lineages each interring in their particular part of the tomb over some seven hundred years. The spatial organization within the tomb was thus a mapping of lineage relationships. The expansion of bone groups from three to eight also suggests that this may represent the creation of sub-lineages at the time of the tomb's last remodelling. As the lineages and their sub-lineages grew, so larger numbers of people had rights of burial within the tomb. While children were normally excluded from burial, the number of adults interred suggests that the living population from which the dead were drawn was initially very small in the tomb's earliest phases, possibly just three small households. However, the same reservations can be made as in the case of Härke's study; postcranial traits especially are influenced by environmental factors such as physical activity and nutritional status, so the patterning within the tomb might signify differences other than kinship.

Blood groups and collagen groups at Mözs

Some remarkable results were obtained on a small fifth century AD Pannonian cemetery near Mözs in Hungary.[136] Blood-typing and collagen-typing linked twenty-five of the twenty-eight skeletons, leading to the identification of three generations of four families. Blood groups were valued over collagen types since the latter could not be clearly related to genetic inheritance and then these results were used to construct probabilities of relationships according to the constraints of their inheritance. The permutation into which most of the burials fitted and which fulfilled the condition of maximum biological probability was determined as a genealogical table (**Figure 5.11**). Three of the four families were considered to have intermarried in the second generation. Children (whether fully grown or not) were buried close to their mothers rather than their fathers, suggesting a strongly matrifocal family structure.[137] Another interesting feature of the cemetery population was the presence of artificially deformed skulls from eleven of the skeletons. This is a bodily alteration performed on infants and is considered to have been common among the Huns and related ethnic groups of the Migration Period. The results indicated that this practice was initiated on one individual within the second generation and was adopted for all ten of the third generation, rather than representing the presence of an entirely separate ethnic or kin group.

DNA: mummies, bog bodies and skeletons

Initial attempts to extract DNA from two Egyptian mummies of the first millennium BC demonstrated that degraded and chemically modified DNA sequences could be obtained from such ancient remains.[138] Later, small quantities of DNA were recovered from three out of an experimental sample of fourteen Egyptian and Peruvian mummies.[139] These first tests used cloning techniques in which a modern DNA sequence was inserted into an existing genome. Subsequently the PCR (polymerase chain reaction) method was adopted, allowing the rapid amplification of any DNA sequence.[140] DNA was also recovered from preserved human brains from North American bog bodies of the Archaic period dating to *c.* 6000 BC at Windover and *c.* 5000 BC at Little Salt Spring.[141] However, tests on British bog bodies indicated that these and their European counterparts would not provide DNA.[142]

As mentioned above, the usual forensic method for establishing familial relationships – chromosomal DNA 'fingerprinting' – is not usually possible with archaeological remains since the relevant DNA sequences are often poorly preserved.[143] Although the retrieval of ancient mitochondrial DNA from archaeological samples of bones and teeth is feasible and well established, the recovery of reliable results is difficult. Chromosonal analysis can

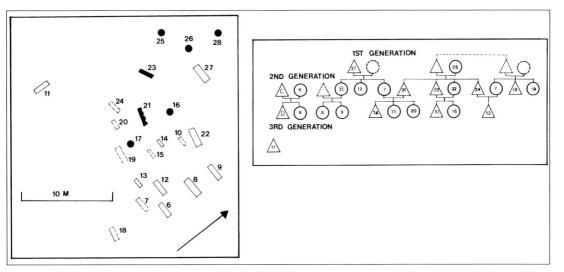

5.11 The plan of the Migration period cemetery of Mözs and the kinship tree derived from blood grouping of skeletal remains (circle = female, triangle = male). The dramatic results must, however, be accepted with caution since the family tree is only a 'best fit' model.

be used to determine sex by identifying products from the X and Y chromosomes, as demonstrated on nineteen out of twenty skeletons from the Norris Farm Native American cemetery dating to c. 1300 AD.[144] An earlier study had successfully recovered mitochondrial DNA sequences from fifty skeletons in this cemetery.[145]

The technique appears, so far, to be most useful in documenting prehistoric migrations such as the possibility of a post-Jomon migration into Japan in the first millennium BC, the nature of Polynesian colonization of the Pacific between c. 1600 BC and AD 700 as far as Easter Island, and the post-glacial populating of the Americas.[146] There are few studies as yet in which kinship and burial practices have been investigated. One of these is Shinoda and Kunisada's combined analysis of mitochondrial DNA sequences and funerary rites from fifty-five burials of the Yayoi period (first century BC–AD) cemetery of Kuma-Nishoda on the Japanese island of Kyushu.[147] Related work on Yayoi period remains from Kyushu has demonstrated a relationship between burial style and haplotype (genetic sequence) which may be interpreted either as burial practices varying according to kinship or as a change in burial styles accompanying a change in the genetic structure of the population.[148] Undoubtedly, funerary archaeology is poised on the edge of a new era of biological reconstruction of kinship and sex. These opportunities also bring with them issues of interpretation which will be complex and often problematic in political and ethical terms.[149] We have opened something of a Pandora's box.

SIX

PLACING THE DEAD

Here lie I by the chancel door;
They put me here because I was poor.
The further in, the more you pay,
But here lie I as snug as they.[1]

The dead are everywhere, inhabiting our memories and forming our world. We read or retell their stories, live in their houses, and work and play in the places that they created and used. Where we put their remains is generally a conscious and carefully thought-out activity by which the dead are both remembered and forgotten, and through which we reaffirm and construct our attitudes to death and the dead and, through these, to place and identity. Whether our loved ones' remains are left on the columbarium shelf, are dumped at sea or are scattered over the football pitch of their favourite team may speak volumes about who we think we are as well as what we felt for them. The act of placement forges and cements relationships between entities and places, often evoking profound emotions of fear, grief, guilt, loathing, anger, embarrassment, relief and joy.

The archaeologist has much to learn from past societies' placing of their dead. We may consider a landscape of the dead in various ways. Firstly, the relationship of the living to the dead can be explored through their spatial and topographic separation and the extent to which the dead occupy the sacred and secular places within the landscape.[2] Secondly, the micro-topographic and landscape setting of the places of the dead may provide further insights into the ways in which the dead were incorporated into cosmologies and social practices. We can discover how barriers (physical and symbolic) are placed to protect the living from the dead, and what places, views and routeways are associated with the dead.[3] Thirdly, the architecture and spatial organization of the place of the dead may also be examined in such terms. We can examine the material culture which is used to set the dead apart from or to bind them to the living.

SEPARATING THE DEAD FROM THE LIVING

For the Pintupi Aborigines of Australia, death leaves its mark on the land. The Pintupi leave the place of an individual's death and should not return for at least a year. This permanent and emotional identification between a deceased person and a locality is also the case for the place of burial. Both places are locations of grief and sorrow which should be avoided so as not to provoke feelings of anger at the loss among mourners. 'Pintupi burial places become one more, rather short-lived, objectification of recent history.'[4]

As part of the rites of passage, the dead must be physically separated from the living. Often this involves the placing of their remains in particular places, across streams, on islands, above, below or at a distance from the places of the living. For the Iban of Borneo, cemeteries are normally located on the opposite side of a stream to the longhouses of the living.[5] Among the Merina, segregation is achieved by ensuring that the tomb and the house are constructed on slightly different alignments to the cardinal points.[6] For the archaeologist, these spatial, topographic and architectural juxtapositions are sometimes recoverable. By examining how these juxtapositions changed through time, we may be able to examine some of the ways in which the dead were conceived of by the living and how much influence and power they were considered to exert.

My first thoughts on this issue came from examining the changes in English funerary practices over the last two centuries. In our idealizing of the past in the present, we often see in the mind's eye our funerals set in leafy country churchyards whereas in reality most British people are cremated and their ashes scattered in the crematorium's garden of remembrance. Churchyards are traditionally at the heart of the community in both physical and spiritual terms. Yet since the 1840s the place of the dead has shifted, for most people, initially to the suburban municipal cemeteries, formerly on the edges of the expanding towns and cities, and now to the even more remote crematoria which are often located in out of town areas (**Figure 2.6**). Most recently, innovative funerary practices such as forest burial may be seen as placing the remains of the dead in settings more positively valued by an environment-conscious society.

The dead have become increasingly invisible and unimportant in British society, culminating in the sale of London cemeteries by certain councils to property developers for the symbolic sum of £1. This change in the significance of the dead is embodied in their spatial dislocation from the heart of society as the disposal of the dead becomes virtually another form of waste management. In any case, our life-affirming culture leaves little room mentally as well as physically for the dead. Even in the highly secular society of modern Britain, the tenets of Anglican Christianity are still powerful. Interpretations of Anglican belief stress that the body is of little consequence in comparison to the immortal soul which will leave this world for another. Such notions are entirely culture-specific and might be taken as indicative of a very troubled and alienated society, adrift from its kinship and its roots, disrespectful of its ancestors and unable to face the sublime mysteries and powerful emotions of the last great rite of passage.

The living and the dead in the Danish Iron Age

For many moments of prehistory we have relatively little idea of the changing placement of the dead in relation to the living. The evidence from the Danish Iron Age is, however, well researched and reasonably representative of former distributions, thanks to 150 years of intensive antiquarian and archaeological investigation, public awareness in reporting finds, and source critical analyses.[7]

Over 160 settlements and 300 cemeteries from the pre-Roman (500 BC–0 BC/AD) and Roman (0 BC/AD–AD 400) periods have been recovered from one small part of Denmark, southern Jutland. These sedentary agricultural communities lived in hamlets and villages of wooden longhouses, each divided into living areas and animal byres. They cremated their dead and buried the ashes in pots. From about AD 50 inhumation burial was adopted and became the dominant rite in the third and fourth centuries AD. The practice of placing human corpses in bogs (described in detail in Chapter 3) died out in the Early Roman period (0 BC/AD–AD 200) and there is no further evidence of any type of funerary deposition other than cemetery burial of the corpse or its ashes.

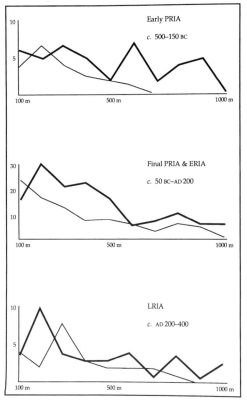

6.1 *The distance of Iron Age cemeteries and settlements from water in southern Jutland, Denmark, divided into three chronological periods. Numbers of cemeteries are marked by the thick line and settlement numbers by the thin line.*

During the early period (500–150 BC), the cremation cemeteries were mostly located at a distance of at least 200–500m from contemporary settlements. The settlements were mostly located within 300m of a watercourse, whereas the cemeteries were between 300m and 900m away, on the upper slopes of hills and on plateaux at some distance from the valleys occupied by the settlements of the living (**Figure 6.1**). Ashes were sometimes buried in miniature round mounds, perhaps copying the forms of the already ancient Middle Bronze Age mounds, which had been constructed around 1700–1200 BC. In almost a third of all cases, the cremations were actually placed within or adjacent to these earlier burial mounds, constructed hundreds or even a thousand years before.

The grave goods accompanying these cremation deposits were restricted to no more than a single metal dress fitting. These were produced in regional forms, defining three style-groups in northern, central and southern Jutland. There are only the slightest hints of differences in mound size and in grave goods which might have signalled social differences among the living. In the absence of osteological studies, nothing can be said about associations of sex and age. The settlement evidence complements that of the cremation cemeteries; there is minor variation in house size and in byre stalls but no single farm in any village was substantially bigger than the others. A few farms possessed no byre space at all, however, perhaps indicative of a distinction between the majority who owned stock and a few who did not. The archaeological remains support the notion that this was a remarkably conformist society which, as revealed by the bog corpses, may not have tolerated the unconventional. The dead were separated from the living in both space and time, placed physically at a distance from the settlements and incorporated into the distant past of the ancient barrows.

From 150 to 50 BC, in the margins between the regional style-groups, there appeared new settlements with overtly hierarchical distinctions of farm size and stock numbers (as indicated by the numbers of byre stalls in each house). The principal farms within each of these communities were further distinguished by their association with black-burnished pottery. Cremation burials also changed from this period onwards. At Kraghede a small group of cremation graves included black-burnished pots along with cremated animals, weaponry and jewellery. Elsewhere in Denmark and Schleswig similar cremations equipped with imported bronze vessels or wheeled vehicles attest to new forms of social organization in the margins between the style-groups. The development of inequalities in life and in

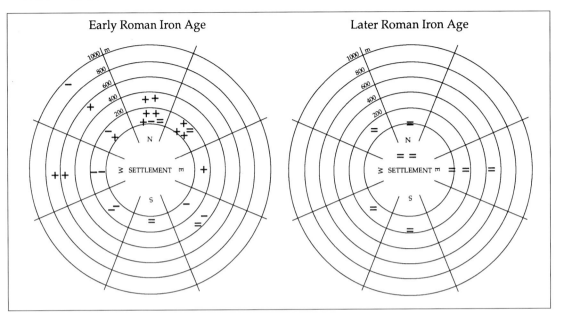

6.2 *Changes in the locations of cemeteries around settlements in southern Jutland between the Early and Later Roman Iron Age. The distance and direction of cemeteries to adjacent settlements is shown in concentric form. Cemeteries above settlements are marked by +, below by -, and those on the same contour by =.*

death in these fringes might represent the formation of new social orders away from the tribal heartlands where ancestral and traditional authority opposed any radical changes. Alternatively or complementarily, these areas may have become increasingly contested between tribal groups, leading to the establishment of new social institutions within them.

Noticeable changes in the placing of the dead occur from this period onwards. In the first century BC there was a relocation of cemeteries closer to settlements and mainly to within 500m of watercourses. The settlements are found on the valley bottoms, sides and tops, whereas the cemeteries in use between 50 BC and AD 200 were mostly placed on hilltops above the valleys or below the settlements. There is evidence that particular cemeteries were, at this time, linked to particular settlements. Locational studies indicate that settlements were evenly spaced 2–4 km apart. In twenty-six cases cemeteries have been found in close proximity to settlements, mostly within a radius of 400m. During this period (50 BC–AD 200) only 11 per cent of burials were placed in or around Bronze Age or earlier burial mounds. The dead were no longer placed far away in space or time but were brought close in to the land around the villages and farms, either looking over the living or placed below them (**Figure 6.2**).

Alongside the profound discontinuity in cemetery location, the burial rite itself began to change. In the first century AD, we begin to find a shift from cremation to inhumation. In contrast to the increasingly lavish cremations, these early inhumations were provided with few grave goods. Élite burials, marked by black-burnished pots and perhaps a single precious item such as a gold finger-ring or silver brooch, adopted this simpler rite. However, further changes during the second century AD led to both cremations and inhumations becoming contexts for conspicuous display in wealth destruction, in grave size and in mound construction.[8]

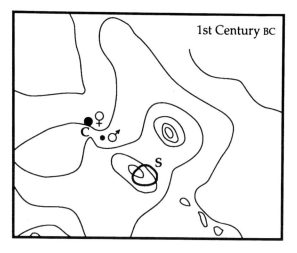

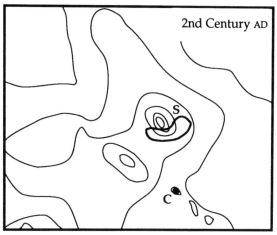

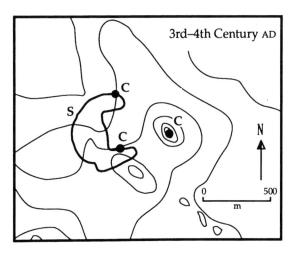

6.3 The Later Roman Iron Age settlement of Vorbasse in Jutland, showing the changing relationship between the settlement (S) and the cemeteries (C) between the first century BC and the fourth century AD.

Around AD 200 there were substantial changes in farm organization, iron, textile and grain production, votive deposition, and political and warfare organization.[9] At settlements like Vorbasse farmsteads were now bigger, within individual large yards, but there was still a main farm among the various farm compounds. The large weapon deposits, thought to be the spoils of battle, from votive contexts such as Nydam and Illerup attest to severe unrest and some of the most populated areas of eastern Jutland seem to have become largely depopulated. Whereas burials in the eastern islands of Denmark and in southern Sweden exhibited huge differences in grave good provision, those in Jutland were relatively standardized and modestly equipped, despite the large quantities of glass and metal items which were imported into Jutland.[10] Inhumation became the dominant burial rite between AD 200 and AD 400. The dead were buried in cemeteries which were in close proximity to the living, within or on the edges of the villages (**Figure 6.3**). The corpse at burial was no longer the locus of wealth disposal even though the women in particular were buried in elaborate costumes.

The placing of the dead over this nine-hundred-year period changed considerably, as did the mode of treatment and the provisioning of the corpse. In the pre-Roman Iron Age the dead were distant from the living and were not elaborately provisioned. Offerings of food, agricultural tools, wealth and people were, instead, made in the bogs and lakes which presumably were gateways to a spirit world associated with fertility and bountifulness. The frequent use of ancient burial mounds suggests that a distant, mythic past was invoked and was associated with the final resting places of the dead.

Through the changes in placement and provisioning of the dead in the late pre-Roman Iron Age, the ancestors took on a new significance for the living. Descent and allegiance may have become especially important. The dead were no longer 'out there' but were buried close by the villages and hamlets, accompanied by valuable grave goods. Membership of the wider ethnic groupings was no longer sufficient in expressing identity; new lineage and village ascriptions were the means by which people defined who they were. The closeness of this topographic relationship between living and dead increased with time, so that living and dead shared the same space in and around the settlement. Such proximity might indicate that the living and the dead were mutually protecting each other at a time of widespread unrest between territorial groupings.

Bronze Age Minoan tombs in southern Crete

Within southern central Crete, in the region known as the Mesara plain, there are about forty cemeteries of the Early Minoan Bronze Age (*c.* 3000–2000 BC). These take the form of circular above-ground stone tombs known as *tholoi* (**Figure 6.4**). Although many have

6.4 The Early Minoan tombs of Crete, known as tholoi, *are located singly or in small groups of two or three. This tomb at Kamilari, one of three, was built* c. 2000 BC *in Middle Minoan I. It faces east and lies about 100m north of its contemporary settlement.*

been disturbed over the millennia, these *tholoi* appear to have been used for communal inhumation burial and subsequent disarticulation, charring and even chopping of bones.[11] The tombs are generally not located in relation to prominent natural features, high topography or significant views, being found mostly on low ground or on mid-slope. Yet they are found in regular spatial association with settlements of this period, being located immediately above or below them.[12] In twenty-four instances, the tombs are found within 250m of the settlement.

There are several aspects which are of interest in examining relationships between the living and the dead.

1. The tombs and the settlements are always at different heights in relation to one another; they are never at the same level but tombs may be higher or lower than settlements.
2. Tombs face eastwards, with some facing the south-east and south.
3. The location of settlements demonstrates a distinct aversion to placing the settlement to the east of the tomb. The settlements of the living might overlook the houses of the dead but the dead could not overlook the living.

Keith Branigan suggests that this controlling of the view of the outside world from within the tomb is also reflected in the construction of antechambers at the front of many tombs. These sometimes contain disarticulated bones but are also associated with large amounts of pottery, stone bowls and figurines, hinting at their use in ancestor ceremonies.[13]

Access in and out of the tomb was further controlled by the construction of small doorways and low, narrow passages. Where intact remains were found in the tomb of Vorou A, many of the dead were placed in clay coffins or jars which were held down by large stones or empty jars and coffins. This constraining treatment of the polluting and dangerous recently dead, before they become disarticulated bones, is a common feature of mortuary practices involving secondary rituals. The construction of tombs so as to emphasize separation in the face of proximity to the living may also be interpreted as a means by which the physically close abodes of the dead were rendered less dangerous to the living.

We might expect that these tomb-settlement complexes were linked in one-to-one relationships where the dead kin of the settlement were interred in an adjacent tomb. Yet there are several reasons why this relationship may have been more complex. The ceramics from the tombs and their settlements are often problematic in terms of their contexts and their quantities (in the case of tombs); we cannot be certain of their dates of construction and use but it seems that a large proportion of complexes have tombs slightly older than the settlement and *vice versa*.[14] In many cases the settlement was abandoned or almost uninhabited for long periods when the adjacent tombs were in use. It is also notable that the settlements were small and remained so during their occupation; it is likely that the population was not static but would have grown over the generations, thus requiring out-migration from these places.

We might envisage the expanded kin groups claiming descent from these places but living some distance away maintaining the right of burial in the ancestral tombs. At the same time there is also the possibility that the construction of settlements next to existing tombs represented the appropriation of these rights to burial by other groups who were not part of the immediate descent group.

SACRED PLACES OF THE DEAD

The Kajemby of the Bay of Boina, on the north-west coast of Madagascar, bury their dead on the beach so that the remains are eventually taken away by the sea. The ancestral spirits of these fishing people give their blessing to the living so that the sea continues to yield its bounty.[15] The beach burial places are sacred not so much because they are liminal spaces between the land and the sea but because they help to define people's relationships to the sea, which is the source of wealth, power and survival. Similar observations can be made in Imerina about the broad relationship of tombs with rice cultivation and in Androy with the relationship between grazing lands and tombs; in both cases, the subsistence products, rice and cattle, are sacred and are implicated in complex associations and metaphorical links with people. For the Tandroy, tombs are placed beyond the cultivated fields. The tombs are not to be visited other than for funerals and the areas around them are protected by taboos forbidding grazing, digging, felling and collecting.

The dead may be placed at locations where the entrances to the next world are thought to be. In other cases, the entrance to the underworld may be quite separate from the place of the dead. An ethnographic example of the link between landscape features and the world of the ancestors comes from the mountainous headwaters of the Sepik River in Papua New Guinea, where there are deep sinkholes in the limestone ridges which the Bimin-Kuskusmin consider to be passages to the underworld of the dead, and out of which ancestral spirits return to haunt and to bless the living. Oil seeping out of a crevice is understood to be the source of fertility and regeneration, whose flow is increased by the ancestral spirits from the underworld. The bodies of the dead are exposed elsewhere in the forests but shrines with human and animal skulls have been constructed near the oil seep.[16]

This dislocation of the place of the ancestral spirits from the places where their remains were put can be suggested for the stone circles of the British Late Neolithic and Early Bronze Age (c. 2800–1800 BC). At Stonehenge the several hundred round barrows within which the dead were buried are mostly restricted to the peripheries of an envelope of visibility around the great circle itself, which contains no burials of this period.[17] This 'doughnut effect', in which round barrows are concentrated in large numbers around a stone monument but on the edges of visibility from it, is found at other stone monuments such as Avebury, Arbor Low and Rudston. With evidence for an association between wood and the living and stone for the ancestors, the stone circles represented certain collectivities of ancestors. Their geographical separation from both the houses of the living and the barrows of the corporeal dead indicates strong distinctions made between living, dead and ancestors.

In New Ireland (an island in the Bismarck Archipelago north-east of Papua New Guinea), funeral rites periodically erase inhabited and worked-upon landscape, ending with the transforming of settlements into burial places, rooting bodies in the ground to create 'burial places of memory'.[18] Suzanne Küchler describes how one side of the settlement is composed of double enclosures which form the burial places. The corpse is presented in one enclosure and buried in the other; funerary sculptures known as *malanggan* are carved in the former and exhibited in the latter. In the mortuary exchange ceremonies held in following years all traces of the deceased person's labour on the land are eradicated. After about two years their house is burnt down, and another two years later a ceremony is held in which the trees planted by the deceased are felled. At the end of the ceremonies the burial place and its settlement are abandoned; they become an empty shell like the corpse and the sculpture which fall apart after death. The secondary forest and garden lands around every settlement are thus realms where anyone passing through encounters burial places of memory. Though the funerary process is one of forgetting the individual dead, rights to former garden land are passed down, paradoxically, through memory of funerary enclosures and other signs of habitation.

The East Yorkshire Iron Age

Burials of the Iron Age in Britain are sparse and hard to identify except in East Yorkshire where the remains of the square barrows which covered individual burials can be seen as cropmarks and occasionally as earthworks. The separation of the dead from the living may have been accomplished in several ways. Large-scale excavations at the settlement sites of Garton Slack and Wetwang Slack have uncovered dispersed groups of unenclosed roundhouses in close proximity to the cemeteries.[19] The abodes of the dead were distinguished from the living by their squareness and, in this region of Britain, by the placing of pig and sheep, but not cattle, with the dead.[20]

Barrows and barrow cemeteries are not placed randomly in the landscape but are closely associated with linear earthworks and with sinkholes and 'gypseys'.[21] The latter are small watercourses which flow seasonally in the chalk valleys. Like the sinkholes, they hold water only in the winter months. The linear earthworks are land boundaries which divide up the chalklands into a myriad different units. Several are major divisions, off which smaller earthworks have been constructed. In certain cases these boundaries follow the line of gypseys. The cemeteries are located predominantly in low-lying parts of the landscape. The large cemeteries often lie along major linear earthworks or at the intersection of several. The large cemetery of Danes' Graves, for example, lies at the intersection of four such linear boundaries where there is also a group of sinkholes.

We can interpret the placing of the dead of Iron Age East Yorkshire as mediating two relationships, the one between different agricultural territories used by the living and the other between the living and the dead. In this latter case the places in which water periodically appeared and disappeared may have been considered as entry points to the underworld.

TOMBS AND TERRITORIES

The formulation of New Archaeological general theories of the relationship between descent, territoriality and placing the dead involved the use of ethnographic analogies. Colin Renfrew formulated a hypothesis that territoriality in segmentary societies may be symbolically expressed through funerary and other monuments. Renfrew's concept of territoriality was borrowed from animal behaviourist notions of ecological adaptation through the regulation of carrying capacity in animal populations, though he emphasized the symbolism of such territorial markers as being a feature only of the human species.[22] Renfrew drew initially on the example of the stone-built *marae* (ceremonial platforms) of the Tuamotu Islands of the Pacific (**Figure 6.5**). The *marae* are material symbols of kinship, binding ancestral spirits and gods to the land occupied by the kindred.[23] Renfrew also drew on Mircea Eliade's structuralist notions that, in order to live in the world, the world must be founded and thus the focal place at the centre of segmentary societies might be considered as the centre of the universe.[24]

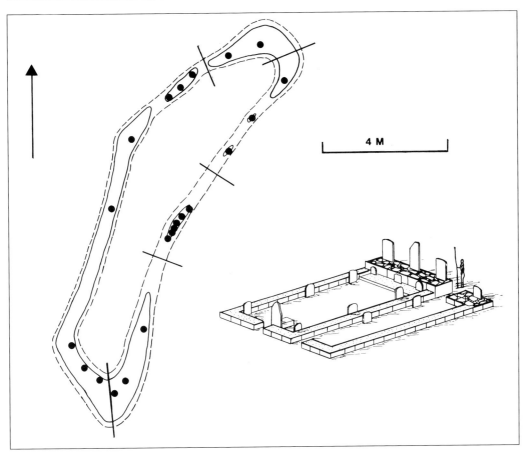

6.5 *The distribution of* marae *(pictured right) on an atoll of the Tuamotu Islands. The straight lines indicate territorial divisions between different lineages.*

Renfrew's ethnographic analogy of Tuamotu *marae* incorporated evidence from one island in which the five segmentary territorial groups each had between two and eight *marae* in its territory. Yet his applications of the model to Neolithic communal tombs on the Scottish islands of Arran and Rousay and in Wessex assumed that single monuments each related to one territorial grouping.[25] Renfrew mapped notional territorial divisions around each tomb, using Thiessen polygons. These are produced by drawing perpendiculars at the midpoints of lines joining adjacent centres, and then linking the perpendiculars, thereby mapping territories around each central place. They became standard fare for a variety of archaeological studies in the 1970s and 1980s.[26]

Renfrew's hypothesis that megalithic monuments were territorial markers was 'tested' according to two conditions to be fulfilled: they should be regularly spaced as single monuments or clusters of monuments, and they should be sited in close relationship with the better soils that might have been farmed by each territorial group. Renfrew believed at the time that his hypothesis plausibly survived these tests but recent research on Arran has resulted in the discovery of more monuments. These not only disrupt his proposed regular spacing but also demonstrate that Arran itself represents an unusual cluster of monuments when compared to the distribution in the rest of western Scotland (**Figure 6.6**).[27]

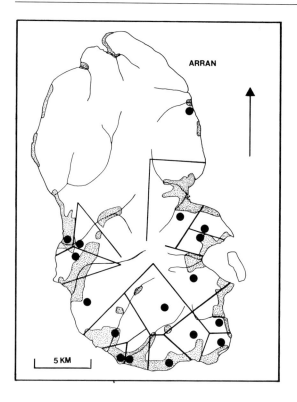

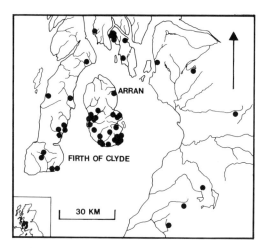

6.6 *The distribution of Neolithic tombs on Arran, Scotland, according to Renfrew's analysis using Thiessen polygons, and as reworked by Hughes in the light of later discoveries of new tombs and in the wider context of the Firth of Clyde.*

His model proposed a certain degree of parity in social evolutionary terms; the cellular and modular nature of certain acephalous segmentary societies in the Pacific and other parts of the world was considered to be a useful analogy for interpreting the evidence from European Neolithic societies estimated to be at similar levels of non-ranked and non-stratified social complexity.[28] Subsequently Chapman has suggested that Neolithic tombs were initially 'places in the landscape' rather than centres of defended areas within firmly sedentary, fully agricultural societies as formerly proposed. Chapman also emphasizes contingency: territoriality may be strongly or weakly marked or even 'turned on and off' in human societies. He highlights Ingold's distinction between territoriality and tenure, the former relating to the location of people dispersed in space and the latter to the claims made by people over resources dispersed in space.[29]

Centres and edges

Taking his cue from Eliade, Renfrew considered that these territorial markers were central and focal places; an equally good, and probably more convincing, hypothesis is that they are boundary markers on edges. 'Centres of the world' may well lie on territorial edges whether for nation states and world religions, as is the case for Jerusalem today, or for subsistence horticulturalists such as the Tewa of New Mexico.[30] In the case of the latter, each village has a 'mother earth navel middle place' while the four mountains that lie at the edges of the Tewa world also have 'earth navels'.

Renfrew later conceded that territorial markers need not be centrally located[31] and fortunately it is often possible to assess whether such monuments were central or peripheral to settlement areas, either by extrapolation from their positioning in relation to the available farming land[32] or in relation to the areas of contemporary settlement.[33] Studies from chronologically later periods also emphasize the significance of political borders or the interplay between edges and centres.

In the European Migration Period (AD 400–800) we often find élite burials, richly equipped and frequently buried under mounds, on the edges of emergent polities. For example, the eastern boundary of the Frankish kingdom along the Rhine valley is marked by many such burials, as is the western frontier region of the Valsgarde-Vendel area in eastern Sweden.[34] Arnold attempted to plot emergent English polities in the late sixth to eighth centuries AD by extrapolating Thiessen polygons around each élite burial or burial group but such an approach is perhaps better rejected in favour of recognizing that the burials were placed explicitly as statements of dominion over borderlands which would have been contested between each polity.[35] Randsborg's distribution map of similar élite burials within late tenth-century Viking Age Denmark is another clear demonstration of how edges constituted centres in these early states, with the boundaries (what Randsborg calls the perimeter of the core) marked by these types of burials and also by military fortresses.[36]

When considering state formation, as above, it is legitimate to consider that concepts of political territory, and thus of boundaries to polities, may have been important. In pre-state societies, as Barrett and Tilley have pointed out, landscapes are not subject to the state's techniques of surveillance and control but are instead encountered as paths, places, locales and boundaries in which mythologies are continually recreated in material form.[37] Boundaries for territories, and even the integrity of such territories, may be ephemeral and fluid. An evident difficulty, then, with Renfrew's use of analogy is that his hypotheses were derived from small Pacific islands where the edges are all too clearly apparent to their relatively isolated populations and may not be applicable to mainland Britain and its inshore islands.

Neolithic Orkney

Renfrew's investigations in Orkney, a group of small islands off the north of Scotland, would seem to be more appropriate for the use of the Pacific analogy. His research was directed towards the study of Neolithic social organization from the ceremonial and funerary monuments which remain today as prominent landmarks. Gordon Childe had postulated an egalitarian society from his excavations at the Late Neolithic village of Skara Brae, whereas Renfrew considered the mobilization of labour required to build the Late Neolithic monuments as possible only in a society which was ruled by a central authority.[38] The large communal chambered tomb of Maes Howe and other Late Neolithic tombs represented, in Renfrew's scheme, the culmination of an evolutionary sequence which began with the smaller tombs of segmentary acephalous communities. As with other parts of the Atlantic facade (the broadly coastal areas of north-west Europe from Sweden to Spain where Early Neolithic funerary monuments were erected), the reason for erecting these monuments was, Renfrew argued, bound up with social stress arising from demographic changes at the interfaces where farming communities came into contact with populations of fisher-gatherer-hunter communities.

Renfrew's social evolutionary model for Neolithic Orkney was expanded by David Fraser's detailed study of tomb distributions and by John Hedges's elaboration of the two-stage sequence as cross-cut by two tribes, the Grooved Ware tribe and the Unstan Ware tribe (named after the two styles of Neolithic pottery in Orkney).[39] Hedges's somewhat bizarre scheme has been brought into question by the stratigraphic sequence of Grooved Ware on top of Unstan Ware at the Neolithic settlement of Pool, and by the more general association of Unstan Ware with the smaller, earlier 'stalled cairns' and Grooved Ware with the larger 'cellular' tombs of later date such as Maes Howe.[40]

Niall Sharples, rejecting the polygon approach to Neolithic social organization, examined the landscape setting of the small stalled tombs and the later large tombs of both cellular and stalled type. The former were built in locations peripheral to the fertile soils where contemporary settlements appear to have been located. These tombs were often visible from the sea and less so from the settled areas. In contrast, the larger tombs were constructed in the centres of settlement areas on land which was fertile but often needed much labour invested for it to be productive. During the early period the ancestors were distant from the living. Subsequently they were brought into the centre of the community within a few large collective monuments. Sharples argues that this transition marked the appropriation of the community's ancestors by a restricted kin group who legitimated their power through their direct line of descent to certain dead and through the control of ancestral remains.

More recently, Colin Richards has excavated a Late Neolithic village at Barnhouse, close to Maes Howe. The 'village hall' and double-roomed house adjacent to it have been considered to be material evidence of Renfrew's Late Neolithic chiefdom though Richards thinks these buildings are community structures.[41] The Barnhouse settlement's open plan contrasts with the closed-off layout of the later village of Skara Brae, which Richards interprets as evidence for a phase of inward-looking and isolationist communities no longer linked by the island-wide organization embodied in the monumental constructions of tombs and other monuments. Richards sees this later phase of settlement as evidence of a devolution in central authority: Late Neolithic society was not becoming evolutionarily more complex and stratified, as Renfrew argued, but was fragmenting into many separate communities which no longer shared the centralizing ideology of previous centuries.[42]

DESCENT GROUPS AND TERRITORIALITY

Arthur Saxe formulated his Hypothesis 8 – formal disposal areas for the dead are used to affirm corporate group rights over crucial but restricted resources – through ethnographic accounts of the Temuan of Malaysia, which linked the advent of cemetery burial to the control of land.[43] This hypothesis was tested cross-culturally by Lynne Goldstein and reformulated:

A. To the degree that corporate group rights to use and/or control crucial but restricted resource(s) are attained and/or legitimated by lineal descent from the dead (i.e. lineal ties to the ancestors), such groups will, by the popular religion and its ritualization, regularly reaffirm the lineal corporate group and its rights. One means of ritualization that is often but not always employed is the maintenance of a permanent, specialized, bounded area for the exclusive disposal of the dead.

B. If a permanent, specialized, bounded area for the exclusive disposal of the group's dead exists, then it is likely that the corporate group has rights over the use and/or control of crucial but restricted resource(s). This corporate control is most likely attained and/or legitimized by means of lineal descent from the dead, either through an actual lineage or through a strong, established tradition that the critical resource passes from parent to offspring.[44]

Hypothesis 8 presents a materialist and cultural ecological perspective on the treatment of ancestral remains. The crucial resources in question, whether land, sea, cattle, water, trade goods or foodstuffs, are conceived of as economic necessities whose control is achieved by a determined, systemic relationship between the economic base and the ideological superstructure. The treatment of the ancestors is relegated to an economic activity in which the ideological basis of reverence is mainly to ensure a sufficient supply of food. Thus this relationship is viewed as an inherent property of certain social systems (so-called 'simple' societies) rather than as a complex of strategies and conflicts carried out by people as social practices. Archaeologists must acknowledge that 'crucial but restricted resources' might be the ancestral myths which are associated with particular locales, or the ancestral remains themselves, or even the abstract concept of 'fertility' which derives from the benediction of the ancestors.

The point at issue is not that the linkages are 'wrong' but that the materialist/cultural ecological formulation of the linkages presents a very limited perspective on the placing of the dead and the variety of ways in which ancestors are implicated in human affairs. Hypothesis 8 has certainly been valuable in directing our attention to the role of ancestors in legitimating structures of power but, as functionalism and cultural materialism have been superseded in the social sciences by theories of agency and practice, so its deterministic formulation hinders its use in exploring the specificities of particular societies and their trajectories. To reduce the significance of ancestors and tombs to a function of subsistence management is to relegate human aspiration and motivation to wondering where the next meal is coming from.

Charles and Hypothesis 8

Working primarily with data on the Woodland period in the American Bottom and the Illinois river valley,[45] Doug Charles has reformulated Hypothesis 8:

- social groups residing in environments in which the natural or culturally modified resource distribution supports a sedentary or restricted mobility mode of subsistence may employ formal disposal areas for the dead to symbolize corporate membership, rights, and inheritance, whereas social groups reliant on a more mobile means of subsistence will not.[46]

He suggests that sedentary agriculturalists may symbolize their rights to territory by establishing a cemetery on or within its boundaries. Mobile communities will tend not to have rigid territoriality and would not routinely return to particular places regularly enough to establish a cemetery in any case.[47] Archaeologically and also ethnographically, mobile groups rarely use cemeteries though there are exceptions such as English Gypsies and the gatherer-hunter Mikea of Madagascar.[48]

While Charles is careful to state that the archaeological absence of cemeteries is no evidence that links between groups and territories were not made, the presence of cemeteries can be interpreted to infer a certain degree of territoriality in which cemeteries can be used to map out the arrangement of each group's subsistence territories. Of course, there are many mobile communities, such as the Pintupi and the Tiwi of Australia, in which a single place of burial legitimates rights for the successors to a particular 'country' or territory; that burial place becomes taboo for other activities and thus technically thereafter a 'formal disposal area for the exclusive disposal of the dead'.[49]

Charles also excludes the sedentary Merina of Madagascar from his formulation of cemeteries built within or on the edges of territories because they are too 'recent' and too historically complex. From my own research among the Betsimisaraka and Tandroy of Madagascar, there are other examples in which corporate groups, namely lineages, use and control cemeteries which lie outside that group's subsistence territory. Charles may be broadly right but there are many question marks over the bridging links and nuances of the overall argument. In addition, much ethnoarchaeological fieldwork remains to be done on the spatial relationships of cemeteries with group territories. The logic of his propositions makes good sense but sometimes the ethnographic results are counter-intuitive.

Descent groups, tombs and land in Madagascar

Using the terms of Hypothesis 8, we could describe the Merina of highland Madagascar as divided into corporate groups controlling the crucial but restricted resource of rice paddy which is attained and legitimated through lineal descent from the dead who are placed in 'permanent, specialized bounded areas for the exclusive disposal of the dead' (quite simply, tombs). Control of the paddyfield resource is enhanced through the common practice of cross-cousin marriage; this type of marriage between members of the same lineage helps to maintain cohesive land plots and prevent their fragmentation. Yet such a definition would leave much unsaid about the relationships of tombs and ancestors to the land and the living society. Furthermore, the proposition that tombs must lie within territories comes seriously unstuck when confronted with the relationship of tombs to the segmentary corporate groups and their territories in Imerina.

The highlands of Imerina are densely settled and exploited for rice cultivation. The visitor to the region would notice, however, that the robust stone and concrete communal tombs (**Figure 2.1**) are concentrated in certain areas and are entirely absent in other areas which are evidently just as populated. Archaeological and historical evidence for the settlement of the highlands reveals the existence of a multitude of hillforts from which independent local leaders controlled villages and the rice-fields around them, until the political unification of Imerina. The latter stages of state formation date to around the end of the eighteenth century. The nineteenth and twentieth centuries have been periods of movement and displacement as new administrative centres were established first by the monarchy and latterly by the French colonial government. People also moved to new locations because of the shortage of paddyfield land, so that their houses would not be too far from their rice-fields. The vast majority of the tombs one sees today are of recent date, having been constructed in the last two hundred years.

Maurice Bloch describes how descent groups retain the corporateness of the past by building it into the landscape of Imerina in the form of tombs.[50] The permanence of these tombs is testament to people's allegiances to an idealized way of life embodied by the hillforts and traditional settlements, known as *tanindrazana* (the places of the ancestors). The corporate groups that constitute this way of life rooted in the past can only really exist for the dead since among the living the web of bilateral descent and the pressures of political and economic changes constantly lead to the formation of discrete groups within existing lineages and the stretching of links with the *tanindrazana*. The landscape of tombs defines the former ancestral lands of the lineages; the tombs are symbols of kinship and links to ancestors. However, the tombs define an idealized and essentially fictive social structure since the people buried together probably never lived together.

The idealized kinship system of segmentary corporate groups for the dead is only articulated with the lived system of bilateral kinship by the *famadihana* (the celebratory 'turning' of bones when the dead are brought outside the tomb). Thus the tombs are generally located many miles away from the individuals who will be interred in them. Furthermore, they may be sited close to communities who have no kinship link with them. Rather than seeing this pattern as an aberration of a tidier model in which territorially fixed, segmentary groups normally have their tombs within their territory, we should understand that the fluidity and change of the last two centuries are responsible in some measure for the popularity of stone tomb construction. They make visible the need to embed fixed points in an ever-changing world.

Were we to pursue our analysis of Merina tombs and territories in terms of Hypothesis 8, we might well miss one of the key articulations of the relationship between ancestors and the living. It is not only death but also fertility which are central concerns in Merina life. The dead and their tombs retain the power of life and the ability to transfer it to the living. In the omnipresence of death, the scarce resource is life itself, provided paradoxically by the dead.

As we have seen in Chapter 2, the pastoralist Tandroy first constructed their tombs within the territory of the Afomarolahy clan in the newly occupied areas on the frontiers of Androy where access to grazing was contested with the neighbouring Bara people. While the tombs of certain lineages and sub-lineages certainly lie within their subsistence territories, others are far away. The reasons for this include the process of gradual migration which has been taking place over the last two hundred years, and the hierarchical relationships between lineages. A single example should illustrate the point. Around 1800 a junior branch of the royal clan established itself some miles to the north of the main group, within a new territory, but the dead had to be returned for burial to the now distant forest cemeteries of the senior branches of the clan. This situation continued until 1976 when the new group began to build its own tombs within the new territory; only now was this junior branch sufficiently powerful and independent to challenge the authority and dominance of the senior branches. Of course, by this time other branches of the clan had moved yet further north but similarly had to return their dead for burial. What is perhaps important is that the right to establish a new cemetery was bound up in social relations of dominance rather than in ecological relationships with subsistence.

A TOMB WITH A VIEW

Ever since Andrew Fleming's discussion of tombs for the living, archaeologists have explored the various ways in which tomb construction and placing relate to social differences and groupings among the living.[51] Recently a number of studies have sought to develop a phenomenology of prehistoric tombs with reference to their contemporary landscapes. Rather than analysing tombs as dots on maps in which space is conceived of as a container abstracted from human affairs, phenomenological approaches seek to understand places, paths and monuments as they are experienced through the perceptions of subjects.[52] Thus places and locales are formed through movement, tasks and activities, the memories of which inform people's biographies and sense of identity.

Contrary to the contemporary understanding of land as a financial resource with an almost exclusively economic utility, the landscapes of pre-capitalist societies might have been infused with meanings and symbolism very different from those of the archaeologist's social context. We cannot understand those landscapes without some appreciation of how they were experienced and lived. Yet how do we begin to explore such a complex situation? As Chris Tilley and Colin Richards point out, archaeologists' maps, plans and elevations give no sense of 'being there' and fail to convey the information relevant to how tombs and other locales were physically experienced.[53] While certain sensory aspects of visibility, sound and touch are directly reconstructable, others are only imaginable as forms of understanding, belief and emotion which are culturally specific and were socially constructed in those circumstances only. For example, while the places of the dead may be feared and avoided in most contemporary societies, we are not able to determine whether such was the case for Neolithic tombs.

Tilley's analyses of the landscape settings of Neolithic tombs in Sweden and in Britain provide good examples of recent approaches.[54] The differences in regional distributions within Sweden reveal varying relationships between megaliths and their landscapes.

- In Skåne, in southern Sweden, the tombs are not positioned for their views, being mostly located on flat terrain. They are close to the sea and to rivers, with a differentiation of tomb orientation either side of the rivers that flow north–south.[55] Tilley interprets their spatial structuring as a series of duplicating references, linking new tombs to pre-existing ones.
- In Västergötland, in south-western Sweden, the megaliths appear to have been sited so as to maximize views towards the mountains and are often arranged in dense north–south rows. Tombs are constructed with different rocks; the uprights are formed by red sedimentary rocks of the plateau and the capstones are invariably of grey igneous rock from the mountains. Here the tombs directly mimic or duplicate the landscape, each forming a microcosm of the landscape in miniature.
- In Bohuslän the tombs are close to areas of potentially arable soils rather than within them as they are in Skåne and Västergötland. These tombs are located on ridge crests and valley edges below bare rock outcrops but are not visible from any distance. From the consistent placing of the tombs to the south of the rock outcrops, Tilley proposes that the north–south axes of the tombs link with the tombs' placing and provide yet another regional variation on the significance of the north–south axis. He further postulates that the Bohuslän monuments do not mimic the landscape but embody commentaries upon it, drawing attention not to their small size and liminal siting but to the settings of bare rock beyond them.

Tilley makes similar observations on the Neolithic monuments of Pembrokeshire and the Black Mountains in Wales and on the chalk downland of Cranbourne Chase in southern England. The chambered tombs of the Black Mountains are large constructions which are orientated either with their major axis in parallel to the main rivers or facing towards prominent spurs on the Black Mountains. In contrast, the smaller and more ephemeral monuments of the Pembrokeshire coast appear to have been situated so as to be made visible by the nearby rock outcrops. Their few finds and siting are suggestive of their use as meeting-places on paths of movement rather than as repositories of successive interments or places of feasting.

The earthen long barrows of Cranbourne Chase form a large group in which the two central clusters are largely intervisible (**Figure 6.7**). The orientations of the long axes of the barrows are closely related to their local topography rather than an overall notion of directionality regardless of place. Tilley concludes that the form of the monument duplicates that of the surrounding landscape, placed parallel to the contour on ridges and escarpments which were perhaps paths of movement.

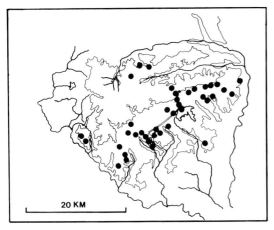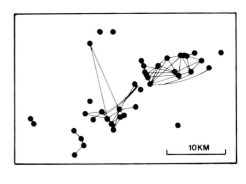

6.7 The distribution (left) of Earlier Neolithic long barrows on Cranborne Chase, Dorset, and lines of intervisibility between them (right). The two groups thus defined are linked by the Middle Neolithic cursus, a long linear enclosure thought to be a routeway for the initiation of spirits entering the realm of the ancestors.

These imaginative ideas provide some interesting ways in which tombs and other funerary monuments might be seen to relate to their landscapes, thereby identifying different regional expressions of people's relationships to land. However, as Fleming has pointed out, the plausibility of Tilley's pattern recognition is not always acceptable.[56] Not only can certain landscape associations be explained in a variety of ways but the arguments often lack a range of corroborative evidence which would help to give validity to a single observation. Yet some of these methods are potentially of great use and Tilley's bold approach serves to remind us that the places the living find for the dead are only elements of complex cosmologies. Archaeologists must attempt some understanding of such aspects of the archaeological record, since without it our delving into those past worlds is limited and banal.

CONCLUSION

Where to put the remains of the dead is generally not a matter of functional expediency. The place of the dead in any society will have significant and powerful connotations within people's perceived social geographies. The dead may still be active members of society – they can inhabit the world as spirits or ancestors – and the abodes of the dead may not always correspond to the places where their physical remains lie. Indeed, mortal remains may indicate liminal spaces between the world of the living and the spirit world. At the same time, the fixing of the dead in the land is a social and political act which ensures access and rights over natural resources. Placing the dead is one of the most visible activities through which human societies map out and express their relationships to ancestors, land and the living.

SEVEN

THE HUMAN EXPERIENCE OF DEATH

Perhaps the whole root of our trouble, the human trouble, is that we will sacrifice all the beauty of our lives, will imprison ourselves in totems, taboos, crosses, blood sacrifices, steeples, mosques, races, armies, flags, nations, in order to deny the fact of death, which is the only fact we have.[1]

The awareness of death and our attempts to transcend it have haunted humanity for at least the last ten thousand years and probably the last million years. As Dr Johnson put it, the prospect of death wonderfully concentrates the mind; the idea of death can be claimed to be the real 'muse of philosophy', the eternal mystery at the core of our religious and philosophical systems of thought.[2] For many philosophers, including Schutz, Heidegger, Becker and Baumann, 'being towards death' provides the context for human action.[3] Our experience of time is shaped by the knowledge of impending death – we strive to comprehend the human condition and to be conscious of life's full meaning in the face of the certainty of our own personal extinction. We construct and participate publicly in a world and its institutions that started before we were born and will continue after we die, yet our experience of time is strictly personal – from womb to tomb – and this private experience is shaped by the knowledge of our impending death. Thus our lives are lived in relation to our finitude:

[T]he idea of death, the fear of it, haunts the human animal like nothing else; it is a mainspring of human activity – activity designed largely to avoid the fatality of death, to overcome it by denying in some way that it is the final destiny for man . . . the fear of death is indeed a universal in the human condition.[4]

Ernest Becker suggests that our being caught up in the public world, beyond the personal, phenomenological experiencing of time, is an act of denying that our deaths must surely come, although this act must be always an unsuccessful attempt to forget the presence of the Grim Reaper at our shoulder. From the moment of our own individual extinction, our death becomes an episode in the 'public time' of others, an opportunity to reflect on death to come and to dwell on the meaning of time and existence.

DEATH AND TIME

The knowledge that we must die gives us our perspective for living, our sense of finitude, our conviction of the value of every moment, our determination to live in such a fashion that we transcend our tragic limitation.[5]

Time is formulated through our human experience which includes our coming to terms with the deaths of others, as well as knowing that our own will come. The deaths of others provide us with the experience of death. Within funerary ritual the passing of time is thrown into relief in three significant ways. Firstly, the processes of decay, caused by death, may be highlighted as markers of duration. Secondly, time may be transcended through metaphorical associations which bring the regeneration of life out of the decay of death. Thirdly, mortal time may be transcended by a symbolic or actual claim for immortality, at a personal or community level, a triumph over death.

Duration

Funerary rites mark duration in various ways. Victor Turner's concept of liminality draws on the use of symbols derived from biological processes such as decomposition and catabolism (destructive metabolism).[6] Huntington and Metcalf refer to Adams's demonstration of metaphorical links in south-east Asian society between the manufacture of dye, the rotting of hemp to make rope, the fermenting of rice to make wine and the rotting of corpses to make clean bones.[7] They also note that the smells of decomposition are an important element of these processes, striking a chord with Susan Kus's observations on the significance of the smell of the decomposing corpse at funerals in highland Madagascar.[8] Edmund Leach illustrates how the mourners' rituals of shaving their heads or, conversely, of not cutting hair during the period of mourning symbolize the passing of time, since the natural growth of hair during the mourning period is a culturally emphasized notion of duration (**Figure 3.1**).[9]

Middleton's analysis of Lugbara notions of time, in Zaire and Uganda, recognizes two kinds of duration. First, there is the 'ordinary time' of growing older and of the passing of the seasons. A death confuses this ordinary time, stopping its orderly passing and leading to the pollution of those affected by the death. Second, in the world outside – in the wilderness and sky – there is no duration, no change and no growth; the order, fertility and hierarchical authority of the ordinary time of the living are lacking. The dead become physically associated with this second mode, moving to the underworld beneath the bush.[10]

Regeneration

The liminal conditions within all sorts of rites of passage involve deathly terminal representations; if the individual is to be 'reborn' their old self must first 'die'. In his study of secondary burial, Hertz noted that changes in the state of the corpse were linked homologically with changes to its soul and to the mourners. The corpse becomes formless and putrescent until only hard, imperishable, dry bones remain; at the same time, the soul is considered homeless and an object of dread until it arrives in the land of the ancestors; and the mourners remain polluted by the death until they are reincorporated into the world of normal relationships.[11] Suzanne Küchler describes how the process of decay works on both corpses and *malanggan* funerary sculptures in northern New Ireland.[12] Carving is described as 'making the skin' so that sculptures are skins which replace the decomposing corpse and contain the life-force liberated at death, such that sculpture and life-force merge together. The sculptures are exhibited for just a few hours and are then themselves left to decay.

Metaphors of regeneration are one route towards the transcendence of death. Barbara Adam suggests that the source of transcendence in human time derives from our reflections on mortality and from our attempts to find meaning in death.[13] By developing concepts of rebirth, people have attempted to negate the finality of death. One of the many examples of regeneration among the world religions can be found in Hindu beliefs, in that every cremation at Varanisi may be seen as an act of self-sacrifice which re-enacts the original cosmogonic sacrifice and rekindles the fires of creation at that very spot where creation began.[14] Bloch and Parry have discussed the significance of symbols of fertility and rebirth in funerary rites whereby death leads to the regeneration of life, and to the birth of the initiate ancestor who becomes a source of continued fertility. They suggest that individuality and unrepeatable time are problems to be overcome if the social order is to be represented as eternal. Individuality and unrepeatable time are thus denied by mortuary rituals in which death is part of a cyclical process of renewal. As a result authority is founded on the orderly and faithful reproduction of the unchanging world of the ancestors.[15] Among the traditions of Laymi society in Bolivia, festivals of the dead mark out the agricultural cycle and divide the year into two, between production and consumption. The dead are effectively socialized as a source of recurrent fertility.[16]

Immortality

A linked notion of transcendence over time is that of personal or community immortality achieved after death. The immortality achieved by individuals has been a central theme of human transcendence since the ancient Mesopotamian *Epic of Gilgamesh* and the time of the early Egyptian pharaohs. It is central to many of the world religions and is evident in Christianity, for example, when the meaning of Christ's crucifixion is restated in the ritual of the Mass, whence the man-god's death becomes an act of universal regeneration which renews time and provides salvation for the living. In the period prior to the appearance of many of the world religions, we know of personal quests for immortality and deification – Egyptian pharaohs, Mesopotamian kings, Roman emperors, Chinese emperors and other rulers all sought immortality, symbolic and actual, as humans sought to become gods. Many dynastic systems have immortalized the institution of rule: the institution of kingship (the body politic) does not die even when the king (the body natural) does. Such notions may lie behind the practice of substituting an effigy for the royal corpse in medieval France and England, the stories of suffocation of ageing Shilluk kings, and the tales of live burial for Dinka 'masters of the fishing spear'.[17]

Societies may create representations of immortality for the entire community, giving themselves an ahistorical existence beyond duration and time. On Normanby Island, off Papua New Guinea, the stone burial platform at the centre of the village is the embodiment of the matrilineage, a place which is formally public, unproblematic, unchanging and ahistorical, in contrast to the historical and short-term personal fame and achievements of its members.[18] For the Tandroy, stone tombs are more permanent than the wooden houses that are burnt after death but eventually tombs themselves become overgrown and fall down (**Figure 2.4**). The tombs provide a measure of duration that goes beyond single generations, even mapping that passing of time by their placing in space, yet the one thing that is actually permanent and continuous, going on forever, is the lineage.

Mike Rowlands points out how memorials to the dead in western society often convert these notions of timelessness into fetishized form. Remembrance of the dead with a monument requires that the monument's form be timeless. Because the monument must never 'die' its style should resonate identity with a distant and remote past.[17] Denials of death, decay and transience may be found even in archaeological heritage management whereby ancient monuments are not allowed to fade away gracefully but must be conserved in perpetuity.

The archaeology of belief

Conceptualizations of the dead and our relationships with them are crucial in the formation of individuals' and societies' historical consciousness. The anthropologist Johannes Fabian asks why colleagues in his discipline have written much which details the funerary practices of many different cultures but have little to say about how the knowledge of death affects the human condition.[20] In this chapter we examine the ways in which the material remains of funerary rites and related practices can provide insights into the changing existential awareness of human beings. I suggest that we can identify a series of experiential transformations over the last million years in the ways that humans have sought transcendence of death.

The history of religious belief is rarely given centre stage in grand narratives of the evolution of civilization and of humanity and yet the urge to comprehend the human condition – the quest for soul food – may be just as great as the quest for food and reproductive success. We need understandings of social change beyond the materialist, functionalist and sociobiological models of evolutionary development which explain away ideology and religion as merely legitimatory mechanisms functioning to ensure reproductive success and control over economic resources and their exploitation. This is not to say that our death awareness has been a prime mover in social change. Rather, if human consciousness is determined by our social being and practice, then we can recognize these transformations in the human experience of death as profound changes which have been embedded in other aspects of social life.

The archaeology of death awareness can potentially provide us with a phenomenological perspective on the changing human condition since the earliest hominids. We can attempt to follow the working through of various ideas about mortality and the transcendence of death, rather than just abstracted notions of ecological adaptation, the evolution of social complexity, or the rise of civilization. To piece together this alternative side to the human story we are heavily reliant on the archaeological understanding of funerary-related material culture – the graves, monuments and material associations which link the treatment of the dead to other aspects of social life. For the last five thousand years, we are also aided by texts, historical sources which have been, themselves, some of the most influential artefacts in effecting these transformations of human understandings. Certain religious traditions may claim impressively long ancestries (Jainism originated 86,000 years ago according to believers) but archaeologists must seek out the material traces of such beliefs.

FUNERARY RITES AND THE ORIGINS OF HUMANITY

Awareness of death and the marking of its occurrence among our fellow humans is supposedly something which is specific to our species. We might consider our awareness of this aspect of the human condition as a fundamental defining characteristic of what it is to be human, at the very core of our being and self-consciousness. According to Voltaire:

> The human race is the only one that knows it must die, and it knows this only through its experience. A child brought up alone and transported to a desert island would have no more idea of death than a cat or a plant.

We may ask ourselves whether this awareness of being in the face of death is truly the preserve of humans, and whether we can identify the moment in human evolution when our species developed the level of self-consciousness that indicates such awareness. Equally, we must ask ourselves exactly what is the significance of the appearance of undeniably purposeful funerary practices, not only for the awakening of ritual, symbolism and death awareness but also for the construction of self, society and cosmology.

Do animals know of death?

Like tool making, tool using, symbolic communication and language, characteristics which were formerly thought to be watersheds between our own species and other animals, death awareness is shared with other species to various degrees.[21] All animals, even the mischaracterized lemming, attempt to avoid death yet relatively few species appear to be deeply affected by the death of one of their own. Dogs, jackdaws, orang-utans, geese and chimpanzees are all said to exhibit signs of bereavement.[22] Disruption of the mother-infant bond in other primates can lead to behavioural disturbances, such as showing signs of depression. Among chimpanzees, dependent young become listless and lethargic after the death of their mothers, even leading to retardation of their physical development; we might say that chimps grieve for their dead.[23] Jane Goodall records how the death of an adult male chimp, who broke his neck falling out of a tree, led the others to display intense excitement and anxiety around the corpse, even throwing stones at it and behaving aggressively towards each other.[24] Yet, as close as chimps and the other higher-order primates are to us biologically, they appear not to indulge in any elaborated behaviour towards the corpse, which is simply discarded and left.

It is to the largest-brained land mammals that we must look for anything approximating to the human concern of treating the corpse. According to Cynthia Moss, probably the most extraordinary fact about African elephants is that they seem to have some concept of death.[25] They may not have graveyards but they do react in a particular way to the carcass or even the bleached old bones of one of their own species (while being unconcerned with the dead of other species). Elephants will stop before a carcass, reaching towards the body with their trunks. They will touch the body and sometimes lift and turn the bones, especially the head and tusks, with their feet and trunks. Moss suggests that, by running their trunk tips along the tusks and lower jaw and into the hollows of the skull, they are trying to recognize the individual. They may even pick up and carry the bones for some distance. In one instance Moss watched an elephant family gather around the carcass of a young female:

> They stopped, became tense and very quiet, and then nervously approached. They smelled and felt the carcass and began to kick at the ground around it, digging up the dirt and putting it on the body. A few others broke off branches and palm fronds and brought them back and placed them on the carcass.

Moss reckons that if the elephants had not then been disturbed by a plane flying overhead, they would have nearly buried the body. She suspects that elephants may also be capable of grief, having seen group disintegration after the death of a matriarch and females lagging behind the group and looking lethargic for many days after the death of their young calves. However, this apparent care for the remains of the dead may be driven by aspects other than emotion. For example, it might also be advantageous for elephants, from a natural selection perspective, to bury their dead in order to discourage scavengers and predators.

The significance of mortuary rites

Of course, the inadequacies of our communication with other species and the problems inherent in interpreting their actions and thoughts render our understanding of their self-consciousness shallow and inconclusive. How much better can we do with early humans? Physical traces of their bodies and faint residues of their activities are all that we have, remains which have survived in only the most serendipitous circumstances. Perhaps the hermeneutic problem of 'understanding the understanding' of early hominids is greater than with animals with which we can interact and communicate, if only partially. We are hindered not only by the paucity of remains from the Palaeolithic but also by our own intellectual and ethnocentric preconceptions about what constitutes funerary ritual. For example, an archaeologist of Yanomamö or Guayakí descent might understand evidence for cannibalism as formal, ritualized respect for the dead whereas a European or North American archaeologist might choose to recognize only the deliberate interment of the corpse below ground.

Archaeologists have concentrated on looking for early treatment of the dead to shed light on the origins of symbolism, ritual and religion. Some have considered the provision of grave goods as evidence of the concept of an afterlife and even of the concept of the soul. The latter are problematic questions, bound up with the cultural and religious backgrounds of the researchers, and there may be more mileage in exploring how far treatment of the dead may have articulated new concepts of the self and the social, through the development of a sophisticated awareness of the nature of death and hence of human existence. Roger Grainger suggests that death and religion always imply each other because of death's 'urgent demand for answers to ontological and teleological questions, questions about the origin and the purpose of living'.[26] Funerary rites are basic to our apprehension of our own final destinies and their actions import their own meanings into existence, so that death reveals the meaning of life rather than religion giving meaning to death:[27]

> The awareness of the reality of death, its final and uncompromising nature as an event outside life . . . heightens the significance of living human gestures, those actions which proclaim a belief in the innate value of being human and being alive.[28]

What funerals are really about, Grainger argues, is a common human dignity, a worthwhile celebration of humanness, the statement of a person's value and worth, an existential landmark locating the dead in space and time and dividing the living from the dead. Grainger suggests that such issues are clearest at the deaths of neglected people rather than the rich, famous and loved. When someone dies without traceable relatives or friends, these are the times when the funeral really counts.[29] There is no display, power-play or even expression of grief; it is neither an individual nor a community that is bereaved but humanity:

> [A]ny man's death diminishes me, because I am involved in mankind; and therefore, never send to know for whom the bell tolls; it tolls for thee. (*Meditation XVII*, John Donne [1572–1631]).

BURIALS OF THE MIDDLE AND UPPER PALAEOLITHIC

[A] person who has ceased to be is as compelling a prospect as it was when the Neanderthal first dug holes for his dead, shaping the questions we still shape in the face of death: 'Is that all there is?', 'What does it mean?', 'Why is it cold?', 'Can it happen to me?'[30]

Recent debates among archaeologists about the development of human awareness of death have located the issue mainly within the last 100,000 years, in the Middle and Upper Palaeolithic. The period between 60,000 and 30,000 years ago, the Middle/Upper Palaeolithic transition, has even been described as a 'big bang' in terms of the evolution of human culture and consciousness.[31] Others suggest that the big change in symbolic behaviour occurred even later, around 25,000–20,000 BP ('before present'), since all but three of the seventy-four dated Upper Palaeolithic burials are from the period 25,000–12,000 BP, especially the later part.[32] Yet, as we shall see, perhaps all of these dates are far too late for pinpointing that significant moment when humans not only became aware of their own deaths but devised elaborate treatments for the dead and, reflexively, created new understandings of the self and of what it is to be human.

The Middle Palaeolithic burial controversy

Although a number of Neanderthal remains were found during the nineteenth century, most archaeologists of the time did not consider that *Homo sapiens neanderthalensis* (anatomically a pre-modern human) was capable of deliberate and ritualized interment of its dead. Although intentional burial was suggested for the two Neanderthal skeletons found at Spy in Belgium in 1886, it was not until discoveries at La Chapelle-aux-Saints and Le Moustier in France in 1908 that scholars felt certain that Neanderthals shared this human trait.[33]

The Le Moustier remains were described as a skeleton that had been buried in an attitude of sleep, while the skeleton at La Chapelle-aux-Saints was described as lying east–west in a trench or grave with his head beneath three or four large fragments of longbone, themselves lying under the articulated bones of a bovid's lower leg. Since then, more than two hundred skeletons of Neanderthals have been excavated and at least thirty of these have been considered to provide evidence of mortuary practices in the form of body positioning, grave construction, placing of artefacts and animal parts in the grave, the arrangement of stones around the grave, and even the placing of flowers in the grave.[34]

That Neanderthals might bury their dead was initially extremely controversial yet, much later, the growing acceptance of this notion – that funerary rites were a Neanderthal innovation appearing 60,000 years ago – received two bombshells. One was the publication of Robert Gargett's taphonomic reappraisal of some of the classic Neanderthal burials. He claimed that all of them could be accounted for through natural events, requiring the Neanderthals only to crawl into these caves to die, thereby denying any physical evidence for purposeful disposal of the dead.[35] Since none of the Neanderthal burials has ever produced bodily ornaments of the sort found on so many Upper Palaeolithic burials of 25,000 years ago and afterwards, Gargett's extreme reasoning struck a chord with some archaeologists. But there were problems with his approach.

Not only did Gargett's study omit a large proportion of the total known sample of Neanderthal burials but his special pleading required dismissal of competent observations by earlier excavators (at La Ferrassie, France), dismissal of grave cuts as either natural scoops (at Kebara, Israel) or pre-existing pits (at La Chapelle-aux-Saints, Le Moustier, La Ferrassie), dismissal of burials as merely a consequence of cave collapse (Regardou, France, and Shanidar, Iraq), and dismissal of grave goods as naturally derived (goat horns at Teshik-Tash, Uzbekistan; pollen from flowers in the Shanidar 4 grave). One sympathetic commentator even suggested that the pollen in the Shanidar 4 grave had been brought in not by the wind, as Gargett suggested, but on the boots of the workmen during excavation.[36]

Subsequently archaeological opinion has swung away from Gargett's minimalist view. His argument does not explain why so many Neanderthal remains are wholly or partially articulated, rather than scattered bones broken up by scavengers of carcasses, and it also conflicts with the evidence.[37] The pollen from Shanidar was ancient and was from plants which flower only in early summer (the grave was excavated in August).[38] Neanderthal burials show a strong orientational preference for east–west orientation, an unlikely chance occurrence. There is also more recent, telling evidence from cave sites at Amud in Israel and Dederiyeh in Syria. At Amud an infant was found within a small niche with an apparent grave good, a red deer maxilla (upper jaw), lying on its pelvis.[39] The Dederiyeh infant lay on its back with arms extended and legs flexed. At its head was a slab of limestone, of a rock type rare in the cave deposits, while a triangular piece of flint lay on the infant's chest, in the most sterile layer of the burial fill.[40]

The second jolt to archaeological knowledge of early funerary behaviour was the thermoluminescence redating of *Homo sapiens sapiens* cave burials at Mugharet es-Skhul to *c.* 96,000–66,000 BP and the dating of others at Qafzeh to *c.* 115,000–92,000 BP, taking the date of these early burials of anatomically modern humans in Israel back even further than those of the Neanderthals.[41]

At Mugharet es-Skhul the bodies of four individuals (I, IV, V and VII) appear to have been purposefully arranged with folded and flexed limbs (**Figure 7.1**). Skhul V, an adult male, was laid on his back with the mandible of a wild boar placed within his arms, while Skhul IX lay with the skull of a bovid.[42] The Qafzeh burials include a child, Qafzeh II, whose left hand rests on a fallow deer's skull and antlers placed across the child's neck. Qafzeh IX is the burial of a young adult with a child laid across its feet.[43] Critics have suggested that the boar mandible and deer skull were accidental intrusions into the Skhul V and Qafzeh II burials and were thus not intentional grave goods, but the likelihood of these and the Amud maxilla – all parts of the head – being chance inclusions is not high, especially since these bones from the graves were much better preserved than animal bones in surrounding layers.[44]

There are still questions that remain open. Why are all the Neanderthal and earliest modern human burials from caves, with none found on open-air sites? Why are there relatively so few of them, given the considerable volume of Middle Palaeolithic cave deposits archaeologically excavated? Why do the grave goods of these burials prior to 30,000 BP consist of little more than bits of animals' heads or odd stone artefacts when these early humans could have placed well-made stone tools in the grave? Indeed, why do the dead not have bone and shell ornaments to adorn their bodies? Why do so many of the burials appear to have had bones removed after death?

Upper Palaeolithic burials

It is with burials of the Upper Palaeolithic after 28,000–25,000 BP that we have no doubts that humans were recognizing the state of death as succeeding life (though that does not imply that they realized that it was inevitable or universal). Bodies were placed in clearly defined grave pits and are regularly accompanied by grave goods, many of which constitute ornaments worn by the corpse.[45] The burials found at Sunghir near Moscow

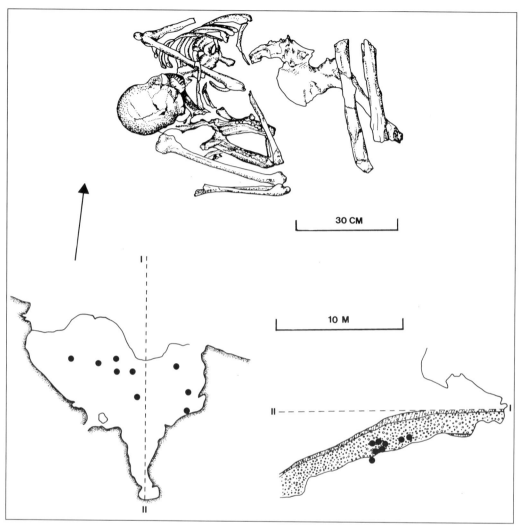

7.1 A plan and section of the excavations of the rock shelter at Mugharet es-Skhul (dots are burials) and the Skhul V burial with a wild boar mandible. The seven partial skeletons and remains of three others from Mugharet es-Skhul and the fifteen skeletons from Qafzeh cave constitute small cemeteries of anatomically modern humans.

(c. 28,000 BP) and Dolní Věstonice in the Czech Republic (28,000–26,000 BP) are truly extraordinary.

One of the Sunghir burials (**Figure 7.2**) is a double interment of two juveniles (possibly one female and the other male) with over ten thousand ivory beads, mammoth ivory pins, disks and pendant, a mammoth ivory figurine, a belt of fox teeth, antler batons, a polished human femur containing red ochre, and ivory lances made from straightened mammoth tusks. The other burial is that of an old man whose thousands of ivory beads appear to have decorated his cap, tunic, trousers and moccasins – a Palaeolithic 'pearly king' adorned from head to foot.[46]

The Dolní Věstonice triple burial, like others of its period, employs the use of red ochre, in this case on the heads of the two men either side of the woman and on the woman's groin where one man's hands were placed (**Figure 7.3**). Charred wood fragments were found in the grave, along with unperforated shells and perforated teeth of wolf and fox. The three individuals present an extraordinary tableau, as the excavator comments, suggestive of the eternal triangle: the woman looks towards the man on her left who looks away from her while the man on her right looks towards her as well as reaching for her genitals. She is further remarkable because her spine is deformed, inhibiting her movements while alive.[47]

These and other Upper Palaeolithic burials highlight some of the problems for understanding earlier burials of the Middle Palaeolithic. Firstly, their low numbers draw attention to the fact that inhumation below ground, during both the Middle and Upper Palaeolithic, was most probably a very special and restricted minority rite reserved only for individuals or circumstances that must have been highly unusual. As Sally Binford states, most Neanderthal human remains – wherever they are found – may be regarded as burials in the sense that the word 'burial' signifies deliberate mortuary treatment and not necessarily the placement of the remains in a covered grave.[48] Most people's bodies were evidently disposed of in some other fashion which has left no trace, presumably on the ground's surface rather than hidden away and

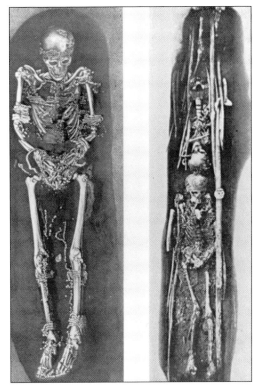

7.2 *The two best preserved burials from Sunghir, near Moscow. The beads ornamenting the adult male (left) can be seen wrapped around the skeleton. The double burial of two children shows the large ivory lances to the right.*

wholly removed from the realm of the living. The fragmentary and partial nature of most Middle Palaeolithic skeletons, together with the 'femur artefact' in the Sunghir grave, hints at a series of rites in which the bones were disaggregated and dispersed after death. The Kebara 2 adult male had his skull removed yet his mandible and hyoid bone remained undisturbed.[49] Other cases are suggestive of skull removal (La Ferrassie 6, Qafzeh VI) and possibly defleshing (Skhul I).[50] Smirnov suggests that post-mortem manipulation of the bones in the Middle Palaeolithic reflects intricate patterns of burial treatment, presupposing relatively complex social relations and religious conception.[51]

The reason why Middle Palaeolithic burials are restricted to caves is uncertain but may be linked to the lack of excavations of well-preserved open-air occupation sites of this period. The discovery of a shallow burial from 19,000 BP, close to an Upper Palaeolithic open-air occupation site at Ohalo II on the shore of the Sea of Galilee, illustrates the problem: Palaeolithic graves in general may just not have been dug very deep and, given the long time periods involved, such deposits will have been prone to wholesale erosion and truncation.[52] As for the lack of ornaments before this date, Middle Palaeolithic people can be assumed to have worn clothes but their dress attachments and ornaments seem not to have been made of durable materials. They used animal portions in their burials but they did not modify the bones of animals to any significant degree to make ornaments and decorative pieces.

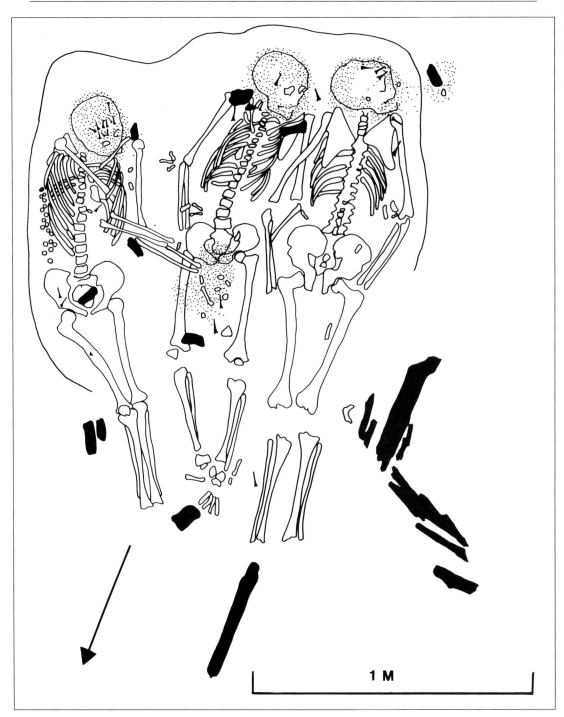

7.3 The triple burial from Dolní Věstonice in Moravia, in the Czech Republic, thought to symbolize an unsuccessful delivery. The woman lies between the two men. They have red ochre on their heads and in her groin and are ornamented with tooth pendants, ivory beads and shells. The charred wood (black) may derive from a grave cover.

THE LOWER PALAEOLITHIC: FORMAL DISPOSAL AND CANNIBALISM?

In recent years fast and furious events have changed many people's conceptions of the capabilities of anatomically pre-modern humans, specifically archaic *Homo sapiens* (the predecessor of Neanderthals and modern humans). Many archaeologists now argue that they were skilful hunters able to plan ahead, rather than being mere brutish, expedient scavengers. Within the later stages of the Lower Palaeolithic (*c.* 800,000–150,000 BP) we find intriguing hints that *Homo erectus* and archaic *Homo sapiens* were more sophisticated creatures than had hitherto been imagined. At Schöningen in Germany eight perfectly weighted wooden javelins, carefully carved from spruce, have been found in association with other artefacts of the Lower Palaeolithic, dating from *c.* 400,000 BP.[53] At Boxgrove in England a wild horse's scapula, excavated within an activity area dating to *c.* 500,000 BP, was found to have a small hole through it, probably made by the impact of a wooden javelin.[54]

The Atapuerca caves

The human remains at Boxgrove consist of just a tibia and a few teeth but cave sites in the Sierra de Atapuerca in Spain have produced two spectacular groups of skeletal remains, one from 780,000 BP, from Gran Dolina cave, and the other from 300,000–200,000 years ago, from La Sima de los Huesos (the Pit of Bones).[55] It is not simply the quantity of the 300,000-year-old human bones, deriving from a minimum of thirty-two individuals, but their remarkable situation in a deep cave system which is of interest.

Most of the bones from La Sima de los Huesos were found in a pit or gallery at the base of a ramp to which access today and probably in ancient times was gained down a 13m deep vertical shaft (**Figure 7.4**). Given the depth of the shaft, it can be assumed that neither animals nor people were living in the pit at its foot. There are no tools or occupation debris. Some animal bones – of bears – were found on the ramp with others in the pit, on top of the human remains, not mingled with them. The human bones show no sign of carnivore gnawing. The evidence suggests that this was not an animal den – the dead people were not brought here by predators. The small number of bears is explained by their having fallen down the shaft.

The human bones were not just thrown down the shaft, since they are found only in the pit and not on the ramp which leads to it. Although the skeletons were not articulated they had not been moved far from their places of deposition. This was not casual dumping of corpses down a hole, simply removing human 'rubbish' from the cave area above.

So how did they get there? A case could possibly be made for a catastrophic Palaeolithic version of 'follow my leader' – a group of people, including three children under the age of ten, fell down the shaft, getting stuck there and dying on the spot. Alternatively, if a number of fatally clumsy people fell in one by one over the years, unlike the bears each must have survived the fall to crawl away from the shaft and possible rescue, down into the pit to die. For the excavators the most compelling explanation, because of the large number of individuals, is that these bodies were purposefully disposed of, either all at once or over a period of time. This may be the earliest example in the world where depositional activities provide evidence for formal mortuary practices.

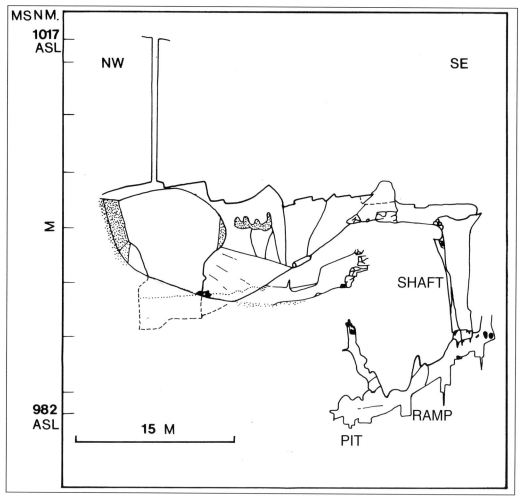

7.4 A section through the cave system at Atapuerca, at the base of which is La Sima de los Huesos. Palaeolithic human remains pose excavation problems. At La Sima de los Huesos the air in the chamber at the base of the cave shaft becomes stale after just a few hours' work each day.

Cannibalism as mortuary ritual

The Atapuerca site is so far unique and, once again, as in the case of Middle Palaeolithic cave burials, it can hardly be taken as an example of the dominant mortuary practice at that time even if it constitutes a formal disposal of the corpse. The 780,000–700,000-year-old bones from the other site at Atapuerca, the cave of Gran Dolina, number some eighty fossil remains. Many of the bones are covered in cut marks and appear to have been split and treated in just the same ways as the bones of other butchered mammals in the deposit. This indicates that they were defleshed and chopped up in a fashion which the excavators interpret as cannibalism.[56]

Elsewhere in the world, among the fragmentary remains of human bones from just over thirty main find sites of this mid-Quaternary period, 400,000-year-old archaic *Homo sapiens* skull fragments from Bilzingsleben in Germany and a *Homo erectus* skull from

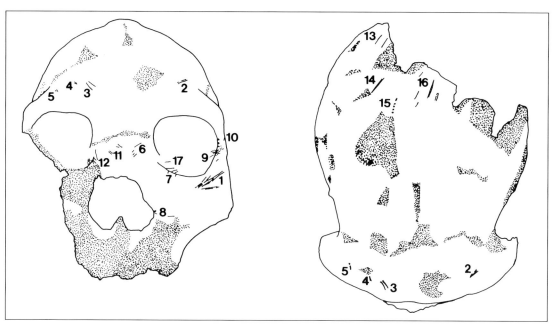

7.5 *The seventeen areas of cut marks on the front and top of the Bodo skull. Shading indicates later surface damage.*

Bodo in Ethiopia exhibit cut marks (**Figure 7.5**). According to Tim White, the cut marks on the outside of the Bodo skull, dated to 300,000 BP, must have been caused by the extraction of the brain which he considers would have been eaten as part of a cannibalistic meal.[57] Perhaps these early humans were simply preying on each other for food, hunting or scavenging any passing stranger.

Similar interpretations of cannibalism were first mooted many years ago when the bones of *Homo erectus* were recovered from breccia and ash deposits within caves at Zhoukoudian near Peking in China. The long bones were broken in such a way as to extract the marrow and many bones were burnt and broken. The case for Peking Man's cannibalism has, however, been discredited by recent taphonomic studies.[58] It has now been demonstrated that intermittent occupation of the caves by humans between 450,000 and 350,000 BP overlapped with their being used as dens by hyenas, whose chewing of bones produced the damage to human remains formerly identified as the results of cannibalism and thus mistaken for human activity.

Whatever or whoever ate Peking Man, the other finds from Atapuerca, Bodo and possibly Bilzingsleben appear to be good candidates for indications of deliberate post-mortem treatment, possibly cannibalism, by archaic *Homo sapiens* and related hominids. That these find sites represent a small but significant proportion of all those with human bones known from that broad period (800,000–150,000 BP) suggests that defleshing may have been widespread. If these traces resulted from cannibalism, then we are left with the $64,000 question. In Nigel Barley's words, when ancient man 'split open human long bones and crania in 400,000 BC should we see him as practising ennobling funerary ritual or primitive cannibalism? They are, of course, the same thing. Once the line to humanity has been crossed, eating the dead is as much a ritual act as burying them, for both . . . are merely culturally different ways of dealing with the problem that fellow humans are made of meat.'[59]

The higher primates and other large mammals generally do not cannibalize their dead.[60] Yet why are there cut marks on these bones? Perhaps they were accidental rather than deliberate and perhaps they were made after the flesh had rotted away. If we reject the argument for Lower Palaeolithic cannibalism because of the gap between defleshing and eating, there being many a slip between cup and lip, we have still to explain these cut marks. In most cases they are consistent with the process of defleshing the corpse, an activity performed by no other species. We are left to ponder whether early hominids of the mid-Quaternary period, and possibly earlier, had crossed that line to humanity whereby defleshing the dead can be considered as a formal funerary treatment, with all its implications for the development of self-consciousness, ritual and symbolism. Did these human characteristics really emerge as late as 60,000–30,000 BP, as some would have it, or did they come into being much earlier, within the last million years or so? There is no doubt that certain features of human culture did not floresce until the beginning of the Upper Palaeolithic, notably artistic representation on artefacts and on cave walls, personal ornaments, elaborate hunting technologies and complex tool technologies.[61] Yet the Schöningen and Boxgrove discoveries demonstrate that humans were very complex creatures considerably earlier.

We will undoubtedly argue for a long time to come about these issues but, in my view, *Homo erectus* and archaic *Homo sapiens* were more like us than we might care to consider. Their gory post-mortem treatments were deliberate and significant acts which demonstrate an awareness of death, along with the attendant implications for self-consciousness, the development of symbolic gestures and the rituals of closing a life.

THE ORIGINS OF MONUMENTALITY

Burials like the two at Sunghir are doubly intriguing. Firstly, these were large and deep cuts into the earth. Secondly, the dead were provisioned with a startling array of grave goods. According to theories of ascribed and achieved status, as examined in Chapter 4, the association of such artefacts with children might suggest that they were members of a complex, hereditarily ranked hierarchical society equivalent to a chiefdom, although all other evidence of social and economic behaviour in this period of the Upper Palaeolithic indicates a mobile, hunter-gatherer society, characteristic in social evolutionary terms of an egalitarian band-type society and not a chiefdom.

The 'pearly costumes' worn by the dead seem unlikely everyday wear. Equally, the mammoth tusk javelin would have been too big for a child to throw and is probably too heavy to have been an effective projectile. Instead, we may be looking at ornaments, costumes and weaponry with special and ceremonial significance. It may well be that Sunghir, at *c.* 28,000 BP, represents the glimmering beginnings of something which has become a global obsession today: the mobilization of resources to construct a container to house the dead and the associated expenditure of further resources for reasons that go beyond mundane practicality – in a nutshell, considerable effort and ostentation.

The earliest examples of what we might call monumental architecture were constructed around 10,000 BP. One is an 8.2m high and 9m diameter stone tower in the earliest deposits at Jericho, built during the Pre-Pottery Neolithic 'A' (known as the PPNA) (**Figure 7.6**).[62] The other, in southern England, comprises the traces of a line of pine tree trunks, each approaching a metre in diameter, set into pits close to the site of what was to become Stonehenge five thousand years later.[63]

Probably all societies have lived in a world which contains natural monuments – waterfalls, mountains, trees, lakes and other features – whose significance is recognized as awesome in some way, created by natural, supernatural or ancestral forces. We might think that the difference between a 'natural' monument and one physically constructed by people is immaterial if people consider both to have been brought into being by the same entities. Yet there is a very important difference in that, while both exist – and may be said to have always existed – as landmarks in the world and in the mind, built monuments are the product of human actions, the results of particular people's intervention with the given world to change it in such a way that the act itself as well as the monument will be remembered and recalled for generations to come.

In one way, the beginning of monumentality may indicate a sea-change in the human condition: rather than inheriting the world as it is, people seek actively to modify and change it. Humans become part of the forces around them and direct the

7.6 The PPNA stone tower at Jericho. The top of the internal stairway is visible between the two workmen, and the earliest town wall can be seen at the bottom right.

shaping of their environment. Today we expect and accept such urges to change the natural world, and live with the consequences on an unprecedented scale.

The Stonehenge posts were put up by Mesolithic people who were hunter-gatherers, driving home the point that it is not just agriculturalists whose social complexity drives them to construct dramatic edifices that dwarf the human scale. The Jericho tower was built by people who farmed as well as hunted and gathered. We can say much more about this tower's context and use than the enigmatic post row on Salisbury Plain. Firstly, the Jericho tower is preceded by a tradition of circular and semi-circular building in stone for houses and other structures going back to the beginning of the Natufian period c. 12,800 BP. Secondly, the tower contains a passage with a stairway which the excavators found to be packed with twelve skeletons, deposited there probably five hundred years after its construction. Some have thought the tower to be solely defensive, the first element of those famous city walls that Joshua's trumpets eventually flattened, whereas more recently it is considered to have been associated with public storage and ritual activities.[64] Whatever its purpose, this great tower was incorporated into the walls of Jericho and was eventually buried under the dissolved mudbricks used by the hundreds of generations who inhabited the place continuously for five thousand years after the tower was built.

THE CONSTRUCTION OF ANCESTORHOOD

In the Near East human remains are scarce from the Upper Palaeolithic and from the following period, known as the Early Epipalaeolithic (seven skeletons, and bones from perhaps another twenty individuals), but more than four hundred burials have been found in sites of the subsequent Natufian period. The Natufian burials are closely associated with settlements, both open and in caves. Natufian burials show tremendous diversity in stone-lining of the grave, body position and posture, numbers of inhumations per grave, disturbance or non-disturbance of the corpse, grave good provision and decorations of the body, and it is not surprising that there has been a long-running debate as to whether Natufian society was ranked or relatively egalitarian.[65] Currently, it appears that the burials do not show evidence of social stratification yet their elaborate treatment indicates that they were the focus of complex ceremonials.[66]

The concentration of burials under settlements can be partially explained by these Natufian communities becoming increasingly sedentary, in contrast to their Palaeolithic predecessors who had inhabited the region during the preceding millennia. The origins of agriculture lie in this period, and Ian Hodder has suggested that the placing of burials and human remains in houses, under houses and in pits and graves within the settlements may relate to a growing concern with the symbolic importance of the house in 'domesticating' people as well as their animals and crops.[67] Yet there is probably an altogether more significant aspect underlying the elaborate treatments, the digging of proper grave pits and the keeping of the dead beneath the community of the living. What we may be seeing for the first time in the human experience is the explicit construction of ancestorhood.[68]

Ancestor cults: living with the dead

Living with ancestors has probably been a continuous feature of humankind since the Lower Palaeolithic, in that people recall their parents, grandparents and beyond. Yet to formalize that relationship into what could be called ancestor cults requires certain features. Firstly, there must be awareness of – and expression given to – the permanence of death which can be contrasted with the transitory nature of life. Secondly, there will exist a set of beliefs relating to the supernatural presence and powers of the ancestors. Certain people, normally elders or ritual specialists, will have abilities to contact the spirit world of the ancestors, often at particular times and places.

Within most ancestor religions, both the living and the dead are subordinate to greater divine forces such as the sun and the moon, or more abstract entities such as fertility or the elements. The spirit world, ontologically between the living and these divine forces, may also include spirits of the trees, hills, earth, stones and other natural features. The ancestors may be considered to dwell apart from the living or in their presence, often occupying actual or imagined houses of the dead. In many ancestor-worshipping societies elaborate monuments are constructed to the glory of the ancestral collectivity. In contrast, individual ancestors are represented as small images which may only have short currency during the mortuary rites in which the individual makes the transition from corpse to ancestor. Ancestor cults are localized and are characteristic of farming communities which rely on seasonal mobilization of communal labour, requiring unity among the living.

What we appear to be witnessing in the Near East between 12,800 and 10,000 BP, when farming had its origins, is the beginning of a human obsession with the material presencing of the dead among the living.[69] We cannot be sure that these material manifestations were accompanied by spiritual ideas that the dead were somehow active supernatural forces affecting the world of the living but this seems likely. Materializations of ancestors may have first begun many thousands of years earlier. It is simply that the

Natufian and subsequent PPNA periods provide a variety of corroborative clues to indicate that ancestors were the focus for a variety of material practices and physical activities. The high degree of regional differences in funerary behaviour suggests a range of ancestor cults, perhaps unsurprising given that people, and their ancestors, were increasingly becoming linked to specific localities where they lived and died. One of these places, Mallaha (Eynan), dating to *c.* 12,000 BP, was a large settlement with two cemeteries. One of these cemeteries contained the burials of at least twelve women, men and children. Built over the burials was a large semi-circular stone-walled structure 8m in diameter. Excavation revealed a series of floor layers and hearths which had built up over a long period of use. This was probably a roofed building whose reconstruction on the same spot again and again suggests that it was marking a special place and thereby linking its living occupants to the dead buried below.[70]

Skulls and the living dead

The most convincing evidence for ancestor cults is found in the Late Natufian and PPNA periods (*c.* 11,000–9,300 BP) when increasingly a major distinction in mortuary treatment was being drawn between children and adults. Normally, dead children are excluded from becoming ancestors because they have not procreated and thus are not part of the maintaining of an unbroken chain of being across the generations. Although this distinction is apparent in the Late Natufian, it is during the PPNA period in particular that it is most manifest. Children's bodies were buried intact. Adults invariably had their skulls removed (and occasionally their mandibles) (**Figure 7.7**). There is a handful of removed child skulls from sites like Jericho but otherwise this is treatment reserved for adults.

Grave goods were rarely placed in the adults' simple graves, which were located inside the settlements. At Jericho they are found under the floors of houses or courtyards. At Netiv Hagdud they were buried in the yards, open spaces or fills of abandoned houses. The skulls were being kept above ground, often in groups or caches. At Jericho they were found singly on the abandoned floors of houses.[71] At Quermez Dere a group of six skulls was found placed in the north-western half of a PPNA house.[72] At Netiv Hagdud three skulls were found on the floor of a probable house though they may possibly have been put in a later pit.[73] In contrast, the cache of infants' skulls from Jericho were buried underneath a plastered basin, perhaps as a foundation offering.

Skulls from the subsequent Pre-Pottery Neolithic 'B' (PPNB) period have created much interest since the first discoveries by Kathleen Kenyon at Jericho. These skulls were provided with new faces made of plaster and eyes of seashells (**cover picture**). We do not know if these faces were designed to copy the remembered visage of each deceased individual though the preference for only certain shapes of skulls for plastering suggests a more complex relationship.[74] As well as the eyes, the nose and eyebrows are carefully modelled and painted. The mouth, however, is either omitted or is modelled only minimally. This may be explained by the fact that many of the plastered skulls lack the mandible, though even when the mandible is present the mouth is still missing or played down.

These skulls provide us with dramatic images of individuals from nearly ten millennia ago. We can be confident that, although these plaster faces are not portraits, they are representations of dead people who were formerly alive and they constitute an embodiment of how the living perceived their ancestral dead. While the corpses lay buried directly beneath the feet of the living, their skulls continued to share the surface world of the living until they were deposited in caches within pits, on house floors or other

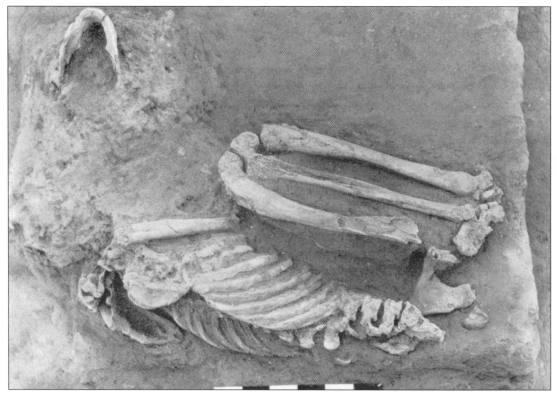

7.7 *A headless burial at Jericho, with cranium missing but mandible still present. We know that the skull was removed some time after the corpse had rotted since there are no cut marks and the other bones are not displaced.*

contexts. Both corpse and skull, however, shared the spatial locale of the living. Such was people's concern with maintaining this thread of place and space that generations on generations lived in the same place, building their mudbrick houses on top of previous dwellings until the surface of their inhabitation, human-made hills of mud known as *tells*, towered above the surrounding plain.

The stone tower at Jericho, that earliest monumental edifice, contains some unusual remains in that the twelve adults and children stuffed into its stairway all retain their heads. Kuijt suggests that their burial here was related to ritual use of the tower. He suggests that either burial in this unusual place served to differentiate these people as special or that it symbolically replaced the need for actual cranial removal. Alternatively, they may have been buried here as victims of some mass catastrophic death.[75] Unfortunately we know little about the tower's use before this moment or about what lies beneath its foundations. It was certainly a very important structure, built close to a spring and associated with storage facilities and structures of ceremonial significance, which was finally used for a very unusual burial rite some centuries after it was constructed.

Why did these ancestral practices come into being at that time and why did they take the form that they did? One explanation, albeit a functionalist one, is that these rituals of skull removal served to emphasize collective community beliefs and identity at a time of considerable economic and social change when opportunities for unequal accumulation of food surpluses abounded.[76] Yet functionalist arguments like this suffer from viewing ritual merely as a corrective mechanism. Such arguments are essentially ahistorical and ultimately incapable of explaining the specifics of the practices – *why* were burial under houses and skull removal adopted?

Ian Hodder has suggested that people, in the process of 'domesticating' themselves, were foregrounding the dead in order to emphasize the *domus*, the household, as a highlighted realm of activity.[77] Yet the skull cult needs to be considered within a wider context of social competition and conflict. There was not only post-mortem removal of the skulls of dead kin but probably the taking of heads by non-kin. On the floor of a burnt-down PPNA house at Jerf el Ahmar in Syria was found the burnt body of an individual, sprawled in a supine position, whose head appears to have been removed before the house was set alight.[78] This exciting discovery suggests that head-hunting and raiding may have accompanied these Neolithic ancestral skull cults. Within the twentieth century similar activities documented among the Naga of eastern India emphasize the importance of removing the skulls of dead kin so that they are not taken by enemies.[79]

We need to consider the bizarre practices of the PPN period as the culmination of a long period of ritual changes within a broad continuity of emphasis on the placing of bodies beneath the living and on the secondary treatment of the dead. Ancestors of specific kin groups were becoming increasingly important for several reasons. Their physical remains served to tie people to the very earth itself, during a time when the seasonal exploitation of that earth, in the planting and harvesting of crops, was becoming a principal feature of people's lives. For such seasonal tasks, mobilization of large enough groups was essential and, in drawing on each other's labour, people needed to recall and demonstrate the ancestral genealogies which bound the living together. In the Natufian prelude to agriculture, it was not just the ancestries of humans that mattered. Crops and animals also had ancestries which could now be carefully managed, controlled and exchanged. Even though the Natufian burial practices provide little evidence of social inequalities, people were probably engaged in highly competitive interactions over land and the products of that land.

What we see in the PPNA and PPNB is a profusion of ancestors. Rather than a few founding ancestors remembered only in memory, there were now strings of thousands of them brought into actual physical being in a clamour for the claims of the living to be heard. The passage from life into death and beyond may not have been the abrupt transition between two states – alive and dead – that we often consider it to be. Death was not in opposition to life but a stage in the continuation of existence.

FROM PLASTERED SKULLS TO FIGURINES: THE MOTHER-GODDESS MYTH REJECTED

After the PPNB period in the Near East, the dead were by and large no longer buried under house floors but were probably disposed of in cemeteries outside the tells. In Anatolia the dead continued to be buried beneath houses and settlements in the ninth millennium BP, although skull removal was less common. Around this time Neolithic communities of the Near East began producing statuettes and figurines of baked clay. These extraordinary pieces of art, among the earliest representations of the human form, first appeared in the Upper Palaeolithic but it is in Neolithic settlements that they are found in large numbers (**Figure 7.8**). There are clay statuettes from PPNB levels at Jericho, and others are known from the same period at 'Ain Ghazal and Tell Ramad. The largest stand nearly a metre high; facial details are painted on and seashells may be used for eyes. These statuettes are

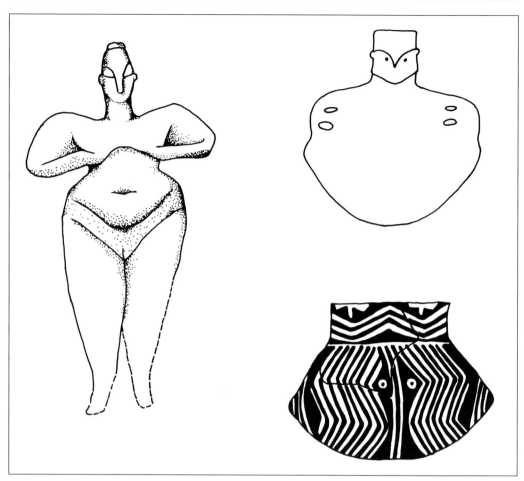

7.8 A Neolithic ceramic statuette from Haçilar in Turkey, with anthropomorphic pots from the same site. The figurine is 11cm high; the pots are 30cm high (bottom) and 24cm high (top).

part of a wide tradition of figurines and statuettes found in large numbers on Neolithic and Chalcolithic (Copper Age) settlements in south-west Asia, the Balkans and the eastern Mediterranean. For over a hundred years, since the time of Bachofen, they have been considered as evidence that people across Europe and the Near East worshipped a mother-goddess and made small effigies in her image.[80]

Although several archaeologists backed this interpretation earlier this century, there is now relatively little agreement on the meanings of this figurine symbolism.[81] One of the problems of the mother-goddess theory is that the proportion of female to male figurines (and to quadruped figurines) varies from region to region; for example, female representations dominate the Anatolian Neolithic while male and female are more evenly portrayed in the Greek Neolithic. Ultimately the theory relies on a process of back-projection in which scholars have assumed that all prehistoric religions before the era of literate state religions must have hinged on similar beliefs relating to personified deities who lived well beyond the realm of mortals. In such ways the religion of the Neolithic is interpreted in the image of the state religions of the Bronze and Iron Ages.

Figurines and ancestors

A stronger alternative idea is that the ancestor cults evident in the earlier Neolithic developed new forms and new representations. There are powerful reasons why we should consider Neolithic baked clay figurines as linked very closely to the plastered skulls, and as representations of dead ancestors, bound up with the world of the living.

1. No children or infants are portrayed except when they are modelled as adjuncts of adults, physically attached to the adult in question. As I have explained above, children cannot fulfil the criteria to become ancestors.
2. The figurines appear to be portrayals of individuals rather than attempts at duplicating the image of a single deity. For example, figurines from south-east Europe and Cyprus bear physical and decorative characteristics which suggest that each embodies an individual.[82]
3. The faces of the vast majority of Neolithic figurines are like the plastered skulls, lacking mouths or with them only weakly accentuated, all the more strange when we consider that eyes, eyebrows, noses, genitalia and ears are all carefully crafted.
4. Caches combining only human skulls and statuettes have been found at Tell Ramad, indicating a direct contextual association between figurines and skulls.[83] It can also be noted that most figurines are found without their heads, perhaps echoing the former practice of skull removal at some point after death, although this might be due to 'wear and tear'.
5. The figurines are made of a clay not dissimilar to that plastered on to the PPNB skulls.
6. They are made of fired clay (though occasionally of stone and unburnt clay), thereby embodying a materiality which links people to the earth into which the dead are placed. Clay was a rich metaphor for the cycle of life and death, the plasma from which living things were modelled, the matrix out of which crops grew and from which houses were built, the material which housed the dead beneath the feet of the living. Mesopotamian myths from later millennia document the importance of clay – it created life and was the food of the dead.[84]
7. Figurines are rarely found in burials but are found within settlement tells, placed on house floors, in grain silos, in house fills, in pits 'where they were buried after use in some ceremony', in crannies within house walls and in the joins between abutting buildings.[85] In these latter cases their positioning in the joins between houses may have served to articulate the ancestral relationships of descent between adjacent households.

If we interpret the figurines as indicators of an ancestor-based social and religious organization, the implications for understanding Neolithic social structure are several. The dominance of female figurines is revelatory: it suggests that in many communities, especially in Anatolia at settlements like Çatalhöyük and Haçilar, only women were considered to be suitable ancestors. If descent was reckoned through the female line, these societies were matrilineal and probably matrilocal, perhaps even matriarchal in ideology and practice. Elsewhere, where males and females are equally represented, then we may be looking at societies with bilateral systems of descent. The portrayal of quadrupeds, probably cattle, in baked clay is more problematic until we bear in mind the significance of ancestry in the rearing of stock, linked to the symbolism of cattle at ninth millennium

BP sites like Çatalhöyük and the practice of providing tombs for cattle in eighth–seventh millennium BP sites like Nabta in Egypt.[86]

If Neolithic clay figurines can now be understood as representations of ancestors, their manufacture represents a transformation from the representation of ancestors in a literal sense, using the actual skull, to a more figurative sense, portraying the deceased individual separately from their physical elements. By the eighth millennium BP at Haçilar, when clay figurines were still in use, certain pottery vessels were being made in the same shapes as the figurines (**Figure 7.8**).[87] Some pots even sport the arms, faces and other features otherwise found on figurines. These anthropomorphized pots, as skeuomorphs of figurines, can be interpreted as an even more abstracted representation of ancestors. Thus, during the tenth to eighth millennia BP, we see a process of metaphorical elaboration in which the relationship between the signified (dead ancestor) and the signifier (skull > figurine > pot) is made manifest by an increasingly abstract representation.

Every settlement tell was a visual metaphor of the community, with the generations of ancestors embodied by or actually incorporated into the clay of the permanent and ever-growing mound while the living spent their short and transient lives inhabiting its surface. In many of the Near Eastern and Anatolian tells, mudbrick houses were constructed directly on top of one another, ensuring that the dwellings of the ancestors lay directly below those of their living descendants. The tells of the Balkan Neolithic provide a different picture; at sites of the Körös culture, the houses of the recently dead were avoided for a generation or two, a regional variation which may have been due to an alternative conception of the ancestral dead as initially requiring some form of separation from the living.[88]

At Çatalhöyük we find the evidence for a flourishing ancestor cult between 7000 and 6000 BC. Skeletons, some of them secondarily treated, lie beneath the floors. Occasional human skulls lie on the floors of abandoned houses. These houses were two-storey constructions; people probably lived most of the time on the rooftops, entering by ladder the lower rooms which lay between the living and the dead. Many of these lower rooms are the places identified as 'shrines' by an early excavator, James Mellaart, and are decked out with images of cattle heads and horns, vulture beaks set in clay 'breasts', paintings of felines, vultures and headless human corpses, and even a drawing of an erupting volcano. Rather than following Hodder's reading of the iconography as the wild 'foregrounded' in order to emphasize the *domus*, the domesticity of the house,[89] we should perhaps understand this vibrant symbolism as relating to the significance of passing from life to death and of the associated creatures who were symbolically instrumental in effecting that transition.

THE QUEST FOR IMMORTALITY

When the gods created humankind they appointed death for humankind, kept eternal life in their own hands. *The Epic of Gilgamesh*

Early hominids may have had little or no awareness of the biological inevitability of death. They may have reckoned that all that could stop them from living forever was accidental death of one sort or another. Today there are many traditional societies in which people consider that death is due to witchcraft or other spiritual malpractices, and that otherwise people would live for eternity. Even in western society the quest for immortality on earth goes on as doctors search for anti-ageing formulae. In California groups of self-styled immortals believe that death can be fended off indefinitely so long as one thinks the correct positive thoughts. Perhaps awareness of death is also a feature of growing up – most children are untrammelled by the burden of knowledge of their own inevitable death.

Ancestors are broadly considered, in many cultures, to be immortal beings (or at least living until the end of the world) whose ontological position lies somewhere between deities and mortals. While we can never know whether ancestors in the Palaeolithic and Neolithic attained a deified status, the absence of any material expression of the dead as gods until the third millennium BC means that their position in any cosmology prior to this period is open to argument.

The elevation of certain ancestors to a status comparable with deities appears to have occurred at around 3100 BC in Egypt and 2500 BC in Mesopotamia and rather later, around 1400 BC, in China. In Egypt the first pyramid, built by Zoser around 2650 BC, may mark the beginning of a redefinition of the pharaoh's relationship to his people in life and in death. Yet pyramid building was a relatively short phenomenon, lasting only a few centuries. Mummification was much longer lasting, being continued and modified as a process for body preservation over two thousand years, initially for the gods and goddesses who were formerly pharaohs, and spreading to the nobility, the greater populace and to millions of sacred animals. From the Egyptian Pyramid Texts and the Book of the Dead we find that the pre-existing deities take human form, or modified versions of human form (**Figure 3.5**), with the newly dead pharaoh becoming initiated into the pantheon of human-like deities.

Mesopotamia: kings, gods and ancestors

Around 2500 BC in Mesopotamia, the sixteen royal graves found at Ur formed part of a much larger cemetery set within the city's sacred walled enclosure in a central area among temples (**Figure 1.6**).[90] The royal graves are complex constructions of chambers entered by sloping passages. Each contains the elaborately decked-out royal corpse laid on a bier and surrounded by a host of grave goods and sometimes the bodies of retainers. One tomb contained the bodies of seventy-four people. In a manner reminiscent of the recent Jonestown mass suicide, death was effected by drinking poison: beside each body lay a small pottery cup which presumably contained the fatal draught that killed them. These graves are among the most spectacular ever found and they bear witness to the absolute power of Mesopotamia's ruling élite, as displayed by their fabulous wealth and their ability to command human sacrifices. We know something about the link between the Mesopotamians' relationship with their deities and their ancestors from archaeology and from later texts.

Each Mesopotamian city was associated with a particular deity. There were large temple complexes at the centre of each city, and individual houses often contained a special altar or place of worship. Written records indicate that adjacent households were related through kinship so that the spatial layout of the city may have formed a map of the kin relationships between the large family lineages which inhabited each of the large courtyard houses. A possible explanation of Mesopotamian religion at this time, in the fourth and third millennia BC, is that it was undergoing a transformation from ancestor worship to the worship of supernatural divinities. Not only might we see the domestic shrine as a means of worshipping the lineage's ancestors but the individual god of each city may have come into being as the founding ancestor of the people of that city, now deified.

The state on earth was perceived as a mirror and a component of the divine cosmic state, ruled over by Anu and his assistant Enlil. The gods chose who should rule and the king ruled as a mortal but carried a superhuman responsibility which the gods could remove at any time.[91] Dead rulers seem not to have become deities although we have the story of King Urnammu visiting the underworld after his death, presenting gifts to the seven gods, making sacrifices to the important dead, and taking on dead servants appropriate to his position.[92] It may well be that the later myths do not relate to the period of the mid-third millennium BC and thus our interpretation of the royal graves at Ur, and whether they embody notions of living beyond death, must derive solely from the archaeological evidence.

Thorkild Jacobsen considers that Mesopotamian religion went through three stages. In the earliest, in the fourth millennium BC, the deities were those of grain and the storehouse, while life, death and rebirth were seen as part of a continuous cycle. In the second stage, in the third millennium BC, the fertility deities were replaced by ruler and hero gods. They were considered as taking human form and they ruled the heavens like kings. By the third stage, in the second millennium, individuals had personal gods among the enormous pantheon of nearly three thousand deities, to whom they could unburden their problems and ask for forgiveness, as if the gods were supernatural parents.[93]

Monumentality and human sacrifice

The remarkable mid-third millennium burials of the early pharaohs and Mesopotamian élite can be understood as an early state phenomenon. As the pharaohs built the pyramids, so the pyramids built the state. At the same time the intention behind the monumentality and excessive destruction of resources was to ensure that the deceased became a deity, a godly ancestor for the successors so that their earthly power might be beyond reproach, god-given. In an exaggerated image of the world of the living, the afterworld also took on a rigidly hierarchical form, shaping and determining the lives of mortals.

Even where the afterworld distinctions were not drawn as sharply as those in ancient Egypt, between deified ancestors and other ancestors, the statements of difference among the dead are clear and establish hierarchical relationships among the ancestral dead, in whose light the living bathe.

The phenomenon of monumental, lavish burials accompanied by human sacrifices appeared throughout the world, in at least thirteen different cultures (see Chapter 1), between 3100 BC and the early nineteenth century. The sacrifice of living humans, whether willing or not, is an expression of the supreme power that rulers exercise over the ruled. In China the practice of human sacrifice may date to the period between 3000 and 2000 BC at Wang-ch'eng-kang but the first royal graves with mass sacrifices are from Anyang around 1400 BC. The Xibeigang graves at Anyang, dating to the Shang period (c. 1400–1000 BC), are probably the graves of the last of the Shang royalty. One contained 165 human sacrifices, perhaps the bodies of prisoners of war, and all these tombs were built in monumental proportions consisting of a rectangular burial pit entered by one or more ramps.[94] Much later, in 210 BC, China's first emperor, Qin Shi huang, was buried in a 76m high tomb, 485m by 515m, known as Mount Li. It has never been excavated but according to written records it contains members of the emperor's harem and all the artisans and craftsmen who had built the tomb. Outside it to the east three huge pits were dug; here the excavators discovered the extraordinary army of 800 terracotta warriors. Like later Chinese emperors, Qin Shi huang was engaged in a quest for immortality, sending out missions to all corners of the known world in search of the elixir of eternal life.[95]

We may define this phenomenon of building tombs for immortals as cults of deities and heroes. These deity and hero cults are regional and are characteristic of early city states where cities were formed around large temple complexes and where gross social inequalities meant certain individuals wielded the power of life and death over others. The funerary monuments of rulers are elaborate and human sacrifices and copious grave goods accompany the royal dead to the afterworld. Their bodies may be preserved through mummification, jade suits and other magical means to make possible this transcendence of death. Pantheons of deities are represented as personified individuals while certain living individuals have divine or heroic ancestries and personages. Absolute power on earth is translated into, and bolstered by, the eternal rule of heavenly deities. Earthly rulers are their representatives, maintaining the harmony of integration within the cosmos.

The monumentality and pomp of the élite's funerary rites may be matched by representations of individuals in monumental size (**Figure 7.9**). In contrast to the small ancestor figurines of the Neolithic and Chalcolithic, statues of the third millennium's early states come to dwarf the human scale. Ruler gods, heroes and deities are embodied individually by large statues and imagery. In Mesopotamian mythology statues were not simply representations of people and other creatures but were entities in their own right, made from the same materials as the living. Living creatures are created by mixing dust with water – in other words, from clay. When they die they revert to the materials from which they were made, silt and dust. Statues were considered to be 'raised' or 'given birth' in the same way as living beings. Death was likened to the breaking of a statue, in which the pieces are scattered and strewn in the soil.[96]

7.9 *The rock-cut New Kingdom temple facade at Abu Simbel with its monumental representations of Ramses II (1290–1244 BC), subsequent to its modern relocation away from the floodwaters of the Aswan Dam.*

'The Epic of Gilgamesh'

One of the world's earliest texts, preserved on Late Babylonian cuneiform tablets from around 700 BC but probably deriving from a story many centuries older, from around 2000 BC, is the *Epic of Gilgamesh*.[97] It is a remarkable document, capturing the sorrow of the human plight of coming to terms with our unavoidable mortality, telling of the fruitless search for the transcendence of death.

A shepherd who becomes king of Uruk, Gilgamesh is terrified by the thought of dying and entering 'the house of darkness' as a weak and powerless ghostly being of shadows. For the dead 'dust is their food and clay their nourishment: they see no light where they dwell in darkness' in the underground city of Arulla, enclosed by seven walls and gates and engulfed in darkness.[98]

Gilgamesh sets out on a quest to find everlasting life. He travels to the end of the world, through the dark passage where the sun goes at night, to the shore of the waters of death, whence a boatman takes him to Utnapishtim and his wife, the last two humans to have been granted immortality by the gods. Utnapishtim explains that this unique gift of immortality, given for saving life on earth from a flood by building a big boat, will never be bestowed on anyone again and he attempts to convince Gilgamesh to accept his fate. Gilgamesh succumbs to a magic form of sleep which is but death, and is woken back to the living by Utnapishtim's wife.

His quest over, Gilgamesh prepares to return to Uruk, yet the wife urges her husband to give him a parting gift. Utnapishtim tells him of a secret plant of rejuvenation that grows at the bottom of the sea. Gilgamesh finds the spot and dives down to grab the plant. He and the boatman sail towards Uruk, reach the Persian Gulf and continue on foot. Coming to a pool, Gilgamesh goes for a swim and a snake comes and snatches away the plant which he has left on the bank. The only immortality left to Gilgamesh is either ancestral transcendence (through his offspring) or cultural transcendence (though memory of his accomplishments).

The story is of particular interest, not just because it is the very first written account of the human condition in the face of death but also because it provides an insight into the self-questioning mind of four thousand years ago, addressing not only personal concerns about dying but also the ideological basis – an immortal afterlife – on which the power of the kings rested. The story is ultimately one of frustration. 'An inner turmoil is left to rage on, a vital question finds no answer.'[99] That dissatisfaction with the failure to transcend death may have been a crucial prelude to the next series of massive changes in human spirituality.

THE RISE OF THE WORLD RELIGIONS

It is broadly in the two thousand-year period of the first millennia BC and AD that we can identify a new current of human belief about the nature of death and immortality. Yet the earliest beginnings of these myriad interpretations and reinterpretations of what happens when we die can be traced to the mid-second millennium BC.[100] The Hindu Rig Veda was in existence by *c.* 1380 BC and it reveals polytheist worship of creation, rain and thunder, fire, air, water, the dawn, the moon and the sky, in which the correct sacrifices would ensure comfort in the heavens above.[101] Recent appraisals of the remarkable Indus civilization cities such as Mohenjo-daro and Harappa, dating to *c.* 2500–1500 BC, have suggested that there are symbolic elements in the architecture and material culture which can be seen to prefigure later Hindu beliefs, such as possible yogic figures and representations of deities.[102]

The exodus of Moses and his people to follow their god Yahweh can also be dated to the second millennium BC, with these early experiences passed down orally before being written down after 1000 BC.[103] Within the first millennium BC we find many of the core elements of the world religions appearing, such as the Hindu *Upanishads* and the teachings of Parsva (Jainism), Zoroaster, Buddha, Confucius and Lao Tzu. Late-comers are the spread of belief in Jesus Christ, the emergence of Shinto in the early centuries AD and the coming of the prophet of Allah, Muhammad, in the sixth century AD.

There are two questions that should be asked about those groups of religious beliefs that we commonly classify as world religions. Are the 'world religions' qualitatively any different to what came before? Secondly, are these 'world religions' simply acknowledged as such because they exist today, the survivors of a series of historical conjunctures and contingencies? The world religions can be distinguished from the deity and hero religions through their universal membership. Even with Judaism and Hinduism, where incorporation depends on birth rather than conversion, these are religions which promise salvation or enlightenment for the masses, and not just the élite, regardless of wealth or social position. Most of their prophets and leaders were men who were either from among the poor or were princes who renounced their worldly wealth; in contrast to the deity and hero religions, earthly power and wealth are not conducive to successfully achieving transcendence of death.

The origins of these world-renouncing religious movements may lie between *c.* 600 BC and *c.* 600 AD, a period when large states and multi-ethnic empires from Asia to Europe and North Africa established wide-ranging hegemonies over countless ethnic groups, and created new classes of the rootless and the rural and urban poor and dispossessed. At the same time the emergent world religions also accompanied phases of 'democratization' or at least lapses in autocracy. Initial phases of materialist rejection, after the earliest generations of believers and followers rejected earthly wealth and power, were followed several centuries later by global expansion and massive monumentality in the form of temples, mosques, cathedrals, stupas and towers of silence. For some religions the superhumans who are credited with initiating the way are represented in human form at a whole variety of personalized and monumental scales. For others, such as Islam and Judaism, there is a complete ban on the representation of the deity.

In terms of the contributions that world religions have made to the human experience of death, they have certain characteristics in common which suggest a qualitative change from earlier religions. All are beholden to an all-powerful supernatural entity or involve worship within a pantheistic monism. A common thread through many is that eternal salvation may be sought through moral improvement and can be realized by supernatural judgement. Monumentality is directed towards the worship of the supreme entity or the transcendent idea. The human body in death is treated with simplicity or is even annihilated.[104]

Transcendence of death is possible for all converts or chosen ones. This transcendence is achieved in various ways. Among the Abrahamic religions of Judaism, Christianity and Islam, as well as in Zoroastrianism (originating in the seventh–sixth centuries BC), time is not conceived of in cosmic cycles but focuses on a goal, progressing from creation to an end which promises a universal salvation and everlasting life after the cosmic last judgement.[105] In contrast, followers of the Buddha (*c.* 563–483 BC) aimed for extinction of the self and release from space and time. Death is not inevitable but a sign that something has gone wrong, caused by Mara 'the killer' who diverts us from the path and from our true immortal selves. By shedding our material attachments, we move beyond death's realm and win relief from an endless series of repeated deaths. By attaining a state of self-extinction (*nirvana*), Buddhists may overcome the error that is death and enter the 'doors to the deathless', 'the gates of the undying'.[106]

THE RISE OF SECULAR BELIEFS

It is also in the first millennium BC, in ancient Greece and Egypt and in Confucian China, that we can find the beginnings of the secular religions which ultimately have provided the basis for the broad scientific enquiry into the nature of belief and transcendence which includes archaeology. Secular thought entails either the rejection of the notion of transcendence of death, or the adoption of an agnostic uncertainty, or merely the loss of interest in the possibility of life after death. The search for salvation becomes the quest for solutions in this world rather than the next, while people live to moral codes of universal human rights, individualism, common welfare and secular humanism.

The monuments of secular belief are municipal buildings which promote public interest and well-being – libraries, museums, lighthouses, pleasure gardens, universities and hospitals. The handling of death becomes increasingly a technical problem of disposal and hygiene as the corpse becomes unwanted matter of little spiritual significance. We might also add that the secular religions of communism and fascism during the twentieth century subscribed to many of these notions yet promulgated hero cults in which the leaders of the revolution and of the party were given god-like status after death with their monumental images placed throughout the state. The embalmed body of Lenin still lies in his tomb outside the Kremlin at the sacred centre of the former Soviet state in Red Square in a manner not unlike the treatment of pharaohs and Mesopotamian kings over four thousand years ago.

One of the principal legacies of the ancient Greek world has been the belief in science and philosophy at the expense of religion. Working broadly within the traditions of secular humanism, archaeologists have come into conflict with indigenous societies and religious communities for whom the archaeological excavation, analysis and curation of human remains is not a worthy quest for knowledge but a major affront to human dignity.

EIGHT

THE POLITICS OF THE DEAD

Once you are dead, put your feet up, call it a day, and let the husband or the missus or the kids or a sibling decide whether you are to be buried or burned or blown out of a cannon or left to dry out in a ditch somewhere. It's not your day to watch it, because the dead don't care.[1]

It used to be said that archaeologists dealt exclusively with the dead, and were lucky that the subjects of their study could not answer back. Since the 1970s it has become apparent, sometimes painfully so, that even the ancient dead are tied to the living through political, religious, economic, social and ancestral links that archaeologists meddle with at their peril. The dead don't care but the living most certainly do. Archaeologists have had to accommodate in their work respect for the living traditions of indigenous peoples all around the world, the deeply held beliefs of members of the world religions, the moral sensibilities of local people, and the political manipulations of communities unhappy with archaeologists' interference. In addition, archaeologists have come into conflict with the illicit looters of the dead whose trappings become commodities for collectors on a global scale. Archaeologists have also been involved in the exhumation of recent massacre victims, collecting evidence to authenticate accounts of atrocities and bring war criminals to trial.

All around the world museums are full of cultural remains gathered far and wide over the last few centuries by antiquarians, archaeologists, adventurers and treasure hunters. Local communities and even nation states have had the material remains of their past and even their dead taken away for storage and exhibition in a faraway museum. Archaeology grew up with European colonialism and, during the nineteenth and early twentieth centuries in particular, those archaeologists working in the colonies had little to stop them from investigating and removing whatever they saw as being of cultural value, regardless of local sensitivities. Along with social anthropologists, they were merely one arm of the colonial administration's control over the colonized. With the end of colonial rule in many countries between the 1940s and 1960s, respect for local views on ancient human remains and other archaeological finds did not appear automatically; indigenous rural communities were still beholden to the wishes of the state and its representatives.

The greatest conflict over the treatment of human remains has generally occurred in those colonial countries where the European population dominated, notably in North America, Australasia and South Africa. Since the 1960s indigenous peoples have waged campaigns for the redressing of injustices, which include requests for the restitution of their cultural property, the non-disturbance of graves, and the reburial of their ancient and sometimes not-so-ancient dead. At the same time some archaeologists and physical anthropologists began to question the morality of their discipline.

Within the positivist-influenced philosophies of scientific method adopted by Australian and North American archaeologists, research was conducted with the aim of finding out

8.1 *During a meeting in 1989 of the World Archaeological Congress at Vermillion, South Dakota, a skull from Madagascar was handed over for return to its country of origin, followed by the reburial, shown here, of Native American bones from Wounded Knee.*

objectively what happened in the past. The ancient remains of indigenous cultures were a legitimate subject for scientific research, conceived of as laboratories for understanding culture change and process. Oral histories, native testimonies and written texts were considered as biased 'emic' representations, tainted by the subjectivity of the observer, and inferior to the objective 'etic' view that archaeology might bring. The indigenes might say that their ancestors fell from the sky or sprouted out of the land but archaeology would be able to show that they arrived from another continent so many thousands of years ago. Indigenous groups with different perspectives on time and with traditions which were still relevant in the contemporary world considered that they already knew their own history and did not need outsiders to tell them a different version, let alone to desecrate the dead in order to do so.[2]

The issues are most visible in the post-colonial nations but there are also concerns in countries such as Britain where there are few such distinctions between indigenous people and outsider archaeologists. There have been ethical dilemmas and confrontations in Britain though such events are minor in comparison with those to be faced by some other nations. While scientific techniques applicable to the study of human remains have mushroomed since 1950, the more recent world-wide concern for reburial and non-disturbance is likely to stop such research in its tracks in many parts of the world.

There has been a sea-change in the opinions of many archaeologists since the early 1980s. Firstly, a small minority began to campaign vociferously on behalf of a more politically aware and ethical consideration of the impacts of disturbing human remains. Secondly, the issues were taken up and aired on the world stage at the Southampton World Archaeological Congress in 1986 and at the Vermillion Inter-Congress in 1989 (**Figure 8.1**). Thirdly, archaeologists were catching up with their colleagues in the other human sciences in realizing that interpreting the past depended on the situatedness of the observer, as much as on any claim for objectivity. Archaeologists could not be free agents, unfettered by their relationship to the rest of society, but were enmeshed in a network of social and economic relationships in which intellectual knowledge was power. The study of the past could be understood as being conducted with reference to the political concerns of the present by present-minded academics whose results would be used, by them and by others, towards a variety of ends.[3]

Archaeologists' relationships with the wider community are now necessarily reflexive. They have a duty to interpret the past not for their own edification but for the communities which they serve, and they also have obligations towards the living, those who claim the people of the past as their ancestors, as well as the dead. This is especially true in the treatment of human remains, where archaeological interests may conflict with spiritual or religious disquiet about the archaeologists' activities.

NATIVE AMERICANS AND ARCHAEOLOGISTS

Reburial, restitution, repatriation and non-disturbance of human remains have become key issues in North America where indigenous groups are reclaiming their ancestors from museum displays and stores.[4] The conflict has been brewing since the 1960s and came to a head after a long series of events. During the 1970s archaeologists were still excavating burial sites without any reference to the Native American communities living in the vicinity. In 1971 archaeologists excavated a nineteenth-century white pioneers' cemetery in Iowa. One of the burials contained grave goods and was thus considered to be Native American. The skeletons of the settlers were removed by undertakers for reburial whereas the Native American skeleton was lifted by the archaeologists for storage in a museum. Local Native Americans, led by Maria Pearson (Running Moccasins), were outraged at this racist treatment in which their dead were no more than museum specimens while the whites' remains were considered sacred.

Similar events occurred at the site of Custer's last stand at the Little Bighorn where the remains of the US Army soldiers found during archaeological excavation were reburied while those of the Lakota warriors were not. With a history of genocide, starvation, discrimination and loss of tribal lands, Native Americans were suffering another form of exploitation by which they were made to feel like second-class citizens. Their past was displayed in museums of natural history, as though they were merely part of the flora and fauna before the 'historical era' when the settlers realized their 'manifest destiny'.[5] They were portrayed as a people on the verge of extinction with a culture that had virtually disappeared.

The American Indian Movement (AIM) and American Indians Against Desecration (AIAD), directed by Jan Hammil, campaigned against these injustices and took their case to the annual conference of the Society for American Archaeology (SAA) in Minneapolis in 1982. The response from the archaeologists was not encouraging. The SAA's committee postponed consideration of a resolution opposing reburial but most archaeologists remained unreceptive and intransigent. During the early 1980s most were against any form of compromise. The scientific importance of excavating and retaining human bones outweighed any concerns of minority groups. If anything, archaeologists were surprised that they were not being thanked for providing Native Americans with a past through archaeology to replace their existing histories which were based only on myth. The ancient ancestors of the Native Americans had a right for their story to be told and their present-day descendants were preventing this knowledge of the past by demanding non-disturbance and reburial.[6] To be told that Native Americans already knew their past through myth and spiritual communication since it was alive in the present caused immense frustration to the academic community, and archaeologists increasingly despaired of Native American lack of interest and disbelief in their scientific results.

The Archaeological Committee for the Preservation of Archaeological Collections (ACPAC) defended their curatorial policy in the face of AIAD's requests for the return of an estimated half a million skeletons held in American collections. They considered that archaeologists should oppose reburial to protect the database of their discipline, and that it was not ethical to accede to wishes for reburial unless the request came from living members of the dead person's tribe. Similar positions were taken by the SAA and by SoPA (the Society of Professional Archaeologists). Most archaeologists accepted this principle of 'demonstrable genetic kinship'; if members of the Lakota, for example, demanded reburial then they should demonstrate that the burials in question were Lakota.

The colonization by European Americans of Native American land – a painful history of betrayal and bad faith beyond the scope of this book – eventually led to the reservation system and the relocations of the last hundred years. Few tribes now live in the places their ancestors inhabited, and burial grounds on Native American land frequently belong to other groups, now departed. Thus most claims for reburial being made by tribal groups were for the human remains of other groups. AIAD were a pan-Indian movement and for them tribal affiliation was outweighed by a broader Native American heritage. In any case the burials of the dead should not be disturbed because they are inherently sacred, and not simply because of any respect for the feelings of surviving family members.

Larry Zimmerman was one of the first archaeologists to question the ethical stand of his colleagues. He has written about the critical, abusive and uncooperative attitudes of his fellow archaeologists when he gave his support to the Native American cause at the 1982 SAA conference and earlier, in 1981, when he was involved with the reburial of nearly five hundred victims of the Crow Creek massacre.[7] Many have subsequently relented from their former views and there have been significant advances in cooperation and mutual understanding in many parts of North America. For example, the disastrous events in Iowa in the early 1970s were rectified by a series of efforts. In 1975 the Iowa State Archaeologist requested Maria Pearson's help in persuading other Native Americans of the desirability of excavating an ossuary threatened by development, and this was given after it became known that the undertaker contracted to arrange the reburial was intending to use a bulldozer. In 1976 the State of Iowa passed 'reburial' legislation which provided a contingency fund for recovering human remains and established a state cemetery for the reinterment of 'ancient' (more than 150 years old) human remains.[8]

Nationally the debate continued to rage among archaeologists but the matter was taken out of their hands by the passing of pro-Indian legislation, the National Museum of the American Indian Act 1989 and the Native American Graves Protection and Repatriation Act 1990 (NAGPRA).[9] Under NAGPRA museums have been required to return all Native American human remains to the appropriate tribal group for reburial. None the less, each case for repatriation has had to be argued on its own merits. By a curious twist, physical anthropologists have had to fall back on highly debatable techniques of using cranial and post-cranial measurement in order to assign prehistoric individuals to contemporary tribal groupings. Yet the controversy is still not settled. Feelings run high on both sides and tribes such as the Lakota have come to distrust the archaeologists profoundly. The *impasse* has recently come to a head in an extraordinary case from Washington State, in the north-west of the United States, which has brought out all of the issues and set them in an explosive nutshell.

The Kennewick discovery and its consequences

In July 1996 a skull and some bones were found by two students on the bank of the Columbia River near Kennewick in Washington State, on land which was the responsibility of the Army Corps of Engineers.[10] During the day several people turned up more parts of the skeleton. After subsequent archaeological excavation, required by law on federal land, it was discovered that this skeleton was not that of a white settler, as an initial study of its physical characteristics had concluded, but was much more ancient. The individual sported a remarkable healed-over injury, caused by a stone projectile point which was still lodged in the bone. A radiocarbon determination corroborated the typological dating of the point, of a type known as a Cascade projectile point, to around 7600–7300 BC. This was a truly outstanding find, made all the more unusual by the fact that the initial assignment to a broad ethnic grouping made from details of the individual's skeletal characteristics was confirmed. He was of Caucasoid type, with skeletal features clearly different from the Mongoloid traits of historical and modern Native Americans.

The Army Corps of Engineers realized that they were dealing with a very hot potato and confiscated the bones from James Chatters, the forensic anthropologist who had been studying the remains. With more human bones coming out of the same site, they dropped a large quantity of soil to protect the river bank from further erosion and to seal it for good. The skeleton was to be reburied by the Confederated Tribes of the Umatilla Indian Reservation, in whose territory it was found. Archaeologists were outraged at what they saw as the wanton destruction of what is one of the most significant archaeological finds in the world in recent years. Not only is this one of just a handful of Palaeoindian skeletons but its physical traits suggest that this individual may have been part of a hitherto unrecognized migration from Asia some ten thousand years ago.

In October 1996 eight archaeologists and anthropologists filed for an injunction to halt the reburial of the remains and to study them in order to verify their relationship to contemporary Native Americans, since they considered that there was insufficient evidence for cultural affiliation, proof of which is a legal requirement under NAGPRA. In June 1997 the Corps' decision to return the skeleton for reburial was overturned by a court which ordered a reassessment of the case by a federal agency and criticized the Corps for failing to act impartially. Meanwhile, another party, the Asatru Folk Assembly, a group of Norse pagans, filed for restitution of the remains to them on the basis that this was one of their ancestors. Both they and representatives of the Umatilla Confederation were permitted to carry out religious ceremonies over the skeleton, potentially causing contamination that might affect any future analysis of the bones. Archaeologists, since they were not a self-constituted religious organization, were barred from undertaking further study or even from viewing the skeleton. After much discussion,[11] the bones were examined in 1999 at the Burke Museum in Seattle by five government-appointed scientists, but the taking of samples for DNA analysis and radiocarbon dating was not permitted.

Just as attitudes were relaxing on both sides of the reburial issue, this case has caused fierce antagonism. Native Americans consider that there is no reason to doubt that the Kennewick man is an ancestor. Just because they are of a certain physical type today does not mean that their ancestors had always been of this type. Representatives of the Umatilla are particularly angry and distressed that their hard-won right to dignified treatment of sacred remains is under attack. On the other side, the SAA have been lobbying the federal government to modify the NAGPRA legislation, recommending that, in cases with this degree of archaeological significance, the scientific value to all American people should outweigh the sacred and religious importance to Native Americans. The SAA do not wish to question tribal authority over the disposition of cultural items found on tribal lands but Native Americans now fear that the legislation will be weakened and that, after all they have striven for, they will be let down by the government and stabbed in the back by archaeologists.

A bill has been introduced into Congress to modify NAGPRA, 'to provide for appropriate study and repatriation of remains for which a cultural affiliation is not readily ascertainable'. Its main features are that finds should be recorded to scientific standards except where ownership by lineal descendants is established, that even when cultural affiliation has been established scientific study may be conducted if the outcome is expected to provide new information on the history or prehistory of the United States, and that such study should be completed within 180 days after the material is made available. Finally, study may not be permitted if the potential scientific benefit of such study is considered by the federal body with custody of the material to be outweighed by curatorial, cultural or other reasonable considerations.

ABORIGINALS AND ATROCITIES IN AUSTRALIA

If we Aborigines cannot control our own heritage, what the hell can we control?[12]

It was only a few generations ago that Australian Aboriginals were hunted, massacred, mutilated, raped and enslaved by white colonists. This history of colonial atrocities, perpetrated in the late eighteenth, nineteenth and early twentieth centuries, makes heart-rending reading. It can be no surprise that Aboriginals have become anxious about the archaeological excavation of their ancestors' remains, among other concerns for social justice. Like the Native Americans, they have been subjected to intellectual imperialism, classified as Neanderthal throwbacks whose corpses and skeletons were preserved in museums while the cemeteries of white people remained undisturbed by the archaeologists and scientists.

As in the United States and Canada the problem developed over many years owing to a woeful lack of communication. Aboriginals became suspicious and resentful while archaeologists never asked permission for removal and study of human remains. Non-disturbance and reburial became the focus for the bitterness that remained over the memory of nineteenth-century atrocities and over the poor and landless economic position of many Aboriginals today. At first only a few academics were prepared to support the Aboriginals' case and these, among them the physical anthropologist Steven Webb, were subjected to verbal abuse and ostracism by their colleagues.[13] The Australian Archaeological Association (AAA) produced a working document in the early 1980s which stressed the importance of research, the reburial of remains only if they were named individuals, and the requirement that no other remains should be destroyed by burial or cremation. Such faint-hearted moves paralleled those in the United States.

This academic intransigence ignored the cultural legacy of episodes which appear monstrous in retrospect. In 1907 the German scientist Hermann Klaatsch sealed an Aboriginal corpse in a tank of preserving fluid and shipped it to Germany for dissection. In the 1920s Sir John Cleland, professor of pathology at the South Australian Museum, preserved the corpses of four 'pure-blooded' Aboriginals as scientific specimens. The bodies received burial in 1985. William Lanney, the last Tasmanian male of unmixed genetic descent, was dissected within twenty-four hours of his death in 1869. His skull was taken away by William Crowther, a member of the Royal College of Surgeons, who is also said to have taken his nose, ears and facial skin and made his skin into a tobacco pouch. George Stokell, a member of the Royal Society of Tasmania, removed Lanney's hands and feet; Stokell thought he would prove that Tasmanian Aboriginals were the missing link between apes and modern humans.[14]

The history of Truganini's corpse is similarly sordid. She was regarded as the last pure-blooded Tasmanian and she almost certainly knew that, on her death, her body would be prized as the last remains of an extinct race. As a result Truganini specified that her body should be cremated. The day after her death in May 1876, the Royal Society of Tasmania requested that her body should be preserved; this was turned down and she was in fact buried. Two years later, however, she was dug up and her bones were sent to Melbourne and London for study. On return, they remained on display in the Tasmanian Museum until 1947 when they were transferred to the museum's store. In 1974 the Australian Institute for Aboriginal Studies (AIAS) persuaded the Tasmanian government that her last wishes should be observed. In 1976 Truganini's bones were cremated and scattered at sea.[15] Such cases are just the tip of the iceberg. Many thousands of skeletons and skulls were taken from Tasmania, Australia and New Zealand for museums and private collections in Australasia and throughout the world.

In recent years substantial collections of Aboriginal bones have been returned from museums such as the Pitt-Rivers Museum in Oxford. Even Palaeolithic bones have been returned and cremated. The problem of what to do with other similarly ancient remains from Lake Mungo may well be resolved by their being curated by Australian Aboriginal groups in 'keeping places', sacred locked stores to which scholars may be admitted. In the early 1980s Michael Mansell, a Tasmanian Aboriginal, made the first of several visits to Britain to request the return of the skull of William Lanney which, it seemed, had ended up in the collections of the University of Edinburgh. In 1991, after six years of negotiation, the university handed over a skull and remains of other skeletons to the Australian consulate. Yet the university staff were worried that they were not convinced that the skull was Lanney's; it might still be lodged, unidentified, in the collection of the Royal College of Surgeons in London.

THE POLITICS OF BONES AROUND THE WORLD

The issue of non-disturbance and reburial is a global one because human remains from so many indigenous groups have been housed in museums throughout the world and because the problems posed by archaeological excavation have occurred in many nations. In Zimbabwe, for example, the national museum service halted excavation of a burial ground on the grounds that it was disturbing the Shona spirits. Indigenous archaeologists in countries such as Papua New Guinea, Cameroon and the Philippines all face difficult dilemmas, balancing responsibility to the profession and responsibility to their communities.[16] Many museums in Britain and elsewhere had in their collections tattooed Maori heads which have now been returned to New Zealand, regardless of the situation that led to their curation. For example, tattooed heads brought to the UK as gifts by a Maori doctor during the nineteenth century have recently been taken back by his grandson. Such items used to be sold in the London auction houses but recently a Maori head was withdrawn prior to auction at Sotheby's. Most recently the 1999 World Archaeological Congress in Cape Town called for the return of 2,500 Khoisan skeletons from museums in South Africa and elsewhere for reburial.[17]

Israel is a nation under siege not only from the outside world but also from the activism of some of its Orthodox Jewish communities who have been campaigning for many years to prevent archaeologists excavating human remains. In 1983 a law was passed, but later rescinded, giving any rabbi power to intervene on archaeological excavations if human remains likely to be of Jewish origin were found. Recently, the political right, which includes Orthodox Jews, succeeded in lobbying the government to issue a new interpretation of the Antiquities Act which has led to the reburial of all human remains younger than five thousand years old.[18] Currently, archaeologists and police regularly come into conflict with protest groups of young, jobless Orthodox men who try to prevent and hamper the archaeologists' work in the hope of stopping them from disturbing human remains.

The African Burial Ground

In North America there has been a major political row involving the descendent community of African Americans reclaiming their heritage in New York.[19] Enslaved Africans were brought to New York from 1626 by the Dutch and later, after 1664, by the English. In 1697 the black community was refused the right of burial in the churchyards, and from before 1712 to 1794 the African Burial Ground, outside the city, was used for ten to twenty thousand burials of blacks and outcast whites. When this area of the city came up for redevelopment in the 1980s, the developers, the General Services Administration (the federal agency dealing with government buildings), commissioned an impact assessment which drew attention to the presence of the cemetery but concluded that the burials had already largely been destroyed by later cellars and foundations. As a result the GSA made no contingency plans for construction in the event of burials being found. When burials were discovered and subsequently announced at a press conference, there was outrage.

The site was only two blocks from City Hall, occupied by New York's first black mayor. African Americans were unhappy that they had no control over their heritage which was being dug up by white people, sanctioned by white bureaucrats. They had not been informed about what might lie under the ground in this area. Worse was to come when a mechanical excavator accidentally destroyed several burials while constructing foundations. In 1991 archaeologists began excavating and 427 skeletons were eventually recovered from the site of the African Burial Ground. In 1992 there was a one-day blockade of the site. President Bush approved legislation to halt part of the development project and approved finance for the building of a museum to honour the contribution of African Americans to colonial New York. The last of the exposed burials were excavated and plans were made for reburial after analysis, for a burial ground exhibition, and for an African Burial Ground memorial (**Figure 8.2**).

8.2 The signboard erected by Howard University's African Burial Ground Project on the site of the excavated cemetery in New York City.

To carry out the analysis the GSA hired Michael Blakey, a professor of physical anthropology at Howard University, an African American institution. His team's results brought to light shocking details about the slaves' treatment as well as raising fascinating questions about how far they were fully Christianized, with many retaining elements of African religions in funerary practice and grave good provision of beads, crystals and shells.[20] Comparison with census data shows that enslaved women's fertility was very low and that there was very little natural increase in the African population in New York, in contrast to the Europeans. The bones of over three-quarters of the cemetery population also exhibited traces of infectious diseases and nutritional stress such as osteomyelitis, hyperostosis, enamel hypoplasia, rickets and lesions from active infection. Women as well as men were carrying out physically strenuous activities, sometimes causing horrific skeletal damage such as the splitting of thoracic vertebrae, breaking of pelvic and cranial bones, and bone damage from tearing of tendons.

Mitochondrial DNA analysis suggests that many of the people buried in the African Burial Ground originated in West Africa, with others from West Central Africa and some from Madagascar. The results have overturned ideas that the English/white American urban community of New York treated their slaves more humanely than their southern neighbours. The whole affair has been described as a microcosm of the wider issues of racism and economic exploitation in New York City. It is also a success story of descendent-community involvement in rescue archaeology and subsequent political and intellectual empowerment.[21]

The case of Jewbury

About 600,000 people have been buried since Roman times in the city of York in northern England. They fill the churchyards, the minster's yard and many other parts of a remarkable two thousand-year accumulation of urban deposits. Major excavations of medieval cemeteries have been conducted at Fishergate and at St Helen-on-the-Walls, providing an exceptional insight into the health, social life and battle injuries of medieval townsfolk.[22] The human bones are kept as a reference collection, along with other archaeological material, for scholarly study. Among the population of medieval York there was a small community of Jews. In their daily lives they suffered discrimination, abuse and physical violence from the other townsfolk and, despite being nominally under the protection of the king, were victims of a massacre in 1190. Attacked by a mob the Jews fled to the castle keep of Clifford's Tower, where many died when the building was set on fire. The Jewish community, however, remained in York and prospered over the next fifty years but then declined. In 1290 when all Jews were expelled from England, only six households remained.

In 1982/3, in advance of a supermarket development, archaeologists excavated a cemetery in that part of York named Jewbury, the name of the former Jewish cemetery which was known from a medieval document of c. 1230.[23] The cemetery expanded into new land bought by the Jewish communities of York and Lincoln around 1230. The graves, 496 in total, were immaculately laid out in rows, oriented south–north, and contained some coffins with iron fittings, a complete contrast to the crowded, intercutting medieval churchyard burials which lay west–east and were generally buried in shrouds. Male and female burials were mixed throughout the cemetery though there was some degree of spatial grouping of the sexes and for children. The osteological analysis revealed an interesting picture of the health of this small population constituting probably two-thirds of York's Jewry between *c.* 1180 and 1290. Though no burials could be directly linked to the massacre of 1190, there were wounds visible on the bones of twenty-five individuals although in only six of these were they certainly deliberately induced. A number of children had atrophied limbs. The bones also yielded evidence of Paget's disease, anaemia and osteomas including tuberculosis.

The York Archaeological Trust had realized the potentially sensitive nature of the site as early as 1980, when they drew the ethical and legal considerations to the attention of the owners, York City Council, and the developers.[24] In 1981 they informed the Chief Rabbi, Sir Immanuel Jakobovits, of their proposal to carry out rescue excavations. He replied to the city council, registering the Jewish community's 'grave religious concern . . . if the site were to in fact contain Jewish graves' which should be treated with the utmost reverence. He supported the need for trial excavation and suggested that remains which could not be preserved *in situ* be disinterred and reburied. Despite the documentary evidence, he was uncertain as to whether these could be Jewish burials since some of the coffins were made with iron nails and the burials were oriented south–north and not west–east (as they should be to face Jerusalem). The supermarket chain Sainsbury's, who had acquired the site, referred the matter of removal of burials to the London Beth Din, the Court of the Chief Rabbi, which concluded that there was no proof that these were Jewish burials. The necessary Home Office licence to remove the burials was obtained, giving a minimum of a year for analysis subsequent to excavation.

However, following a report in the *Guardian* newspaper, members of the Jewish College at Gateshead presented arguments to the Chief Rabbi that the remains were almost certainly Jewish. The Chief Rabbi then made representations to the Home Office:

> Whatever the scientific and historical loss, I hope you and the general public will appreciate our paramount concern for the reverence due to mortal remains which once bore the incorruptible hallmark of the divine image, and which, we believe, have an inalienable right to stay undisturbed. We are convinced that the dignity shown to human remains, even centuries after death, could contribute more than any scientific inquiry to the advancement of human civilization and the enhancement of the respect in which human beings hold each other.

The Home Office responded by requiring immediate reburial and the osteological analyses were ended prematurely. In 1984 the bones were reburied in the presence of the Chief Rabbi on the edge of the original cemetery in the supermarket's car park, a location which has become a place of pilgrimage. Today the York Archaeological Trust regret the loss of this research opportunity but consider that they acted with propriety throughout and in good faith. They had been caught in the middle between parties who had difficult decisions to make – whether development was acceptable, whether the burials really were Jewish, and whether a licence once granted should be revoked.

LEGAL REQUIREMENTS AND PROBLEM CASES IN BRITAIN

In England and Wales exhumation of human remains, whether for archaeological purposes or not, falls largely within the legislation of the Burial Act 1857 or the Disused Burial Grounds (Amendment) Act 1981 (amending the 1884 legislation).[25] Section 25 of the 1857 Act concerns exhumation:

[It is] not lawful to remove any body, or remains of any body, which may have been interred in any place of burial, without licence under hand of one of Her Majesty's principal Secretaries of State, and with such precautions as such Secretary of State may prescribe as the condition of such licence.

The legislation in Britain was initially drafted during the Victorian era with its concerns about the violation of sepulture by 'resurrection men' snatching corpses for anatomical research and teaching.[26] This was particularly the case in Scotland, in the wake of the infamous Burke and Hare who were resorting to murder in order to obtain corpses to sell to Edinburgh's medical schools. Anatomists had been using human corpses since the seventeenth century and, prior to the Anatomy Act 1832, the penalty for murder specified not only death by hanging but also dissection by anatomists! After the 1832 Act some 50,000 corpses, mainly those of the institutional poor, ended up on the anatomist's slab within the next hundred years. More recently, the supply has come from those who donate their bodies to science. One of the oddest donations was that made to University College, London, by Jeremy Bentham, the nineteenth-century social thinker and philanthropist, who requested that his body be preserved after public dissection. Student rag week fun in the past has involved the kidnapping of his head, detached from its body. His dressed and stuffed skeleton is still on display in the college though the head has been placed in the college safe and is replaced in the glass-fronted case by a wax substitute.[27]

There have been very few recent prosecutions concerning corpses. One of the more bizarre was a case in 1960 when a man exhumed the corpse of his mother and tried to bring her back to life by attaching the body to the mains electricity supply. In less drastic circumstances, licences for exhumation are granted by the Secretary of State at the Home Office (**Figure 8.3**). Human remains may also be exhumed by order of the coroner or by a faculty of the Ordinary. The former is a warrant to exhume and is issued only in cases where there is doubt about the cause of death. The latter is granted by a diocesan bishop and concerns transfer of remains from consecrated ground to another location. A faculty of the Ordinary was granted to Dante Gabriel Rossetti in 1869 when he decided to recover the manuscript of poems that he had placed in his wife's coffin.

The Secretary of State's licence is regularly obtained by archaeologists on finding human remains or in advance of their likely discovery, and is usually used for unconsecrated ground. In the case of known recent cemeteries the Disused Burial Grounds (Amendment) Act is the more appropriate legislation. This requires that prior notice of the removal of remains must be given by the developers both in the newspapers and on the land in question. Clearances of church crypts prior to development are similarly governed by the 1981 Act.

The public are probably unaware that most cemetery excavations are carried out not by archaeologists but by commercial enterprises such as Necropolis who carry out large-scale clearance of cemeteries in advance of development. The latter are not popular with archaeologists because their low-cost methods of exhumation involve heavy machinery, very often on cemetery sites of archaeological significance. In a recent case London archaeologists, wishing to excavate a medieval burial ground, had to carry out the excavation for the same cost that a clearance firm had quoted to the developers.

The procedure for obtaining a licence for exhumation is relatively straightforward. However, a lack of communication and understanding has sometimes led to unfortunate results. Coroners are not always fully apprised of what situations require archaeological intervention. Church authorities have also consented to highly damaging works affecting ancient burials in churchyards without any archaeological provision. The issuing of

Licence Number: 0938

File Number: BCR/98 5/6/1

LICENCE FOR THE REMOVAL OF HUMAN REMAINS

In virtue of the power vested in me by Section 25 of the Burial Act, 1857 (20 & 21 Vic., cap.81), I hereby grant licence for the removal of the remains of **persons unknown** from the place in which they are now interred, in the place known as ████████, ████████, ████████, South Yorkshire (NGR SE ██ ██).

2.   It is a condition of this licence that the following precautions shall be observed:-

    (a)   The removal shall be effected with due care and attention to decency.

    (b)   The ground in which the remains are interred shall be screened from the public gaze while the work of removal is in progress.

    (c)   The remains, if of sufficient scientific interest shall be examined by **Dr A Chamberlain and Dr Pia Nystrom**.

    (d)   The remains shall, if of sufficient scientific interest, be conveyed to **Doncaster Museum** for archival storage or they shall be conveyed to a burial ground in which interments may legally take place and there be reinterred.

3.   This licence merely exempts those from the penalties which would be incurred if the removal took place without a licence. It does not in any way alter civil rights. It does not confer the right to bury the remains in any place where such right does not already exist.

4.   This licence expires on **30 APRIL 1998**.

HOME OFFICE   **One of Her Majesty's Principal**
17 March 1998   **Secretaries of State**

8.3 A Home Office licence. Conditions such as the screening of remains from the public and the reburial of Christian remains after a sufficient period of study are usually specified.

licences by the Home Office does not require any consultation with English Heritage or its Welsh counterpart Cadw, the government's advisory bodies on heritage matters. A recent example of this lack of consultation was revealed when builders were constructing an extension to a private house at Towton in North Yorkshire. This was on the site of the battle of Towton in 1461, the bloodiest battle on British soil, which was fought between the armies of Edward IV and Henry VI during the Wars of the Roses. The slain were buried in a series of large pits and one of these lay directly under the house.

A licence to exhume the battle-scarred skeletons had been obtained without any requirement for archaeological investigation; fortunately one of the building contractors realized the extent of the damage being caused in construction and called in the archaeologists. As a result a considerable amount was learned about medieval face-to-face combat, such as the concentration of injuries to the head in the form of crushing (mace, flail or morning star), slashing (sword or dagger) and piercing (poleaxe or battleaxe) traumas, probably inflicted when the victim was already lying on the ground. Previously wounded soldiers were also killed in combat, one suffering from a severely damaged lower jaw. The rugged muscle attachments on their bones also indicate physically strenuous lives and 'occupational injuries' are documented by traumatic lesions probably caused during archery practice on the longbow.[28]

In Scotland the police should be informed of the find.[29] The Procurator Fiscal then decides what action should be taken. However, the legal situation is murkier than in England and Wales: all human remains have the 'right of sepulture' and deliberate violation of a burial is a criminal act. Disturbance of remains where public decency is considered to have been offended is also an offence. Archaeologists have no legal right to excavate human remains, a situation which has even led to Historic Scotland themselves, the government agency, being refused permission to excavate. In 1991 Stranraer Sheriff Court responded to local objections and prevented the disinterring of medieval bodies at Whithorn Priory, where Historic Scotland had intended to excavate in order to repair the fabric of historic buildings.[30]

ARCHAEOLOGY AND THE PUBLIC IN BRITAIN

British attitudes to dead bodies are ambivalent, contradictory and volatile.[31] Any archaeological enquiry into human remains must take on board the values, beliefs and social context of that work and attempt to understand and mould public attitudes. What has been called the pornography of death may create, on the one hand, a grim fascination and morbid voyeurism and, on the other, a prudish prurience and fear of obscenity.[32] There is no doubt that skeletons are crowd-pullers but people often become extremely worried when those remains retain flesh and skin. Another contradiction lies in our medical treatment of the dead. We do not want to confront our mortality and, to that end, death is treated as a medical failure and is hidden from society at large. Yet there is a 500-year old tradition of scientific, post-mortem 'violation' for determining cause of death and the health of the nation. We do and we don't want to know about death; archaeology is the only medium by which many people will ever see or touch the remains of dead bodies.

Two newspaper items published on the same day, 24 May 1991, illustrate the contradictory nature of the British public's reaction to ancient human remains. One is from the *Guardian*, a national newspaper, about the discovery of a 1200–1500-year old skeleton in Southwark in south London, found during archaeological excavations in advance of development. Alongside a close-up photograph of a trepanned skull, the article enthuses about the discovery and what may be learned from it. The other report is from the local *North Norfolk News* about 500–1000-year-old human bones from a ruined medieval churchyard eroding out of the sea cliff at Eccles. There appears to have been no archaeological involvement but some of the bones had been taken by souvenir hunters. The manager of a nearby holiday camp is quoted as saying that people who took the bones 'must be sick'.

Spiritual notions about the dead may be equally confused. On one hand, spirituality and mysticism may foster fears and beliefs about violation of sepulture and resting in peace. On the other, the decline in belief in the resurrection of the body has contributed to the removal of the dead, physically and spiritually, from the world of the living. The Church of England has no particular or strong line on the disturbance of human remains. Most clerics would consider that mortal remains are but a shell vacated by the soul and thus of little spiritual significance. Doctrine and practice in England do not hold the disturbance of human remains as especially serious. In any case, many Christian and pre-Christian burials in Britain have never been allowed to 'rest in peace' since removal and disturbance have been regular and necessary aspects of churchyard burial and of earlier forms of funerary treatment involving secondary rites. Yet there are always small minorities who will be deeply offended by any disturbance of the dead.

Finally, the physical body is often a metaphor for the body social. For many social and ethnic groups, disturbance of the dead is disturbance of society at large, its traditions, beliefs and security. For groups that feel marginalized, threatened or oppressed, disturbance of even their ancient dead may be unthinkable. Conversely, during excavations in the crypt of Spitalfields Church, descendants of some of the dead were involved in researching their ancestors who died in eighteenth- and nineteenth-century London. Many were members of the Huguenot Society of Great Britain and the Australian Society of Genealogists and were not only deeply interested in the project but were able to contribute valuable historical information about their dead ancestors.[33]

Richard Morris, the director of the Council for British Archaeology (CBA), has warned of archaeologists crossing the boundary between science and voyeurism by digging post-medieval graveyards simply because they are rescue sites.[34] It has also been suggested by developers that archaeological consultants don't always seem to know the purpose or value of investigating these cemetery groups. Archaeologists have to be clear about their research questions and about communicating these to the public. Not only do we need to ask what life was like in the past but we should also be asking what we can learn about us from these studies.

Scientific analyses of nutrition, health, disease, injury and mortality in past populations may well benefit our understanding of current ailments such as arthritis and bone cancer or trends such as environmental and dietary changes. Studies of past attitudes to death, attitudes to the body, social structure, ethnicity, gender and class will also have an impact on how we see ourselves, perhaps coming to terms with our own mortality and providing a new perspective on the short-term present, reflecting on the strangeness of our own beliefs and practices today.

Archaeologists are particularly sensitive to bad public relations and are likely to back down in the face of orchestrated criticism over issues such as disturbance and reburial. Post-modernist thought has tended to cause a loss of nerve among practitioners rather than discussion of how best to harness the power relations in which archaeologists are involved. Some archaeologists in Britain hold religious beliefs and a few are genuinely uncomfortable with human remains, but for others, wavering about where they stand, adoption of a spurious sanctimoniousness is not an acceptable position. Unlike in North America and Australia, archaeologists in Britain are themselves indigenous, with a share and a say in our cultural life, past and present. Equally, archaeology is itself a cultural tradition in Britain rather than the second wave of colonialism that it has been in other countries. We have no right to tell other nations' indigenous groups what to do but we have every right to change the way that people think in our own culture.

CODES OF ETHICS FOR THE TREATMENT OF HUMAN REMAINS

International guidance for museums which have human remains in their collections is provided by the International Council on Museums (ICOM) in its 1986 code of ethics. Human remains should be securely housed and carefully maintained. They should be available to qualified researchers and educators 'but not to the morbidly curious'. Research and curation should be to standards acceptable to professionals and to those of various beliefs 'in particular members of the community, ethnic or religious groups concerned'. On the question of the public display of human remains, they say 'Although it is occasionally necessary to use human remains and other sensitive material in interpretive exhibits, this must be done with tact and with respect for the feelings of human dignity held by all peoples.'

The Vermillion Accord

In August 1989, at the University of South Dakota in Vermillion, the World Archaeological Congress held its first Inter-Congress. The subject was 'Archaeological Ethics and the Treatment of the Dead'. Among the two hundred participants were Native Americans, Australian and Tasmanian Aboriginals, Saami, Maori, Cameroonian, Zimbabwean and Indian representatives. Michael Day, a senior British physical anthropologist, drafted a series of six statements calling for mutual respect for the beliefs of indigenous peoples as well as the importance of science and education.[35] This accord was accepted by the conference. Although it can be criticized for its ambiguities,[36] the accord has been a successful basis for negotiation and reconciliation.

1. Respect for the mortal remains of the dead shall be accorded to all irrespective of origin, race, religion, nationality, custom and tradition.
2. Respect for the wishes of the dead concerning disposition shall be accorded whenever possible, reasonable and lawful, when they are known or can be reasonably inferred.
3. Respect for the wishes of the local community and of relatives or guardians of the dead shall be accorded whenever possible, reasonable and lawful.
4. Respect for scientific research value of skeletal, mummified and other human remains (including fossil hominids) shall be accorded when such value is demonstrated to exist.
5. Agreement on the disposition of fossil, skeletal, mummified and other remains shall be reached by negotiation on the basis of mutual respect for the legitimate concerns of communities for the proper disposition of their ancestors, as well as the legitimate concerns of science and education.
6. The express recognition that the concerns of various ethnic groups, as well as those of science, are legitimate and to be respected, will permit acceptable agreements to be reached and honoured.

Towards a code of ethics for human remains in the British Isles

In Britain the responses to archaeological excavation of human remains have varied from outrage and demands for instant reburial, as at Jewbury, to cooperation in analysis, as at Spitalfields Church, to archaeological analysis and museum retention of remains. Archaeologists themselves are divided about these issues. Recent articles and letters in *British Archaeological News* indicate that this problem continues to arise, especially for burial sites of the eighteenth and nineteenth centuries in Britain.[37] Unless a coherent and agreed ethical code is adopted for the treatment of human remains throughout the British Isles, we shall continue in a rather haphazard and confused manner which will cause further blunders, misunderstandings and distrust among archaeologists and their public.

Examples of suitable codes and good practice are the policy and guidance notes produced by Historic Scotland and English Heritage. The Institute of Field Archaeologists (IFA) has published a technical paper on the legal position but its Code of Practice does not make any reference to the treatment of human remains.[38]

Historic Scotland's policy document *The Treatment of Human Remains in Archaeology* covers six objectives and associated policies to achieve them. These are:

- to require the lawful and respectful treatment of human remains by staff, contractors and grantees;
- to ensure that human remains are not needlessly damaged, disturbed or destroyed at protected monuments;
- to ensure that human remains are carefully excavated and removed prior to damaging development;
- to ensure that a decision is made after proper study, normally for museum curation but recognizing that remains of late medieval-modern Christians will occasionally be reburied, that religions such as Judaism have a strong need for immediate reburial, and considering the views of the local community;
- to ensure best working practices in recording and recovery;
- to encourage discussion of issues relating to human remains, including the sensitive handling of resulting controversies.

English Heritage's 1990 policy note on *Human Remains on Historic Properties* was drafted in association with their proposal to rebury skeletal remains from the medieval churches of Wharram Percy and Barton-on-Humber. These bones are to be retrievable for research purposes, sealed in plastic containers in a watertight vault within the excavated and conserved historic property of the Saxon church at Barton-on-Humber (**Figure 8.4**). The policy note outlines the archaeological importance of studying human remains, the legal obligations during investigation, and the need for sensitive handling, reburial and non-disturbance where possible. It emphasizes the needs of academic research for maintaining accessibility for future study and for reburial in contexts which are easily recoverable. Finally, consideration should be given to reburial with appropriate religious rites.

The reburial of Christian remains has been a prominent feature of archaeological excavations in recent years. At Butt Road in Colchester a probable Roman church was associated with a Roman cemetery of west–east inhumations.[39] The issue of reburial becomes complex in such situations because it highlights the problem of deciding what constitutes a 'Christian' archaeologically and whether such a distinction between Christians and non-Christians should be observed.

8.4 *After analysis of the medieval and later Christian burials excavated from around the Saxon church of Barton-on-Humber, the bones were stored in a vault inside the church.*

The situation in Britain has derived from various contexts and causes which are unique to the culture. Consequently the various codes and guidelines, both international and national, should provide a framework for devising a code of ethics specific to the particular circumstances of law, attitudes, practices and working relationships within the British Isles. Archaeologists in Britain will never be able to dictate terms to local communities on this subject, but the formulation of such a code should make it clear what our goals are and what we hope to achieve. It should provide a line in the sand or a base point from which we can negotiate and, it is hoped, reach mutually acceptable solutions.[40]

1. Legal requirements, both civil and ecclesiastical, must be observed in full by archaeologists and others involved on their behalf.
2. There must be a clear statement of research objectives prior to disturbance of burial grounds. Where groups claim an actual or cultural link with the dead then they may wish to contribute to, or have an interest in, the formulation of this research. Disturbance should be kept to a minimum in accordance with research priorities and subsequent works.
3. The archaeological excavation, analysis and deposition of human remains must be undertaken with due propriety and respect. Where burials can be identified to a particular faith or community, consideration must be given to their views on reburial with appropriate religious rites.
4. Human remains are an important archaeological resource and should normally be curated according to the standards laid down for all archaeological finds. If reburial is unavoidable it should take place after completion of specialist study

and be retrievable, i.e. the remains must be adequately recorded and labelled in permanent containers deposited in a secure, watertight vault from which they can easily be recovered.

5. Respect for the wishes of the dead concerning disposition shall be accorded whenever possible, reasonable and lawful, when they are known.

6. Agreement on the disposition of human remains shall be reached by negotiations between archaeologists and any group expressing a concern, where conventional procedures of investigation and deposition are not considered to apply.

7. Archaeologists must be committed to public education and interest in the value of studying human remains.

8. Exhibition of human remains should be handled tactfully and with respect for feelings of human dignity.

9. Human remains in museum and vault storage should be made available to *bona fide* researchers, students and other legitimately interested persons.

10. Requests for the restitution of human remains collected from other nations should be honoured, after negotiation and agreement on appropriate conditions of reburial, curation or exhibition.

PLUNDERING AND PILLAGING THE DEAD – THE PROBLEM OF LOOTING

In 1987 looters (*huaqueros*) broke into and pillaged one of the most spectacular burials ever found. The 1750-year-old tomb at Sipán, in Peru, contained hundreds of gold artefacts along with the central grave of a Moche nobleman, accompanied by several graves of retainers. Archaeologists managed to reach the site and disturb the *huaqueros*, thereby salvaging something of the context of this remarkable find.[41] The Sipán incident is just one case in a worldwide epidemic of disturbing burials for the valuable artefacts that they might contain. Throughout countries in South and Central America such as Ecuador, Colombia, Peru and Guatemala, *huaqueros* are often better armed than the police who may not always be enthusiastic about catching up with them. In North America pothunters dig Native American burials as well as settlements for artefacts to collect and sell, especially from sites on private land which cannot be protected. The Mediterranean countries have been home to indigenous and foreign looters for centuries. Nations caught up in wars and other political upheavals, such as Iran, Afghanistan and Iraq, have similarly suffered from looting of ancient tombs, often by local populations.[42]

It is often the poverty-stricken local communities who are involved in the looting, making only a little money to supplement their agricultural activities. The middlemen dealers buy cheap and sell dear while poorly paid government officials may make a bit by turning a blind eye. The real profits are made in Europe and North America. Auction houses take a percentage from the seller and buyer; governments collect tax and also like to encourage people to come to their country to buy and sell; collectors amass large collections and even larger fortunes. If the collectors didn't want these things we wouldn't have a problem. In Ricardo Elia's words, 'The truth is that collectors are the real looters.'[43] Of course, they compete in a market where they will be bidding against respectable museums and where beautiful publications and esteemed academics lend credibility, exclusivity and élan to their activities.

Most nations have legislation restricting removal or export of cultural property.[44] But international smuggling is rife. In 1990 Geraldine Norman, an art correspondent, estimated that 80 per cent of antiquities on the market were illegally excavated and smuggled. The USA, a signatory to the 1970 UNESCO Convention on Cultural Property, will not allow the import of stolen objects such as those from Central America,[45] so they are flown to London or other European cities and sold at auction houses or direct to American dealers and collectors, thus ending up in the United States. Moves have been made to restrict the sale of pilfered artefacts. The British Museum supports the spirit of the UNESCO convention, and most museums in the west have collecting policies which prevent them from acquiring stolen and undocumented material. British auctioneers and dealers even have a code of practice for the control of international trading in works of art (1984) by which members of the UK fine art and antiques trade undertake not to import, export or transfer the ownership of objects which they believe have been acquired in or exported from their country of origin in violation of that country's laws. The problem, of course, is that proof is usually hard to come by since all unprovenanced antiquities are tainted with suspicion.[46] As Oscar Muscarella stated in 1983, 'Every object that surfaces on the art market is plundered . . . End of discussion.'[47]

Compromises and climb-downs have been attempted in many countries. In Ecuador the state's Anthropology Museum has tried to work with the *huaqueros* rather than ignoring them, by buying their looted antiquities so as to keep them in the country, putting them on display for local people, and attracting foreign archaeologists to come and see them even though they are without context. In one area of Ecuador *huaqueros* have even been taught to use archaeological techniques.[48]

Until a few years ago the Oxford Archaeological Laboratory used to validate the authenticity of any artefact brought to them by techniques such as thermoluminescence; the fees from this service raised money which could be used to fund other aspects of the laboratory's research. Many West African 2000-year-old terracotta statuettes, thought to represent the spirits of the dead in prehistoric Mali, have been looted by villagers and sold on by international merchants to collectors and museums, and were previously dated by the OAL without their needing to see an export licence.[49] In 1993 the Metropolitan Museum of Art in New York finally returned a group of 363 artefacts, mostly of gold and silver, which had been looted from a group of sixth-century BC burial mounds in the Manisa and Usak regions of Turkey in 1966. The looters had been prosecuted but the artefacts were sold to dealers in Switzerland and New York who sold them to the Metropolitan Museum for $1.5 million. For twenty-five years the Turkish authorities were stonewalled by the Metropolitan whose staff consistently denied that they had the material and even displayed it with a misleading provenance.[50]

Collecting is a multi-million pound industry and governments and their archaeological advisors are often powerless to intervene effectively since proof of illicit removal within one country is difficult to obtain when the artefacts arrive in another country. Archaeologists feel very strongly about the problem of looting. Not only are archaeological sites destroyed worldwide but the remains of the past are stripped of their contexts and revered for their financial worth rather than their cultural value. The problem is compounded by public perceptions of archaeology and its practitioners, since there is still a predominant view that archaeologists are themselves treasure hunters who are simply trying to keep others off their lucrative patch. The market-place morality of the 1980s has also contributed to the erosion of notions of public ownership, replaced by feelings that private ownership of the past is perfectly acceptable. Archaeologists and government officials may be somewhat out on a limb in condemning the looting of burials, the illicit sale of artefacts and the subsequent collecting by enthusiasts.

Solutions need to be found in many different directions. Museums should be more cooperative in cases of restitution. Auction houses and importing countries must require better documentation. Nations where looting occurs will need to curtail the looting of sites, and archaeologists must put across their message clearly and forcefully to the public at large.[51]

The antiquities trade results in the deprivation of local communities' heritage, the damage and destruction of archaeological sites, the loss of knowledge specifically about context and more generally about the past, the loss of public access to treasures in publicly accountable museums, the alienation of indigenous people from their cultural traditions, and the fostering of links among *huaqueros* and middlemen to organized crime.

THE ARCHAEOLOGY OF TWENTIETH-CENTURY ATROCITIES

Another political arena in which archaeologists have found themselves is that of documenting the atrocities committed during the wars of the twentieth century. In the face of government denials, official cover-ups, and intimidation of local survivors, it has often been extremely difficult to document and verify accounts of massacres. Only in recent years were the mass graves of victims of German Nazis and Soviet Stalinists uncovered by archaeologists to establish once and for all who was responsible and who died.[52] At Serniki in the Ukraine Richard Wright and his Australian team excavated the remains of 550 Jewish victims of a Nazi massacre during the Second World War. Similar excavations have been conducted on the mass graves of those murdered by the Soviets. Mass graves from three sites in western Russia have been excavated by a team led by Marek Urbanski, yielding the remains of 25,700 Poles killed in April and May 1940. Most of them were Polish army officers captured at the beginning of the war; 14,700 of the bodies have been identified by their uniforms and equipment. Exhumation has also begun on the thirty thousand political victims of Stalin's secret service, the NKVD, who were buried in hundreds of mass graves in the Kuropaty Woods near Minsk.

More recently archaeologists and forensic anthropologists have been involved in recovering the remains of victims of military human rights violations over the last thirty years. Between 1976 and 1983 more than a thousand people 'disappeared' under the Argentinian military regime.[53] With the restoration of democracy in 1983 investigations began immediately. In 1984 the American forensic anthropologist Clyde Snow began supervising the excavation and exhumation of the victims, providing testimony which resulted in the sentencing of five out of nine generals and admirals on trial. Snow also led teams in Guatemala and Mexico in 1994.[54] Similar projects to recover those murdered by military forces have been set up in El Salvador, Haiti, Honduras, the Philippines and Rwanda.[55]

Much of this work is carried out under the auspices of the Physicians for Human Rights (PHR), a Boston-based organization of scientists using forensics to investigate and prevent violations of international human rights and humanitarian law. In ten years it has been involved in exhumations and autopsies of alleged torture and non-judicial execution victims in Brazil, Israel, the former Czechoslovakia, Iraq, Kurdistan, Kuwait, Panama and Thailand as well as the nations mentioned above.

Recently PHR forensic teams have worked for the United Nations excavating mass graves in the former Yugoslavia at sites like Vukovar and Srebrnica, to validate the accounts of the victims' relatives and provide evidence that will lead to prosecutions of war criminals.[56] In 1991 two hundred Croatian soldiers and hospital workers disappeared near Ovcara, while in the hands of the Serbian Yugoslav National Army (JNA). Eleven months later Snow and members of UNPROFOR discovered a grave site south-east of Ovcara and identified the exposed bones of three adult males. Two of these surface skeletons had gunshot wounds to the head. Snow's PHR team, including the archaeologist

Rebecca Saunders, returned to carry out a preliminary survey. A test trench located nine skeletons along with cartridges in a mass grave. In 1993 a PHR team, under the auspices of the UN War Crimes Commission, began full excavation. In 1995 the International Criminal Tribunal for the former Yugoslavia (ICTY) issued indictments for the killing of 260 men against three high-ranking JNA officers.[57]

WHO OWNS THE DEAD?

In 1998 an unusual court case in London centred around the use of human body parts in an exhibition of sculpture. An artist, Anthony-Noel Kelly, had obtained portions of cadavers from the Royal College of Surgeons' stores and had used them to make moulds from which he had produced casts. The trial was problematic because in Britain there is no ownership in a corpse.[58] In a historic ruling, the judge declared that the human remains 'having undergone a process of skill . . . with the object of preserving it for the purpose of medical or scientific examination' did constitute property and had thus been unlawfully removed. On appeal, the judge's verdict was upheld.[59] Up until this particular case, it could have been claimed that the collections of human remains in the many museums in Britain were not the property of those museums and that, subsequently, they had no right to keep them.

Yet who really 'owns' the ancient dead? Do they belong to the whole of humanity, whose representatives and institutions maintain their remains and learn from the past to enlighten the present? Or do they belong to the descendent communities who claim them as direct ancestors to the exclusion of everyone else? What about the remains of ancestors so ancient that they are likely to have passed on genes to everyone on the planet? Do they belong to any one ethnicity or nation?

The 'reburial' issue has come a long way since the 1970s and the tide is turning in favour of the rights of indigenous and other minority groups to decide the fate of ancestral remains. Closer cooperation and mutual respect has led to compromise and to the development of trust so that archaeologists and other academics can represent local groups as expert witnesses. There has also been a growth in numbers of indigenous archaeologists in various countries. By and large archaeologists and developers know to ensure that there is prior consultation with indigenous groups before undertaking rescue and research projects. There are also local successes in establishing 'keeping places' where local custodians may ensure the sanctity of the bones' resting place while controlling access by researchers.

There seems little doubt that the 'reburial' issue has developed out of specific historical conditions of exploitation and unequal relationships of power, albeit in many different parts of the world. It is among those communities who feel most discriminated against and under threat from the secular authorities, and often most powerless to control their own political and economic destinies, that the concerns of tampering with the ancestral dead are strongest. For indigenous groups whose ancestors were victims of atrocities and exploitation, archaeologists and anthropologists have constituted a second wave of colonialism in which science, like Christianity, has been viewed as just another vehicle of oppression. Many live with the contradiction of inhabiting and working the land yet not owning it, full citizens but of second-class status. There is a genuine desire to protect the dead and to release them from their 'prisons' in museum stores and, for many, this is a moral stance linked to a different understanding of history, in which the past lives on in the present.

At the same time, and without denying the sincerity of these concerns, the 'reburial' issue has been a rallying point for political activism, seeking to establish control over bones as symbols of power, serving to legitimize ethnicity, equality and rights over land, and challenging the racism of the colonial majority. Sometimes respect for the dead has been imported through western Christian teachings to indigenous peoples who traditionally were unconcerned by the fate of human remains.[60] In broader political terms, indigenous peoples have not managed to gain back the lands and resources that were taken from them by governments and settlers but they have won a symbolic victory which has helped to restore pride and respect in indigenous identity. In many cases the general public acknowledges the histories of oppression and dislocation suffered by indigenous minorities and has been broadly sympathetic to their aims in restricting the activities of archaeologists. At the same time archaeologists have had cause to remember that they should always put the living first.

Yet the future is far from certain. How far can the pendulum of redress swing before extreme demands prompt a backlash in archaeological and public opinion? Clement Meighan points to the case of an excavation in West Virginia in 1991 where not just the bones but also the artefacts, pollen samples and other material evidence in association with a 2000-year-old Adena burial mound were to be given up for reburial within a year, while Indian representatives were paid to censor 'objectionable' photographs or data from the final report. The excavation agreement also stipulated that no remains would be touched by menstruating women.[61] The Kennewick case has opened old wounds on both sides. In Australia there is growing resentment towards government support for Aboriginal land claims. The problem with emphasizing ancestral heritage, at the expense of a shared heritage of humankind, is that it seeks exclusivity and raises one ethnic group above others as somehow more 'human', leading us back into the politics of racial hatred and intolerance in a mirror image of the former situation.

The archaeologist is also enmeshed in relationships of power concerning the world of looting and illicit trading of antiquities. On the one hand there are groups who wish to prevent burials being desecrated, on the other there are local people who cannot dig them up fast enough. Here is a far greater problem which is infinitely more difficult to solve because archaeologists are not in the positions of power that they once held, and have been able to relinquish, in the 'reburial' issue. Instead, the power is very much in the hands of those who benefit from the trade at every level. Having been on the receiving end of the efforts of political activists who have campaigned effectively for their goals, it is now time for archaeologists to apply the lessons learned. By joining with indigenous and local groups whose heritage is being plundered, archaeologists can engage actively in limiting the looting and the collecting.

Archaeology is a means of studying the past so that we may know more about ourselves and about the present. As such, it is a moral pursuit in which we change not only our own views and attitudes about what it is to be fair and just but we also strive to unmask power and its effects, both past and present. Dealing with the dead, recent and ancient, inevitably must serve the living.

NINE

EPILOGUE: DEATH AND MEMORY

[A]rchitectural and ceremonial forms are frequently integrated into the descriptive imagery and paradigms used in classifying Batammaliba cosmological structure and order. Architectural representations function both as mnemonic aids and as more permanent and concrete expressions of the underlying principle on which Batammaliba cosmogony itself rests.[1]

To some people's minds, matters concerning ritual and the supernatural will, by definition, leave little or no material trace. To advance any notions about these aspects of past, and especially prehistoric societies, is to work with a minimum of evidence. Yet very often the treatment of the dead and their subsequent veneration are given material form in ways that are impossible for anyone to miss. Beliefs and rituals did not reside solely in prehistoric minds but were actualized – made real – by people's reflexive relationships with material culture, building, shaping and weaving the imaginary and incorporeal into material existence. For many past societies it is often only the material culture for the dead that has survived. Many of humanity's greatest monuments over the last ten thousand years have been religious structures built for the dead and for other supernatural forces.

Furthermore, ritual is not wholly separable from the political, social and economic aspects of life. As Gordon Childe pointed out long ago, funerary rituals can be political activities intimately associated with the grabbing of power by emergent classes and élites.[2] Tombs are not simply symbolic markers but are real components of political actuality, forming a principal means of acquiring and demonstrating power.

Faced with the universal event of a human death, people's experiences of the world during and after a death may differ individually and culturally. Funerary rituals demand participation in acknowledging the death, sharing in a sense of a common humanity, and mending the torn fabric of a bereaved community. Death forces a change in social relations: life for the living will never be the same again. The living can also profit as well as they may from both the death itself and from the opportunities presented by holding a funeral. The deceased may not actually be considered to be gone from the world, merely transformed into an ancestor, thereby providing further opportunities for the living to manipulate their relationships with each other through their relationships to the dead.

After all the rituals are completed, after new social relations have been created, after social practice has been restated or reinvented during the performance of the funeral, there remains the placing of the dead. This may relate to where someone died, where their body rested temporarily or was transformed during the rites of passage, where the remains were eventually deposited, or where their spirit ultimately resides. Any or even all of these places may be invisible and quickly forgotten, but often such places are marked or monumentalized so as to be distinctive and visible. Death is engraved on the landscape. It is re-experienced by the living whenever we see (or even think about) the event and its location. Death is never over. Business is always unfinished, because the meaning of the death and of its memory, whether enhanced or not by a monument, will forever be reworked, even by societies distant in space or time from the actual corpse. The bones of the man from Kennewick have lain forgotten in the mud for nine thousand years but he is probably more important now than he ever was in life.

Searching to interpret past societies' attempts to render ritual into material form or to provide artificial and constrained settings within which ritual might be enacted, archaeologists have frequently disagreed on what the term 'ritual' means and whether there is any value in a blanket definition which works cross-culturally as opposed to specific meanings applicable to particular cultural circumstances.

RITUAL

We may dispose of human corpses, and use or display human remains, without any intimations of ritual but such situations are often perceived as remarkable, undignified or even depraved, precisely because the prescribed, formal, dignified and emotionally affective practices which constitute ritual are missing. Indeed, the very presence of a corpse or human remains may serve to define the practices directed towards them as ritualized. It may be that the origins of ritual for the human species lie in disposing of the corpse, helping the bereaved and adjusting to the community's loss. Death is the most significant of the rites of passage in our progress from womb to tomb.

Funerary rituals commonly involve powerful emotions, appeals to the supernatural, ceremonial performances and tie-breaking acts, yet there is profound disagreement over definitions as to where ritual ends and the secular or mundane begins.[3] Returning to Ibn Fadlan's story in Chapter 1, we can recognize aspects of ritual in the naked kinsman's torching of the ship, the making of the dead man's costume, the violent death of the slave girl and many other acts. Normal social life is effectively suspended for the mourners as they take part in activities that draw on traditions and obligations, preparing the dead for the afterlife.

Ritual is one form of customary practice – in which participants are aware of socially agreed conventions from brief matters of politeness to long and elaborate religious rites – in which procedure is prescribed and explicit even though meanings may be ambiguous, mysterious or implicit. It is performance with what Gilbert Lewis calls a peculiar fixity, not always involving public ceremony.[4] It is differentiated from other social practices by its formalization and periodicity, by the centrality of emphasis on the human body, and by the invocation of representations which direct bodily posture and movement (such as praying) and redefine the body's immediate and conceptual environment.[5] Ritual performance often reveals other worlds of spirits, deities and ancestors to the participants, serving up declared truths about the meaning of life and death, speaking of worlds beyond the boundaries of the here and now, and seeking to establish seemingly autonomous social categories and distinctions such as between living and dead, ritual and mundane, or sacred and profane.[6]

Rituals are also intensely charged political moments in which the social order may be legitimized or even subverted. Ritual mastery is displayed and often contested while the ritual process involves the negotiation of power as participants seek to define and appropriate the hegemonic order. Yet the meanings of rituals may be understood differently according to position and perspective. The same ritual can be interpreted by certain participants as bringing the community together and by others as emphasizing different statuses and distinctions. Equally, participants may not understand many or all of the symbolic pointers and flourishes within a ritual but they may still be deeply affected by it emotionally.

Ritual is not something altogether removed from the everyday but is situated in constant reference to other daily and seasonal activities. It is a particular form of practice which draws on other aspects of human experience from everyday life but through more stringent, formal and prescribed conventions.[7] It demands knowledge of the conditions for its performance and focuses attention on individuals' statuses and identities. In doing so, it summons up representations of the past and an altered sense of time and change, heightening realizations that social life is not as it was, since the people playing various roles have changed.[8] These roles are expressions of status, perhaps embodied by ceremonial clothing or bodily mutilation, which may relate to, rather than directly reflect, social position. Within ritual the past pervades the present. Lists of genealogies, titles and obligations may be recited and the existence of invisible entities – roles and corporate groups as well as ghosts and spirits – proclaimed. It may be considered as time out of time, betwixt and between the normal passing of time; it may make time go backwards or even make time continue in ensuring the rising of the sun.

Rituals are normally conservative, preserving ways of doing things – speaking, gesturing, dressing – while these things change in everyday life. The practices involved in funerary rites may be the most conservative of all; we might dress in outmoded mourning clothes and use coffins whose basic design has not changed substantially for hundreds of years. Yet funerary fashions can change very quickly. Undertakers' and stonemasons' catalogues are full of constantly changing styles of coffins and tombstones. Even outside the capitalist commercialism of death, traditional societies may be not so traditional after all when it comes to funerary ritual – it can be a context for innovation and change. Certain aspects of funerary ritual change very quickly and in non-linear directions, particularly those things that leave no visible mark, such as the order of a funeral procession. Other changes may be longer lasting or may progress in a more linear way, such as methods of tomb construction and the architectural styles involved. Indeed, funerary monumentality is ritual materialized and petrified, visible for all to see centuries after the event.

ARCHITECTURE, DEATH AND MONUMENTS

In an interesting study of architecture in prehistory, Peter Wilson suggests that the grave and the house have been powerful symbolic features in human evolution, firstly with the house and its symbolism after ten thousand years ago and secondly with the tomb.[9] Within Wilson's scheme, gatherer-hunter societies have no funerary architecture and thus it has been absent for all but the last ten thousand years of human history, becoming significant after five thousand years ago.

He sees monumental funerary architecture as succeeding the 'house' phenomenon of domestication, a view similar to that put forward by Ian Hodder in his study of the European Neolithic.[10] Wilson identifies a particular phase, broadly after five thousand years ago, when tombs became more substantial than houses, when the deceased and their tombs were made the centre and focus of life itself. Tombs had become literally 'power houses'.

There has been a tendency to view funerary architecture in isolation from domestic and other forms of architecture. Suzanne Preston Blier's insightful analysis of Batammaliba architecture, quoted above, illustrates some of the metaphorical connections that are possible between house and tomb. Tombs may be houses of the ancestors or, alternatively, the living may consider themselves to dwell within the houses of the ancestors. The tombs of the pharaohs and nobles in the Valley of the Kings replicate and exaggerate the passageways, staircases and ramps of their above-ground palaces and temples and are adorned with paintings in which the life above ground is replicated in the tomb. The architectures of life and death are not simply metaphorical transformations of each other and of the cosmos – they form part of a greater whole, humanity's understanding and quest for the meaning of life in the face of death.

9.1 The Great Pyramid of Khufu built c. *2540* BC. *It stands 147m high and was constructed of 2.3 million carved stone blocks each weighing an average of 2.5 tonnes.*

Death has inspired some of the world's greatest architecture. Two of the ancient world's great wonders were tombs: the great pyramids (**Figure 9.1**) and the mausoleum of Halicarnassus. The latter was the resting place of Mausolus, the Persian satrap of Caria (Asia Minor) who died in 353 or 352 BC, and was built either by him or by his sister and wife Artemisia. Although under Islamic tradition stone memorials should be erected only if it is feared that the grave might not be recognized, the Taj Mahal ('abode of the chosen one') at Agra is another tomb synonymous with architectural magnificence and beauty. It was built between 1631 and 1653 by the Mogul emperor Shah Jahan, as a mausoleum for his favourite wife Mumtaz Mahal, who bore him fourteen children and was buried here in 1632. Supposedly a monument inspired by his grief, it is one of a series of massive building projects, including forts, mosques, trunk roads and other public edifices, through which he built Mogul rule into the landscape of northern India. The Taj Mahal and its garden may additionally be a materialization of heaven on earth, constructing conceptions of the afterlife in solid form as an ultimate symbol of Mogul rule under Shah Jahan.

Tombs are not just somewhere to put dead bodies: they are representations of power (**Figure 9.2**). Like ritual, funerary architecture legitimizes and extends the hegemonic order. Tombs can be the focus of a society's economy, towards which the accumulation of wealth and surplus are directed. They are artefacts which must have profoundly altered prehistoric peoples' comprehension of space and time. Tombs are often vast, substantial and beautiful, massively constructed from many smaller elements to provide an effect of permanence which appears to overcome death. This monumental permanence also changes the lived landscape forever, forming a fixed point in time and space for future generations.

9.2 Outside the Kremlin two soldiers stand guard at the door of Lenin's tomb. From on top of the tomb, which contains his embalmed body, Soviet dignitaries used to watch the May Day parades.

The Rus of the tenth century might have kept alive the memory of that remarkable funeral of their kinsman, passed down over several generations, but the mound served as a visible, physical manifestation of the event, the culmination of the funerary process but also the beginning of remembrance and commemoration. In constructing the burial mound with its great birch post, the Rus were fixing their dead firmly in that Volga landscape so that it would remain for many centuries after they departed.

CONCLUSION

I have ended this book by focusing on the two major facets of the archaeology of funerary practices – the rituals which accompany death and the monuments which reveal its presence to the world. Ritual – the intangible indicator of a death – has in the past been dismissed as an irretrievably lost aspect of prehistory but, as this book has shown, we can today approach the study of human behaviour in past societies with new theories and new understanding. On the other hand, funerary architecture – the most enduring sign of a past life – has sometimes been treated with a certain theoretical simplicity. Archaeologists have in recent years refined their approaches to the meaning and causes of monumentality, by keeping ever-present in their theories the individuals whose diverse motivations led to the construction of the tombs and burial places which still mark our landscape.

Archaeology has grown beyond attempts to explain all human life according to universal laws of behaviour. We now move towards the understanding and explanation of the past through more subtle ideas about human experience and perception. Archaeology can range across space and time to excavate and understand the many paths we make but, immanent in the diversity of life, there is one universal – death. We are all ultimately going in the same direction.

EXCAVATING HUMAN REMAINS

Contrary to popular belief, archaeologists no longer behave like Indiana Jones or Lara Croft, the animated heroine of *Tomb Raider*. When we venture to disturb the dead, archaeology requires both meticulous excavation and recording and also sensitive handling and dignified treatment to accommodate the feelings of the living. Archaeologists and other researchers have developed many techniques and approaches for recovering different kinds of information from human remains and the particular structures and environments in which they have survived the centuries and millennia. There is now a huge international body of literature on excavation and recording techniques and standards, archaeological project organization and management, legal requirements and scientific analytical techniques.[1] What is provided here is a summary of excavation techniques to give the reader an idea of the procedures involved.

PRE-EXCAVATION

All fieldwork should have a project design which includes research objectives, methodology, timetable, costing and provision for post-excavation analysis and writing-up.[2] All site workers should be fully briefed and familiarized with methods of recording and excavating, and identification of different archaeological materials including human bone. There is no excuse for not knowing the relevant legislation and obtaining the necessary licences, agreements and permissions from, in England, the Home Office, the local authority, the land owner, the tenant and the county archaeologist. It is always worth making sure that all parties with a potential interest in the work are informed before beginning the excavation. This includes the parish council, the police, the local public and, where appropriate, the local clergy. Nobody likes to feel left in the dark and very often difficulties and misunderstandings can be nipped in the bud with adequate prior consultation.

Arrangements must be made for on-site specialists and specialist equipment; if sampling for DNA surviving in human bones, sterile suits and gloves are recommended though they are no guarantee of sterile conditions. Arrangements for eventual deposition of bones and other finds should also be made before excavation. The site safety officer should ensure that site workers are inoculated against tetanus – other diseases are very unlikely to survive more than fifty years on sites where bodies have become skeletonized. However, if sealed lead coffins are expected then consultation with the local Health and Safety Executive is essential since there may well be risks from lead poisoning, smallpox, anthrax and fungal diseases. Additionally some site workers may be in danger of suffering psychologically where soft tissue on the remains survives largely intact.

On cemetery sites identified for development, it is rare that gravestones have not been previously cleared. Where they remain *in situ* and can be recorded prior to excavation, the

CBA have published a manual for their recording.[3] Occasionally, there may be a plan of the graveyard which identifies the named plots of individuals and families.

EXCAVATING INHUMATIONS

When excavating cemetery burials, excavation should be conducted in an atmosphere of respect and dignity. This does not mean that everyone walks about looking like Victorian mutes. It does mean that you don't put cigarettes in the skeletons' mouths, wrap them in scarves, do impersonations of 'Alas poor Yorick', or re-enact *Clan of the Cave Bear* by waving a femur over your head. A Home Office licence will normally specify that the human remains are to be screened from public view. This does not mean that the public aren't allowed to see them or should be kept at bay; visitors can be asked if they would like to see the skeletons and they will certainly want to. The screening, which can be done with wooden panels or with fine-meshed, coloured netting, should satisfy those who do not wish to see exposed bones.

Ancient human remains are fragile. When excavating a skeleton, delicate tools such as a plasterer's leaf, plastic spatulae, paintbrushes and wooden toothpicks are used to gently prise away the soil without dislodging the bones (**Figure 10.1**). The soil from around the hands and feet, the abdomen and chest, and the head is later sieved through a 2mm mesh (this will invariably mean wet-sieving) to recover the tiny hand and feet bones, any gall, kidney or urinary stones, any foetal bones in the pelvic area, the occasionally ossified cartilage of the larynx, loose teeth and the tiny ear bones and hyoid bone of the throat. The soil from around and under infant burials should also be sieved. In the adult human skeleton there are 206 bones, many fewer than the unfused bones of infants and juveniles. While the skeleton is in the ground it may display visible signs of abnormalities such as a twisted spine or a slipped joint which might not be apparent later and can be recognized on site by the osteological specialist.

Extremely fragile or composite grave goods (such as necklaces or box fittings) should be left *in situ* after recording and then lifted in a soil block for detailed excavation in the laboratory. Block removal of human remains should be carried out only in special circumstances; bog bodies and frozen bodies are examples.

10.1 *Excavating a Pictish burial (c. AD 500) at Kilpheder, South Uist. The body of this forty-year-old woman was, for reasons unknown, interfered with some months after death. Her sternum was removed and her right hand moved from her chest to her waist – the bones of part of her hand were left in the chest cavity. The corpse was also tilted on one side.*

In non-calcareous soils bodies may be reduced to stains and silhouettes or may leave no trace at all. In acidic sands these stains can be identified either by digging a sequence of thin spits and recording at each spit level, or by attempting to remove the clean sand from around the stain, as in the case of the Sutton Hoo 'sandmen'.[4] In such cases other stains may be identifiable as items additional to the corpse, such as coffin planks, animal skins and pieces of organic grave goods. The stained sand should be sprayed with a chemical consolidant as soon as it is exposed. In one of the burial pits from Sutton Hoo there was no visible trace at all of the corpse but close interval sampling of the basal layer of the grave led to the identification of concentrations of certain trace elements which may have resulted from a wholly decayed body.

Sampling

Soil samples should be taken on the advice of an environmental specialist, normally to test pH (to assess how soil acidity may have affected bone preservation and diagenesis), to provide samples for trace element analyses (either as controls or to confirm the presence of a corpse if its physical traces have gone), to recover pollen potentially from floral tributes (if the soil is sufficiently acid or waterlogged), to recover fly and beetle remains (if the soil has remained waterlogged or if their impressions survive in clay around the corpse), and to recover snails (if the soil is sufficiently alkaline). The latter may provide evidence for lengthy post-mortem pre-burial treatment. Even in soils where pollen does not normally survive, pollen samples can be taken from the copper-stained soil around copper alloy grave goods.

Recent advances in the recovery of ancient DNA indicate that much may be learned from sampling inhumations. However, a specialist's advice is always needed. Sterile suits and gloves are recommended to minimize the amount of contaminating DNA which is continuously shed by the excavator. DNA is best preserved in very dry or frozen conditions. Otherwise it will occasionally survive in well-preserved bone and is best sampled from canine or molar teeth where the enamel is not worn through. In this way samples can be extracted under laboratory conditions, irrespective of prior handling; in any case, laboratory contamination is always the biggest problem. Such analyses are most worthwhile on large cemetery groups and may not yield meaningful results on individuals or small populations.

Radiocarbon samples should be collected on site, selecting bones – such as an upper rib – that are likely to have sufficient collagen, for immediate foil wrapping within sealed plastic bags. Human bones from coastal areas, where people have been eating seafood, may be affected by the marine reservoir effect, which leads to radiocarbon determinations older than the true age on account of the intake of ancient marine carbon, although this seems to apply only in extreme cases where seafoods are a staple diet. Radiocarbon samples should also be considered from the wooden hafts of spears and other grave goods or the residues inside ceramic or metal containers if they survive.

Problems of stratigraphy and excavation method

In densely packed medieval and later churchyards there are likely to be stratigraphic problems; the excavator will be unable to see the individual grave cuts at any height above the skeleton itself. Occasionally there will be mortar spreads and surfaces which will show where graves have been cut though them and which also seal earlier burials. These and the evidence of skeletons cut through by later burials may be the only retrievable stratigraphic relationships for churchyard burials. The mortar spreads may be dateable by linking them to the particular build of the church to which they relate and dating that build by its architectural style. Each burial should, where possible, be dug in a day. They should not be left overnight because of their fragility and the possibility of vandalism.

Medieval and later grave cuts are not normally dug with a section left across the middle but there are circumstances when a section across the grave cut, rather than just a profile, is needed. Prehistoric skeletons and grave fills sometimes exhibit post-mortem damage and intrusion which may go unnoticed if a grave cut is not dug in half section. When digging down towards the skeleton, the fill layer should be dug in spits, commencing at the likely head end so that the skull will be found first, before encountering the smaller bones.

Palaeolithic human remains can pose their own excavation problems (**Figure 7.4**). Most are found in cave sediments which require modified techniques of excavation. Fossil human bones are often held in a hard matrix which must be carefully chiselled away, normally after lifting and moving to the laboratory.

Survival of soft tissue

Soft tissue decays at different rates according to conditions of soil type and climate.[5] There are few exceptional circumstances in which the excavator of remains older than a hundred years can expect to find surviving tissue. Lead coffins create an anaerobic environment, like that found in the well preserved medieval burial at St Bees in Cumbria.[6]

In certain boggy conditions corpses can survive in peat so that the skin is preserved even though most or all of the bones have dissolved away. The stomach and intestines may contain a mine of information about the individual's last meal, internal parasites, and surrounding environment. The cut of the hair – head, facial and body – and the treatment of the skin, whether tattooed, scarred, pierced or painted, may speak reams about past conceptions of personal appearance and identity. Hands, feet, skin and nails may even hold secrets about occupations and status.

Frozen or freeze-dried corpses, though not always from funerary contexts as in the case of the Alpine Iceman, may provide even more spectacular glimpses into past cultures. Similar situations may be found in dry environments where natural or artificial mummification has resulted in extraordinary conditions of preservation. It appears that these frozen or dry conditions provide the best circumstances for the likely survival of biomolecular material such as DNA.

EXCAVATING CREMATIONS

Cremated bones can turn up in all sorts of contexts (single fragments, scatters in a ditch fill or on a pyre surface) but are mostly encountered as deposits in small pits, with or without pottery or organic containers. Burnt bones are extremely fragile and must be disturbed as little as possible during excavation. Cremation deposits not placed in a container or in a pot that has been smashed should be excavated with similar care to digging inhumations. Undisturbed cremation deposits can be dug in 20mm spits to recover the deposition sequence of the bones and grave goods. The whole cremation pit fill should be sampled by flotation, wet-sieved through a 2mm mesh to recover charred plant and wood remains as well as small pieces of bone. The same goes for pyre deposits, if they can be located by using magnetic susceptibility and magnetometry after initial stripping of the site. Cremations in pots or other containers should be bandaged and lifted for excavation in the laboratory.

Burnt bone is unlikely to have much potential for DNA or other molecular analyses, chemical analysis or radiocarbon dating because of the diagenetic effects of the cremation fire but approximate age and often sex of the deceased can be ascertained with some certainty. The size of the bone fragments, their weight and quantity, the remains of items burnt on the pyre, and the presence of charcoal may allow the archaeologist to identify many aspects of the pyre technology and ritual, such as the heat of the fire, its size and effectiveness, the fuel and timber used, the grave goods and animal offerings, and the process of selection of bones and other items from the pyre's aftermath.

RECORDING

Skeletons are treated as individual contexts (and not as small finds) and are recorded on a skeleton sheet, giving details of bones present, the cross-referencing of plan, section, sample and photograph numbers, and details about the orientation and position of the body (**Figure 10.2**). For example, the corpse may be lying on its back (supine), on its front (prone) or on its left or right side, in an extended (straight), flexed (knees bent), crouched (knees brought up towards the chest) or contracted (knees up under the chin) position. Any unusual features or associated grave goods are photographed and recorded in closer detail. The grave cut and the grave fill(s) will also have their own context sheets.

Skeletons are normally recorded in plan at a scale of 1:10 with vertical black and white and colour photography, along with detailed oblique shots of special pathological features or grave goods. The grave cuts and other excavated features will normally be planned at 1:20.

Cremation burials are recorded on context sheets and are drawn in plan and in section (at 1:10) and photographed. Associated grave goods and pyre debris, along with bone quantities and maximum bone fragment size, are recorded on the context sheet. During excavation of the cremation pit, attention should be paid to any traces of burning or scorching from hot ashes and pyre debris and to traces of vanished organic containers for the ashes (in the shape of the deposit as revealed in section).

LIFTING AND TEMPORARY STORAGE

It is not always appropriate to lift inhumations and there are circumstances where they are best left *in situ* after initial recording and osteological analysis of age, sex and evidence of pathologies. Such might be the case on rescue excavations where only a small number of medieval or later burials are encountered and where they may remain undisturbed by proposed development. If it is decided that the skeletons should be removed, the bones must be carefully lifted. It is often thought that fragile bones must always be consolidated with a glue such as polyvinyl acetate (PVA) but such treatment will affect any subsequent chemical or molecular analyses and is only carried out if the bones are liable to break into tiny pieces. Bones are best cleaned by slow and gentle drying and brushing but less fragile ones may be washed in tepid water. They should also be marked and given adequate labelling of site, context and skeleton number, prior to bagging and careful, loose packing in acid-free cardboard boxes, padded with acid-free tissue paper. Skulls may be packed in smaller 'skull boxes'. Fragile bones should be individually wrapped in acid-free paper before being placed in plastic bags.

ARCUS Skeleton Context Record

Research School of Archaeology, Sheffield University, S1 4DT

| Sheet | of |

| Site Code | Grid ref. E N | Sub-division | Context no. | Skeleton Number |

| Associated Samples | Associated Finds | Condition | Drawing No. | Category: |
| | | | Photo No. | Human ☐ Animal ☐ |

Position of:

Skull

Arms

Legs

Descripton

Human Bones Present   (indicate north)

Length Right		Length Left		Levels (no. or AOD in metres)
Hum		Hum		
Rad		Rad		Cranium:
Uln		Uln		Sacrum:
Fem		Fem		Feet:
Tib		Tib		Completed by:
Fib		Fib		Date: PTO.

10.2 A skeleton recording sheet for use in the field. A more detailed sheet and checklist is used later in the laboratory.

POST-EXCAVATION

The moment between finishing excavation and beginning analysis and writing-up provides time for an appraisal of the project's research strategy in which to set out objectives, requirements, costs, timetabling and personnel. This should establish a closely monitored timetable of specialist reporting and interaction so that specialists are aware of the project's various research directions and are provided with the necessary contextual information that they will require in interpreting their results. This is also the time for ensuring that the finds will be appropriately curated or, if necessary, reburied. Museum curation and storage is a long-term commitment that costs money and resources which the project, normally through its sponsors, can be expected to find.

Post-excavation tasks on inhumations will include: ageing and sexing; recording of metrical and non-metrical traits; palaeopathology; palaeodemography of the cemetery group; and analysis of skin, hair, brain matter or other soft tissue which may happen to survive. Additional techniques that might be applicable are chemical analysis of bone (trace element and stable isotope analyses) and molecular analysis (DNA and blood-typing). The strategy for disarticulated remains is different. It includes calculation of minimum numbers, and perhaps of skeletal part representation and spatial analysis of the assemblage.

Post-excavation tasks for cremation burials include: ageing and sexing; palaeopathology (where recoverable); study of any burnt soft tissue if it survives; analysis of charcoal, carbonized plant remains and fuel ash from the pyre; and study of cremation technology.

Selection of radiocarbon samples for dating prehistoric sites later than 40,000 BP will need to consider human bone, articulated animal bone, organic elements of grave goods and other material such as charcoal. It will be crucial to establish the likely timespan prior to the sample's deposition in the ground and the directness of its relationship to what is being dated. Considerations must also be made about possible sources of contamination and the likelihood of old carbon being incorporated into the sample.

Stylistic and technological studies of artefacts will be needed for the many types of grave goods: coffins and coffin fittings, shroud pins, body ornaments, weaponry, pottery, etc. Environmental analyses of samples taken during the excavation may be required for a wide range of materials: pollen, beetles, snails, magnetic susceptibility, pH, soil micromorphology, wood, charcoal and plant remains.

The structural reporting of the site, whether a cemetery, tomb or burial mound, along with the reconstruction of funerary practices and the synthesis of specialist reports is also required. Post-excavation costs for cemetery sites may be as much as four times the cost of excavation. It can also take many years because of lengthy conservation costs of metal and other unstable artefacts, large assemblages of human remains to study (which are best analysed by one specialist, rather than a team, to ensure standardized observations), and complex analytical procedures which may be very time-consuming. The whole enterprise is not to be entered into lightly.

NOTES

CHAPTER ONE

1. His account of his journey, known as the *Risala*, survives in several transcriptions. This description is based primarily on the translation from a probable eleventh-century manuscript with additional material from a version transcribed in 1593. The complete text can be found in Jones 1968: 425–30.
2. Good textbooks which cover these subjects include Boddington *et al.* 1987; Brothwell 1981 [1963]; Chamberlain 1994; Hunter *et al.* 1996; Mays 1998; and Roberts and Manchester 1995.
3. Archaeological books on this topic which are useful overviews or collections of papers include Chapman *et al.* 1981; Humphreys and King 1981; Gnoli and Vernant 1982; Pader 1982; Roberts *et al.* 1989; Morris 1993; Bahn 1996; Kjeld Jensen and Høilund Nielsen 1997; and Downes and Pollard 1999.
4. Spindler 1994.
5. Spindler 1994: 205.
6. Atkinson 1968; 1972.
7. Preston Blier 1987.
8. Whimster 1981; Wilson 1981; Wait 1985; Hill 1995.
9. Cunliffe 1993.
10. Rees Jones 1994: 308.
11. Wells and Green 1973; Rahtz 1978.
12. Doxtater 1990.
13. Hirst 1985.
14. Pader 1982.
15. McKinley 1997: 142.
16. McKinley 1997.
17. Møhl 1977.
18. Wilson 1985: 247.
19. Cunnington and Lucas 1972.
20. Pers. comm. from HM Coroner, Sheffield, of statistics from the Home Office Statistical Bulletin.
21. MacClancy 1992: 5.
22. Farb and Armelagos 1980: 93.
23. Fortune 1932.
24. Vlach 1978: 144.
25. Henshall 1966; Dickson 1978; Tipping 1994.
26. Gittings 1984: 110–17; Goody 1993: 284; Litten 1991: 144.
27. Jørgensen 1975.
28. Champion *et al.* 1984: 274.
29. See Demoule 1982 for French Iron Age examples.
30. Rega 1997; O'Shea 1996; Mokrin is discussed in detail in Chapter 5.
31. Goldstein 1980; 1981; the Mississippian culture is discussed in detail in Chapter 4.
32. Good books on this are Shennan 1988 and Drennan 1996.
33. Lilley *et al.* 1994: fig. 99; for more information on Jewbury, see Chapter 8.
34. Harrington 1996: 223; for more information on the African Burial Ground, see Chapter 8.
35. Aufderheide *et al.* 1981.
36. Daniell 1997: 95–109.
37. Morley 1971: 37.
38. Shay 1985.
39. Johnson 1917; Daniell 1997: 105–6.
40. Carver 1998.
41. Orme 1981: 239–45.
42. Thomas 1988.
43. Rees Jones 1994: 308.
44. Parker Pearson 1982.
45. Clarke 1979; see also Reece 1977; 1988; Baldwin 1985; Phillpott 1991.
46. Parker Pearson 1993a.
47. Sjøvold 1959; Ingstad 1982. Ingstad questions the traditional identification of the elderly female as Queen Asa.
48. Randsborg 1980; Roesdahl 1982.
49. The example of a woman apparently thrown into another woman's grave at Sewerby has already been mentioned; Hirst 1985.
50. Burkert 1987; Girard 1977; 1987; Smith 1987.
51. Hubert and Mauss 1964 [1899]; Leach 1976: 81–93.
52. Burkert 1983.
53. The relevant literature includes Boone 1984, Davies 1981 and Green 1975. Maccoby (1982) considers that biblical stories such as Cain's murder of Abel hide a central theme of human sacrifice which runs through Judaeo-Christian belief.
54. Paredes and Purdum 1990.
55. Childe 1945; Flinders Petrie 1902–1904; Emery 1961; Kemp 1967; Woolley 1934; Pollock 1991a; Li Chi 1977; Chang 1980.

56. Alva and Donnan 1993; Schreiber 1996a.
57. Greene Robertson 1983; Cortez 1996.
58. Kendall 1997; Pauketat and Emerson 1997; Cotterell 1981; Roscoe 1911: 103–12.
59. Sugiyama 1989; Cabrera Castro *et al.* 1991.
60. Reinhard 1996; Schreiber 1996b.
61. Silverblatt 1987: 94–101; Sillar 1992: 112–13.
62. Tierney 1989.

CHAPTER TWO

1. Ucko 1969: 262.
2. Macaulay 1979.
3. Ucko 1969.
4. Among the earliest was Goody 1962, followed by monographs such as Douglass 1969; Bloch 1971; Ahern 1973; Danforth 1982 and Metcalf 1982, along with overviews such as Thomas 1975; Huntington and Metcalf 1979 (2nd edn Metcalf and Huntington 1991); Humphreys and King 1981; Bloch and Parry 1982; Palgi and Abramovitch 1984; Cederroth *et al.* 1987 and Damon and Wagner 1989.
5. Van Gennep 1960 [1908]; Hertz 1907.
6. Van Gennep 1960 [1908]: 21; Turner 1969; Leach 1976.
7. Van Gennep 1960 [1908]: 146.
8. Hertz 1960: 78.
9. Hertz 1960: 79.
10. Carr 1995: 191; Metcalf and Huntington 1991: 12, 111–12.
11. Metcalf and Huntington 1991: 113–30; Huntington 1973; 1987.
12. Metcalf and Huntington 1991: 112.
13. Radcliffe-Brown 1952: 178–87; Giddens 1984: 1.
14. Malinowski 1948: 29–35; Radcliffe-Brown 1964 [1922]: 240; Evans-Pritchard 1948: 200.
15. Malinowski 1948: 34–5.
16. Geertz 1973: 142–69.
17. Goody 1962: 197.
18. Goody 1962: 69–75.
19. Goody 1962: 142, 303.
20. Metcalf and Huntington 1991: 144–51; Metcalf 1982.
21. Bloch 1971: 72, 114, 166–70.
22. Douglas 1966; see also Leach 1976.
23. Okely 1983; Hodder 1982a; 1982b; Donley 1982; Moore 1982; Parker Pearson 1982; Shanks and Tilley 1982.
24. Okely 1983: 227–8.
25. Huntington and Metcalf 1979.
26. Disorientation of the coffin is found throughout Madagascar, for example (Mack 1986); burials across running water and the provision of blades are found among the Iban (Uchibori 1978). The remainder are all documented within Madagascar.
27. Battaglia 1990.

28. Van Gennep 1960 [1908]: 157–60.
29. Turner 1969; Hodder 1982c.
30. Bloch 1982: 227.
31. Dureau 1991; Strathern 1987; Metcalf and Huntington 1991: 7–8.
32. Dureau 1991: 34–40.
33. Metcalf and Huntington 1991: 73–4.
34. Ucko 1969.
35. Leach 1976.
36. Grinsell 1961. Some of the more elaborate Iron Age burials from east Yorkshire (*c.* 400–200 BC) contain grave goods which have been reversed or inverted, such as a chainmail suit, shields and a sword; Stead 1991.
37. Mack 1986; Newell 1976.
38. Watson and Rawski 1988; Ahern 1973; Chidester 1990: 125–36.
39. Kopytoff 1971.
40. Lehmann and Myers 1993; Steadman, Palmer and Tilley 1996: 63–4; Swanson 1964.
41. Descola 1996: 363–83.
42. Metcalf 1982; Metcalf and Huntington 1991: 96.
43. For detailed discussion of the origins and expression of ancestor veneration, see Chapter 7.
44. Saxe 1970; Binford 1971; Brown 1971b.
45. Binford 1977; Schiffer 1987.
46. Binford 1971.
47. Goodenough 1965 cited in Binford 1971.
48. Binford 1971; his study was an attack on Kroeber's (1927) propositions that disposal of the dead had little connection to biological or primary necessities and that it was not closely integrated with law, religion or social organization.
49. The Human Relations Area Files have been regularly updated since Binford's study. His reference is to Murdoch 1957. Binford also drew on other ethnographic accounts, principally from Bendann's survey of 1930.
50. Saxe 1970.
51. Because attributes are correlated, 'information' is being repeated unnecessarily; some of the attributes are 'redundant' because what they signify is duplicated by other associated attributes. Saxe uses 'entropy' to mean few correlations between attributes; 'information' is evenly distributed rather than concentrated, with no duplication. See Chapter 4 pp. 74–5 for more on redundancy and entropy.
52. Meggitt 1965.
53. Goldstein 1976.
54. Goldstein 1976: 61.
55. Goldstein 1976: 60.
56. Hodder 1982c: 196–9; Morris 1991; Carr 1995: 182.
57. Ucko 1969: 270 cited in Chapman 1977: 20.
58. Tainter 1975; 1977. See Chapter 4 for more on Tainter's analyses.

59. Tainter 1978: 121.
60. Carr 1995: 178–80.
61. Carr 1995: 122.
62. Carr 1995: fig. 2.
63. Hertz 1907; Carr 1995: 193.
64. Hodder 1982c; Pader 1982; Parker Pearson 1982; Metcalf and Huntington 1991: 14–19.
65. Rowlands 1989.
66. Shanks and Tilley 1987.
67. Geertz 1973.
68. Metcalf and Huntington 1991: 133–88.
69. Bloch 1971; 1977: 287.
70. Tarlow 1992.
71. Barrett 1994.
72. For example, Bourdieu 1977; 1984; Giddens 1984.
73. Pader 1982: 56.
74. Fabian 1991: 174.
75. Fabian 1991: 177.
76. For example Giddens 1984 in contrast to Binford 1981b.
77. Metcalf and Huntington 1991: 74–5.
78. Gould 1980; Stiles 1977; Binford 1981b.
79. Yellen 1977.
80. Hodder 1982d.
81. Wylie 1985; 1988; 1989.
82. Hodder 1982c.
83. Parker Pearson and Ramilisonina 1998.
84. As in his analysis of Ilchamus calabash decoration; Hodder 1986.
85. Hodder 1982c.
86. An example of such a study is David 1992.
87. Musée d'Art et d'Archéologie 1989.
88. Parker Pearson 1999a: 14.
89. Heurtebize 1986a; Parker Pearson 1992.
90. Drury 1743 [1729]: 175–6.
91. Heurtebize 1986b: 139–66; Parker Pearson 1999a: 14.
92. Heurtebize 1997.
93. Parker Pearson 1999a: 11–12.
94. Heurtebize 1986a; Parker Pearson et al. 1996; Parker Pearson 1999a.
95. Heurtebize 1986a.
96. Parker Pearson 1982.
97. Barley 1990: 116.
98. Barley 1990: 113–16.
99. The archaeological works are by Dethlefsen and Deetz 1966; Deetz and Dethlefsen 1967; 1971; Rahtz 1981; Gould and Schiffer 1981; Parker Pearson 1982; Cannon 1989; Finch 1991; Tarlow 1992; 1998 and Cox 1998. The sociological and historical studies include Ariès 1974; 1981; Bassett 1995; Bennett 1992: 173–270; Chidester 1990: 251–90; Clarke 1993; Colvin 1991; Curl 1972; 1980; Dempsey 1975; Fulton 1965; Gittings 1984; Gorer 1965; Habenstein and Lamers 1955; Jackson 1977; Kalish and Reynolds 1976; Kübler-Ross 1975; Litten 1991; Llewellyn 1991; Mack 1973; Mitford 1965; Morley 1971; Pine 1975; Rawnsley and Reynolds 1977; Sheskin 1979; Stannard 1974; 1977; Sudnow 1967; Warner 1959; and Whaley 1981.
100. Burman 1988; Cox 1996; 1998; Jones 1979; Molleson and Cox 1993; Rahtz and Watts 1983; Reeve and Adams 1993.
101. Finch 1991: 113.
102. Parker Pearson 1982; in 1996 the figure for cremations in Britain, recorded by the National Association of Funeral Directors, was 72.2 per cent.
103. See Parker Pearson 1982; Tarlow 1992.
104. Cannadine 1981: 191–3; Tarlow 1992: 132–3; 1998.
105. Jupp 1993: 190.
106. Parker Pearson 1982: 105; Jupp 1993: fig. 1.
107. Parker Pearson 1982.
108. Cannon 1989.
109. Gittings 1984; Daniell 1997: 46; Weever 1631 quoted in Finch 1991.
110. Finch 1991: 105–6.
111. Finch 1991: 110–11.
112. Bennett 1992; Ennew 1980; Vallee 1957.
113. Vallee 1957: 127.
114. Formerly the tassels were cut and retained by the chief mourner. Today they remain attached and are dropped into the grave.
115. Buchanan 1793 quoted in Bennett 1992: 243.
116. Vallee 1955: 129–30.
117. Cannadine 1981: 242.
118. Orme 1981: 284.

CHAPTER THREE

1. Prior 1989: 21.
2. Among the many works on the social anthropology of the body, see Polhemus 1973; 1988; Beck 1975; Blacking 1977; Turner 1984; 1992; Brown 1988; O'Hanlon 1989; Featherstone et al. 1991; Synnott 1993 and Connor 1995.
3. Prior 1989: 14.
4. Shilling 1993: 12.
5. Van Gennep 1960 [1908]: 72.
6. Douglas 1966; 1973; see also Tuan 1974.
7. Foucault 1977; 1979.
8. Observed by Spencer and Gillen 1899 and reported by Durkheim 1965 [1912]: 435–6.
9. Leach 1958.
10. Barrett 1994: 123.
11. Leach 1977: 169.
12. Douglas 1973.
13. Leach 1977: 171.
14. Douglas 1973.
15. Kristeva 1982 but see Lowenhaupt Tsing for a critique.
16. Leach 1977: 171–3.
17. See Hodder 1982c.
18. Shanks and Tilley 1982.

19. Parker Pearson 1982: 110.

20. Tarlow 1998.

21. For New England, see Dethlefsen and Deetz 1966; Deetz and Dethlefsen 1967; 1971.

22. Rodwell and Rodwell 1982.

23. For example, Cox 1996.

24. Gittings 1984; Johnson 1996.

25. Cannon pers. comm.; see also Tarlow 1998 and Chapter 2.

26. Albery *et al.* 1993; Bradfield 1994.

27. Bradfield 1994: 6.

28. *Monty Python's Flying Circus* cited in Chapman and Randsborg 1981: 1.

29. Illich 1975.

30. Downes 1999.

31. Chidester 1990: 87–102; Parry 1982; 1994.

32. Chagnon 1992: 135–7.

33. Hertz 1907.

34. Danforth 1982.

35. Among groups such as the Merina, Bezanozano and Betsimisaraka; Mack 1986.

36. Pardo 1989.

37. Carr and Knüsel 1997.

38. Piggott 1962; Smith 1965.

39. Shanks and Tilley 1982; 1987.

40. This seems to have been the case for the Neolithic chambered tombs of the British Isles: the emptied tombs of Orkney were probably reused in the Late Neolithic or Bronze Age; the tombs of the Outer Hebrides were reworked in the Iron Age (Hingley 1996); bones from the West Kennet long barrow were probably removed in the 1670s or 1680s by Robert Toope, a local physician, who was selling ground-up ancient human bones as a medicinal powder (Burl 1979: 127).

41. Brothwell 1961; Hogg 1958; Helmuth 1973; Sagan 1974; Arens 1979; Brown and Tuzins 1983; Elgar and Crespi 1992.

42. Arens 1979; Lewis 1986: 64–6.

43. Gordon-Grube 1988; Peacock 1896: 270–1.

44. Glasse 1977; Gajdusek 1977; Steadman and Merbs 1982.

45. Sahlins 1983: 88.

46. Such as the 1972 Andean plane crash (Read 1974), the Donner party's catastrophe (Gzowski 1980; Grayson 1990), the archaeologically documented Franklin expedition (Beattie and Geiger 1987; Beattie 1999), and the crew of the *Mignonette*'s eating of the 'cabin boy' Richard Parker in 1884 (Simpson 1984).

47. Dornstreich and Morren 1974.

48. Lévi-Strauss 1966.

49. Shankman 1969; Vayda 1970; Garn and Block 1970; Walens and Wagner 1971; Bygott 1972; Dornstreich and Morren 1974.

50. Harner 1977; Harris 1977; 1986; but see Ortiz de Montellano 1978; 1983 and Castile 1980 for rebutting arguments.

51. Lewis 1986: 77; Fiddes 1991: 171–9.

52. Strathern 1982; Sahlins 1983; Bowden 1984; Lewis 1986.

53. Sanday 1986: 3. *Cf* Sutton 1995.

54. Such as Yanamamö consumption of cremated bones (Chagnon 1992: 135–7) and Trobriand demonstrations of filial piety in which sons sucked the flesh of the exhumed and dismembered corpses of their fathers (Malinowski 1929: 133 cited in Lewis 1986: 73).

55. Strathern 1982.

56. It has been practised often as a means of acquiring the power of one's enemies. It may also be characterized as aggressive cannibalism as noted among the Etoro, Kaluli and Daribi of Papua New Guinea (Strathern 1982) and in Fiji (Sahlins 1983). Traditional eating of enemies' eyeballs by Maori warriors was historically a means of taking on their opponents' *mana* or spirit (Bowden 1984).

57. Clastres 1998: 211–35.

58. Sutton Phelps and Burgess 1964; Roper 1969; Turner and Morris 1970; Flinn *et al.* 1976; Branigan 1982; Trinkhaus 1985; Wall *et al.* 1986; White, T.D. 1992; Villa and Mahieu 1991; Turner 1993; Owsley *et al.* 1994; Melbye and Fairgrieve 1994.

59. Villa *et al.* 1986.

60. White, T.D. 1992; Turner 1993; Turner and Turner 1992; Turner *et al.* 1993.

61. Turner 1993; Turner *et al.* 1993; Flinn *et al.* 1976: 308.

62. Binford 1981a; Behrensmeyer *et al.* 1986; Trinkhaus 1985; White and Toth 1991.

63. This point was made by Bahn (1990) but recently a human coprolite from the bottom of a pit structure on the Anasazi site of 1001 0 at Cowboy Wash, Ute Mountain, has tested positive for myoglobin, a protein found in high concentrations in humans only in the heart muscle; Whittell 1998.

64. Anon. 1960.

65. Shennan 1975; O'Shea 1981a; 1996; Rega 1997.

66. Though this style is of recent origin within the last two decades, the coffins' origin lies in the carving of the chief's palanquin; one was constructed for a chief but, as a result of his untimely death, served as his coffin; Secretan 1995.

67. Schneider and Weiner 1989.

68. Feeley-Harnik 1989.

69. Barley 1990: 115.

70. Ingersoll and Nickell 1987: 219.

71. Borg 1991; Davies 1994; Ignatieff 1984; McIntyre 1990; Mayo 1988; Moriarty 1995; Mosse 1990; Scruggs 1985.

72. Bruce-Mitford 1975.

73. Parker Pearson *et al.* 1994. Some archaeologists are reluctant to accept this interpretation and

point to the possibilities of a body's complete disappearance due to chemical decomposition in acidic soil; East 1984; Carver 1998. There is certainly no evidence for a dressed body even though high-status corpses were normally clothed at this period.

74. Partridge 1994: 12.
75. Elliot Smith 1933.
76. Leca 1979.
77. Partridge 1994: 10.
78. This is suggested by the large entourages of individuals accompanying the pharaohs of the 1st Dynasty to the grave, as mentioned in Chapter 1.
79. Partridge 1994: 11–12.
80. Wallis Budge 1987 [1893]: 340–1; Andrews 1985: 12; Hornung 1992.
81. The Book of the Dead sets out the passage into the afterlife including the judgement of the dead. In the Papyrus of Ani (a scribe in the royal priesthood of Thebes, *c.* 1300 BC; Wallis Budge 1987 [1893]: 338–51), the gods Anubis and Thoth are represented by the side of a balance. Osiris-Ani is shown to have passed the test and is admitted into the divine court of Osiris. Such judgement is supposed to be impersonal and absolute yet the story on papyrus is a human artefact which was composed by a scribe's hand; thus it was the living who declared the fate of the dead, under the pretence of an appeal to a supernatural authority.
82. See Carter and Mace 1923; Desroches-Noblecourt 1965; Edwards 1979 and El Mahdy 1989.
83. In dynastic Egypt's convoluted political and kinship manoeuvrings, Tutankhamen's widow (also probably his sister) Ankhesenamun and the throne were taken by Ay, Commander of the King's Horse and father-in-law of Akhenaten – as well as grandfather of Ankhesenamun! She was to have married a Hittite prince but he was murdered *en route* to Egypt (Aldred 1988: 297–8).
84. Tutankhamen's head was shaved, in the manner of a temple priest, possibly because of treatment to a skull injury, perhaps caused by an arrow penetrating his skull around his left ear (Aldred 1988: 297).
85. Geary 1986; 1994; Brown 1981.
86. Geary 1986: 176.
87. Geary 1986: 179.
88. Brown 1981: 222.
89. Rudenko 1970; Polosmak 1994; Bogucki 1996.
90. Rudenko 1970: 279.
91. Kristeva 1982.
92. Rudenko 1970: 114.
93. Rudenko 1970: 113; Polosmak 1994; Bogucki 1996.
94. Tannenbaum 1987: 693; Gell 1993: 21.
95. Gell 1993: 22.

96. Gell 1993: 314.
97. Shanks 1993; Green 1997: 906.
98. Zavitukhina and Barkova 1978: 42–3. The slicing of the skin may have been carried out at any one of three moments: when the man was scalped, when his body was prepared for burial or when the tomb was robbed. Whatever the moment, this act demonstrates a certain concern with rupturing this boundary.
99. Zavitukhina and Barkova 1978; Rudenko 1970: 113.
100. Vernant 1991a; 1991b; Treherne 1995: 128.
101. Tauber 1979; Sellevold *et al.* 1984.
102. Van der Sanden 1996; see also Dieck 1972; 1986. At least nine other bog corpses or skeletons date to the Earlier Neolithic; Bennike 1985; 1999; Thorpe 1996: 134. For British and Irish bog bodies, see Turner and Scaife 1995.
103. The 'bog men, after their brief time as god and husband of the goddess – the time of the spring feasts and the wanderings through the villages – fulfilled the final demand of religion. They were sacrificed and placed in the sacred bogs; and consummated by their death the rites that ensured . . . luck and fertility in the coming year. At the same time, through their sacrificial deaths, they were themselves consecrated for all time to Nerthus, goddess of fertility – to Mother Earth.' (Glob 1969: 190–2). Glob also refers to Tacitus's observations that the Germanic tribe, the Semmones 'celebrate the grim initiation of their barbarous rites with a human sacrifice for the good of the community', while Germanic law requires that '[t]raitors and deserters are hung from trees; cowards, shirkers and notorious evil-livers are plunged in the mud of marshes with a hurdle on their heads: the difference of punishment has regard to the principle that crime should be blazoned abroad by its retribution, but abomination hidden'. Tacitus also relates that a woman found guilty of adultery had her hair cut off in the presence of her relatives and was then scourged out of the village.
104. Cited in van der Sanden 1996: 166–7.
105. Vogelius Andersen 1958.
106. Van der Sanden 1996: 118–19, 141; Renfrew, J.M. 1973.
107. Laurence and Bennett 1980: 782–3.
108. Van der Sanden 1996: 155–65.
109. Stead *et al.* 1986; Brothwell and Bourke 1995.
110. Glob 1969: 113.
111. Bender Jørgensen 1979; Parker Pearson 1984b.
112. Sellevold *et al.* 1984.
113. Analysis of Lindow Man revealed that his skin may have been painted; Pyatt *et al.* 1991; 1995; Cowell and Craddock 1995.
114. Van der Sanden 1996: 124–34.
115. For Bronze Age dress see Glob 1974; Hald 1980; Bender Jørgensen 1986; 1992. The Dutch

bog body clothing is described in van der Sanden 1996: 124.

116. Bender Jørgensen 1979.

117. Bender Jørgensen 1979.

118. Iron Age people may have appreciated that after long exposure to peat human skin is transformed through a process of natural tanning into something akin to leather; the leather animal skins might be associated with a symbolism surrounding the whole meaning and process of deposition in peat bogs. Ann Ross has pointed out that druids and seers of early Irish tradition wrapped themselves in bull-hides so that they might communicate with the gods and see into the future (Ross 1986: 164). This is a possible explanation but the differences in time, space and tradition and the specificity of bull-hide render any direct parallel unlikely. The leather garments on bog bodies were made from the hides of sheep, calves and deer.

119. Parker Pearson 1993a; see Chapter 6 for further discussion of the funerary landscape of Iron Age Denmark.

120. Glob 1969; Parker Pearson 1984b.

121. Parker Pearson 1984b.

122. For example, Gebühr (1979) argues that the Windeby girl is a normal burial and does not indicate unusual deposition. See also Munksgaard 1984 and Fischer 1999.

123. Connolly 1985; Parker Pearson 1986.

124. Briggs 1995; Parker Pearson 1986.

125. Interpretations of ritual regicide are also possible; see Frazer 1911.

126. Brothwell and Bourke 1995: 56–7; Magilton 1995: 186.

127. Van der Sanden 1995: 155; 1996: 138–42.

CHAPTER FOUR

1. From Thomas Gray (1716–71) 'Elegy in a Country Churchyard'.

2. Smith 1955.

3. Lubbock 1865; Childe 1951; McNairn 1980.

4. Fried 1967; Sahlins 1958; 1968; Sahlins and Service 1960.

5. Ingold 1986.

6. Renfrew 1973a; Renfrew and Shennan 1982; Bintliff 1984; Earle 1987; 1991; Yoffee and Sherratt 1993; Wason 1994.

7. Leach 1979.

8. Clastres 1977; Giddens 1979; 1984; Leach 1982; Shanks and Tilley 1987; Rowlands 1989; Shennan 1993; Yoffee 1993; Barrett 1994: 161–4; Whittle 1997: 146–7.

9. Whittle 1997: 147.

10. Saxe 1970: 4.

11. Binford 1971; O'Shea 1984.

12. Peebles 1971: 69.

13. See Chapter 2 for more information on how New Archaeology used role theory.

14. Saxe 1970: 9.

15. Parsons 1951.

16. Fried 1967: 109.

17. Sahlins 1958; Service 1962; Earle 1987; 1991.

18. Peebles and Kus 1977.

19. Peebles 1971; Peebles and Kus 1977.

20. Tainter 1975; 1977. See also Tainter 1980; 1981.

21. See Chapter 2 for an explanation of energy expenditure in mortuary ritual.

22. O'Shea 1984: 15–20; Pader 1982: 60–1.

23. Brown 1971a.

24. O'Shea 1984: fig. 2.2.

25. O'Shea 1981a; 1984.

26. O'Shea 1984: 280–3.

27. O'Shea and Zvelebil 1984.

28. O'Shea and Zvelebil 1984: 35.

29. Jacobs 1995: 395.

30. Jacobs 1995: 395–6.

31. Jupp 1993: 190.

32. Hart and Pilling 1966; Goodale 1971.

33. Chapman 1977: 27–9; 1981; 1990: 176–207.

34. Almagro and Arribas 1963: 45–6; Chapman 1981: 405.

35. Shennan 1975.

36. See Chapter 5 for discussion of the gender and kinship implications of Shennan's work.

37. Frankenstein and Rowlands 1978; Biel 1986.

38. Dietler 1990: 386–7.

39. Randsborg 1973; 1974. A similar study by Arnold (1988a; 1988b) estimated grave good values by their scarcity.

40. Renfrew 1986. See also Chapman 1991.

41. Binford 1962.

42. Buikstra 1981.

43. Wood et al. 1992; Roberts and Manchester 1995: 164.

44. Giddens 1984.

45. Goodman and Armelagos 1988; Sillens et al. 1989; Ezzo 1994; Pate 1994.

46. Roberts and Manchester 1995: 173; Martin et al. 1985.

47. Cook 1981; Goodman 1991; Skinner and Goodman 1992 for enamel hypoplasia; Lallo et al. 1977; Martin et al. 1985: 266; Stuart-Macadam 1989; Mays 1985 for Harris lines; and Roberts and Manchester 1995 for stunted growth.

48. Cook 1981: 143–4.

49. Huss-Ashmore et al. 1982.

50. Buikstra et al. 1989; Ezzo 1994.

51. Sillens and Kavanagh 1982; Aufderheide 1989; Pate 1994; Burton and Wright 1995.

52. Blakely and Beck 1981.

53. Schoeninger 1979.

54. Ezzo 1994.

55. Burton and Price 1990; Larson et al. 1992.

56. Aufderheide 1989: 254.

57. Vogel and van der Merwe 1977; 1978; Tauber 1981; Walker and DeNiro 1986; Burger and van

der Merwe 1990; Schwarcz and Schoeninger 1991; Katzenberg 1992.

58. Hastorf and Johannessen 1993.
59. Richards and van Klinken 1997; Richards, M. 1998.
60. Turner 1988: 10.
61. Bourdieu 1984; Turner 1988.
62. Lukács 1971.
63. Weber 1958; Turner 1988: 20–1.
64. For example, Pader 1982: 54–6.
65. Bloch 1977; Parker Pearson 1982; Giddens 1984; Barrett 1994.
66. O'Shea 1984: 20–1.
67. Parker Pearson 1982.
68. Leach 1979: 122. See also Härke 1997.
69. Bloch 1971; Parker Pearson 1982; Barrett 1990.
70. Pader 1982: 60–1; O'Shea 1984: 17.
71. Pader 1982: 59, citing Hugh-Jones 1979: 109.
72. Gittings 1984.
73. For example, in ancient Egypt (see Chapter 3).
74. Parker Pearson 1993b: 78–81.
75. Glob 1974; Broholm 1943–47.
76. Rubertone 1989.
77. Bradley 1990; O'Shea 1984.
78. Chapman 1983.
79. Sheridan and Davis 1998.
80. O'Shea 1981b; Halstead and O'Shea 1982; 1985.
81. Miller and Tilley 1984; Bloch 1977.
82. Childe 1945.
83. Piggott 1979.
84. Parker Pearson 1982; 1984b. See Chapters 2 and 6 for detailed case studies.
85. Bradley 1984; 1990.
86. Morris 1991; 1993: 128–55.
87. For general works on the Mississippian, see Peebles 1979; 1987; Drennan and Uribe 1987; Milner 1990; Steponaitis 1991; Welch 1991 and Barker and Pauketat 1992.
88. Knight and Steponaitis 1998.
89. Peebles and Kus 1977.
90. Peebles and Kus 1977: 439–44.
91. As argued earlier in this chapter; Metcalf 1982; Hart and Pilling 1966; Jupp 1993.
92. Steponaitis 1983; Knight and Steponaitis 1998.
93. Steponaitis 1983: 168.
94. Knight and Steponaitis 1998.
95. Bradley 1990; Knight and Steponaitis 1998.
96. Steponaitis 1983: 172–3.
97. See Michals 1981 for dietary evidence.
98. *Cf.* Lévi-Strauss 1962.
99. Blakely and Beck 1981; Powell 1992; Blitz 1993a: 176–8.
100. Saitta 1994.
101. Steponaitis 1983: 162–3.
102. Lévi-Strauss 1962: 162.
103. Bauer 1996.
104. Coe 1993.
105. Hall 1976; Knight 1986.
106. Steponaitis 1986: 387–8.
107. Blitz 1993b; Pauketat and Emerson 1991.
108. Emerson 1997: 195–212.
109. Prentice 1986.
110. For the role of agency see Smith 1990; Saitta 1994; Cobb and Garrow 1996; for ideology as legitimatory mechanism see Steponaitis 1986: 392.
111. Hall 1976; Knight 1986; 1989; Pauketat and Emerson 1991; see Coe 1993 for Mesoamerica.
112. Knight 1986: 678; Pauketat and Emerson 1991: 932–5.
113. Knight 1986: 677–9.
114. Knight 1986: 685.
115. Cushman 1899; Fundaburk 1958; Swanton 1967.
116. In British archaeology the debate around chiefdoms, status and social complexity has often centred on the monuments and elaborate burials of Late Neolithic and Early Bronze Age Wessex. For a variety of interpretations see Piggott 1938; Childe 1940; Fleming 1971; 1973a; 1973b; 1996; Renfrew 1973a; Startin and Bradley 1981; Clarke *et al.* 1985; Barrett 1990; 1994; Bradley 1993; Parker Pearson 1993b; Edmonds 1995 and Whittle 1996; 1997.

CHAPTER FIVE

1. Gilchrist 1991: 497.
2. Important works include Gordon 1986; Cannon 1991; Conkey 1991; Eisher 1991; Englestad 1991; Hastorf 1991; Pollock 1991b and Dommasnes 1992.
3. Rubin 1975: 179.
4. Moore and Scott 1997: 259.
5. Wylie 1991: 22–9.
6. Sørensen 1987; 1991: 122.
7. Meskell 1996.
8. Taylor 1996; Yates 1993: 46; Yates and Nordbladh 1990.
9. Chamberlain 1994.
10. Rega 1997; Holcomb and Konigsberg 1995.
11. Weiss 1972.
12. Schwartz 1995: 16–17.
13. Taylor 1996: 56.
14. Rega 1997: 242; Moore 1988; Taylor 1996: 63–5.
15. Rega 1997: 242.
16. Taylor 1996: 212–14.
17. De Lauretis 1986: 14–15.
18. Sørensen 1992: 34.
19. Conkey and Spector 1984: 11; Winters 1968.
20. Wylie 1991; Gilchrist 1997; MacCormack and Strathern 1980; Gibbs 1987; Hurcombe 1995.
21. Hodder 1991.
22. Rubin 1975; Collier and Yanagisako 1987.
23. Joffroy 1954; 1962.
24. Charles in Joffroy 1954; Sauter 1980.
25. Spindler 1983.

26. Pauli 1972: 133.
27. Langlois 1987; Arnold 1991: 369. A recent unpublished analysis by Knüsel confirms the Vix princess's sex and identifies osteological defects in the skull and hip joint, indicating that she had distinctly assymetrical facial features and walked with a shuffling gait, perhaps aspects which might have contributed to her possible combined roles as priestess and shaman.
28. Lucy 1997.
29. Brush 1988.
30. See also Rahtz et al. 1980; Richards, J.D. 1988.
31. Knüsel and Ripley in press; Whitehead 1981; Williams 1986; Whelan 1991a.
32. Webster 1975: 150; de Beauvoir 1953; Firestone 1970.
33. Ehrenberg 1989: 168–71.
34. Ingstad 1982; Dommasnes 1992: 2.
35. Hodder 1982c: 77–83.
36. Strathern 1972: 156.
37. Hodder 1991.
38. Webster 1975; Brown 1975.
39. Fortune 1932.
40. Gimbutas 1974; 1989; 1991.
41. Ehrenberg 1989; Hodder 1990; Meskell 1995; Taylor 1996: 148–64.
42. Chapman 1997; Hitchcock 1997; Kokkinidou and Nikolaidou 1997; Bender 1997: 179. See Chapter 7 for discussion about the meaning of these figurines.
43. Ehrenberg 1989.
44. See Hugh-Jones 1979.
45. Van de Velde 1979a; 1979b.
46. Rolle 1989; Rolle et al. 1991; Taylor 1996: 199–205.
47. Taylor 1996: 202.
48. Taylor 1996: 202.
49. Bender 1997: 179.
50. Meigs 1984; 1990.
51. Wilson 1985.
52. Ehrenberg 1989; Sherratt 1981; Barrett 1989.
53. Moore 1988: 35.
54. Hurcombe 1995.
55. Stalsberg 1991.
56. Stalsberg 1991: 77.
57. Dommasnes 1982.
58. Dommasnes 1982; 1991: 67.
59. Dommasnes 1991: 70.
60. Sofaer Derevenski 1994; 1997; Meskell 1994; 1996; Baker 1997.
61. For example, Lucy 1994; Rega 1997; Lillie 1997.
62. Chamberlain 1997: 249; Rega 1997: 235–6.
63. Pader 1982: 129–31.
64. Pader 1982: 167–70.
65. Rega 1997.
66. Lillie 1997: 222.
67. Lucy 1994: 24–5.
68. Gosden 1994: 108.
69. Meskell 1996: 9, citing Connell 1995: 64.
70. Meskell 1994; 1996: 11–14.
71. Dettwyler 1991; Silk 1992.
72. Mays 1993; Lee 1994; Sillar 1994; Smith and Kahila 1992.
73. Sillar 1994: 56–8; Smith and Kahila 1992; see Chapter 1 for more information on human sacrifice.
74. Taylor 1996: 223–6.
75. Mann 1986: 31.
76. Whelan 1991b.
77. Harrold 1980: 202.
78. Randsborg 1974; 1984; Levy 1982; Kristiansen 1984; Gibbs 1987; Sørensen 1987; 1991; 1992; Ehrenberg 1989: 130–9; Damm 1991a; 1991b; Parker Pearson 1993a; Meiklejohn et al. 1997.
79. Sørensen 1992.
80. Albrethsen and Petersen 1976; Clark and Neeley 1987; Meiklejohn et al. 1997; Thorpe 1996: 76–87.
81. Contra Orme 1981 who wrongly considers that the grave good distributions at Vedbaek indicate that age was signalled more strongly than gender.
82. Thorpe 1996: 129–34.
83. Damm 1991a: 132.
84. See also Sjögren 1986.
85. Shennan 1975; Shennan 1993; Cf. Rega 1997 and O'Shea 1996.
86. Damm 1991a.
87. Sørensen 1992; see also Randsborg and Nybo 1984.
88. Broholm and Hald 1948; Sørensen 1991.
89. See Chapter 4 for more discussion of Randsborg 1973; 1974.
90. Kristiansen 1984; Gibbs 1987; Sørensen 1992.
91. Sellevold et al. 1984; Breitsprecher 1987.
92. Breitsprecher 1987: tables 1 and 2.
93. Hedeager 1990.
94. Taylor 1996.
95. Shennan 1975: 286.
96. Shennan 1993; O'Shea 1996.
97. Rega 1997: 241.
98. O'Shea 1996: 20.
99. The original sources for Mokrin are Giric 1971 and Tasic 1972.
100. O'Shea 1996: 264–6.
101. O'Shea 1996: 281, 288.
102. Rega 1997: 232.
103. Rega 1997: 233–5.
104. O'Shea 1996: 294.
105. Binford 1972, first reported in 1964.
106. Binford calls this category 'grouped' burials (1972: 409) but it is not clear what the term signifies.
107. Allen and Richardson 1971: 42.
108. Saxe 1971.
109. Wright 1978, subsequently challenged by Crabtree 1991 and Byrd and Monahan 1995. See also Hayden 1990.
110. King 1978.

111. Allen and Richardson 1971.
112. Pader 1982: 64.
113. Dommasnes 1991: 70.
114. Darvill 1987: 91.
115. Needham 1988.
116. Mizoguchi 1992.
117. Green and Rollo-Smith 1984; Davis and Payne 1993; Parker Pearson 1993b: 78–81.
118. Heurtebize 1986b: 139–66; Parker Pearson 1999a: 14. See Chapter 2 for a detailed case study.
119. Louwe Kooijmans 1993.
120. Wahl and König 1987; Whittle 1996: 170–1; Taylor 1996: 168–70. The Talheim grave contained a jumbled mass of bodies, identified as 7 children, 9 juveniles, 10 men and 6 women.
121. Mays 1998 lists, for example, the metopic suture, lambdoid ossicles, ossicle at lambda, shovel-shaped incisors, palatine torus and parietal foramina.
122. Mays 1998: 112–14; see Sheilagh Stead's analysis of non-metric traits in the Iron Age cemeteries of east Yorkshire, in Stead 1991. Other examples are cited by Higham and Bannanurag 1990 and Masset 1993.
123. Hunter *et al.* 1996: 128.
124. Connolly 1969.
125. See Mays 1998: 197–206 for a good summary.
126. Hagelberg and Clegg 1991.
127. Evison 1997: 65.
128. Higham and Bannanurag 1990.
129. Härke 1990.
130. Gilchrist 1997: 49.
131. Boyle *et al.* 1995.
132. Härke 1990.
133. A major problem with identifying Germanic migrations is that had DNA been recovered, it is likely that no significant genetic differences would have been found between 'British' and 'German' skeletons.
134. Masset 1993; Scarre 1984.
135. Fleming 1973b.
136. Salamon and Lengyel 1980.
137. Salamon and Lengyel 1980: 99.
138. Pääbo 1985.
139. Pääbo 1986.
140. Pääbo *et al.* 1989.
141. Doran *et al.* 1986; Pääbo *et al.* 1988.
142. Hughes *et al.* 1986.
143. DNA analysis was successful in identifying the remains of the Romanovs; Radzinsky 1992; Gill *et al.* 1994; 1995.
144. Stone *et al.* 1996.
145. Stone and Stoneking 1993.
146. Horai *et al.* 1991; Hagelberg and Clegg 1993; Hagelberg *et al.* 1994; Stone and Stoneking 1993.
147. Shinoda and Kunisada 1994.
148. Oota *et al.* 1995.
149. Evison 1996.

CHAPTER SIX

1. From a Devon tombstone.
2. Parker Pearson 1982; 1993a; Tilley 1984; Sharples 1985.
3. Tilley 1993; 1994.
4. Myers 1986: 133–5.
5. Uchibori 1978.
6. Ruud 1960.
7. Jensen 1982; Hedeager 1985; 1990; Parker Pearson 1984a; 1984b; 1985; 1993a.
8. Parker Pearson 1984b; see also Hedeager and Kristiansen 1981; Hvass 1985.
9. Hedeager 1990.
10. Hedeager 1976; Parker Pearson 1984b.
11. Branigan 1993.
12. Branigan 1998.
13. Murphy 1998.
14. Peter Day pers. comm.
15. Radimilahy 1994.
16. Poole 1986: 171–5.
17. Little is known about the twenty barrows within this visibility envelope but the one that has been excavated was built after *c.* 2100 BC and may represent a later encroachment into this ancestral zone; Parker Pearson and Ramilisonina 1998.
18. Küchler 1993.
19. Brewster 1982; Dent 1982; 1983.
20. Parker Pearson 1999b.
21. Bevan 1999.
22. Renfrew 1976.
23. Renfrew 1976, citing Emory 1947.
24. Renfrew 1976, citing Eliade 1965.
25. Renfrew 1973a; 1973b; 1976.
26. For example Hodder and Orton 1976; Madsen and Jensen 1982; Hedges 1984: 118; Darvill 1979; 1982; Arnold 1988b.
27. Hughes 1988; Chapman 1995: 41–5.
28. See Sahlins 1961; 1968.
29. Chapman 1995: 39–40, citing Ingold 1986 and Sack 1986.
30. Ortiz 1969.
31. Renfrew 1979: 222.
32. As in the case of Cooney's analysis of megalithic tombs' proximity to the fertile 'rockland' soils of South Leitrim, Ireland; Cooney 1983.
33. Such as Holgate's identification of Neolithic chambered tombs around spring lines and watersheds at some distance from the lower-lying settlement areas of the Thames Valley in southern England; Holgate 1988.
34. Müller-Wille 1983; Parker Pearson *et al.* 1994.
35. Arnold 1988b.
36. Randsborg 1980.
37. Barrett 1994; see Chapter 4; Tilley 1994.
38. Childe 1931; Renfrew 1979.
39. Fraser 1983; Hedges 1984.
40. Hunter in press; Sharples 1985.
41. Richards forthcoming.

42. Richards, C. 1998.
43. Saxe 1970; Saxe and Gall 1977. See Chapter 2 for full discussion of Saxe's hypotheses.
44. Goldstein 1976: 61.
45. Charles 1992; 1995; Charles and Buikstra 1983; Charles *et al.* 1986. See also Rothschild 1979; Buikstra 1984 and Milner 1984.
46. Charles 1995: 78–9.
47. Charles 1995: 79.
48. Okely 1983; Parker Pearson 1982.
49. Myers 1986: 133–4, 303; Goodale 1971: 99–100.
50. Bloch 1971.
51. Fleming 1973b.
52. For example, Edmonds 1999.
53. Tilley 1995; Richards 1995.
54. Tilley 1993; 1994.
55. Tilley 1993: 59.
56. Fleming 1996.

CHAPTER SEVEN

1. Baldwin 1962.
2. Feifel 1959; Becker 1973: 12; Choron 1963.
3. Schütz 1967; Heidegger 1962; Becker 1973; Baumann 1993. See also Gosden 1994.
4. Becker 1973: ix.
5. McManners 1981: 2.
6. Turner 1969.
7. Metcalf and Huntington 1991: 72–4; Adams 1977.
8. Kus 1992.
9. Leach 1958.
10. Middleton 1960; 1982.
11. Hertz 1907.
12. Küchler 1988.
13. Adam 1990.
14. Parry 1982; 1994.
15. Bloch and Parry 1982.
16. Harris 1982.
17. Huntington and Metcalf 1979, citing Kantorowicz 1957; Giesey 1960; Evans-Pritchard 1948; Deng 1972; Lienhardt 1961.
18. Thune 1989.
19. Rowlands 1993.
20. Fabian 1991: 187.
21. Laughter is considered a distinguishing feature of humanness, as recognized by Aristotle over two thousand years ago, but there are indications that chimpanzees and other animals have their own expressions akin to laughter. Suicide is another, as Childe noted self-referentially. 'To end his life deliberately is in fact something that distinguishes Homo sapiens from other animals even better than ceremonial burial of the dead.' From Childe's farewell letter, cited in Green 1981: 154.
22. Murray Parkes 1972: 58, citing Bowlby 1961: 328–31. Darwin (1872) also discusses this phenomenon.
23. Goodall 1986: 101–4; 1989.
24. Goodall 1986: 320.
25. Moss 1988: 270–1. See also Joubert 1991.
26. Grainger 1998: 54.
27. Grainger 1998: 66, 97.
28. Grainger 1998: 105.
29. Grainger 1998: 128, 136.
30. Lynch 1997: 24.
31. Mithen 1996: 151–84. See also Botscharow 1989; Marshack 1991; Hayden 1993 and d'Errico 1995.
32. Lindley and Clark 1990: 239.
33. Trinkhaus and Shipman 1993: 128–9, 177–8, 186–7.
34. Leroi-Gourhan 1975; Trinkhaus 1983; Peyrony 1934; Solecki 1971.
35. Gargett 1989.
36. Gamble 1989.
37. Hayden 1993: 120–1.
38. Leroi-Gourhan 1989.
39. Rak *et al.* 1994.
40. Akazawa *et al.* 1995.
41. Stringer 1990. See also Grün *et al.* 1990.
42. McCown 1937.
43. Vandermeersch 1970; 1981.
44. Lindley and Clark (1990: 235) are critical of the bones being interpreted as grave goods, in contrast to Stringer 1990.
45. Harrold 1980; May 1986.
46. McBurney 1975.
47. Klima 1987a; 1987b.
48. Sally Binford 1968: 141.
49. Bar-Yosef *et al.* 1992.
50. Smirnov 1989.
51. Smirnov 1989: 223.
52. Nadel 1995: 2–3.
53. Dennell 1997.
54. Pitts and Roberts 1998: 257–61.
55. Arsuaga *et al.* 1997. The date of 780,000 BP for Gran Dolina is not universally accepted; Pitts and Roberts (1998: 280–3) consider it contemporary with Boxgrove, around 500,000 BP.
56. Bermudez de Castro *et al.* 1997.
57. White 1986.
58. Binford and Ho 1985: 415–16; Binford and Stone 1986: 468.
59. Barley 1995: 14.
60. See Chapter 3 for more discussion of cannibalism.
61. White, R. 1982; 1992; 1993.
62. Kenyon 1981.
63. Burl 1979b; Allen in Cleal *et al.* 1995.
64. Bar-Yosef 1986; Kenyon 1981.
65. Wright 1978; Henry 1985; 1989; Belfer-Cohen 1995; Byrd and Monahan 1995.
66. Belfer-Cohen 1995; Kuijt 1996.
67. Hodder 1990.
68. Amiran 1962; Bienert 1991; Kenyon 1957; Kuijt 1996.
69. See Wright 1988.

70. Boyd 1995.
71. Kenyon 1981.
72. Watkins 1990.
73. Bar-Yosef *et al.* 1991.
74. Arensburg and Hershkovitz 1988; Garfinkel 1994: 166.
75. Kuijt 1996: 324–5.
76. Kuijt 1996.
77. Hodder 1990.
78. Stordeur *et al.* 1997.
79. Jacobs 1990.
80. See Chapter 5 for information on the background and rise of mother-goddess theories.
81. Crawford 1957; Hawkes 1968; Mellaart 1970: 167–85 and Gimbutas 1974; 1989; 1991, have all supported the mother-goddess theory. Recently articles by Bailey 1994, Knapp and Meskell 1997, Kokkinidou and Nikolaidou 1997 and Hitchcock 1997 have attempted to critique earlier ideas about figurines and move forward.
82. Bailey 1996; Knapp and Meskell 1997.
83. Garfinkel 1994: 162–3.
84. Cassin 1982.
85. Mellaart 1970: 166. The houses from these sites are built tightly up against each other to form a mass of attached buildings.
86. Mellaart 1967; McKim Malville *et al.* 1998.
87. Mellaart 1970.
88. Chapman 1994: 60.
89. Hodder 1990.
90. Woolley 1934; Pollock 1991a.
91. Frankfort 1948.
92. Ringgren 1973: 46–8.
93. Jacobsen 1976; O'Brien and Major 1982: 139–40.
94. Li Chi 1977.
95. Cotterell 1981.
96. Cassin 1982: 355–6.
97. Anon. 1960.
98. Ringgren 1973: 46–8, 121–3.
99. Frankfort *et al.* 1946: 212.
100. According to Hans Küng, '[o]nly for about 5,000 years, since the beginning of the third millennium BCE [before Christian era], were there early historical high cultures and high religions'. (1992: 4).
101. Sen 1961; Zaehner 1966.
102. Sen 1961; Zaehner 1966.
103. Küng 1992: 19.
104. See Murray Parkes *et al.* 1997 for case studies of present-day funerary practices for the world religions.
105. Küng 1992: 17–18; Nigosian 1993: 90–7.
106. Conze 1993: 1–8.

CHAPTER EIGHT

1. Lynch 1997: 9.
2. Zimmerman 1996.

3. Jenkins 1991. See White 1991, Vitelli 1996 and Salmon 1997 on archaeology and ethics.
4. Cheek and Keel 1984; Hubert 1989; McGuire 1989; Echo-Hawk 1992.
5. See Bieder 1992 and Riding In 1992 for the history of anthropological head-hunting in the US.
6. Meighan 1985.
7. Zimmerman 1989; 1992.
8. Anderson 1985.
9. Talmage 1982; Bahn 1984; Bahn and Paterson 1986; Deloria 1992; Klesert and Powell 1993; Powell *et al.* 1993; Jones and Harris 1998.
10. Minthorn 1996; Chatters 1997; Sampson 1997; Slayman 1997; Asatru Folk Assembly 1997; Morell 1998.
11. Lee 1998.
12. Langford 1983.
13. Webb 1987.
14. Richardson 1989; Maslen 1991.
15. Hubert 1989: 150.
16. Hubert 1989.
17. The Khoisan are one of the indigenous peoples of southern Africa. Many of these earliest inhabitants were wiped out by Dutch and British colonists in the seventeenth to nineteenth centuries. Jordan 1999.
18. Jones and Harris 1997: 15. Human remains older than this are considered by Orthodox Jews to lie beyond the beginning of Creation and are thus not 'human'.
19. Harrington 1996.
20. Pers. comm. from Michael Blakey, Mark Mack, Edna Medford and Warren Perry.
21. In addition to the post-excavation team, 150 volunteers have been working on the project's presentation to the public; Blakey pers. comm.
22. Dawes and Magilton 1980; Stroud and Kemp 1993.
23. Lilley *et al.* 1994.
24. Rahtz 1985: 42–6; Lilley *et al.* 1994: 298–300.
25. The 1857 Act is just one of several versions of the Burial Act, the others being the Burial Acts of 1852, 1853, 1854, 1855, 1900 and 1906.
26. Richardson 1988.
27. Bentham's will of 30 May 1832 stipulates that 'my executor will from time to time cause to be conveyed to the room in which [my friends and disciples] meet the said box or case with the contents therein to be stationed . . .'.
28. Boylston *et al.* 1997.
29. The same is the case for Northern Ireland and the Isle of Man.
30. Historic Scotland 1997: 4.
31. See Clarke 1993.
32. Gorer 1965.
33. Reeve and Adams 1993; Cox 1996.
34. Morris 1994.
35. Day 1990; Zimmerman 1992.
36. Houtman 1990.

37. Anon. 1994; Morris 1994; Cox 1994; Huggins 1994. This journal is now *British Archaeology*.
38. Garrett-Frost *et al.* 1992. The Code of Practice refers only to the need for ethical behaviour generally to be observed by archaeologists.
39. Crummy 1997: 120–2.
40. Parker Pearson 1995. See also Reeve 1998, which addresses historical period material and sets out the correct scientific procedures of investigation and recording of human remains as well as recommending that normal disposal should consist of reinterment on the site where they were discovered except where there are good reasons for reburial elsewhere or storage for research and teaching.
41. Alva and Donnan 1993; Schreiber 1996a.
42. See case studies in Mauch Messenger 1989; Vitelli 1996.
43. Elia 1996: 61.
44. Herscher 1989.
45. Guthrie Hingston 1989; Harris 1989.
46. Cook 1991.
47. Cited in Koczka 1989: 196.
48. Howell 1996.
49. Brent 1994.
50. Hoving 1993; Rose and Acar 1996.
51. See Warren 1989 on the ethical dilemmas.
52. Harrington 1997; Wright 1995.
53. Di Lonardo *et al.* 1984; Joyce and Stover 1991; Snow 1982.
54. Barry 1992; Boles *et al.* 1995; Gibbons 1992.
55. Physicians for Human Rights 1996a.
56. Physicians for Human Rights 1996b.
57. There seems no end to such work. Forensic teams are now attempting to work in Kosovo on massacres of ethnic Albanians.
58. See Harte 1994.
59. Stomberg 1998.
60. Barley 1995: 205.
61. Meighan 1996.

CHAPTER NINE

1. Preston Blier 1987: 36.
2. Childe 1945.
3. Mandelbaum 1959; Rosenblatt 1959; Lewis 1980; Gerholm 1988; Parkin 1992. See Barrett 1994, Wilson 1996 and Hill 1996 for recent archaeological definitions.
4. Lewis 1980: 7–8, 21.
5. Bell 1992.
6. Barrett 1994.
7. Barrett 1994: 77–81; Hill 1996.
8. Bloch 1977; Lewis 1980.
9. Wilson 1989.
10. Hodder 1990.

APPENDIX

1. More detailed advice can be found in McKinley and Roberts 1993; Brothwell 1981: 1–19; Barker 1993: 125–6; Buikstra and Ubelaker 1994; Hunter *et al.* 1996: 40–57; and some of the contributions in Roberts *et al.* 1989.
2. A good guide to putting together a project design is English Heritage's *Management of Archaeological Projects*, known as MAP 2.
3. Jones 1979. See Wilsher 1995a; 1995b for Scotland.
4. Carver 1998.
5. Janaway 1996.
6. O'Sullivan 1982.

BIBLIOGRAPHY

Adam, B. 1990 *Time and Social Theory*. Cambridge: Polity Press.

Adams, M.J. 1977 Style in southeast Asian materials processing: some implications for ritual and art. In H. Lechtman and R. Merrill (eds) *Material Culture: studies, organisation, and dynamics of technology*. St Paul: West Publishing, 21–52.

Ahern, E. 1973 *The Cult of the Dead in a Chinese Village*. Stanford: Stanford University Press.

Akazawa, T., Muhesen, M., Dodo, Y., Kondo, O. and Mizoguchi, Y. 1995 Neanderthal infant burial. *Nature* 377: 585–6.

Albery, N., Elliot, G. and Elliot, J. (eds) 1993 *The Natural Death Handbook: a manual for improving the quality of living and dying*. London: Virgin Books.

Albrethsen, S. and Petersen, E.B. 1976 Excavation of a Mesolithic cemetery at Vedbaek, Denmark. *Acta Archaeologica* 47: 1–28.

Aldred, C. 1988 *Akhenaten: King of Egypt*. London: Thames and Hudson.

Allen, W.L. and Richardson, J.B. III 1971 The reconstruction of kinship from archaeological data: the concepts, the methods, and the feasibility. *American Antiquity* 36: 41–53.

Almagro, M. and Arribas, A. 1963 *El Poblado y la Necrópolis Megalíticos de Los Milliares (Santa Fe de Mondújar, Almería)*. Madrid: Bibliotheca Praehistorica Hispana 3.

Alva, W. and Donnan, C. 1993 *Royal Tombs of Sipán*. Los Angeles: Fowler Museum of Cultural History, University of California Los Angeles.

Amiran, R. 1962 Myths of the creation of man and the Jericho statues. *Bulletin of the American Schools of Oriental Research* 167: 23–5.

Anderson, D. 1985 Reburial: is it reasonable? *Archaeology* 38: 48–51.

Andrews, C.A.R. 1985 Introduction. In R.O. Faulkner *The Ancient Egyptian Book of the Dead*. London: British Museum, 11–16.

Anon. 1960 *The Epic of Gilgamesh*. Introduction by N.K. Sandars. Harmondsworth: Penguin.

Anon. 1994 Church reveals secrets of the grave. *British Archaeological News* 16: 1.

Arens, W. 1979 *The Man-Eating Myth: anthropology and anthropophagy*. New York: Oxford University Press.

Arensburg, B. and Hershkovitz, I. 1988 Neolithic human remains. In O. Bar-Yosef and D. Alon (eds) *Nahal Hemar Cave*. Jerusalem: Israel Department of Antiquities and Museums, 50–8.

Ariès, P. 1974 *Western Attitudes toward Death from the Middle Ages to the Present*. Baltimore: Johns Hopkins University Press.

Ariès, P. 1981 *The Hour of our Death*. Harmondsworth: Penguin.

Arnold, B. 1991 The deposed princess of Vix: the need for an engendered European prehistory. In D. Walde and N.D. Willows (eds) *The Archaeology of Gender: proceedings of the 22nd Annual Chacmool Conference*. Calgary: Archaeological Association of the University of Calgary, 366–74.

Arnold, C.J. 1980 Wealth and social structure: a matter of life and death. In P. Rahtz, T. Dickinson and L. Watts (eds) *Anglo-Saxon Cemeteries 1979*. Oxford: BAR British Series 82, 81–142.

Arnold, C.J. 1988a *An Archaeology of the Early Anglo-Saxon Kingdoms*. London: Routledge.

Arnold, C.J. 1988b Territories and leadership: frameworks for the study of emergent polities in early Anglo-Saxon England. In S.T. Driscoll and M.R. Nieke (eds) *Power and Politics in Early Medieval Britain and Ireland*. Edinburgh: Edinburgh University Press, 111–27.

Arsuaga, J.L., Martínez, I., Gracia, A., Carretero, J.M., Lorenzo, C. and García, N. 1997 Sima de los Huesos (Sierra de Atapuerca, Spain). The site. *Journal of Human Evolution* 33: 109–27.

Asatru Folk Assembly. 1997 Ancient Caucasian in North America. www.runestone.org/km.html.

Atkinson, R.J.C. 1956 *Stonehenge*. London: Hamilton.

Atkinson, R.J.C. 1968 Old mortality: some aspects of burial and population in Neolithic England. In J.M. Coles and D.D.A. Simpson (eds) *Studies in Ancient Europe*. Leicester: Leicester University Press, 83–93.

Atkinson, R.J.C. 1972 Burial and population in the British Bronze Age. In F. Lynch and C. Burgess (eds) *Prehistoric Man in Wales and the West: essays in honour of Lilley F. Chitty*. Bath: Adams & Dart, 107–16.

Aufderheide, A.C. 1989 Chemical analysis of human remains. In M.Y. Iscan and K.A.R. Kennedy (eds) *Reconstruction of Life from the Skeleton*. New York: Liss, 237–60.

Aufderheide, A.C., Neiman, F.D., Wittmers, L.E. and Rapp, G. 1981 Lead in bone II: skeletal lead content as an indicator of lifetime lead ingestion and the social correlates in an archaeological population. *American Journal of Physical Anthropology* 55: 285–91.

Bachofen, J.J. 1973 [1861] *Myth, Religion and Mother Right*. Princeton: Princeton University Press.

Bahn, P.G. 1984 Do not disturb? Archaeology and the rights of the dead. *Oxford Journal of Archaeology* 3: 127–39.

Bahn, P.G. 1990 Eating people is wrong. *Nature* 348: 395.

Bahn, P.G. (ed.) 1996 *Tombs, Graves and Mummies: 50 discoveries in world archaeology*. London: Weidenfeld & Nicolson.

Bahn, P.G. and Paterson, R.W.K. 1986 The last rights: more on archaeology and the dead. *Oxford Journal of Archaeology* 5: 255–71.

Bailey, D. 1994 Reading prehistoric figurines as individuals. *World Archaeology* 25: 321–31.

Bailey, D. 1996 The interpretation of figurines: the emergence of illusion and new ways of seeing. *Cambridge Archaeological Journal* 6: 291–5.

Baker, M. 1997 Invisibility as a symptom of gender categories in archaeology. In J. Moore and E. Scott (eds) *Invisible People and Processes: writing gender and childhood into European archaeology*. Leicester: Leicester University Press, 183–91.

Baldwin, J. 1962 Letter from a region in my mind. *The New Yorker* 17 November 1962.

Baldwin, R. 1985 Intrusive burial groups in the late Roman cemetery at Lankhills, Winchester. *Oxford Journal of Archaeology* 4: 93–104.

Barker, A. and Pauketat, T. (eds) 1992 *Lords of the Southeast: social inequality and the native elites of southeastern North America*. Washington, DC: American Anthropological Association.

Barker, P. 1993 *Techniques of Archaeological Excavation*. Third edition. London: Batsford.

Barley, N. 1990 *Native Land: the bizarre rituals and curious customs that make the English English*. Harmondsworth: Penguin.

Barley, N. 1995 *Dancing on the Grave: encounters with death*. London: John Murray.

Barrett, J.C. 1989 Food, gender and metal: questions of social reproduction. In M.L. Sørensen and R. Thomas (eds) *The Bronze Age–Iron Age Transitions in Europe: aspects of continuity and change in European societies c. 1200 to 500 BC*. Oxford: BAR International Series 483: 304–20.

Barrett, J.C. 1990 The monumentality of death: the character of Early Bronze Age mortuary mounds in southern Britain. *World Archaeology* 22: 178–89.

Barrett, J.C. 1994 *Fragments from Antiquity: an archaeology of social life in Britain, 2900–1200 BC*. Oxford: Blackwell.

Barry, T. 1992 *Inside Guatemala*. Albuquerque: The Inter-Hemispheric Education Resource Center.

Bar-Yosef, O. 1986 The walls of Jericho: an alternative explanation. *Current Anthropology* 27: 157–62.

Bar-Yosef, O., Gopher, A., Tchernov, E. and Kislev, M.E. 1991 Netiv Hagdud: an early Neolithic village site in the Jordan valley. *Journal of Field Archaeology* 18: 405–24.

Bar-Yosef, O., Vandermeersch, B., Arensburg, B., Belfer-Cohen, A., Goldberg, P., Laville, H., Meignen, L., Rak, Y., Speth, J.D., Tchernov, E., Tillier, A.-M. and Weiner, S. 1992 The excavations in Kebara cave, Mt Carmel. *Current Anthropology* 33: 497–551.

Bassett, S. (ed.) 1995 *Death in Towns: urban responses to the dying and the dead, 100–1600*. Leicester: Leicester University Press.

Battaglia, D. 1990 *On the Bones of the Serpent: person, memory, and mortality in Sabarl Island society*. Chicago: University of Chicago Press.

Bauer, B.S. 1996 Legitimization of the state in Inca myth and ritual. *American Anthropologist* 98: 327–37.

Baumann, Z. 1993 *Mortality, Immortality and Other Life Strategies*. Oxford: Polity Press.

Beattie, O. 1999 Sleep by the shores of those icy seas: death and resurrection in the last Franklin expedition. In J. Downes and T. Pollard (eds) *The Loved Body's Corruption: archaeological contributions to the study of human mortality*. Glasgow: Cruithne Press, 52–68.

Beattie, O. and Geiger, J. 1987 *Frozen in Time: unlocking the secrets of the Franklin Expedition*. London: Collins.

Beck, B.E.F. 1975 The anthropology of the body. *Current Anthropology* 16: 486–7.

Becker, E. 1973 *The Denial of Death*. New York: Free Press.

Behrensmeyer, A., Gordon, K. and Yanagi, G. 1986 Trampling as a cause of bone surface damage and pseudo-cut marks. *Nature* 319: 768–71.

Belfer-Cohen, A. 1995. Rethinking social stratification in the Natufian culture: the evidence from burials. In S. Campbell and A. Green (eds) *The Archaeology of Death in the Ancient Near East*. Oxford: Oxbow Monograph 51, 9–16.

Bell, C. 1992 *Ritual Theory, Ritual Practice*. Oxford: Oxford University Press.

Bendann, E. 1930 *Death Customs: an analytical study of burial rites*. London: Dawson.

Bender, B. 1997 Commentary: writing gender. In J. Moore and E. Scott (eds) *Invisible People and Processes: writing gender and childhood into European archaeology*. Leicester: Leicester University Press, 178–80.

Bender Jørgensen, L. 1979 Cloth of the Roman Iron Age in Denmark. *Acta Archaeologica* 50: 1–60.

Bender Jørgensen, L. 1986 *Forhistoriske Textiler i Skandinavien: prehistoric Scandinavian textiles*. Copenhagen: Nordiske Fortidsminder.

Bender Jørgensen, L. 1992 *North European Textiles until AD 1000*. Copenhagen: Nordiske Fortidsminder.

Bennett, M. 1992 *Scottish Folk Traditions from the Cradle to the Grave*. Edinburgh: Polygon.

Bennike, P. 1985 *Palaeopathology of Danish Skeletons*. Copenhagen: Akademisk Forlag.

Bennike, P. 1999 The Early Neolithic Danish bog finds: a strange group of people! In B. Coles, J. Coles and M. Schou Jørgensen (eds) *Bog Bodies, Sacred Sites and Wetland Archaeology*. Exeter: University of Exeter WARP Occasional Paper 12, 27–32.

Benthall, J. and Polhemus, E. 1975 *The Body as a Medium of Expression*. London: Allen Lane.

Bermudez de Castro, J.M., Arsuaga, J.L. and Carbonell, E. 1997 A hominid from the lower Pleistocene of Atapuerca, Spain: possible ancestor to Neanderthals and modern humans. *Science* 276: 1392–5.

Bevan, W. 1999 The landscape context of the Iron-Age square-barrow burials, East Yorkshire. In J. Downes and T. Pollard (eds) *The Loved Body's Corruption: archaeological contributions to the study of human mortality*. Glasgow: Cruithne Press, 69–93.

Bieder, R.E. 1992 The collecting of bones for anthropological narratives. *American Indian Culture and Research Journal* 16: 21–35.

Biel, J. 1986 *Der Keltenfürst von Hochdorf*. Stuttgart: Konrad Theiss.

Bienert, H.D. 1991 Skull cult in the prehistoric Near East. *Journal of Prehistoric Religion* 5: 9–23.

Binford, L.R. 1962 Archaeology as anthropology. *American Antiquity* 28: 217–25.

Binford, L.R. 1971 Mortuary practices: their study and their potential. In J. Brown (ed.) *Approaches to the Social Dimensions of Mortuary Practices*. Washington DC: Memoir of the Society for American Archaeology 25, 6–29.

Binford, L.R. 1972 Galley Pond mound. In L.R. Binford *An Archaeological Perspective*. New York: Seminar Press, 390–420.

Binford, L.R. 1977 General introduction. In L. Binford (ed.) *For Theory Building in Archaeology*. New York: Academic Press, 1–10.

Binford, L.R. 1981a *Bones: ancient men and modern myths*. New York: Academic Press.

Binford, L.R. 1981b *Nunamiut Ethnoarchaeology*. New York: Academic Press.

Binford, L.R. and Ho, C.K. 1985 Taphonomy at a distance: Zhoukoudian, 'the cave home of Beijing Man'? *Current Anthropology* 26: 413–42.

Binford, L.R. and Stone, N.M. 1986 Zhoukoudian: a closer look. *Current Anthropology* 27: 453–75.

Binford, S.R. 1968 A structural comparison of disposal of the dead in the Mousterian and the Upper Paleolithic. *Southwestern Journal of Anthropology* 24: 139–54.

Bintliff, J. (ed.) 1984 *European Social Evolution: archaeological perspectives*. Bradford: University of Bradford.

Blacking, J. (ed.) 1977 *The Anthropology of the Body*. London: Academic Press.

Blakely, R.L. and Beck, L.A. 1981 Trace element, nutritional status and social stratification at Etowah, Georgia. *Annual of the New York Academy of Science* 376: 417–31.

Blitz, J. 1993a *Ancient Chiefdoms of the Tombigbee*. Tuscaloosa: University of Alabama Press.

Blitz, J. 1993b Big pots for big shots: feasting and storage in a Mississippian community. *American Antiquity* 58: 80–96.

Bloch, M. 1971 *Placing the Dead: tombs, ancestral villages, and kinship organisation in Madagascar*. London: Seminar Press.

Bloch, M. 1977 The past and the present in the present. *Man* 12: 278–92.

Bloch, M. 1982 Death, women and regeneration. In M. Bloch and J. Parry (eds) *Death and the Regeneration of Life*. Cambridge: Cambridge University Press, 211–30.

Bloch, M. and Parry, J. (eds) 1982 *Death and the Regeneration of Life*. Cambridge: Cambridge University Press.

Boddington, A., Garland, A.N. and Janaway, R.C. (eds) 1987 *Death, Decay and Reconstruction: approaches to archaeology and forensic science*. Manchester: Manchester University Press.

Bogucki, P. 1996 Pazyryk and the Ukok princess. In P.G. Bahn (ed.) *Tombs, Graves and Mummies: 50 discoveries in world archaeology*. London: Weidenfeld & Nicholson, 146–51.

Boles, T.C., Snow, C.C. and Stover, E. 1995 Forensic DNA testing on skeletal remains from mass graves: a pilot project in Guatemala. *Journal of Forensic Science* 20: 149–53.

Boone, E.H. (ed.) 1984 *Ritual Human Sacrifice in Mesoamerica: a conference at Dumbarton Oaks, October 13–14, 1979*. Cambridge MA: Harvard University Press.

Borg, A. 1991 *War Memorials*. London: Leo Cooper.

Botscharow, L.J. 1989 Sites as texts: an exploration of Mousterian traces. In I. Hodder (ed.) *The Meanings of Things*. London: Unwin Hyman, 50–5.

Bourdieu, P. 1977 *Outline of a Theory of Practice*. Cambridge: Cambridge University Press.

Bourdieu, P. 1984 *Distinction: a social critique of the judgement of taste*. London: Routledge & Kegan Paul.

Bowden, R. 1984 Maori cannibalism: an interpretation. *Oceania* 55: 81–99.

Bowlby, J. 1961 Processes of mourning. *International Journal of Psychoanalysis* 42: 317–40.

Boyd, B. 1995 Houses and hearths, pits and burials: Natufian mortuary practices at Mallaha (Eynan), upper Jordan valley. In S. Campbell and A. Green (eds) *The Archaeology of Death in the Ancient Near East*. Oxford: Oxbow Monograph 51, 17–23.

Boyle, A., Dodd, A., Miles, D. and Mudd, A. 1995 *Two Oxfordshire Anglo-Saxon Cemeteries: Berinsfield and Didcot*. Oxford: Oxford University Committee for Archaeology.

Boylston, A., Holst, M., Coughlan, J., Novak, S., Sutherland, T. and Knüsel, C. 1997 Recent excavations of a mass grave from Towton. *Yorkshire Medicine* 9: 25–6.

Bradfield, J.B. 1994 *Green Burial: the d-i-y guide to law and practice*. Second edition. London: The Natural Death Centre.

Bradley, R. 1984 *The Social Foundations of Prehistoric Britain: themes and variations in the archaeology of power*. London: Longman.

Bradley, R. 1990 *The Passage of Arms*. Cambridge: Cambridge University Press.

Bradley, R. 1993 *Altering the Earth: the origins of monuments in Britain and continental Europe*. Edinburgh: Society of Antiquaries of Scotland Monograph Series 8.

Brandt, S.A. 1988 Early Holocene mortuary practices and hunter-gatherer adaptations in southern Somalia. *World Archaeology* 20: 40–56.

Branigan, K. 1982 The unacceptable face of Minoan Crete. *Nature* 5580: 201–2.

Branigan, K. 1993 *Dancing With Death: life and death in southern Crete c. 3000–2000 BC*. Amsterdam: Hakkert.

Branigan, K. 1998 The nearness of you: proximity and distance in Early Minoan funerary landscapes. In K. Branigan (ed.) *Cemetery and Society in the Aegean Bronze Age*. Sheffield: Sheffield Academic Press, 13–26.

Breitsprecher, U. 1987 *Zum Problem der geschlechtsspezifischen Bestattungen in der Römischen Kaiserzeit: ein Beitrag zur Forschungsgeschichte und Methode*. Oxford: BAR International Series 376.

Brent, M. 1994 The rape of Mali and the plight of ancient Jenne. *Archaeology* 47(3): 26–35.

Brewster, T.C.M. 1982 *The Excavation of Garton and Wetwang Slacks*. London: National Monuments Record (microfiche).

Briggs, C.S. 1995 Did they fall or were they pushed? Some unresolved questions about bog bodies. In R.C. Turner and R.G. Scaife (eds) *Bog Bodies: new discoveries and new perspectives*. London: British Museum, 168–82.

Broholm, H.C. 1943–7 *Danmarks Bronzealder I–IV*. Copenhagen.

Broholm, H.C. and Hald, M. 1948 *Bronze Age Fashion*. Copenhagen: Gyldendalske.

Brothwell, D. 1961 Cannibalism in early Britain. *Antiquity* 35: 304–7.

Brothwell, D. 1981 *Digging up Bones: the excavation, treatment and study of human skeletal remains*. Third edition. Oxford: British Museum (Natural History) and Oxford University Press.

Brothwell, D. and Bourke, J.B. 1995 The human remains from Lindow Moss 1987–8. In R.C. Turner and R.G. Scaife (eds) *Bog Bodies: new discoveries and new perspectives*. London: British Museum, 52–8.

Brown, J.A. 1971a The dimensions of status in the burials at Spiro. In J.A. Brown (ed.) *Approaches to the Social Dimensions of Mortuary Practices*. Washington DC: Memoir of the Society for American Archaeology 25, 92–112.

Brown, J.A. (ed.) 1971b *Approaches to the Social Dimensions of Mortuary Practices*. Washington DC: Memoir of the Society for American Archaeology 25.

Brown, J.K. 1975 Iroquois women: an ethnohistoric note. In R.R. Reiter (ed.) *Toward an Anthropology of Women*. New York: Monthly Review Press, 235–51.

Brown, P. 1981 *The Cult of Saints*. London: SCM Press.

Brown, P. 1988 *The Body and Society: men, women, and sexual renunciation in early Christianity*. New York: Columbia University Press.

Brown, P. and Tuzins, D. (eds) 1983 *The Ethnography of Cannibalism*. Washington DC: Society for Psychological Anthropology.

Bruce-Mitford, R. 1975 *The Sutton Hoo Ship-Burial Volume 1: excavations, background, the ship, dating and inventory*. London: British Museum.

Brush, K. 1988 Gender and mortuary analysis in pagan Anglo-Saxon archaeology. *Archaeological Review from Cambridge* 7: 76–89.

Buchanan, J.L. 1793 *Travels in the Western Hebrides: from 1782 to 1790*. London.

Buikstra, J.E. 1981 Mortuary practices, palaeodemography and palaeopathology: a case study from the Koster site (Illinois). In R. Chapman, I. Kinnes and K. Randsborg (eds) *The Archaeology of Death*. Cambridge: Cambridge University Press, 123–32.

Buikstra, J.E. 1984 The lower Illinois river region: a prehistoric context for the study of ancient diet and health. In M.N. Cohen and G.J. Armelagos (eds) *Palaeopathology at the Origins of Agriculture*. London: Academic Press, 215–34.

Buikstra, J.E., Frankenberg, S., Lambert, J.B. and Xue, L. 1989 Multiple elements: multiple expectations. In T.D. Price (ed.) *The Chemistry of Prehistoric Human Bone*. Cambridge: Cambridge University Press, 155–210.

Buikstra, J.E. and Ubelaker, D.H. (eds) 1994 *Standards for Data Collection from Human Skeletal Remains*. Fayetteville AK: Arkansas Archaeological Survey.

Burger, R.L. and van der Merwe, N.J. 1990 Maize and the origins of highland Chavin civilisation: an isotopic perspective. *American Anthropologist* 92: 85–95.

Burkert, W. 1983 *Homo Necans: the anthropology of ancient Greek sacrificial ritual and myth*. Berkeley: University of California Press.

Burkert, W. 1987 The problem of ritual killing. In R.G. Hamerton-Kelly (ed.) *Violent Origins: ritual killing and cultural formation*. Stanford: Stanford University Press, 149–76.

Burl, A. 1979a *Prehistoric Avebury*. New Haven CT: Yale University Press.

Burl, A. 1979b *Rings of Stone*. London: Frances Lincoln and Weidenfeld.

Burman, P. 1988 *The Churchyards Handbook: advice on the history and significance of churchyards*. London: Church House.

Burton, J.H. and Price, T.D. 1990 The ratio of barium to strontium as a paleodietary indicator of consumption of marine resources. *Journal of Archaeological Science* 17: 547–57.

Burton, J.H. and Wright, L.C. 1995 Nonlinearity in the relationship between bone Sr/Ca and diet: paleodietary implications. *American Journal of Physical Anthropology* 96: 273–82.

Bygott, J.D. 1972 Cannibalism among wild chimpanzees. *Nature* 238: 410–11.

Byrd, B.F. and Monahan, C.M. 1995 Death, mortuary ritual, and Natufian social structure. *Journal of Anthropological Archaeology* 14: 251–87.

Cabrera Castro, R., Sugiyama, S. and Cowgill, G.L. 1991 The Templo de Quetzalcoatl Project at Teotihuacán: a preliminary report. *Ancient Mesoamerica* 2: 77–92.

Cannadine, D. 1981 War and death, grief and mourning in modern Britain. In J. Whaley (ed.) *Mirrors of Mortality: studies in the social history of death*. London: Europa, 187–242.

Cannon, A. 1989 The historical dimension in mortuary expressions of status and sentiment. *Current Anthropology* 30: 437–58.

Cannon, A. 1991 Gender, status, and the focus of material display. In D. Walde and N.D. Willows (eds) *The Archaeology of Gender: proceedings of the 22nd Annual Chacmool Conference*. Calgary: Archaeological Association of the University of Calgary, 144–9.

Carr, C. 1995 Mortuary practices: their social, philosophical-religious, circumstantial, and physical determinants. *Journal of Archaeological Method and Theory* 2: 105–200.

Carr, G. and Knüsel, C. 1997 The ritual framework of excarnation by exposure as the mortuary practice of the early and middle Iron Ages of central southern Britain. In A. Gwilt and C. Haselgrove (eds) *Reconstructing Iron Age Societies: new approaches to the British Iron Age*. Oxford: Oxbow, 167–73.

Carter, H. and Mace, A.C. 1923 *The Tomb of Tutankhamen*. London: Cassell.

Carver, M.O.H. 1998 *Sutton Hoo: burial ground of kings?* London: British Museum.

Cassin, E. 1982 Le mort: valeur et représentation en Mésopotamie ancienne. In G. Gnoli and J.-P. Vernant (eds) *La Mort, Les Morts dans les Sociétés Anciennes*. Cambridge: Cambridge University Press, 355–72.

Castile, G.P. 1980 Purple people eaters? A comment on Aztec elite class cannibalism à la Harris-Harner. *American Anthropologist* 82: 389–91.

Cederroth, S., Corlin, C. and Lundstrom, J. (eds) 1987 *On the Meaning of Death*. Uppsala: Uppsala Studies in Cultural Anthropology 8.

Chagnon, N.A. 1992 *Yanomamo: the last days of Eden*. San Diego: Harcourt Brace Jovanovich.

Chamberlain, A.T. 1994 *Human Remains*. London: British Museum.

Chamberlain, A.T. 1997 Commentary: missing stages of life – towards the perception of children in archaeology. In J. Moore and E. Scott (eds) *Invisible People and Processes: writing gender and childhood into European archaeology*. Leicester: Leicester University Press, 248–50.

Champion, T.C., Gamble, C., Shennan, S.J. and Whittle, A. 1984 *Prehistoric Europe*. London: Academic Press.

Chang, K.-C. 1980 *Shang Civilization*. New Haven: Yale University Press.

Chapman, J. 1991 The creation of social arenas in the Neolithic and Copper Age of S.E. Europe: the case of Varna. In P. Garwood, D. Jennings, R. Skeates and J. Toms (eds) *Sacred and Profane: proceedings of a conference on archaeology, ritual and religion, Oxford 1989*. Oxford: Oxford University Committee for Archaeology Monograph 32, 152–71.

Chapman, J. 1994 The living, the dead and the ancestors: time, life cycles and the mortuary domain in later European prehistory. In J. Davies (ed.) *Ritual and Remembrance: responses to death in human societies*. Sheffield: Sheffield Academic Press, 40–85.

Chapman, J. 1997 Changing gender relations in the later prehistory of eastern Hungary. In J. Moore and E. Scott (eds) *Invisible People and Processes: writing gender and childhood into European archaeology*. Leicester: Leicester University Press, 131–49.

Chapman, R.W. 1977 Burial practices: an area of mutual interest. In M. Spriggs (ed.) *Archaeology and Anthropology: areas of mutual interest*. Oxford: BAR Supplementary Series 19, 19–33.

Chapman, R.W. 1981 Archaeological theory and communal burial in prehistoric Europe. In I. Hodder, G. Isaac and N. Hammond (eds) *Pattern of the Past: studies in honour of David L. Clarke*. Cambridge: Cambridge University Press, 387–411.

Chapman, R.W. 1983 Archaeology after death. *Scottish Archaeological Review* 2: 88–96.

Chapman, R.W. 1990 *Emerging Complexity: the later prehistory of south-east Spain, Iberia and the west Mediterranean*. Cambridge: Cambridge University Press.

Chapman, R.W. 1995 Ten years after – megaliths, mortuary practices, and the territorial model. In L. Anderson Beck (ed.) *Regional Approaches to Mortuary Analysis*. New York: Plenum, 29–51.

Chapman, R.W., Kinnes, I. and Randsborg, K. (eds) 1981 *The Archaeology of Death*. Cambridge: Cambridge University Press.

Chapman, R.W. and Randsborg, K. 1981 Perspectives on the archaeology of death. In R.W. Chapman, I. Kinnes and K. Randsborg (eds) *The Archaeology of Death*. Cambridge: Cambridge University Press, 1–24.

Charles, D.K. 1992 Woodland demographic and social dynamics in the American Midwest: analysis of a burial mound survey. *World Archaeology* 24: 175–97.

Charles, D.K. 1995 Diachronic regional social dynamics: mortuary sites in the Illinois Valley/American Bottom region. In L. Anderson Beck (ed.) *Regional Approaches to Mortuary Analysis*. New York: Plenum, 77–99.

Charles, D.K. and Buikstra, J.E. 1983 Archaic mortuary sites in the central Mississippi drainage: distribution, structure, and behavioral implications. In J.L. Phillips and J.A. Brown (eds) *Archaic Hunters and Gatherers in the American Midwest*. New York: Academic Press, 117–45.

Charles, D.K., Buikstra, J.E. and Konigsberg, L.W. 1986 Behavioral implications of Terminal Archaic and Early Woodland mortuary practices in the lower Illinois Valley. In K.B. Farnsworth and T.E. Emerson (eds) *Early Woodland Archaeology*. Kampsville IL: Kampsville Seminars in Archeology 2, Center for American Archeology.

Chatters, J. 1997 Kennewick Man. nmnhwww.si.edu/arctic/html/kennewick_man.html.

Cheek, A.L. and Keel, B.C. 1984 Value conflicts in osteo-archaeology. In E. Green (ed.) *Ethics and Values in Archaeology*. New York: Free Press, 194–207.

Chidester, D. 1990 *Patterns of Transcendence: religion, death, and dying*. Belmont CA: Wadsworth.

Childe, V.G. 1931 *Skara Brae: a Pictish village in Orkney*. London: Kegan Paul, Trench, Trubner.

Childe, V.G. 1940 *Prehistoric Communities of the British Isles*. London: W. and R. Chambers.

Childe, V.G 1945 Directional changes in funerary practices during 50,000 years. *Man* 4: 13–19.

Childe, V.G. 1951 *Social Evolution*. London: Watts.

Choron, J. 1963 *Death and Western Thought*. New York: Collier.

Clark, G.A. and Neeley, M. 1987 Social differentiation in European Mesolithic burial data. In P. Rowley-Conwy, M. Zvelebil and H.P. Blankholm (eds) *Mesolithic Northwest Europe: recent trends*. Sheffield: Department of Archaeology, University of Sheffield, 121–7.

Clarke, D. (ed.) 1993 *The Sociology of Death*. Oxford: Blackwell.

Clarke, D.V., Cowie, T. and Foxon, A. 1985 *Symbols of Power at the Time of Stonehenge*. Edinburgh: National Museum of Antiquities of Scotland.

Clarke, G. 1979 *Pre-Roman and Roman Winchester. Part 2: The Roman cemetery at Lankhills*. Oxford: Clarendon Press.

Clastres, P. 1977 *Society Against the State*. Oxford: Blackwell.

Clastres, P. 1998 *Chronicle of the Guayaki Indians*. Translated by P. Auster. London: Faber & Faber.

Cleal, R.M.J., Walker, K.E. and Montague, R. 1995 *Stonehenge in its Landscape: twentieth-century excavations*. London: English Heritage.

Cobb, C.R. and Garrow, P.H. 1996 Woodstock culture and the question of Mississippian emergence. *American Antiquity* 61: 21–37.

Coe, M.D. 1993 *The Maya*. Fifth edition. London: Thames & Hudson.

Collier, J.F. and Yanagisako, S.J. 1987 *Gender and Kinship: essays toward a unified analysis*. Stanford: Stanford University Press.

Colvin, H. 1991 *Architecture and the After-life*. New Haven: Yale University Press.

Conkey, M.W. 1991 Does it make a difference? Feminist thinking and archaeologies of gender. In D. Walde and N.D. Willows (eds) *The Archaeology of Gender: proceedings of the 22nd Annual Chacmool Conference*. Calgary: Archaeological Association of the University of Calgary, 24–33.

Conkey, M.W. and Spector, J.D. 1984 Archaeology and the study of gender. *Advances in Archaeological Method and Theory* 7: 1–38.

Connell, R.W. 1995 *Masculinities*. Sydney: Allen & Unwin.

Connolly, R.C. 1969 Kinship of Smenkhkare and Tutankhamen affirmed by serological micromethod. *Nature* 224: 325.

Connolly, R.C. 1985 Lindow Man – a prehistoric bog corpse. *Anthropology Today* 1: 15–17.

Connor, L.H. 1995 The action of the body on society: washing a corpse in Bali. *Journal of the Royal Anthropological Institute* (n.s.) 1: 537–59.

Conze, E. 1993 *A Short History of Buddhism*. Oxford: Oneworld.

Cook, D.C. 1981 Mortality, age-structure and status in the interpretation of stress indicators in prehistoric skeletons: a dental example from the Lower Illinois valley. In R. Chapman, I. Kinnes and K. Randsborg (eds) *The Archaeology of Death*. Cambridge: Cambridge University Press, 133–44.

Cook, B.F. 1991 The archaeologist and the art market: politics and practice. *Antiquity* 65: 533–7.

Cooney, G. 1983 Megalithic tombs in their environmental setting: a settlement perspective. In T. Reeves-Smyth and F. Hamond (eds) *Landscape Archaeology in Ireland*. Oxford: BAR British Series 116, 179–94.

Cortez, C. 1996 The tomb of Pacal at Palenque. In P.G. Bahn (ed.) *Tombs, Graves and Mummies: 50 discoveries in world archaeology*. London: Weidenfeld & Nicolson, 126–9.

Cotterell, A. 1981 *The First Emperor of China*. London: Macmillan.

Cowell, M.R. and Craddock, P.T. 1995 Addendum: copper on the skin of Lindow Man. In R.C. Turner and R.G. Scaife (eds) *Bog Bodies: new discoveries and new perspectives*. London: British Museum, 74–5.

Cox, M. 1994 On excavating the recent dead. *British Archaeological News* 18: 8.

Cox, M. 1996 *Life and Death in Spitalfields 1700 to 1850*. York: Council for British Archaeology.

Cox, M. (ed.) 1998 *Grave Concerns: death and burial in England 1700 to 1850*. London: Council for British Archaeology Research Report 113.

Crabtree, P.J. 1991 Gender hierarchies and the sexual division of labor in the Natufian culture of the southern Levant. In D. Walde and N.D. Willows (eds) *The Archaeology of Gender: proceedings of the 22nd Annual Chacmool Conference*. Calgary: Archaeological Association of the University of Calgary, 384–91.

Crawford, O.G.S. 1957 *The Eye Goddess*. London: Phoenix House.

Crummy, P. 1997 *City of Victory: the story of Colchester – Britain's first Roman town*. Colchester: Colchester Archaeological Trust.

Cunliffe, B.W. 1993 *Danebury*. London: Batsford and English Heritage.

Cunnington, P. and Lucas, C. 1972 *Costume for Births, Marriages and Death*. London: Black.

Curl, J.S. 1972 *The Victorian Celebration of Death*. Newton Abbott: David & Charles.

Curl, J.S. 1980 *A Celebration of Death: an introduction to some of the buildings, monuments, and settings of funerary architecture in the western European tradition*. London: Constable.

Cushman, H.B. 1899 *History of the Choctaw, Chickasaw and Natchez Indians*. Greenville TX: Headlight Printing House.

Damm, C.B. 1991a Burying the past. An example of social transformation in the Danish Neolithic. In P. Garwood, D. Jennings, R. Skeates and J. Toms (eds) *Sacred and Profane: proceedings of a conference on archaeology, ritual and religion, Oxford 1989*. Oxford: Oxford University Committee for Archaeology Monograph 32, 43–9.

Damm, C.B. 1991b From burials to gender roles: problems and potentials in post-processual archaeology. In D. Walde and N.D. Willows (eds) *The Archaeology of Gender: proceedings of the 22nd Annual Chacmool Conference*. Calgary: Archaeological Association of the University of Calgary, 130–5.

Damon, F.H. and Wagner, R. (eds) 1989 *Death Rituals and Life in the Societies of the Kula Ring*. De Kalb: Northern Illinois Press.

Danforth, L. 1982 *The Death Rituals of Rural Greece*. With photographs by Alexander Tsiaras. Princeton: Princeton University Press.

Daniell, C. 1997 *Death and Burial in Medieval England: 1066–1550*. London: Routledge.

Darvill, T.C. 1979 Court cairns, passage graves and social change in Ireland. *Man* 14: 311–27.

Darvill, T.C. 1982 *The Megalithic Chambered Tombs of the Cotswold-Severn Region*. Highworth, Wilts.: Vorda.

Darvill, T.C. 1987 *Prehistoric Britain*. London: Batsford.

Darwin, C. 1872 *The Expression of the Emotions in Man and Animals*. London: John Murray.

David, N. 1992 The archaeology of ideology: mortuary practices in the central Mandara highlands, northern Cameroon. In J. Sterner and N. David (eds) *An African Commitment*. Calgary: University of Calgary Press, 181–210.

Davies, J. 1994 Reconstructing enmities: war and war memorials, the boundary markers of the west.

History of European Ideas 19: 47–52.

Davies, N. 1981 *Human Sacrifice: in history and today*. New York: William Morrow.

Davis, S. and Payne, S. 1993 A barrow full of cattle skulls. *Antiquity* 67: 12–22.

Dawes, J.D. and Magilton, J.R. 1980 *The cemetery at St Helen-on-the-Walls, Aldwark. The Archaeology of York Volume 12: The Medieval Cemeteries*. London: Council for British Archaeology.

Day, M. 1990 Archaeological ethics and the treatment of the dead. *Anthropology Today* 6: 15–16.

de Beauvoir, S. 1953 *The Second Sex*. New York: Alfred Knopf.

de Lauretis, T. 1986 Feminist studies/critical studies: issues, terms, and contexts. In T. de Lauretis (ed.) *Feminist Studies: critical studies*. Bloomington: Indiana University Press, 1–19.

Deetz, J. and Dethlefsen, E.N. 1967 Death's head, cherub, urn, and willow. *Natural History* 76(3): 28–37.

Deetz, J. and Dethlefsen, E.N. 1971 Some social aspects of New England colonial mortuary art. In J. Brown (ed.) *Approaches to the Social Dimensions of Mortuary Practices*. Washington DC: Memoir of the Society for American Archaeology 25, 30–8.

Deloria, V. Jr. 1992 Indians, archaeologists, and the future. *American Antiquity* 57: 595–8.

Demoule, J.-P. 1982 L'analyse archéologique des cimetières et l'exemple des necropoles celtiques. In G. Gnoli and J.-P. Vernant (eds) *La Mort, Les Morts dans les Sociétés Anciennes*. Cambridge: Cambridge University Press, 319–37.

Dempsey, D. 1975 *The Way We Die: an investigation of death and dying in America today*. New York: McGraw-Hill.

Deng, F.M. 1972 *The Dinka of the Sudan*. New York: Holt, Rinehart and Winston.

Dennell, R. 1997 The world's oldest spears. *Nature* 385: 767–8.

Dent, J.S. 1982 Cemeteries and settlement patterns of the Iron Age on the Yorkshire Wolds. *Proceedings of the Prehistoric Society* 48: 437–57.

Dent, J.S. 1983 A summary of the excavations carried out in Garton Slack and Wetwang Slack, 1964–80. *East Riding Archaeologist* 7: 1–14.

d'Errico, F. 1995 A new model and its implications for the origin of writing: the La Marche antler revisited. *Cambridge Archaeological Journal* 5: 163–206.

Descola, P. 1996 *The Spears of Twilight: life and death in the Amazon jungle*. London: HarperCollins.

Desroches-Noblecourt, C. 1965 *Life and Death of a Pharaoh: Tutankhamun*. Harmondsworth: Penguin.

Dethlefsen, E.N. and Deetz, J. 1966 Death's heads, cherubs and willow trees: experimental archaeology in colonial cemeteries. *American Antiquity* 31: 502–10.

Dettwyler, K.A. 1991 Can palaeopathology provide evidence for 'compassion'? *American Journal of Physical Anthropology* 84: 375–84.

Di Lonardo, A., Darlu, P., Baur, M. and Orrego, C. 1984 Human genetics and human rights. *American Journal of Forensic Medicine and Pathology* 5: 339–47.

Dickson, J.H. 1978 Bronze Age mead. *Antiquity* 52: 108–13.

Dieck, A. 1972 Stand und Aufgaben der Moorleichenforschung. *Archäologisches Korrespondenzblatt* 2: 365–8.

Dieck, A. 1986 Der Stand der europäischen Moorleichen im Jahr 1986 sowie Materialvorlage von anthropologischen und medizinischen Sonderbefunden. *Telma* 16: 131–58.

Dietler, M. 1990 Driven by drink: the role of drinking in the political economy and the case of Early Iron Age France. *Journal of Anthropological Archaeology* 9: 352–406.

Dommasnes, L.H. 1982 Late Iron Age in western Norway. Female roles and ranks as deduced from an analysis of burial customs. *Norwegian Archaeological Review* 15: 70–84.

Dommasnes, L.H. 1991 Women, kinship, and the basis of power in the Norwegian Viking Age. In R. Samson (ed.) *Social Approaches to Viking Studies.* Glasgow: Cruithne Press, 65–73.

Dommasnes, L.H. 1992 Two decades of women in prehistory and in archaeology in Norway. A review. *Norwegian Archaeological Review* 25: 1–14.

Donley, L.W. 1982 House power: Swahili space and symbolic markers. In I. Hodder (ed.) *Symbolic and Structural Archaeology.* Cambridge: Cambridge University Press, 63–73.

Doran, G.H., Dickel, D.N., Ballinger, W.E. Jr, Agee, O.F., Laipis, P.J. and Hauswirth, W.W. 1986 Analytical, cellular and molecular analysis of 8,000-yr-old human brain tissue from the Windover archaeological site. *Nature* 223: 803–6.

Dornstreich, M.D. and Morren, E.B. 1974 Does New Guinea cannibalism have nutritional value? *Human Ecology* 2: 1–11.

Douglas, M. 1966 *Purity and Danger. An analysis of concepts of pollution and taboo.* London: Routledge & Kegan Paul.

Douglas, M. 1973 *Natural Symbols: explorations in cosmology.* Harmondsworth: Penguin.

Douglass, W.A. 1969 *Death in Murelaga: funerary ritual in a Spanish Basque village.* Seattle: University of Washington Press.

Downes, J. 1999 Cremation: a spectacle and a journey. In J. Downes and T. Pollard (eds) *The Loved Body's Corruption: archaeological contributions to the study of human mortality.* Glasgow: Cruithne Press, 19–29.

Downes, J. and Pollard, T. (eds) 1999 *The Loved Body's Corruption: archaeological contributions to the study of human mortality.* Glasgow: Cruithne Press.

Doxtater, D. 1990 Socio-political change and symbolic space in Norwegian farm culture after the Reformation. In M. Turan (ed.) *Vernacular Architecture: paradigms of environmental response.* Aldershot: Avebury Press, 183–218.

Drennan, R.D. 1996 *Statistics for Archaeologists: a commonsense approach.* New York: Plenum Press.

Drennan, R.D. and Uribe, C.A. (eds) 1987 *Chiefdoms in the Americas.* Lanham MD: University Press of America.

Drury, R. 1743 [1729] *Madagascar: or Robert Drury's Journal during fifteen years captivity on that island.* London: Meadows.

Dureau, C.M. 1991 Death, gender and regeneration: a critique of Maurice Bloch. *Canberra Anthropology* 14: 24–44.

Durkheim, E. 1965 [1912] *The Elementary Forms of the Religious Life.* New York: Free Press.

Earle, T. 1987 Chiefdoms in archaeological and ethnohistorical perspective. *Annual Review of Anthropology* 16: 279–308.

Earle, T. (ed.) 1991 *Chiefdoms: power, economy, and ideology.* Cambridge: Cambridge University Press.

East, K. 1984 The Sutton Hoo ship burial: a case against the coffin. *Anglo-Saxon Studies in Archaeology and History* 3: 139–52.

Echo-Hawk, W. (ed.) 1992 Repatriation of American Indian remains. (Special issue.) *American Indian Culture and Research Journal* 16: 1–268.

Edmonds, M. 1995 *Stone Tools and Society.* London: Batsford.

Edmonds, M. 1999 *Ancestral Geographies of the Neolithic: landscape, monuments and memory.* London: Routledge.

Edwards, I.E.S. 1979 *Tutankhamun, his Tomb and its Treasures.* London: Victor Gollancz.

Ehrenberg, M. 1989 *Women in Prehistory.* London: British Museum.

Eisner, W.R. 1991 The consequences of gender bias in mortuary analysis: a case study. In D. Walde and N.D. Willows (eds) *The Archaeology of Gender: proceedings of the 22nd Annual Chacmool Conference.* Calgary: Archaeological Association of the University of Calgary, 352–7.

El Mahdy, C. 1989 *Mummies, Myth and Magic.* London: Thames & Hudson.

Elgar, M. and Crespi, B. 1992 *Cannibalism: ecology and evolution among diverse taxa.* New York: Oxford University Press.

Elia, R.J. 1996 A seductive and troubling work. In K.D. Vitelli (ed.) *Archaeological Ethics.* Walnut Creek: Altamira Press, 54–62.

Eliade, M. 1965 *Le Sacré et le Profane.* Paris: Gallimard.

Elliot Smith, G. 1933 *The Diffusion of Culture.* London: Watts & Co.

Emerson, T.E. 1997 *Cahokia and the Archaeology of Power.* Tuscaloosa AL: University of Alabama Press.

Emery, W.B. 1961 *Archaic Egypt.* Harmondsworth: Penguin.

Emory, K.P. 1947 *Tuamotuan Religious Structures and Ceremonies.* Honolulu: Berenice Pauahi Bishop Museum Bulletin 191.

Engels, F. 1891 *The Origin of the Family, Private Property and the State.* Fourth edition. Moscow: Foreign Languages Publishing House.

Engelstad, E. 1991 Images of power and contradiction: feminist theory and post-processual archaeology. *Antiquity* 65: 502–14.

English Heritage 1990 *Human Remains on Historic Properties*. London: English Heritage.

English Heritage 1991 *The Management of Archaeological Projects (MAP 2)*. London: English Heritage.

Ennew, J. 1980 *The Western Isles Today*. Cambridge: Cambridge University Press.

Evans-Pritchard, E.E. 1948 *The Divine Kingship of the Shilluk of the Nilotic Sudan*. Cambridge: Cambridge University Press.

Evison, M.P. 1996 Genetics, ethics and archaeology. *Antiquity* 70: 512–14.

Evison, M.P. 1997 Ancient HLA: a preliminary investigation. PhD thesis, University of Sheffield.

Ezzo, J.A. 1994 Putting the 'chemistry' back into archaeological bone chemistry analysis: modelling of potential paleodietary indicators. *Journal of Anthropological Archaeology* 13: 1–34.

Fabian J. 1991 How others die – reflections on the anthropology of death. In J. Fabian, *Time and the Work of Anthropology: critical essays 1971–1991*. Amsterdam: Harwood, 173–90.

Farb, P. and Armelagos, G. 1980 *Consuming Passions: the anthropology of eating*. Boston: Houghton Mifflin.

Faulkner, R.O. 1996 *The Ancient Egyptian Book of the Dead*. London: British Museum.

Featherstone, M., Hepworth, M. and Turner, B.S. (eds) 1991 *The Body: social process and culture theory*. London: Sage.

Feeley-Harnik, G. 1989 Cloth and the creation of ancestors in Madagascar. In J. Schneider and A.B. Weiner (eds) *Cloth and Human Experience*. Washington DC: Smithsonian Institution Press, 73–116.

Feifel, H. (ed.) 1959 *The Meaning of Death*. New York: McGraw-Hill.

Fiddes, N. 1991 *Meat: a natural symbol*. London: Routledge.

Finch, J. 1991 'According to the qualitie and degree of the person deceased': funeral monuments and the construction of social identities 1400–1750. *Scottish Archaeological Review* 8: 105–14.

Firestone, S. 1970 *The Dialectic of Sex: the case for feminist revolution*. New York: Bantam.

Fischer, C. 1999 The Tollund man and the Elling woman and other bog bodies from central Jutland. In B. Coles, J. Coles and M. Schou Jørgensen (eds) *Bog Bodies, Sacred Sites and Wetland Archaeology*. Exeter: University of Exeter WARP Occasional Paper 12, 93–7.

Fleming, A. 1971 Territorial patterns in Bronze Age Wessex. *Proceedings of the Prehistoric Society* 37: 138–64.

Fleming, A. 1973a Models for the development of the Wessex culture. In A.C. Renfrew (ed.) *The Explanation of Culture Change: models in prehistory*. London: Duckworth, 571–85.

Fleming, A. 1973b Tombs for the living. *Man* 8: 177–93.

Fleming, A. 1996 Tomb with a view. *Antiquity* 69: 1040–2.

Flinders Petrie, W.M. 1902–4 *Abydos*. Volumes 1 and 2. London: Egypt Exploration Fund.

Flinn, L., Turner, C.G. and Brew, A. 1976 Additional evidence for cannibalism in the southwest: the case of LA 4528. *American Antiquity* 41: 308–18.

Fortune, R. 1932 *The Sorcerers of Dobu*. New York: E.P. Dutton.

Foucault, M. 1977 *Discipline and Punish. The birth of the prison*. London: Allen Lane.

Foucault, M. 1979 *The History of Sexuality*. Volume 1. London: Allen Lane.

Frank, A.W. 1990 Bringing bodies back in: a decade review. *Theory, Culture and Society* 7: 131–62.

Frankenstein, S. and Rowlands, M.J. 1978 The internal structure and regional context of Early Iron Age society in southwestern Germany. *Bulletin of the Institute of Archaeology London* 15: 73–112.

Frankfort, H. 1948 *Kingship and the Gods: a study of ancient Near Eastern religion as the integration of society and nature*. Chicago: Chicago University Press.

Frankfort, H., Frankfort, H.A., Wilson, J.A., Jacobsen, T. and Irwin, W.A. 1946 *The Intellectual Adventure of Ancient Man: an essay on speculative thought in the ancient Near East*. Chicago: Chicago University Press.

Fraser, D. 1983 *Land and Society in Neolithic Orkney*. Oxford: BAR British Series 117.

Frazer, J.G. 1911 *The Golden Bough: a study in magic and religion*. London: Macmillan.

Fried, M.H. 1967 *The Evolution of Political Society: an essay in political anthropology*. New York: Random House.

Fulton, R. (ed.) 1965 *Death and Identity*. New York: Wiley.

Fundaburk, E.L. (ed.) 1958 *Southeastern Indians: life portraits. A catalogue of pictures 1564–1860*. Metuchen NJ: Scarecrow Reprint Corporation.

Gajdusek, D.C. 1977 Unconventional viruses and the origin and disappearance of kuru. *Science* 197: 943–60.

Gamble, C. 1989 Comments on 'Grave shortcomings: the evidence for Neanderthal burial by R. Gargett'. *Current Anthropology* 30: 181–2.

Garfinkel, Y. 1994 Ritual burial of cultic objects: the earliest evidence. *Cambridge Archaeological Journal* 4: 159–88.

Gargett, R.H. 1989 Grave shortcomings: the evidence for Neanderthal burial. *Current Anthropology* 30: 157–90.

Garn, S.M. and Block, W.D. 1970 The limited nutritional value of cannibalism. *American Anthropologist* 72: 106.

Garrett-Frost, S., Harrison, G. and Logie, J.G. 1992 The law and burial archaeology. *Institute of Field Archaeologists Technical Paper* 11.

Geary, P.J. 1986 Sacred commodities: the circulation of medieval relics. In A. Appadurai (ed.) *The Social*

Life of Things: commodities in cultural perspective. Cambridge: Cambridge University Press, 169–91.

Geary, P.J. 1994 *Living with the Dead in the Middle Ages.* Ithaca: Cornell University Press.

Gebühr, M. 1979 Das Kindergrab von Windeby. Versuch einer 'Rehabilitation'. *Offa* 36: 75–107.

Geertz, C. 1973 *The Interpretation of Cultures: selected essays.* New York: Basic Books.

Gell, A. 1993 *Wrapping in Images: tattooing in Polynesia.* Oxford: Clarendon Press.

Gerholm, G. 1988 On ritual: a postmodernist view. *Ethnos* 53: 190–203.

Gibbons, A. 1992 Forensic medicine – scientists search for 'the disappeared' in Guatemala. *Science* 257: 479.

Gibbs, L. 1987 Identifying gender representation in the archaeological record: a contextual study. In I. Hodder (ed.) *The Archaeology of Contextual Meanings.* Cambridge: Cambridge University Press, 79–89.

Giddens, A. 1979 *Central Problems in Social Theory.* London: Macmillan.

Giddens, A. 1984 *The Constitution of Society: outline of the theory of structuration.* London: Polity Press.

Giesey, R.E. 1960 *The Royal Funeral Ceremony in Renaissance France.* Geneva: Librairie E. Droz.

Gilbert, R.I. and Mielke, J.H. (eds) 1985 *The Analysis of Prehistoric Diets.* New York: Academic Press.

Gilchrist, R. 1991 Women's archaeology? Political feminism, gender theory and historical revision. *Antiquity* 65: 495–501.

Gilchrist, R. 1997 Ambivalent bodies: gender and medieval archaeology. In J. Moore and E. Scott (eds) *Invisible People and Processes: writing gender and childhood into European archaeology.* Leicester: Leicester University Press, 42–58.

Gill, P., Ivanov, P.L., Kimpton, C., Piercy, R., Benson, N., Tully, G., Evett, I., Hagelberg, E. and Sullivan, K. 1994 Identification of the remains of the Romanov family by DNA analysis. *Nature Genetics* 6: 130–5.

Gill, P., Kimpton, K., Aliston-Greiner, R., Sullivan, K., Stoneking, M., Melton, T., Nott, J., Barritt, S., Roby, R., Holland, M. and Weeden, V. 1995 Establishing the identity of Anna Anderson Manahan. *Nature Genetics* 9: 9–10.

Gimbutas, M. 1974 *The Goddesses and Gods of Old Europe: myths and cult images.* London: Thames & Hudson.

Gimbutas, M. 1989 *The Language of the Goddess.* London: Thames & Hudson.

Gimbutas, M. 1991 *The Civilization of the Goddess.* New York: HarperCollins.

Girard, R. 1977 *Violence and the Sacred.* Baltimore: Johns Hopkins University Press.

Girard, R. 1987 Generative scapegoating. In R.G. Hamerton-Kelly (ed.) *Violent Origins: ritual killing and cultural formation.* Stanford: Stanford University Press, 73–105.

Girič, M. (ed.) 1971 *Mokrin, the Early Bronze Age Necropolis. I, Dissertationes et Monographie.* Kikinda: Narodai Museum Volume 11.

Gittings, C. 1984 *Death, Burial and the Individual in Early Modern England.* London: Croom Helm.

Glasse, R. 1977 Cannibalism in the kuru region of New Guinea. *Transactions of the New York Academy of Sciences* 29: 748–54.

Glob, P.V. 1969 *The Bog People: Iron-Age man preserved.* London: Faber & Faber.

Glob, P.V. 1974 *The Mound People: Danish Bronze-Age man preserved.* London: Faber & Faber.

Gnoli, G. and Vernant, J.-P. (eds) 1982 *La Mort, les Morts dans les Sociétés Anciennes.* Paris and Cambridge: Editions de la Maison des Sciences de l'Homme and Cambridge University Press.

Goldstein, L.G. 1976 Spatial structure and social organization: regional manifestations of Mississippian society. PhD thesis, Northwestern University.

Goldstein, L.G. 1980 *Mississippian Mortuary Practices: a case study of two cemeteries in the lower Illinois Valley.* Evanston IL: Scientific Papers 4, Northwestern Archeological Program.

Goldstein, L.G. 1981 One-dimensional archaeology and multidimensional people: spatial organization and mortuary analysis. In R. Chapman, I. Kinnes and K. Randsborg (eds) *The Archaeology of Death.* Cambridge: Cambridge University Press, 53–69.

Goodale, J. 1971 *Tiwi Wives: a study of the women of Melville Island, North Australia.* Seattle: University of Washington Press.

Goodall, J. 1986 *The Chimpanzees of Gombe: patterns of behavior.* Cambridge MA: Belknap Press of Harvard University Press.

Goodall, J. 1989 Gombe: highlights and current research. In P.G. Heltne and L.A. Marquardt (eds) *Understanding Chimpanzees.* Cambridge MA: Harvard University Press.

Goodenough, W.H. 1965 Rethinking 'status' and 'role': toward a general model of the cultural organisation of social relationships. In M. Banton (ed.) *The Relevance of Models for Social Anthropology.* London: Tavistock, 1–24.

Goodman, A.H. 1991 Stress, adaption and enamel developmental defects. In D.J. Ortner and W.G.J. Putschar (eds) *Human Palaeopathology: current synthesis and future options.* Washington DC: Smithsonian Institution Press, 280–7.

Goodman, A.H. and Armelagos, G. 1988 Childhood stress and decreased longevity in a prehistoric population. *American Anthropologist* 90: 936–44.

Goody, J. 1962 *Death, Property and the Ancestors: a study of the mortuary customs of the Lo Dagaa of West Africa.* London: Tavistock.

Goody, J. 1993 *The Culture of Flowers.* Cambridge: Cambridge University Press.

Gordon, L. 1986 What's new in women's history. In T. de Lauretis (ed.) *Feminist Studies: critical studies.* Bloomington: Indiana University Press, 20–30.

Gordon-Grube, K. 1988 Anthropophagy in post-Renaissance Europe: the tradition of medicinal cannibalism. *American Anthropologist* 90: 405–9.

Gorer, G. 1965 *Death, Grief and Mourning in Contemporary Britain*. London: Cresset.

Gosden, C. 1994 *Social Being and Time*. Oxford: Blackwell.

Gould, R.A. 1980 *Living Archaeology*. Cambridge: Cambridge University Press.

Gould, R.A. and Schiffer, M.B. (eds) 1981 *Modern Material Culture: the archaeology of us*. New York: Academic Press.

Grainger, R. 1998 *The Social Symbolism of Grief and Mourning*. London: Jessica Kingsley Publishers.

Grayson, D.K. 1990 Donner Party deaths: a demographic assessment. *Journal of Anthropological Research* 46: 223–42.

Green, A.W. 1975 *The Role of Human Sacrifice in the Ancient Near East*. Missoula: Scholars Press.

Green, C. and Rollo-Smith, S. 1984 The excavation of eighteen round barrows near Shrewton, Wiltshire. *Proceedings of the Prehistoric Society* 50: 255–318.

Green, M.J. 1997 Images in opposition: polarity, ambivalence and liminality in cult representation. *Antiquity* 71: 898–911.

Green, S. 1981 *Prehistorian: a biography of V. Gordon Childe*. Bradford-on-Avon: Moonraker.

Greene Robertson, M. 1983 *The Sculpture of Palenque, I: the Temple of the Inscriptions*. Princeton NJ: Princeton University Press.

Grinsell, L.V. 1961 The breaking of objects as a funerary rite. *Folk-lore* 72: 475–91.

Grün, R., Beaumont, P. and Stringer, C. 1990 ESR dating evidence for early modern humans at Border Cave in South Africa. *Nature* 344: 537–9.

Guthrie Hingston, A. 1989 U.S. implementation of the UNESCO cultural property convention. In P. Mauch Messenger (ed.) *The Ethics of Collecting Cultural Property: whose culture? whose property?* Albuquerque: University of New Mexico Press, 129–47.

Gzowski, P. 1980 *The Sacrament: a true story of survival*. New York: Atheneum.

Habenstein, R.W. and Lamers, W.M. 1955 *History of American Funeral Directing*. Milwaukee: Bulfin Press.

Hagelberg, E. and Clegg, J.B. 1991 Isolation and characterization of DNA from archaeological bone. *Proceedings of the Royal Society of London Series B* 244: 45–50.

Hagelberg, E. and Clegg, J.B. 1993 Genetic polymorphisms in prehistoric Pacific islanders determined by analysis of ancient bone DNA. *Proceedings of the Royal Society of London Series B* 252: 163–70.

Hagelberg, E., Quevedo, S., Turbon, D. and Clegg, J.B. 1994 DNA from ancient Easter Islanders. *Nature* 369: 25–6.

Hald, M. 1980 *Ancient Danish Textiles from Bogs and Burials: a comparative study of costume and Iron Age textiles*. Copenhagen: National Museum of Denmark.

Hall, R.L. 1976 Ghosts, water barriers, corn, and sacred enclosures in the eastern woodlands. *American Antiquity* 41: 360–4.

Halstead, P.J. and O'Shea, J. 1982 A friend in need is a friend indeed: social storage and the origin of social ranking. In A.C. Renfrew and S.J. Shennan (eds) *Ranking, Resources and Exchange: aspects of the archaeology of early societies*. Cambridge: Cambridge University Press, 92–9.

Halstead, P.J. and O'Shea, J. (eds) 1985 *Bad Year Economics: the archaeology of risk and uncertainty*. Cambridge: Cambridge University Press.

Harding, A.F. 1984 Aspects of social evolution in the Bronze Age. In J. Bintliff (ed.) *European Social Evolution: archaeological perspectives*. Bradford: University of Bradford, 135–45.

Härke, H. 1990 Warrior graves? The background of the Anglo-Saxon weapon burial rite. *Past and Present* 126: 22–43.

Härke, H. 1997 The nature of burial data. In C. Kjeld Jensen and K. Høilund Nielsen (eds) *Burial and Society: the chronological and social analysis of archaeological burial data*. Aarhus: Aarhus University Press, 19–28.

Harner, M. 1977 The ecological basis for Aztec sacrifice. *American Ethnologist* 4: 117–35.

Harrington, S.P.M. 1996 Bones and bureaucrats: New York's great cemetery imbroglio. In K.D. Vitelli (ed.) *Archaeological Ethics*. Walnut Creek: Altamira Press, 221–36.

Harrington, S.P.M. 1997 Unearthing Soviet massacres. http://www.archaeology.org/9707/newsbriefs/massacres.html.

Harris, L.J. 1989 From the collector's perspective: the legality of importing pre-Columbian art and artifacts. In P. Mauch Messenger (ed.) *The Ethics of Collecting Cultural Property: whose culture? whose property?* Albuquerque: University of New Mexico Press, 155–75.

Harris, M. 1977 *Cannibals and Kings: the origins of culture*. New York: Random House.

Harris, M. 1986 *Good to Eat*. London: Allen & Unwin.

Harris, O. 1982 The dead and the devils among the Bolivian Laymi. In M. Bloch and J. Parry (eds) *Death and the Regeneration of Life*. Cambridge: Cambridge University Press, 45–73.

Harrold, F. 1980 A comparative analysis of Eurasian Palaeolithic burials. *World Archaeology* 12: 195–210.

Hart, C.W.W. and Pilling, A. 1966 *The Tiwi of North Australia*. New York: Holt, Rinehart & Winston.

Harte, J.D.C. 1994 Law after death, or 'what body is it?' The legal framework for the disposal and remembrance of the dead. In J. Davies (ed.) *Ritual and Remembrance: responses to death in human societies*. Sheffield: Sheffield Academic Press, 200–37.

Hastorf, C.A. 1991 Gender, space, and food in prehistory. In M. Conkey and J. Gero (eds) *Engendering Archaeology*. Oxford: Blackwell, 132–59.

Hastorf, C.A. and Johannessen, S. 1993 Pre-Hispanic political change and the role of maize in the central Andes of Peru. *American Anthropologist* 95: 115–38.

Hawkes, J. 1968 *Dawn of the Gods*. London: Chatto & Windus.

Hayden, B. 1990 Nimrods, piscators, pluckers and planters: the emergence of food production. *Journal of Anthropological Archaeology* 9: 31–69.

Hayden, B. 1993 The cultural capacities of Neanderthals: a review and re-evaluation. *Journal of Human Evolution* 24: 113–46.

Hedeager, L. 1976 Processes towards state formation in Early Iron Age Denmark. In K. Kristiansen and C. Paludan-Müller (eds) *New Directions in Scandinavian Archaeology*. Copenhagen: National Museum of Denmark, 217–23.

Hedeager, L. 1985 Grave finds from the Roman Iron Age. In K. Kristiansen (ed.) *Archaeological Formation Processes: the representativity of archaeological remains from Danish prehistory*. Copenhagen: Nationalmuseets Forlag, 152–74.

Hedeager, L. 1990 *Iron-Age Societies: from tribe to state in northern Europe, 500 BC to AD 700*. Oxford: Blackwell.

Hedeager, L. and Kristiansen, K. 1981 Bendstrup – en fyrstegrav fra aeldre romersk jernalder, dens sociale og historiske miljø. *Kuml*: 81–164.

Hedges, J.W. 1984 *Tomb of the Eagles: a window on Stone Age tribal Britain*. London: John Murray.

Heidegger, M. 1962 *Being and Time*. London: SCM Press.

Helmuth, H. 1973 Cannibalism in palaeoanthropology and ethnology. In A. Montagu (ed.) *Man and Aggression*. New York: Oxford University Press.

Henry, D.O. 1985 Preagricultural sedentism: the Natufian example. In T.D. Price and J.A. Brown (eds) *Prehistoric Hunter-Gatherers: the emergence of cultural complexity*. New York: Academic Press, 365–84.

Henry, D.O. 1989 *From Foraging to Agriculture*. Philadelphia: University of Pennsylvania Press.

Henshall, A.S. 1966 A dagger-grave and other cist burials at Ashgrove, Methilhill, Fife. *Proceedings of the Society of Antiquaries of Scotland* 97: 166–79.

Herscher, E. 1989 International control efforts: are there any good solutions? In P. Mauch Messenger (ed.) *The Ethics of Collecting Cultural Property: whose culture? whose property?* Albuquerque: University of New Mexico Press, 117–28.

Hertz, R. 1907 Contribution à une étude sur la représentation collective de la mort. *Année Sociologique* 10: 48–137.

Hertz, R. 1960 *Death and the Right Hand*. London: Cohen & West.

Heurtebize, G. 1986a *Histoire des Afomarolahy (extrême-sud de Madagascar)*. Paris: CNRS.

Heurtebize, G. 1986b *Quelques aspects de la vie dans l'Androy*. Antananarivo: Musée d'Art et d'Archéologie.

Heurtebize, G. 1997 *Mariage et Deuil dans l'Extrême-Sud de Madagascar*. Paris: Harmattan.

Higham, C. and Bannanurag, R. 1990 The princess and the pots. *New Scientist* 126(1718): 50–4.

Hill, J.D. 1995 *Ritual and Rubbish in the Iron Age of Wessex: a study on the formation of a specific archaeological record*. Oxford: BAR British Series 242.

Hill, J.D. 1996 The identification of ritual deposits of animals. A general perspective from a specific study of 'special animal deposits' from the southern English Iron Age. In S. Anderson and K. Boyle (eds) *Ritual Treatment of Human and Animal Remains*. Proceedings of the First Meeting of the Osteoarchaeological Research Group. Oxford: Oxbow, 17–32.

Hingley, R. 1996 Ancestors and identity in the later prehistory of Atlantic Scotland – the reuse and reinvention of Neolithic monuments and material culture. *World Archaeology* 28: 231–43.

Hirst, S. 1985 *An Anglo-Saxon inhumation cemetery at Sewerby, East Yorkshire*. York: York University.

Historic Scotland 1997 *The Treatment of Human Remains in Archaeology*. Edinburgh: Historic Scotland Operational Policy Paper 5.

Hitchcock, L.A. 1997 Engendering domination: a structural and contextual analysis of Minoan Neopalatial bronze figurines. In J. Moore and E. Scott (eds) *Invisible People and Processes: writing gender and childhood into European archaeology*. Leicester: Leicester University Press, 113–30.

Hodder, I. (ed.) 1982a *Symbolic and Structural Archaeology*. Cambridge: Cambridge University Press.

Hodder, I. 1982b Theoretical archaeology: a reactionary view. In I. Hodder (ed.) *Symbolic and Structural Archaeology*. Cambridge: Cambridge University Press, 1–16.

Hodder, I. 1982c *Symbols in Action: ethnoarchaeological studies of material culture*. Cambridge: Cambridge University Press.

Hodder, I. 1982d *The Present Past: an introduction to anthropology for archaeologists*. London: Batsford.

Hodder, I. 1986 *Reading the Past: current approaches to interpretation in archaeology*. Cambridge: Cambridge University Press.

Hodder, I. 1990 *The Domestication of Europe*. Oxford: Blackwell.

Hodder, I. 1991 Gender representation and social reality. In D. Walde and N.D. Willows (eds) *The Archaeology of Gender: proceedings of the 22nd Annual Chacmool Conference*. Calgary: Archaeological Association of the University of Calgary, 11–16.

Hodder, I. and Orton, C. 1976 *Spatial Analysis in Archaeology*. Cambridge: Cambridge University Press.

Hogg, G. 1958 *Cannibalism and Human Sacrifice*. London: Hale.

Holcomb, S.M.C. and Konigsberg, L.W. 1995 Statistical study of sexual dimorphism in the human fetal sciatic notch. *American Journal of Physical Anthropology* 97: 113–26.

Holgate, R. 1988 *Neolithic Settlement of the Thames Basin*. Oxford: BAR British Series 194.

Horai, S., Kondo, R., Murayama, K., Hayashi, S., Koike, H. and Nakai, N. 1991 Phylogenetic affiliation of ancient and contemporary humans inferred from mitochondrial DNA. *Philosophical Transactions of the Royal Society of London Series B* 333: 407–17.

Hornung, E. 1992 *Idea into Image: essays on Ancient Egyptian thought*. New York: Timken.

Houtman, G. 1990 Human remains and the Vermillion Accord. *Anthropology Today* 6: 23–4.

Hoving, T. 1993 *Making the Mummies Dance: inside the Metropolitan Museum of Art*. New York: Simon & Schuster.

Howell, C.L. 1996 Daring to deal with *huaqueros*. In K.D. Vitelli (ed.) *Archaeological Ethics*. Walnut Creek: Altamira Press, 47–53.

Hubert, H. and Mauss, M. 1964 [1899] *Sacrifice: its nature and function*. London: Cohen & West.

Hubert, J. 1989 A proper place for the dead: a critical review of the 'reburial' issue. In R. Layton (ed.) *Conflict in the Archaeology of Living Traditions*. London: Unwin Hyman, 131–66.

Huggins, P. 1994 Opening lead coffins. *British Archaeological News* 17: 8.

Hughes, D.D. 1991 *Human Sacrifice in Ancient Greece*. London: Routledge.

Hughes, I. 1988 Megaliths: space, time and the landscape. A view from the Clyde. *Scottish Archaeological Review* 5: 41–56.

Hughes, M.A., Jones, D.S. and Connolly, R.C. 1986 Body in the bog but no DNA. *Nature* 323: 208.

Hugh-Jones, C. 1979 *From the Milk River: spatial and temporal processes in Amazonia*. Cambridge: Cambridge University Press.

Humphreys, S.C. and King, H. (eds) 1981 *Mortality and Immortality: the anthropology and archaeology of death*. London: Academic Press.

Hunter, J. In press. The Neolithic settlement at Pool, Sanday. In A. Ritchie (ed.) *Neolithic Orkney and its European Context*. Cambridge: MacDonald Institute.

Hunter, J., Roberts, C. and Martin, A. 1996 *Studies in Crime: an introduction to forensic archaeology*. London: Batsford.

Huntington, R. 1973 Death and the social order: Bara funeral customs (Madagascar). *African Studies* 32: 65–84.

Huntington, R. 1987 *Gender and Social Structure in Madagascar*. Bloomington: Indiana University Press.

Huntington, R. and Metcalf, P. 1979 *Celebrations of Death: the anthropology of mortuary ritual*. Cambridge: Cambridge University Press.

Hurcombe, L. 1995 Our own engendered species. *Antiquity* 69: 87–100.

Huss-Ashmore, R., Goodman, A.H. and Armelagos, G. 1982 Nutritional inference from palaeopathology. *Advances in Archaeological Method and Theory* 5: 395–474.

Hvass, S. 1985 *Hodde: et vestjysk landsbysamfund fra eldre jernalder*. Copenhagen: Universitetsforlaget i København.

Ignatieff, M. 1984 Soviet war memorials. *History Workshop Journal* 17: 157–63.

Illich, I. 1975 *Medical Nemesis: the expropriation of health*. London: Calder & Boyars.

Ingersoll, D.W. and Nickell, J.N. 1987 The most important monument: the Tomb of the Unknown Soldier. In D.W. Ingersoll and G. Bronitsky (eds) *Mirror and Metaphor: material and social constructions of reality*. Lanham MD: University Press of America, 199–223.

Ingold, T. 1986 *The Appropriation of Nature: essays on human ecology and social relations*. Manchester: Manchester University Press.

Ingstad, A.S. 1982 Osebergdronningen – hvem var hun? *Viking* 45: 49–65.

Jackson, C.O. (ed.) 1977 *Passing: the vision of death in America*. Westport: Greenwood.

Jacobs, J. 1990 *The Nagas: society, culture and the colonial encounter*. London: Thames & Hudson.

Jacobs, K. 1995 Returning to Oleni'ostrov: social, economic, and skeletal dimensions of a boreal forest Mesolithic cemetery. *Journal of Anthropological Archaeology* 14: 359–403.

Jacobsen, T. 1976 *The Treasures of Darkness: a history of Mesopotamian religion*. New Haven: Yale University Press.

Janaway, R.C. 1996 The decay of buried human remains and their associated materials. In J.R. Hunter, C. Roberts and A.L. Martin *Studies in Crime: an introduction to forensic archaeology*. London: Batsford, 58–85.

Jenkins, K. 1991 *Re-Thinking History*. London: Routledge.

Jensen, J. 1982 *The Prehistory of Denmark*. London: Methuen.

Joffroy, R. 1954 *La Tombe de Vix (Côte d'Or)*. Paris: Fondation Eugène Piot, Monuments et Mémoires Volume 48 Fascicule 1.

Joffroy, R. 1962 *Le Trésor de Vix: histoire et portée d'une grande découverte*. Paris: Fayard.

Johnson, M. 1996 *The Archaeology of Capitalism*. Oxford: Blackwell.

Johnson, W. 1917. *Byways in British Archaeology*. Cambridge: Cambridge University Press.

Jones, D.G. and Harris, R.J. 1997 Contending for the dead. *Nature* 386: 15–16.

Jones, D.G. and Harris, R.J. 1998 Archaeological human remains: scientific, cultural and ethical considerations. *Current Anthropology* 39: 253–65.

Jones, G. 1968 *A History of the Vikings*. Oxford: Oxford University Press.

Jones, J. 1979 *How to Record Graveyards*. Second edition. London: CBA and Rescue.

Jordan, B. 1999 Row erupts as Khoisan call for return of old bones. *Sunday Times* (South Africa) 17 January 1999.

Jørgensen, E. 1975 Tuernes mysterier. *Skalk* 1: 3–10.

Joubert, D. 1991 Eyewitness to an elephant wake. *National Geographic Magazine* 179: 39–41.

Joyce, C. and Stover, E. 1991 *Witnesses from the Grave*. London: Bloomsbury.

Jupp, P. 1993 Cremation or burial? Contemporary choice in city and village. In D. Clarke (ed.) *The Sociology of Death*. Oxford: Blackwell, 169–97.

Kalish, R. and Reynolds, D. 1976 *Death and Ethnicity: a psychocultural study*. Los Angeles: University of Southern California Press.

Kantorowicz, E. 1957 *The King's Two Bodies*. Princeton: Princeton University Press.

Katzenberg, M.A. 1992 Advances in stable isotope analysis of prehistoric bones. In A.R. Saunders and M.A. Katzenberg (eds) *Skeletal Biology of Past Peoples: research methods*. New York: Wiley-Liss, 109–19.

Kemp, B.J. 1967 The Egyptian 1st Dynasty royal cemetery. *Antiquity* 41: 22–32.

Kendall, T. 1997. *Kerma and the Kingdom of Kush, 2500–1500 BC: the archaeological discovery of an ancient Nubian empire*. Washington DC: National Museum of African Art, Smithsonian Institution.

Kenyon, K.M. 1957 *Digging up Jericho*. London: E. Benn.

Kenyon, K.M. 1981 *Excavations at Jericho. Volume 3: The architecture and stratigraphy of the tell*. London: British School of Archaeology in Jerusalem.

King, T.F. 1978 Don't that beat the band? Nonegalitarian political organization in prehistoric central California. In C.L. Redman, M.J. Berman, E.V. Curtin, W.T. Langhorne Jr, N.M. Versaggi and J.C. Wanser (eds) *Social Archaeology: beyond subsistence and dating*. New York: Academic Press, 225–48.

Kjeld Jensen, C. and Høilund Nielsen, K. (eds) 1997 *Burial and Society: the chronological and social analysis of archaeological burial data*. Aarhus: Aarhus University Press.

Klesert, A.L. and Powell, S. 1993 A perspective on ethics and the reburial controversy. *American Antiquity* 58: 348–54.

Klima, B. 1987a A triple burial from the Upper Palaeolithic of Dolni Vestonice. *Journal of Human Evolution* 16: 831–5.

Klima, B. 1987b Une triple sépulture du Pavlovian à Dolní Věstonice, Tchécoslovaquie. *Anthropologie (Paris)* 91: 329–34.

Knapp, B. and Meskell, L. 1997 Bodies of evidence on prehistoric Cyprus. *Cambridge Archaeological Journal* 7: 183–204.

Knight, V.J. 1986 The institutional organization of Mississippian religion. *American Antiquity* 51: 675–87.

Knight, V.J. 1989 Symbolism of Mississippian mounds. In P.H. Wood, G.A. Waselcov and M.T. Hatley (eds) *Powhatan's Mantle: Indians in the colonial southeast*. Lincoln: University of Nebraska Press, 279–91.

Knight, V.J. and Steponaitis, V.P. 1998 A new history of Moundville. In V.J. Knight and V.P. Steponaitis (eds) *Archaeology of the Moundville Chiefdom*. Washington DC: Smithsonian Institution Press, 1–25.

Knüsel, C. and Ripley, K.M. In press. The *berdache* or man-woman in Anglo-Saxon England and post-Roman Europe. In A. Tyrrell and W. Fraser (eds) *Social Identity in Early Medieval Britain*. Leicester: Leicester University Press.

Koczka, C.S. 1989 The need for enforcing regulations on the international art trade. In P. Mauch Messenger (ed.) *The Ethics of Collecting Cultural Property: whose culture? whose property?* Albuquerque: University of New Mexico Press, 185–98.

Kokkinidou, D. and Nikolaidou, M. 1997 Body imagery in the European Neolithic: ideological implications of anthropomorphic figurines. In J. Moore and E. Scott (eds) *Invisible People and Processes: writing gender and childhood into European archaeology*. Leicester: Leicester University Press, 88–112.

Kopytoff, I. 1971 Ancestors as elders in Africa. *Man* 41: 129–42.

Kristeva, J. 1982 *Powers of Horror: an essay on abjection*. New York: Columbia University Press.

Kristiansen, K. 1984 Ideology and material culture: an archaeological perspective. In M. Spriggs (ed.) *Marxist Perspectives in Archaeology*. Cambridge: Cambridge University Press, 72–100.

Kroeber, A. 1927 Disposal of the dead. *American Anthropologist* 29: 308–15.

Kselman, T.A. 1993 *Death and the Afterlife in Modern France*. Princeton: Princeton University Press.

Kübler-Ross, E. 1975 *Death: the final stage of growth*. Englewood Cliffs NJ: Prentice-Hall.

Küchler, S. 1988 Malangan: objects, sacrifice and the production of memory. *American Ethnologist* 15: 625–37.

Küchler, S. 1993 Landscape as memory: the mapping of process and its representation in a Melanesian society. In B. Bender (ed.) *Landscape: politics and perspectives*. Providence RI: Berg, 85–106.

Kuijt, I. 1996 Negotiating equality through ritual: a consideration of Late Natufian and Prepottery Neolithic 'A' period mortuary practices. *Journal of Anthropological Archaeology* 15: 313–36.

Küng, H. 1992 *Judaism: the religious situation of our time*. London: SCM.

Kus, S. 1992 Toward an archaeology of body and soul. In J.-C. Gardin and C.S. Peebles (eds) *Representations in Archaeology*. Bloomington: Indiana University Press, 168–77.

Lallo, J.W., Armelagos, G.J. and Mensforth, R.P. 1977 The role of diet, disease, and physiology in the origin of porotic hyperstosis. *Human Biology* 49: 471–83.

Langford, R.K. 1983 Our heritage – your playground. *Australian Archaeology* 16: 1–6.

Langlois, R. 1987 Le visage de la Dame de Vix. In *Trésors des Princes Celtes*. Paris: Galeries nationales du Grand Palais, Editions de la Réunion des Musées Nationaux, 212–17.

Larson, C.S. *et al.* 1992 Carbon and nitrogen isotopic signatures of human dietary change in the Georgia Bight. *American Journal of Physical Anthropology* 89: 197–214.

Laurence, D.R. and Bennett, P.N. 1980 *Clinical Pharmacology*. Edinburgh: Churchill Livingstone.

Leach, E. 1958 Magical hair. *Journal of the Royal Anthropological Institute* 88: 147–64.

Leach, E. 1976 *Culture and Communication: the logic by which symbols are connected*. Cambridge: Cambridge University Press.

Leach, E. 1977 A view from the bridge. In M. Spriggs (ed.) *Archaeology and Anthropology: areas of mutual interest*. Oxford: BAR Supplementary Series 19, 161–76.

Leach, E. 1979 Discussion. In B.C. Burnham and J. Kingsbury (eds) *Space, Hierarchy and Society: interdisciplinary studies in social area analysis*. Oxford: BAR Supplementary Series 59, 119–24.

Leach, E. 1982 *Social Anthropology*. London: Fontana.

Leca, A.-P. 1979 *The Cult of the Immortal: mummies and the ancient Egyptian way of death*. London: Souvenir.

Lee, K.A. 1994 Attitudes and prejudices towards infanticide: Carthage, Rome and today. *Archaeological Review from Cambridge* 13: 65–79.

Lee, M. 1998 Interior Department looking at tests for Kennewick Man. www.tri-cityherald.com/bones/041598.html.

Lehmann, A.C. and Myers, J.E. 1997 Ghosts, souls, and ancestors: power of the dead. In A.C. Lehmann and J.E. Myers (eds) *Magic, Witchcraft, and Religion*. Mountain View CA: Mayfield Publishing, 283–6.

Leroi-Gourhan, A. 1975 The flowers found with Shanidar IV, a Neanderthal burial in Iraq. *Science* 190: 562–4.

Leroi-Gourhan, A. 1989 Comments on 'Grave shortcomings: the evidence for Neanderthal burial by R. Gargett'. *Current Anthropology* 30: 183.

Lévi-Strauss, C. 1962 *Totemism*. London: Merlin Press.

Lévi-Strauss, C. 1963 *Structural Anthropology*. Harmondsworth: Peregrine.

Lévi-Strauss, C. 1966 The culinary triangle. *New Society* 166: 937–40.

Levy, J. 1982 *Social and Religious Organization in Bronze Age Denmark: an analysis of ritual hoard finds*. Oxford: BAR International Series 124.

Lewis, G. 1980 *Day of Shining Red: an essay on understanding ritual*. Cambridge: Cambridge University Press.

Lewis, I.M. 1986 *Religion in Context: cults and charisma*. Cambridge: Cambridge University Press.

Li Chi. 1977 *Anyang: a chronicle of the discovery, excavation, and reconstruction of the ancient capital of the Shang dynasty*. Seattle: University of Washington Press.

Lienhardt, R.G. 1961 *Divinity and Experience: the religion of the Dinka*. Oxford: Clarendon Press.

Lilley, J.M., Stroud, G., Brothwell, D.R. and Williamson, M.H. 1994 *The Jewish Burial Ground at Jewbury. The Archaeology of York Volume 12: The Medieval Cemeteries*. London: Council for British Archaeology.

Lillie, M.C. 1997 Women and children in prehistory: resource sharing and social stratification at the Mesolithic-Neolithic transition in Ukraine. In J. Moore and E. Scott (eds) *Invisible People and Processes: writing gender and childhood into European archaeology*. Leicester: Leicester University Press, 213–28.

Lindley, J. and Clark, G. 1990 Symbolism and modern human origins. *Current Anthropology* 31: 233–61.

Litten, J. 1991 *The English Way of Death: the common funeral since 1450*. London: Hale.

Llewellyn, N. 1991 *The Art of Death: visual culture in the English death ritual* c. 1500 – c. 1800. London: Reaktion Books.

Louwe Kooijmans, L.P. 1993 An Early/Middle Bronze Age multiple burial at Wassenaar, the Netherlands. *Analecta Praehistorica Leidensia* 26: 1–20.

Lowenhaupt Tsing, A. 1993 *In the Realm of the Diamond Queen: marginality in an out-of-the-way place*. Princeton: Princeton University Press.

Lubbock, J. 1865 *Prehistoric Times, as Illustrated by Ancient Remains and the Manners and Customs of Modern Savages*. London: Williams & Norgate.

Lucy, S.J. 1994 Children in early medieval cemeteries. *Archaeological Review from Cambridge* 13: 21–34.

Lucy, S.J. 1997 Housewives, warriors and slaves? Sex and gender in Anglo-Saxon burials. In J. Moore and E. Scott (eds) *Invisible People and Processes: writing gender and childhood into European archaeology*. Leicester: Leicester University Press, 150–68.

Lukács, G. 1971 *History and Class Consciousness*. London: Merlin.

Lynch, T. 1997 *The Undertaking: life studies from the dismal trade*. London: Jonathan Cape.

Macaulay, D. 1979 *Motel of the Mysteries*. London: Hutchinson.

McBurney, C.B.M. 1975 Early man in the Soviet Union: the implications of some recent discoveries. *Proceedings of the British Academy* 61: 171–221.

MacClancy, J. 1992 *Consuming Culture*. London: Chapmans.

Maccoby, H. 1982 *The Sacred Executioner: human sacrifice and the legacy of guilt*. London: Thames & Hudson.

MacCormack, C.P. and Strathern, M. (eds) 1980 *Nature, Culture and Gender*. Cambridge: Cambridge University Press.

McCown, T. 1937 Mughâret es-Skhul: description and excavation. In D. Garrod and D. Bate (eds) *The Stone Age of Mount Carmel*. Oxford: Clarendon Press, 91–107.

McGuire, R.H. 1989 The sanctity of the grave: white concepts and American Indian burials. In R. Layton (ed.) *Conflict in the Archaeology of Living Traditions*. London: Unwin Hyman, 167–84.

McIntyre, C. 1990 *Monuments of War*. Hale: London.

Mack, A. (ed.) 1973 *Death in American Experience*. New York: Schocken.

Mack, J. 1986 *Madagascar: island of the ancestors*. London: British Museum.

McKim Malville, J., Wendorf, F., Mazar, A.A. and Schild, R. 1998 Megaliths and Neolithic astronomy in southern Egypt. *Nature* 392: 488–91.

McKinley, J. 1997 Bronze Age 'barrows' and funerary rites and rituals of cremation. *Proceedings of the Prehistoric Society* 63: 129–45.

McKinley, J.I. and Roberts, C. 1993 Excavation and post-excavation treatment of cremated and inhumed human remains. *Institute of Field Archaeologists Technical Paper* no. 13.

McManners, J. 1981 *Death and the Enlightenment: changing attitudes to death among Christians and unbelievers in eighteenth-century France*. Oxford: Oxford University Press.

McNairn, B. 1980 *The Method and Theory of V. Gordon Childe*. Edinburgh: Edinburgh University Press.

Madsen, T. and Jensen, H.J. 1982 Settlement and land use in early Neolithic Denmark. *Analecta Praehistorica Leidensia* 15: 63–86.

Magilton, J.R. 1995 Lindow Man: the Celtic tradition and beyond. In R.C. Turner and R.G. Scaife (eds) *Bog Bodies: new discoveries and new perspectives*. London: British Museum, 183–7.

Malinowski, B. 1929 *The Sexual Life of Savages*. London: Routledge & Kegan Paul.

Malinowski, B. 1948 *Magic, Science and Religion and Other Essays*. Glencoe IL: Free Press.

Mandelbaum, D.G. 1959 Social uses of funerary rites. In H. Feifel (ed.) *The Meaning of Death*. New York: McGraw-Hill, 189–217.

Mann, M. 1986 *The Sources of Social Power. Volume 1: A history of power from the beginning to* AD *1760*. Cambridge: Cambridge University Press.

Martin, L.D., Goodman, A.H. and Armelagos, G.J. 1985 Skeletal pathologies as indicators of quality and quantity of diet. In R.I. Gilbert and J. Mielke (eds) *The Analysis of Prehistoric Diets*. Orlando: Academic Press, 229–74.

Marshack, A. 1991 The Täi plaque and calendrical notation in the Upper Palaeolithic. *Cambridge Archaeological Journal* 1: 25–61.

Maslen, G. 1991 The last Tasmanian. *Times Higher Educational Supplement* 953: 10.

Masset, C. 1993 *Les Dolmens: sociétés néolithiques, pratiques funéraires*. Paris: Editions Errance.

Mauch Messenger, P. (ed.) 1989 *The Ethics of Collecting Cultural Property: whose culture? whose property?* Albuquerque: University of New Mexico Press.

May, F. 1986 *Les Sépultures Préhistoriques: étude critique*. Paris: CNRS.

Mayo, J.M. 1988 War memorials as political memory. *Geographical Review* 78: 62–74.

Mays, S.A. 1985 Relationship between Harris line formation and bone growth and development. *Journal of Archaeological Science* 12: 207–20.

Mays, S.A. 1993 Infanticide in Roman Britain. *Antiquity* 67: 883–8.

Mays, S.A. 1998 *The Archaeology of Human Bones*. London: Routledge.

Meggitt, M.J. 1965 The Mae Enga of the Western Highlands. In P. Lawrence and M.J. Meggitt (eds) *Gods, Ghosts and Men in Melanesia: some religions of Australia, New Guinea and the New Hebrides*. London: Oxford University Press, 105–31.

Meighan, C.W. 1985 Archaeology and anthropological ethics. *Anthropology Newsletter* 26: 20.

Meighan, C.W. 1996 Burying American archaeology. In K.D. Vitelli (ed.) *Archaeological Ethics*. Walnut Creek: Altamira Press, 209–13.

Meigs, A.S. 1984 *Food, Sex, and Pollution: a New Guinea religion*. New Brunswick NJ: Rutgers University Press.

Meigs, A.S. 1990 Multiple gender ideologies and statuses. In P. Reeves Sanday and R. Gallagher Goodenough (eds) *Beyond the Second Sex: new directions in the anthropology of gender*. Philadelphia: University of Pennsylvania Press, 101–12.

Meiklejohn, C., Petersen, E.B. and Alexandersen, V. 1997 Anthropology and archaeology of Mesolithic gender in the western Baltic. In M. Donald and L. Hurcombe (eds) *Gender and Material Culture*. New York: Macmillan.

Melbye, J. and Fairgrieve, S.I. 1994 A massacre and possible cannibalism in the Canadian Arctic: new evidence from the Saunaktuk site (NgTn-1). *Arctic Anthropology* 31: 57–77.

Mellaart, J. 1967 *Çatal Hüyük: a Neolithic town in Anatolia*. London: Thames & Hudson.

Mellaart, J. 1970 *Excavations at Haçilar*. Edinburgh: Edinburgh University Press.

Meskell, L.M. 1994 Dying young: the experience of death at Deir el Medina. *Archaeological Review from Cambridge* 13: 35–45.

Meskell, L.M. 1995 Goddesses, Gimbutas and New Age archaeology. *Antiquity* 69: 74–86.

Meskell, L.M. 1996 The somatization of archaeology: institutions, discourses, corporeality. *Norwegian Archaeological Review* 29: 1–16.

Metcalf, P. 1982 *A Borneo Journey into Death: Berawan eschatology from its rituals*. Philadelphia: University of Pennsylvania Press.

Metcalf, P. and Huntington, R. 1991 *Celebrations of Death: the anthropology of mortuary ritual*. Second edition. Cambridge: Cambridge University Press.

Michals, L. 1981 The exploitation of fauna during the Moundville I phase at Moundville. *Southeastern Archaeological Conference Bulletin* 24.

Middleton, J. 1960 *The Religion of the Lugbara*. London: Oxford University Press.

Middleton, J. 1982 Lugbara death. In M. Bloch and J. Parry (eds) *Death and the Regeneration of Life*. Cambridge: Cambridge University Press, 134–54.

Miller, D. and Tilley, C. (eds) 1984 *Ideology, Power and Prehistory*. Cambridge: Cambridge University Press.

Milner, G.R. 1984 Social and temporal implications of variation among American Bottom Mississippian cemeteries. *American Antiquity* 49: 468–88.

Milner, G.R. 1990 The late prehistoric Cahokia cultural system of the Mississippi River valley: foundations, florescence, and fragmentation. *Journal of World Prehistory* 4: 1–43.

Minthorn, A. 1996 Ancient human remains need to be reburied. www.tri-cityherald.com/bones/1027.html.

Mitford, J. 1965 *The American Way of Death*. London: Hutchinson.

Mithen, S. 1996 *The Prehistory of the Mind: a search for the origins of art, religion and science*. London: Thames & Hudson.

Mizoguchi, K. 1992 A historiography of a linear barrow cemetery: a structurationist's point of view. *Archaeological Review from Cambridge* 11: 39–49.

Møhl, U. 1977 Bjørnekløer og brandgrave. Dyreknogler fra germansk jernalder i Stilling. *Kuml*: 119–30.

Molleson, T. and Cox, M. 1993 *The Spitalfields Project. Volume 2: The anthropology: the middling sort*. York: Council for British Archaeology Research Report 86.

Moore, H.L. 1982 The interpretation of spatial patterning in settlement residues. In I. Hodder (ed.) *Symbolic and Structural Archaeology*. Cambridge: Cambridge University Press, 74–9.

Moore, H.L. 1988 *Feminism and Anthropology*. Cambridge: Polity Press.

Moore, J. 1997 Conclusion: the visibility of the invisible. In J. Moore and E. Scott (eds) *Invisible People and Processes: writing gender and childhood into European archaeology*. Leicester: Leicester University Press, 251–7.

Moore, J. and Scott, E. 1997 Glossary. In J. Moore and E. Scott (eds) *Invisible People and Processes: writing gender and childhood into European archaeology*. Leicester: Leicester University Press, 258–62.

Morell, V. 1998 Kennewick Man: more bones to pick. *Science* 279: 25–6.

Moriarty, C. 1995 The absent dead and figurative First World War memorials. *Transactions of the Ancient Monuments Society* 39: 7–40.

Morley, J. 1971 *Death, Heaven and the Victorians*. London: Studio Vista.

Morris, I. 1991 The archaeology of ancestors: the Saxe/Goldstein hypothesis revisited. *Cambridge Archaeological Journal* 1: 147–69.

Morris, I. 1993 *Death-Ritual and Social Structure in Classical Antiquity*. Cambridge: Cambridge University Press.

Morris, R. 1994 Examine the dead gently. *British Archaeological News* 17: 9.

Moss, C. 1988 *Elephant Memories: thirteen years in the life of an elephant family*. New York: Fawcett Columbine.

Mosse, G.L. 1990 *Fallen Soldiers: reshaping the memory of the World Wars*. New York: Oxford University Press.

Müller-Wille, M. 1983 Royal and aristocratic graves in central and western Europe in the Merovingian period. *Vendel Period Studies*: 109–16.

Munksgaard, E. 1984 Bog bodies – a brief survey of interpretations. *Journal of Danish Archaeology* 3: 120–3.

Murdoch, G.P. 1957 World ethnographic sample. *American Anthropologist* 59: 664–87.

Murphy, J.M. 1998 Ideologies, rites and rituals: a view of Pre-Palatial Minoan tholoi. In K. Branigan (ed.) *Cemetery and Society in the Aegean Bronze Age*. Sheffield: Sheffield Academic Press, 27–40.

Murray Parkes, C. 1972 *Bereavement: studies of grief in adult life*. London: Tavistock.

Murray Parkes, C., Laungani, P. and Young, B. (eds) 1997 *Death and Bereavement Across Cultures*. London: Routledge.

Musée d'Art et d'Archéologie 1989 *Androy*. Antananarivo: Alliance Française/Musée d'Art et d'Archéologie, Université d'Antananarivo.

Myers, F.R. 1986 *Pintupi Country, Pintupi Self: sentiment, place, and politics among Western Desert Aborigines*. Berkeley: University of California Press.

Nadel, D. 1995 The visibility of prehistoric burials in the southern Levant: how rare are the Upper Palaeolithic/Early Epipalaeolithic graves? In S. Campbell and A. Green (eds) *The Archaeology of Death in the Ancient Near East*. Oxford: Oxbow Monograph 51, 1–8.

Needham, S.P. 1988 Selective deposition in the British Early Bronze Age. *World Archaeology* 20: 229–48.

Newell, W.H. (ed.) 1976 *Ancestors*. The Hague: Mouton.

Nigosian, S.A. 1993 *The Zoroastrian Faith: tradition and modern research*. Montreal: McGill-Queen's University Press.

Nordström, H.-Å. 1996 The Nubian A-Group: ranking funerary remains. *Norwegian Archaeological Review* 29: 17–39.

O'Brien, J. and Major, W. 1982 *In the Beginning: creation myths from ancient Mesopotamia, Israel and Greece*. Chico CA: Scholars Press.

O'Hanlon, M. 1989 *Reading the Skin: adornment, display and society among the Wahgi*. London: British Museum.

Okely, J. 1983 *The Traveller-Gypsies*. Cambridge: Cambridge University Press.

Oota, H., Saitou, N., Matsushita, T. and Ueda, S. 1995 A genetic study of 2,000-year-old human remains from Japan using mitochondrial DNA sequences. *American Journal of Physical Anthropology* 98: 133–45.

Orme, B. 1981 *Anthropology for Archaeologists.* London: Duckworth.

Ortiz, A. 1969 *The Tewa World.* Chicago: University of Chicago.

Ortiz de Montellano, B. 1978 Aztec cannibalism: an ecological necessity? *Science* 200: 611–17.

Ortiz de Montellano, B. 1983 Counting skulls: comment on the Aztec cannibalism of Harner and Harris. *American Anthropologist* 85: 403–6.

O'Shea, J. 1981a Social configurations and the archaeological study of mortuary practices: a case study. In R. Chapman, I. Kinnes and K. Randsborg (eds) *The Archaeology of Death.* Cambridge: Cambridge University Press, 39–52.

O'Shea, J. 1981b Coping with scarcity: exchange and social storage. In A. Sheridan and G. Bailey (eds) *Economic Archaeology: towards an integrated approach.* Oxford: BAR International Series 96, 167–83.

O'Shea, J. 1984 *Mortuary Variability: an archaeological investigation.* New York: Academic Press.

O'Shea, J. 1996 *Villagers of the Maros: a portrait of an Early Bronze Age society.* New York: Plenum.

O'Shea, J. and Zvelebil, M. 1984 Oleneostrovski mogilnik: reconstructing the social and economic organization of prehistoric foragers in northern Russia. *Journal of Anthropological Archaeology* 3: 1–40.

O'Sullivan, D. 1982 St Bees man: the discovery of a preserved medieval body in Cumbria. Middelberg: Proceedings of the Palaeopathology Association Fourth European Meeting, 171–7.

Owsley, D.W. *et al.* 1991 Culturally modified human bones from the Edward 1st site. In D.W. Owsley and R.C. Jantz (eds) *Skeletal Biology in the Great Plains: migration, warfare, health and subsistence.* Washington DC: Smithsonian Institution Press.

Pääbo, S. 1985 Preservation of DNA in ancient Egyptian mummies. *Journal of Archaeological Science* 12: 411–17.

Pääbo, S. 1986 Molecular genetic investigations of ancient human remains. *Cold Spring Harbor Symposia on Quantitative Biology* 51: 441–6.

Pääbo, S., Gifford, J.A. and Wilson, A.C. 1988 Mitochondrial DNA sequences from a 7000-year-old brain. *Nucleic Acids Research* 16: 9775–87.

Pääbo, S., Higuchi, R.G. and Wilson, A.C. 1989 Ancient DNA and the polymerase chain reaction. *Journal of Biological Chemistry* 264: 9709–12.

Pader, E.J. 1982 *Symbolism, Social Relations and the Interpretation of Mortuary Remains.* Oxford: BAR Supplementary Series 130.

Palgi, P. and Abramovitch, H. 1984 Death: a cross-cultural perspective. *Annual Review of Anthropology* 13: 385–417.

Pardo, I. 1989 Life, death and ambiguity in the social dynamics of inner Naples. *Man* 24: 103–23.

Paredes, J.A. and Purdum, E.D. 1990 'Bye-bye Ted...': community response in Florida to the execution of Theodore Bundy. *Anthropology Today* 6: 9–11.

Parker Pearson, M. 1982 Mortuary practices, society and ideology: an ethnoarchaeological study. In I. Hodder (ed.) *Symbolic and Structural Archaeology.* Cambridge: Cambridge University Press, 99–113.

Parker Pearson, M. 1984a Social change, ideology and the archaeological record. In M. Spriggs (ed.) *Marxist Perspectives in Archaeology.* Cambridge: Cambridge University Press, 59–71.

Parker Pearson, M. 1984b Economic and ideological change: cyclical growth in the pre-state societies of Jutland. In D. Miller and C. Tilley (eds) *Ideology, Power and Prehistory.* Cambridge: Cambridge University Press, 69–92.

Parker Pearson, M. 1985 Death, society and social change: the Iron Age of southern Jutland 200 BC–600 AD. PhD thesis, University of Cambridge.

Parker Pearson, M. 1986 Lindow Man and the Danish connection. *Anthropology Today* 2: 15–18.

Parker Pearson, M. 1992 Tombs and monumentality in southern Madagascar: preliminary results of the central Androy survey. *Antiquity* 66: 941–8.

Parker Pearson, M. 1993a The powerful dead: relationships between the living and the dead. *Cambridge Archaeological Journal* 3: 203–29.

Parker Pearson, M. 1993b *Bronze Age Britain.* London: Batsford/English Heritage.

Parker Pearson, M. 1995 Ethics and the dead in British archaeology. *The Field Archaeologist* 23: 17–18.

Parker Pearson, M. 1999a Fearing and celebrating the dead in southern Madagascar. In J. Downes and A. Pollard (eds) *The Loved Body's Corruption: archaeological contributions to the study of human mortality.* Glasgow: Cruithne Press, 9–18.

Parker Pearson, M. 1999b Food, sex and death: cosmologies in the British Iron Age with particular reference to East Yorkshire. *Cambridge Archaeological Journal* 9: 43–69.

Parker Pearson, M., Godden, K., Heurtebize, G., Ramilisonina and Retsihisatse 1996 The Androy Project: fourth report. Unpublished manuscript. Universities of Sheffield and Antananarivo.

Parker Pearson, M. and Ramilisonina. 1998 Stonehenge for the ancestors: the stones pass on the message. *Antiquity* 72: 308–26.

Parker Pearson, M., van de Noort, R. and Woolf, A. 1994 Three men and a boat: Sutton Hoo and the Saxon kingdom. *Anglo-Saxon England* 22: 27–50.

Parkin, D. 1992 Ritual as spatial direction and bodily division. In D. de Coppe (ed.) *Understanding Rituals.* London: Routledge, 11–25.

Parry, J. 1982 Sacrificial death and the necrophageous ascetic. In M. Bloch and J. Parry (eds) *Death and the Regeneration of Life.* Cambridge: Cambridge University Press, 74–110.

Parry, J. 1994 *Death in Banaras.* Cambridge: Cambridge University Press.

Parsons, T. 1951 *The Social System.* New York: Free Press.

Partridge, R.B. 1994 *Faces of the Pharaohs: royal mummies and coffins from ancient Thebes*. London: Rubicon Press.

Pate, F.D. 1994 Bone chemistry and palaeodiet. *Journal of Archaeological Method and Theory* 1: 161–209.

Pauketat, T.R. and Emerson, T.E. 1991 The ideology of authority and the power of the pot. *American Antiquity* 93: 919–41.

Pauketat, T.R. and Emerson, T.E. 1997 *Cahokia: domination and ideology in the Mississippian world*. Lincoln: University of Nebraska Press.

Pauli, L. 1972 Untersuchungen zur Späthallstattkultur in Nordwürttemberg: Analyse eines Kleinraumes im Grenzbereich zweiter Kulturen. *Hamburger Beiträge zur Archäologie* 2: 1–166.

Peacock, M. 1896 Executed criminals and folk medicine. *Folk-lore* 7: 268–83.

Peebles, C. 1971 Moundville and surrounding sites: some structural considerations of mortuary practices. II. In J. Brown (ed.) *Approaches to the Social Dimensions of Mortuary Practices*. Washington DC: Memoir of the Society for American Archaeology 25, 68–91.

Peebles, C. 1979 *Excavations at Moundville, 1905–1951*. Ann Arbor: University of Michigan Press.

Peebles, C. 1987 The rise and fall of the Mississippian in western Alabama: the Moundville and Somerville phases, AD 1000 to 1600. *Mississippi Archaeology* 22: 1–31.

Peebles, C. and Kus, S. 1977 Some archaeological correlates of ranked societies. *American Antiquity* 42: 421–48.

Peyrony, D. 1934 La Ferrassie: Moustérien, Périgordien, Aurignacien. *Préhistoire* 3: 1–92.

Phillpott, R.A. 1991 *Burial Practices in Roman Britain: a survey of grave treatment and furnishing AD 43–410*. Oxford: BAR British Series 219.

Physicians for Human Rights 1996a PHR investigates mass graves in Rwanda. gopher.igc.apc.org:5000/00/int/phr/for/2.

Physicians for Human Rights 1996b PHR resumes Vukovar exhumation. gopher.igc.apc.org:5000/00/int/phr/for/yugo/4.

Piggott, S. 1938 The Early Bronze Age in Wessex. *Proceedings of the Prehistoric Society* 4: 52–106.

Piggott, S. 1962 *The West Kennet Long Barrow: excavations 1955–56*. London: HMSO.

Piggott, S. 1979 'Royal tombs' reconsidered. In A. Chmielowska (ed.) *Festschrift Jazdzewski*. Lodz: Muzeum Archeologicznego i Ethnograficznego w Lodzi, Prace i Materialy Seria Archeologiczna 25, 293–301.

Pine, V.R. 1975 *Caretaker of the Dead: the American funeral director*. New York: Wiley.

Pitts, M. and Roberts, M. 1998 *Fairweather Eden: life in Britain half a million years ago as revealed by the excavations at Boxgrove*. London: Arrow.

Polhemus, E. (ed.) 1973 *Social Aspects of the Human Body*. Harmondsworth: Penguin.

Polhemus, E. 1988 *Body Styles*. London: Lennard Books.

Pollock, S. 1991a Of priestesses, princes and poor relations: the dead in the royal cemetery of Ur. *Cambridge Archaeological Journal* 1: 171–89.

Pollock, S. 1991b Women in a men's world: images of Sumerian women. In M.W. Conkey and J.M. Gero (eds) *Engendering Archaeology: women and prehistory*. Oxford: Blackwell, 366–87.

Polosmak, N. 1994 A mummy unearthed from the Pastures of Heaven. *National Geographic* 186 (4): 80–103.

Poole, F.J.P. 1986 The erosion of a sacred landscape: European exploration and cultural ecology among the Bimin-Kuskusmin of Papua New Guinea. In M. Tobias (ed.) *Mountain People*. Norman OK: University of Oklahoma Press, 169–82.

Powell, M.L. 1992 In the best of health? Disease and trauma among the Mississippian elite. In A. Barker and T. Pauketat (eds) *Lords of the Southeast: social inequality and the native elites of southeastern North America*. Washington DC: American Anthropological Association, 81–97.

Powell, S., Garza, C.E. and Hendricks, A. 1993 Ethics and ownership of the past: the reburial and repatriation controversy. *Archaeological Method and Theory* 5: 1–42.

Prentice, G. 1986 An analysis of the symbolism expressed by the Birger figurine. *American Antiquity* 51: 239–66.

Preston Blier, S. 1987 *The Anatomy of Architecture: ontology and metaphor in Batammaliba architectural expression*. Cambridge: Cambridge University Press.

Prior, L. 1989 *The Social Organisation of Death: medical discourse and social practices in Belfast*. London: Macmillan.

Pyatt, F.B., Beaumont, E.H., Buckland, P.C., Lacy, D., Magilton, J.R. and Storey, D.M. 1995 Mobilisation of elements from the bog bodies Lindow II and III, and some observations on body painting. In R.C. Turner and R.G. Scaife (eds) *Bog Bodies: new discoveries and new perspectives*. London: British Museum, 62–73.

Pyatt, F.B., Beaumont, E.H., Lacy, D., Magilton, J.R. and Buckland, P.C. 1991 Non isatis sed vitrum or, the colour of Lindow Man. *Oxford Journal of Archaeology* 10: 61–73.

Radcliffe-Brown, A.R. 1952 *Structure and Function in Primitive Society*. London: Routledge & Kegan Paul.

Radcliffe-Brown, A.R. 1964 [1922] *The Andaman Islanders*. New York: Free Press.

Radimilahy, C. 1994 Sacred sites in Madagascar. In D.L. Carmichael, J. Hubert, B. Reeves and A. Schanche (eds) *Sacred Sites, Sacred Places*. London: Routledge, 82–8.

Radzinsky, E. 1992 *The Last Tsar*. London: Hodder & Stoughton.

Rahtz, P. 1978 Grave orientation. *Archaeological Journal* 135: 1–14.

Rahtz, P. 1981 Artefacts of Christian death. In S.C. Humphreys and H. King. (eds) *Mortality and Immortality: the anthropology and archaeology of death*. London: Academic Press, 117–36.

Rahtz, P. 1985 *Invitation to Archaeology*. Oxford: Blackwell.

Rahtz, P., Dickinson, T. and Watts, L. (eds) 1980 *Anglo-Saxon Cemeteries 1979*. Oxford: BAR British Series 82.

Rahtz, P. and Watts, L. 1983 *Wharram Percy: the memorial stones of the churchyard*. York: Department of Archaeology, University of York.

Rak, Y., Kimbel, W.H. and Hovers, E. 1994 A Neanderthal infant from Amud Cave, Israel. *Journal of Human Evolution* 26: 313–24.

Randsborg, K. 1973 Wealth and social structure as reflected in Bronze Age burials – a quantitative approach. In C. Renfrew (ed.) *The Explanation of Culture Change: models in prehistory*. London: Duckworth, 565–70.

Randsborg, K. 1974 Social stratification in Early Bronze Age Denmark. *Prahistorische Zeitschrift* 49: 38–61.

Randsborg, K. 1980 *The Viking Age in Denmark: the formation of a state*. London: Duckworth.

Randsborg, K. 1984 Women in prehistory: the Danish example. *Acta Archaeologica* 55: 143–54.

Randsborg, K. and Nybo, C. 1984 The coffin and the sun: demography and ideology in Scandinavian prehistory. *Acta Archaeologica* 55: 161–84.

Rawnsley, S. and Reynolds, J. 1977 Undercliffe cemetery, Bradford. *History Workshop Journal* 1: 215–21.

Read, P.P. 1974 *Alive: the story of the Andes survivors*. London: Secker & Warburg.

Reece, R. (ed.) 1977 *Burial in the Roman World*. London: Council for British Archaeology.

Reece, R. 1988 *My Roman Britain*. Cirencester: Cotswold Studies.

Rees Jones, S. 1994 Historical survey. In J.M. Lilley, G. Stroud, D.R. Brothwell, and M.H. Williamson *The Jewish Burial Ground at Jewbury. The Archaeology of York Volume 12: The Medieval Cemeteries*. London: Council for British Archaeology, 301–13.

Reeve, J. 1998 Do we need a policy on the treatment of human remains? *The Archaeologist* 33: 11–12.

Reeve, J. and Adams, M. 1993 *The Spitalfields Project. Volume 1: The archaeology: across the Styx*. York: Council for British Archaeology Research Report 85.

Rega, E. 1997 Age, gender and biological reality in the Early Bronze Age cemetery at Mokrin. In J. Moore and E. Scott (eds) *Invisible People and Processes: writing gender and childhood into European archaeology*. Leicester: Leicester University Press, 229–47.

Reinhard, J. 1996 Peru's ice maidens: unwrapping the secrets. *National Geographic* 189 (6): 62–81.

Renfrew, A.C. 1973a Monuments, mobilization and social organization in Neolithic Wessex. In A.C. Renfrew (ed.) *The Explanation of Culture Change: models in prehistory*. London: Duckworth, 539–58.

Renfrew, A.C. 1973b *Before Civilization: the radiocarbon revolution and prehistoric Europe*. London: Jonathan Cape.

Renfrew, A.C. 1976 Megaliths, territories and populations. In S.J. de Laet (ed.) *Acculturation and Continuity in Atlantic Europe*. Bruges: De Tempel, 198–220.

Renfrew, A.C. 1979 *Investigations in Orkney*. London: Society of Antiquaries.

Renfrew, A.C. 1986 Varna and the emergence of wealth in prehistoric Europe. In A. Appadurai (ed.) *The Social Life of Things: commodities in cultural perspective*. Cambridge: Cambridge University Press, 141–68.

Renfrew, A.C. and Shennan, S.J. (eds) 1982 *Ranking, Resources and Exchange: aspects of the origin of early European society*. Cambridge: Cambridge University Press.

Renfrew, J.M. 1973 *Palaeoethnobotany*. London: Methuen.

Richards, C. 1995 Monumental choreography: architecture and spatial representation. In C. Tilley (ed.) *Interpretive Archaeology*. Oxford: Berg, 143–78.

Richards, C. 1998 Centralising tendencies? A re-examination of social evolution in Late Neolithic Orkney. In M. Edmonds and C. Richards (eds) *Understanding the Neolithic of North-Western Europe*. Glasgow: Cruithne Press, 516–32.

Richards, C. Forthcoming. *Dwelling Among the Monuments: excavations at Barnhouse and Maes Howe*. Cambridge: Macdonald Institute.

Richards, J.D. 1988 Style and symbol: explaining variability in Anglo-Saxon cremation burials. In S.T. Driscoll and M.R. Nieke (eds) *Power and Politics in Early Medieval Britain and Ireland*. Edinburgh: Edinburgh University Press, 145–61.

Richards, M. 1998 Bone stable isotope analysis: reconstructing the diet of humans. In A. Whittle and M. Wysocki, Parc le Breos Cwm transepted long cairn, Gower, West Glamorgan: date, contents, and context. 165–6. *Proceedings of the Prehistoric Society* 64: 139–82.

Richards, M. and van Klinken, G.J. 1997 A survey of European human bone stable carbon and nitrogen isotope values. In A.G.M. Sinclair, E.A. Slater and J.A.J. Gowlett (eds) *Archaeological Sciences 1995*. Oxford: Oxbow, 363–8.

Richardson, L. 1989 The acquisition, storage and handling of Aboriginal skeletal remains in museums: an indigenous perspective. In R. Layton (ed.) *Conflict in the Archaeology of Living Traditions*. London: Unwin Hyman, 185–8.

Richardson, R. 1988 *Death, Dissection and the Destitute*. London: Pelican.

Riding In, J. 1992 Six Pawnee crania: historical and contemporary issues associated with the massacre and decapitation of Pawnee Indians in 1869. *American Indian Culture and Research Journal* 16: 101–19.

Ringgren, H. 1973 *Religions of the Ancient Near East.* London: SPCK.

Rissman, P. 1988 Public displays and private values: a guide to buried wealth in Harappan archaeology. *World Archaeology* 20: 209–28.

Roberts, C., Lee, F. and Bintliff, J. (eds) 1989 *Burial Archaeology: current research, methods and developments.* Oxford: BAR British Series 211.

Roberts, C. and Manchester, K. 1995 *The Archaeology of Disease.* Second edition. Stroud: Sutton.

Robins, D. and Ross, A. 1989 *The Life and Death of a Druid Prince: the story of an archaeological sensation.* London: Rider.

Rodwell, W. and Rodwell, K. 1982 St Peter's Church, Barton-upon-Humber. *Antiquaries Journal* 62: 283–315.

Roesdahl, E. 1982 *Viking Age Denmark.* London: British Museum.

Rolle, R. 1989 *The World of the Scythians.* London: Batsford.

Rolle, R., Müller-Wille, M. and Schietzel, K. (eds) 1991 *Gold der Steppe: Archäologie der Ukraine.* Neumünster: Karl Wachholtz Verlag.

Roper, M. 1969 A survey of the evidence for intrahuman killing in the Pleistocene. *Current Anthropology* 10: 427–59.

Roscoe, J. 1911 *The Baganda: an account of their native customs and beliefs.* London: Macmillan.

Rose, M. and Acar, Ö. 1996 Turkey's war on the illicit antiquities trade. In K.D. Vitelli (ed.) *Archaeological Ethics.* Walnut Creek: Altamira Press, 71–89.

Rosenblatt, P.C. 1959 Uses of ethnography in understanding grief and mourning. In H. Feifel (ed.) *The Meaning of Death.* New York: McGraw-Hill, 41–9.

Ross, A. 1986 Lindow Man and the Celtic tradition. In I.M. Stead, J.B. Bourke and D. Brothwell (eds) *Lindow Man: the body in the bog.* London: British Museum, 162–9.

Rothschild, N. 1979 Mortuary behavior and social organization at Indian Knoll and Dickson Mounds. *American Antiquity* 44: 658–75.

Rowlands, M. 1989 A question of complexity. In D. Miller, M. Rowlands and C. Tilley (eds) *Domination and Resistance.* London: Unwin Hyman, 29–40.

Rowlands, M. 1993 The role of memory in the transmission of culture. *World Archaeology* 25: 141–51.

Rubertone, P.E. 1989 Archaeology, colonialism and seventeenth century Native America – towards an alternative interpretation. In R. Layton (ed.) *Conflict in the Archaeology of Living Traditions.* London: Unwin Hyman, 32–45.

Rubin, G. 1975 The traffic in women: notes on the 'political economy' of sex. In R.R. Reiter (ed.) *Toward an Anthropology of Women.* New York: Monthly Review Press, 157–210.

Rudenko, S.I. 1970 *Frozen Tombs of Siberia: the Pazyryk burials of Iron Age horsemen.* London: Dent.

Ruud, J. 1960 *Taboo: a study of Malagasy customs and beliefs.* Antananarivo: Trano Printy Loterana.

Sack, R.D. 1986 *Human Territoriality: its theory and history.* Cambridge: Cambridge University Press.

Sagan, E. 1974 *Cannibalism: human aggression and cultural form.* New York: Harper & Row.

Sahlins, M.D. 1958 *Social Stratification in Polynesia.* Seattle: University of Washington Press.

Sahlins, M.D. 1961 The segmentary lineage, an organisation of predatory expansion. *American Anthropologist* 63: 322–45.

Sahlins, M.D. 1968 *Tribesmen.* Englewood Cliffs NJ: Prentice Hall.

Sahlins, M.D. 1983 Raw women, cooked men and other 'great things' of the Fiji Islands. In P. Brown and D. Tuzins (eds) *The Ethnography of Cannibalism.* Washington DC: Society for Psychological Anthropology, 72–93.

Sahlins, M.D. and Service, E.R. (eds) 1960 *Evolution and Culture.* Ann Arbor: University of Michigan Press.

Saitta, D.J. 1994 Agency, class, and archaeological interpretation. *Journal of Anthropological Archaeology* 13: 201–27.

Salamon, A and Lengyel, I. 1980 Kinship interrelations in a fifth-century 'Pannonian' cemetery: an archaeological and palaeobiological sketch of the population fragment buried in the Mözs cemetery, Hungary. *World Archaeology* 12: 93–104.

Salmon, M.H. 1997 Ethical considerations in anthropology and archaeology, or relativism and justice for all. *Journal of Anthropological Research* 53: 47–63.

Sampson, D. 1997 Tribal chair questions scientists' motives and credibility. www.unicet.com/"umatribe/kennman2.html.

Sanday, P.R. 1986 *Divine Hunger: cannibalism as a cultural system.* Cambridge: Cambridge University Press.

Sauter, M. 1980 Sur le sexe de la 'Dame de Vix'. *L'Anthropologie* 84: 88–103.

Saxe, A.A. 1970 Social dimensions of mortuary practices. PhD thesis, University of Michigan.

Saxe, A.A. 1971 Social dimensions of mortuary practices in a Mesolithic population from Wadi Halfa, Sudan. In J. Brown (ed.) *Approaches to the Social Dimensions of Mortuary Practices.* Washington DC: Memoir of the Society for American Archaeology 25, 39–57.

Saxe, A.A. and Gall, P.L. 1977 Ecological determinants of mortuary practices: the Temuan of Malaysia. In W. Wood (ed.) *Cultural-Ecological Perspectives on Southeast Asia.* Athens OH: Papers in International Southeast Asia Studies 41, Ohio University, 74–82.

Scarre, C.J. 1984 Kin groups in megalithic burials. *Nature* 311: 512–13.

Schiffer, M.B. 1987 *Formation Processes of the Archaeological Record*. Albuquerque: University of New Mexico Press.

Schneider, J. and Weiner, A. (eds) 1989 *Cloth and Human Experience*. Washington DC: Smithsonian Institution Press.

Schoeninger, M.J. 1979 Diet and status at Chalcatzingo: some empirical and technical aspects of strontium analysis. *American Journal of Physical Anthropology* 51: 295–310.

Schreiber, K. 1996a The lords of Sipán. In P.G. Bahn (ed.) *Tombs, Graves and Mummies: 50 discoveries in world archaeology*. London: Weidenfeld & Nicolson, 118–21.

Schreiber, K. 1996b Inka mountain sacrifices. In P.G. Bahn (ed.) *Tombs, Graves and Mummies: 50 discoveries in world archaeology*. London: Weidenfeld & Nicolson, 160–3.

Schütz, E. 1967 *Collected Papers I*. Edited by M. Natanson. The Hague: Mouton.

Schwarcz, H. and Schoeninger, M.J. 1991 Stable isotope analyses in human nutritional ecology. *Yearbook of Physical Anthropology* 34: 283–321.

Schwartz, J.H. 1995 *Skeleton Keys: an introduction to human skeletal morphology, development, and analysis*. Oxford: Oxford University Press.

Scruggs, J.C. 1985 *To Heal a Nation: The Vietnam Veterans Memorial*. New York: Harper & Row.

Secretan, T. 1995 *Going into Darkness: fantastic coffins from Africa*. London: Thames & Hudson.

Sellevold, B., Lund Hansen, U. and Balslev Jorgensen, J. 1984 *Iron Age Man in Denmark*. Copenhagen: Copenhagen University Press.

Sen, K.M. 1961 *Hinduism*. Harmondsworth: Penguin.

Service, E.R. 1962 *Primitive Social Organization: an evolutionary perspective*. New York: Random House.

Shankman, P. 1969 Le rôti et le bouilli: Lévi-Strauss' theory of cannibalism. *American Anthropologist* 71: 54–69.

Shanks, M. 1993 Style and the design of a perfume jar from an Archaic Greek city state. *Journal of European Archaeology* 1: 77–106.

Shanks, M. and Tilley, C. 1982 Ideology, symbolic power and ritual communication: a reinterpretation of Neolithic mortuary practices. In I. Hodder (ed.) *Symbolic and Structural Archaeology*. Cambridge: Cambridge University Press, 129–54.

Shanks, M. and Tilley, C. 1987 *Re-constructing Archaeology*. Cambridge: Cambridge University Press.

Sharples, N. 1985 Individual and community: the changing role of megaliths in the Orcadian Neolithic. *Proceedings of the Prehistoric Society* 51: 59–74.

Shay, T. 1985 Differentiated treatment of deviancy at death as revealed in anthropological and archeological material. *Journal of Anthropological Archaeology* 4: 221–41.

Shennan, S.E. 1975 The social organisation at Branč. *Antiquity* 49: 279–87.

Shennan, S.J. 1988 *Quantifying Archaeology*. Edinburgh: Edinburgh University Press.

Shennan, S.J. 1993 Settlement and social change in central Europe 3500–1500 BC. *Journal of World Prehistory* 7: 121–61.

Sheridan, A. and Davis, M. 1998 The Welsh 'jet set' in prehistory: a case of keeping up with the Joneses? In A. Gibson and D. Simpson (eds) *Prehistoric Ritual and Religion: essays in honour of Aubrey Burl*. Stroud: Sutton, 148–62.

Sherratt, A. 1981 Plough and pastoralism: aspects of the secondary products revolution. In I. Hodder, G. Isaac and N. Hammond (eds) *Pattern of the Past: essays in honour of David L. Clarke*. Cambridge: Cambridge University Press, 261–305.

Sheskin, A. 1979 *Cryonics: a sociology of death and bereavement*. New York: Irvington.

Shilling, C. 1993 *The Body and Social Theory*. London: Sage.

Shinoda, K.-I. and Kunisada, T. 1994 Analysis of ancient Japanese society through mitochondrial DNA sequencing. *International Journal of Osteoarchaeology* 4: 291–7.

Silk, J.B. 1992 The origins of caregiving behavior. *American Journal of Physical Anthropology* 87: 227–9.

Sillar, W. 1992 The social life of the Andean dead. *Archaeological Review from Cambridge* 11: 107–23.

Sillar, W. 1994 Playing with god: cultural perceptions of children, play and miniatures in the Andes. *Archaeological Review from Cambridge* 13: 47–63.

Sillens, A. and Kavanagh, M. 1982 Strontium and palaeodietary research: a review. *Yearbook of Physical Anthropology* 25: 67–90.

Sillens, A., Sealy, J.C. and van der Merwe, N.J. 1989 Chemistry and palaeodietary research: no more easy answers. *American Antiquity* 54: 504–12.

Silverblatt, I. 1987 *Moon, Sun and Witches: gender ideologies and class in Inca and colonial Peru*. Princeton NJ: Princeton University Press.

Simpson, A.W.B. 1984 *Cannibalism and the Common Law: the story of the tragic last voyage of the Mignonette and the strange legal proceedings to which it gave rise*. Chicago: University of Chicago Press.

Sjögren, K.-G. 1986 Kinship, labour and land in Neolithic southwest Sweden: social aspects of megalithic graves. *Journal of Anthropological Archaeology* 5: 229–65.

Sjøvold, T. 1959 *The Oseberg Find and the Other Viking Ship Finds*. Oslo.

Skinner, M. and Goodman, A.H. 1992 Anthropological uses of developmental defects of enamel. In S.R. Saunders and M.A. Katzenberg (eds) *Skeletal Biology of Past Peoples: research methods*. New York: Wiley-Liss, 153–74.

Slayman, A.L. 1997 A battle over bones. www.archaeology.org/9701/etc/special.html.

Smirnov, Y.A. 1989 Intentional human burial: Middle Palaeolithic (last glaciation) beginnings. *Journal of World Prehistory* 3: 199–233.

Smith, B. (ed.) 1990 *The Mississippian Emergence.* Washington DC: Smithsonian Institution Press.

Smith, I.F. 1965 *Windmill Hill and Avebury: excavations by Alexander Keiller, 1925–1939.* Oxford: Clarendon Press.

Smith, J.Z. 1987 The domestication of sacrifice. In R.G. Hamerton-Kelly (ed.) *Violent Origins: ritual killing and cultural formation.* Stanford: Stanford University Press, 191–205.

Smith, M.A. 1955 The limitations of inference in archaeology. *Archaeological Newsletter* 6: 1–7.

Smith, P. and Kahila, G. 1992 Identification of infanticide in archaeological sites: a case study from the Late Roman–Early Byzantine periods at Askalon, Israel. *Journal of Archaeological Science* 19: 667–75.

Snow, C.C. 1982 Forensic anthropology. *Annual Review of Anthropology* 12: 97–131.

Sofaer Derevenski, J. 1994 Where are the children? Accessing children in the past. *Archaeological Review from Cambridge* 13: 7–20.

Sofaer Derevenski, J. 1997 Engendering children, engendering archaeology. In J. Moore and E. Scott (eds) *Invisible People and Processes: writing gender and childhood into European archaeology.* Leicester: Leicester University Press, 192–202.

Solecki, R.S. 1971 *Shanidar: the first flower people.* New York: Knopf.

Sørensen, M.L.S. 1987 Material order and cultural classification: the role of bronze objects in the transition from Bronze Age to Iron Age in Scandinavia. In I. Hodder (ed.) *The Archaeology of Contextual Meanings.* Cambridge: Cambridge University Press, 90–101.

Sørensen, M.L.S. 1991 Gender construction through appearance. In D. Walde and N.D. Willows (eds) *The Archaeology of Gender: proceedings of the 22nd Annual Chacmool Conference.* Calgary: Archaeological Association of the University of Calgary, 121–9.

Sørensen, M.L.S. 1992 Gender archaeology and Scandinavian Bronze Age studies. *Norwegian Archaeological Review* 25: 31–49.

Spencer, B. and Gillen, F.J. 1899 *The Native Tribes of Central Australia.* London: Macmillan.

Spindler, K. 1983 *Die Frühen Kelten.* Stuttgart: Reclam.

Spindler, K. 1994 *The Man in the Ice.* London: Weidenfeld & Nicolson.

Stalsberg, A. 1991 Women as actors in North European Viking Age trade. In R. Samson (ed.) *Social Approaches to Viking Studies.* Glasgow: Cruithne Press, 75–83.

Stannard, D.W. (ed.) 1974 *Death in America.* Philadelphia: University of Pennsylvania Press.

Stannard, D.W. 1977 *The Puritan Way of Death: a study in religion, culture and social change.* New York: Oxford University Press.

Startin, W. and Bradley, R. 1981 Some notes on work organisation and society in prehistoric Wessex. In C. Ruggles and A. Whittle (eds) *Astronomy and Society in Britain during the Period 4000–1500 BC.* Oxford: BAR British Series 88, 289–96.

Stead, I.M. 1991 *Iron Age Cemeteries in East Yorkshire: excavations at Burton Fleming, Rudston, Garton-on-the-Wolds, and Kirkburn.* London: English Heritage Archaeological Report 22.

Stead, I.M., Bourke, J.B. and Brothwell, D. (eds) 1986 *Lindow Man: the body in the bog.* London: British Museum.

Steadman, L.B. and Merbs, C.F. 1982 Kuru and cannibalism? *American Anthropologist* 84: 611–27.

Steadman, L.B., Palmer, C.T. and Tilley, C.F. 1996 The universality of ancestor worship. *Ethnology* 35: 63–76.

Steponaitis, V.P. 1983 *Ceramics, Chronology, and Community Patterns: an archaeological study at Moundville.* New York: Academic Press.

Steponaitis, V.P. 1986 Prehistoric archaeology in the southeastern United States, 1970–1985. *Annual Review of Anthropology* 15: 363–404.

Steponaitis, V.P. 1991 Contrasting patterns of Mississippian development. In T. Earle (ed.) *Chiefdoms: power, economy, and ideology.* Cambridge: Cambridge University Press, 193–228.

Stiles, D. 1977 Ethnoarchaeology: a discussion of methods and applications. *Man* 12: 87–103.

Stomberg, C. 1998 *R v* Kelly and another. *All England Law Reports* 1998 (3): 741–52.

Stone, A.C., Milner, G.R., Pääbo, S. and Stoneking, M. 1996 Sex determination of ancient human skeletons using DNA. *American Journal of Physical Anthropology* 99: 231–8.

Stone, A.C. and Stoneking, M. 1993 Ancient DNA from a pre-Columbian Amerindian population. *American Journal of Physical Anthropology* 92: 463–71.

Stordeur, D., Helmer, D. and Willcox, G. 1997 Jerf el Ahmar: un nouveau site de l'horizon PPNA sur le moyen Euphrate syrien. *Bulletin de la Société Préhistorique Française* 94: 282–5.

Strathern, A. 1982 Witchcraft, greed, cannibalism and death: some related themes from the New Guinea Highlands. In M. Bloch and J. Parry (eds) *Death and the Regeneration of Life.* Cambridge: Cambridge University Press, 111–31.

Strathern, M. 1972 *Women in Between: female roles in a male world: Mount Hagen, New Guinea.* New York: Seminar Press.

Strathern, M. 1987 Conclusion. In M. Strathern (ed.) *Dealing with Inequality: analysing gender relations in Melanesia and beyond.* Cambridge: Cambridge University Press, 278–300.

Stringer, C. 1990 Comments on 'Symbolism and modern human origins by J. Lindley and G. Clark'. *Current Anthropology* 31: 248–9.

Stringer, C. and Gamble, C. 1993 *In Search of the Neanderthals.* London: Thames & Hudson.

Stroud, G. and Kemp, R.L. 1993 *Cemeteries of St Andrew, Fishergate. The Archaeology of York Volume 12: The Medieval Cemeteries*. London: Council for British Archaeology.

Stuart-Macadam, P.L. 1989 Nutritional deficiency disease: a survey of scurvy, rickets, and iron-deficiency anemia. In M.Y. Iscan and K.A.R. Kennedy (eds) *Reconstruction of Life from the Skeleton*. New York: Liss, 201–22.

Sudnow, D. 1967 *Passing On: the social organization of dying*. Englewood Cliffs NJ: Prentice-Hall.

Sugiyama, S. 1989 Burials dedicated to the old Temple of Quetzalcoatl at Teotihuacán, Mexico. *American Antiquity* 54: 85–106.

Sutton, D.S. 1995 Consuming counterrevolution: the ritual and culture of cannibalism in Wuxuan, Guangxi, China, May to July 1968. *Comparative Studies in Society and History* 37: 136–72.

Sutton Phelps, D. and Burgess, R. 1964 A possible case of cannibalism in the Early Woodland period of eastern Georgia. *American Antiquity* 30: 199–202.

Swanson, G. 1964 *The Birth of the Gods: the origin of primitive beliefs*. Ann Arbor: University of Michigan Press.

Swanton, J.R. 1967 Early accounts of the Natchez. In R.C. Owen, J.J.F. Deetz and A.D. Fisher (eds) *The North American Indians: a sourcebook*. London: Macmillan, 545–54.

Synnott, A. 1993 *The Body Social: symbolism, self and society*. London: Routledge.

Tainter, J.R. 1975 Social inference and mortuary practices: an experiment in numerical classification. *World Archaeology* 7: 1–15.

Tainter, J.R. 1977 Modelling change in prehistoric social systems. In L. Binford (ed.) *For Theory Building in Archaeology*. New York: Academic Press, 327–51.

Tainter, J.R. 1978 Mortuary practices and the study of prehistoric social systems. *Archaeological Method and Theory* 1: 105–41.

Tainter, J.R. 1980 Behavior and status in a Middle Woodland mortuary population from the Illinois valley. *American Antiquity* 45: 308–13.

Tainter, J. 1981 Reply to Braun. *American Antiquity* 46: 416–20.

Talmage, V.A. 1982 The violation of sepulture: is it legal to excavate human remains? *Archaeology* 35: 44–9.

Tannenbaum, N. 1987 Tattoos: invulnerability and power in Shan cosmology. *American Ethnologist* 14: 693–712.

Tarlow, S. 1992 Each slow dusk a drawing-down of blinds. *Archaeological Review from Cambridge* 11: 125–40.

Tarlow, S. 1998 Romancing the stones: the graveyard boom of the later eighteenth century. In M. Cox (ed.) *Grave Concerns: death and burial in England 1700 to 1850*. London: Council for British Archaeology Research Report 113, 33–43.

Tasič, N. (ed.) 1972 *Mokrin, the Early Bronze Age Necropolis. I, Dissertationes et Monographie*. Kikinda: Narodai Museum Volume 12.

Tauber, H. 1979 Kulstof-14 datering af møselig. *Kuml*: 73–8.

Tauber, H. 1981 ^{13}C evidence for dietary habits of prehistoric man in Denmark. *Nature* 292: 332–3.

Taylor, T. 1996 *The Prehistory of Sex: four million years of human sexual culture*. London: Fourth Estate.

Thomas, J. 1988 The social significance of Cotswold-Severn burial practices. *Man* 23: 540–59.

Thomas, L.-V. 1975 *Anthropologie de la Mort*. Paris: Payot.

Thorpe, I.J. 1996 *The Origins of Agriculture in Europe*. London: Routledge.

Thorsen, S. 1980 'Klokkehøj' ved Bøjden. Et sydvestfynsk dyssekammer med velbevaret primaergrav. *Kuml*: 105–46.

Thune C.E. 1989 Death and matrilineal reincorporation on Normanby Island. In F.H. Damon and R. Wagner (eds) *Death Rituals and Life in the Societies of the Kula Ring*. De Kalb: Northern Illinois Press, 153–78.

Tierney, P. 1989 *The Highest Altar: the story of human sacrifice*. New York: Viking.

Tilley, C. 1984 Ideology and the legitimation of power in the Neolithic of southern Sweden. In D. Miller and C. Tilley (eds) *Ideology, Power and Prehistory*. Cambridge: Cambridge University Press.

Tilley, C. 1993 Art, architecture, landscape [Neolithic Sweden]. In B. Bender (ed.) *Landscape: politics and perspectives*. Providence RI: Berg, 49–84.

Tilley, C. 1994 *A Phenomenology of Landscape: places, paths and monuments*. Oxford: Berg.

Tilley, C. (ed.) 1995 *Interpretive Archaeology*. Oxford: Berg.

Tipping, R. 1994 'Ritual' floral tributes in the Scottish Bronze Age – palynological evidence. *Journal of Archaeological Science* 21: 133–9.

Treherne, P. 1995 The warrior's beauty: the masculine body and self-identity in Bronze-Age Europe. *Journal of European Archaeology* 3: 105–44.

Trinkhaus, E. 1983 *The Shanidar Neanderthals*. New York: Academic Press.

Trinkhaus, E. 1985 Cannibalism and burial at Krapina. *Journal of Human Evolution* 14: 203–16.

Trinkhaus, E. and Shipman, P. 1993 *The Neanderthals: changing the image of mankind*. New York: Alfred A. Knopf.

Tuan, Y.F. 1974 *Topophilia: a study of environmental perception, attitudes, and values*. Englewood Cliffs: Prentice-Hall.

Turner, B.S. 1984 *The Body and Society: explorations in social theory*. Oxford: Blackwell.

Turner, B.S. 1988 *Status*. Minneapolis: University of Minnesota Press.

Turner, B.S. 1992 *Regulating Bodies*. London: Routledge.

Turner, C.G. 1993 Cannibalism in Chaco Canyon: the charnel pit excavated in 1926 at Small House Ruin by Frank H.H. Roberts, Jr. *American Journal of Physical Anthropology* 91: 412–39.

Turner, C.G. and Morris, N.T. 1970 A massacre at Hopi. *American Antiquity* 35: 320–31.

Turner, C.G. and Turner, J.A. 1992 The first claim for cannibalism in the Southwest: Walter Hough's 1901 discovery at Canyon Butte Ruin 3, northeastern Arizona. *American Antiquity* 57: 661–82.

Turner, C.G., Turner, J.A. and Green, R.C. 1993 Taphonomic analysis of Anasazi skeletal remains from Largo-Gallina sites in northwestern New Mexico. *Journal of Anthropological Research* 49: 83–110.

Turner, R.C. and Scaife, R.G. (eds) 1995 *Bog Bodies: new discoveries and new perspectives.* London: British Museum.

Turner, V.W. 1969 *The Ritual Process: structure and anti-structure.* London: Routledge & Kegan Paul.

Uchibori, M. 1978 The leaving of this transient world: a study of Iban eschatology and mortuary practices. PhD thesis, Australian National University.

Ucko, P.J. 1969 Ethnography and the archaeological interpretation of funerary remains. *World Archaeology* 1: 262–90.

Vallee, F.G. 1955 Burial and mourning customs in a Hebridean community. *Journal of the Royal Anthropological Institute* 85: 119–30.

Van de Velde, P. 1979a On Bandkeramik social structure: an analysis of pot decoration and hut distributions from the central European Neolithic communities of Elsloo and Hienheim. *Analecta Praehistorica Leidensia* 12: 1–242.

Van de Velde, P. 1979b The social anthropology of a Neolithic cemetery in the Netherlands. *Current Anthropology* 20: 37–58.

Van der Sanden, W.A.B. 1995 Bog bodies on the continent: the developments since 1965, with special reference to the Netherlands. In R.C. Turner and R.G. Scaife (eds) *Bog Bodies: new discoveries and new perspectives.* London: British Museum, 146–65.

Van der Sanden, W.A.B. 1996 *Through Nature to Eternity: the bog bodies of northwest Europe.* Amsterdam: Batavian Lion.

Van Gennep, A. 1960 [1908] *The Rites of Passage.* Chicago: University of Chicago Press.

Vandermeersch, B. 1970 Une sépulture moustérienne avec offrandes découverte dans la grotte de Qafzeh. *Comptes Rendus Hebdomadaires des Séances de l'Académie des Sciences* 270: 298–301.

Vandermeersch, B. 1981 *Les Hommes Fossiles de Qafzeh (Israel).* Paris: CNRS.

Vayda, A.P. 1970 On the nutritional value of cannibalism. *American Anthropologist* 72: 1462–3.

Vernant, J.-P. 1991a Mortals and immortals: the body of the divine. In F.I. Zeitlin (ed.) *Mortals and Immortals: collected essays.* Princeton: Princeton University Press, 27–49.

Vernant, J.-P. 1991b A 'beautiful death' and the disfigured corpse in Homeric epic. In F.I. Zeitlin

(ed.) *Mortals and Immortals: collected essays.* Princeton: Princeton University Press, 50–74.

Villa, P., Bouville, C., Courtin, J., Helmer, D., Mahieu, E., Shipman, P., Belluomini, G. and Branca, M. 1986 Cannibalism in the Neolithic. *Science* 233: 431–6.

Villa, P. and Mahieu, E. 1991 Breakage patterns in human long bones. *Journal of Human Evolution* 21: 27–48.

Vitelli, K.D. (ed.) 1996 *Archaeological Ethics.* Walnut Creek: Altamira.

Vlach, J.M. 1978 *The Afro-American Tradition in Decorative Arts.* Cleveland OH: Cleveland Museum of Arts.

Vogel, J.C. and van der Merwe, N.J. 1977 Isotopic evidence for early maize cultivation in New York State. *American Antiquity* 42: 238–42.

Vogel, J.C. and van der Merwe, N.J. 1978 δC^{13} content of human collagen as a measure of prehistoric diet in Woodland North America. *Nature* 276: 815–16.

Vogelius Andersen, C.H. 1958 Forhistoriske fingeraftryk. *Kuml*: 151–4.

Wahl, J. and König, H.G. 1987 Anthropologisch-traumatologische Unterschung der menschlichen Skelettreste aus dem bandkeramischen Massengrab bei Talheim, Kreis Heilbronn. *Fundberichte aus Baden Württemberg* 12: 65–193.

Wait, G. 1985 *Ritual and Religion in Iron Age Britain.* Oxford: BAR British Series 149.

Walens, S. and Wagner, R. 1971 Pigs, proteins, and people-eaters. *American Anthropologist* 73: 269–70.

Walker, P.L. and DeNiro, M.J. 1986 Stable nitrogen and carbon isotope ratios as indices of prehistoric dietary dependence on marine and terrestrial resources in southern California. *American Journal of Physical Anthropology* 71: 51–61.

Wall, S.M., Musgrave, J.H. and Warren, P.M. 1986 Human bones from a Late Minoan Ib house at Knossos. *Annual of the British School of Archaeology at Athens* 81: 333–88.

Wallis Budge, E.A. 1987 [1893] *The Mummy: a handbook of Egyptian funerary archaeology.* London: Kegan Paul.

Warner, W.L. 1959 *The Living and the Dead: a study of the symbolic life of Americans.* New Haven: Yale University Press.

Warren, K.J. 1989 A philosophical perspective on the ethics and resolution of cultural property issues. In P. Mauch Messenger (ed.) *The Ethics of Collecting Cultural Property: whose culture? whose property?* Albuquerque: University of New Mexico Press, 1–25.

Wason, P.K. 1994 *The Archaeology of Rank.* Cambridge: Cambridge University Press.

Watkins, T. 1990 The origins of house and home? *World Archaeology* 21: 336–46.

Watson, J. and Rawski, E. (eds) 1988 *Death Ritual in Late Imperial and Modern China.* Berkeley: University of California Press.

Webb, S. 1987 Reburying Australian skeletons. *Antiquity* 61: 292–6.

Weber, M. 1958 *The Religion of India*. Glencoe IL: Free Press.

Webster, P. 1975 Matriarchy: a vision of power. In R.R. Reiter (ed.) *Toward an Anthropology of Women*. New York: Monthly Review Press, 141–56.

Weever, J. 1631 *Ancient Funerall Monuments within the United Monarchie of Great Britaine, Ireland, and the Islands adiacent. With the dissolved monastries therein contained*. London.

Weiss, K.M. 1972 On systematic bias in skeletal sexing. *American Journal of Physical Anthropology* 37: 239–50.

Welch, P. 1991 *Moundville's Economy*. Tuscaloosa: University of Alabama Press.

Wells, C. and Green, C. 1973 Sunrise dating of death and burial. *Norfolk Archaeology* 35: 435–42.

Wesler, K.W. 1997 The Wickliffe Mounds Project: implications for Late Mississippi period chronology, settlement, and mortuary patterns in western Kentucky. *Proceedings of the Prehistoric Society* 63: 261–83.

Whaley, J. (ed.) 1981 *Mirrors of Mortality: studies in the social history of death*. London: Europa.

Whelan, M.K. 1991a Gender and historical archaeology: eastern Dakota patterns in the nineteenth century. *Historical Archaeology* 25: 17–32.

Whelan, M.K. 1991b Gender and archaeology: mortuary studies and the search for the origins of gender differentiation. In D. Walde and N.D. Willows (eds) *The Archaeology of Gender: proceedings of the 22nd Annual Chacmool Conference*. Calgary: Archaeological Association of the University of Calgary, 358–65.

Whimster, R. 1981 *Burial Practices in Iron Age Britain*. Oxford: BAR British Series 90.

White, K.D. (ed.) 1991 Archaeology and indigenous peoples: ethical issues and questions. (Special issue.) *Anthropology UCLA* 18: 1–122.

White, R. 1982 Rethinking the Middle/Upper Palaeolithic transition. *Current Anthropology* 23: 169–92.

White, R. 1992 Beyond art: toward an understanding of the origins of material representation in Europe. *Annual Review of Anthropology* 21: 537–64.

White, R. 1993 Technological and social dimensions of 'Aurignacian-age' body ornaments across Europe. In H. Knecht, A. Pike-Tay and R. White (eds) *Before Lascaux: the complex record of the early Upper Palaeolithic*. Boca Raton: CRC Press, 247–99.

White, T.D. 1986 Cut marks on the Bodo cranium: a case of prehistoric defleshing. *American Journal of Physical Anthropology* 69: 503–9.

White, T.D. 1992 *Prehistoric Cannibalism at Mancos 5MTUMR-2346*. Princeton: Princeton University Press.

White, T.D. and Toth, N. 1991 The question of ritual cannibalism at Grotta Guattari. *Current Anthropology* 32: 118–38.

Whitehead, H. 1981 The bars and the burden strap: a new look at institutionalized homosexuality in native North America. In S. Ortner and H. Whitehead (eds) *Sexual Meanings: the cultural construction of gender and sexuality*. Cambridge: Cambridge University Press, 80–115.

Whittell, G. 1998 Tell-tale protein exposes truth about cannibals. *The Times* 28 November 1998.

Whittle, A. 1996 *Europe in the Neolithic: the creation of new worlds*. Cambridge: Cambridge University Press.

Whittle, A. 1997 *Sacred Mound Holy Rings: Silbury Hill and the West Kennet palisade enclosures: a Later Neolithic complex in north Wiltshire*. Oxford: Oxbow Monograph 74.

Williams, W. 1986 *The Spirit and the Flesh: sexual diversity in American Indian culture*. Boston: Beacon Press.

Willsher, B. 1995a *How to Record Scottish Graveyards: a companion to understanding Scottish graveyards*. Edinburgh: CBA Scotland.

Willsher, B. 1995b *Understanding Scottish Graveyards*. Edinburgh: Cannongate.

Wilson, B. 1996 Aspects of the literature on the theory and identification of ritual. In S. Anderson and Boyle, K. (eds) *Ritual Treatment of Human and Animal Remains*. Proceedings of the First Meeting of the Osteoarchaeological Research Group. Oxford: Oxbow, 11–15.

Wilson, C.E. 1981 Burials within settlements in southern Britain during the pre-Roman Iron Age. *Bulletin of the University of London Institute of Archaeology* 18: 127–69.

Wilson, E. 1985 *Adorned in Dreams: fashion and modernity*. London: Virago.

Wilson, P. 1989 *The Domestication of the Human Species*. New Haven: Yale University Press.

Winters, H. 1968 Value systems and trade cycles of the Late Archaic in the Midwest. In L.R. Binford and S.R. Binford (eds) *New Perspectives in Archeology*. Chicago: Aldine, 175–221.

Wood, J.W., Milner, G.R., Harpending, H.C. and Weiss, K.M. 1992 The osteological paradox. Problems of inferring prehistoric health from skeletal samples. *Current Anthropology* 33: 343–70.

Woolley, L. 1934 *Ur Excavations. Volume 2: The royal cemetery*. London: British Museum.

Wright, G.A. 1978 Social differentiation in the early Natufian. In C.L. Redman, M.J. Berman, E.V. Curtin, W.T. Langhorne Jr, N.H. Versaggi and J.C. Wanser (eds) *Social Archaeology: beyond subsistence and dating*. New York: Academic Press, 201–24.

Wright, G.R.H. 1988 The severed head in earliest Neolithic time. *Journal of Prehistoric Religion* 2: 51–6.

Wright, R. 1995 The Sydney Papers Volume 7 Number 3 – Mass graves in the Ukraine. www.soton.ac.uk:80/ ~jb3/war/war.html.

Wylie, A. 1985 The reaction against analogy. *Advances in Archaeological Method and Theory* 8: 63–111.

Wylie, A. 1988 'Simple' analogy and the role of relevance assumptions: implications of archaeological practice. *International Studies in the Philosophy of Science* 2: 134–50.

Wylie, A. 1989 Archaeological cables and tacking: the implications of practice for Bernstein's 'options beyond objectivism and relativism'. *Philosophy of the Social Sciences* 19: 1–18.

Wylie, A. 1991 Feminist critiques and archaeological challenges. In D. Walde and N.D. Willows (eds) *The Archaeology of Gender: proceedings of the 22nd Annual Chacmool Conference*. Calgary: Archaeological Association of the University of Calgary, 17–23.

Yates, T. 1993 Frameworks for an archaeology of the body. In C. Tilley (ed.) *Interpretative Archaeology*. Oxford: Berg, 31–72.

Yates, T. and Nordbladh, J. 1990 This perfect body, this virgin text: between sex and gender in archaeology. In I. Bapty and T. Yates (eds) *Archaeology after Structuralism*. London: Routledge, 222–37.

Yellen, J. 1977 *Archaeological Approaches to the Present*. New York: Academic Press.

Yoffee, N. 1993 Too many chiefs? (or safe texts for the 90s). In N. Yoffee and A. Sherratt (eds) *Archaeological Theory: who sets the agenda?* Cambridge: Cambridge University Press, 53–9.

Yoffee, N. and Sherratt A. (eds) 1993 *Archaeological Theory: who sets the agenda?* Cambridge: Cambridge University Press.

Zaehner, R.C. 1966 *Hinduism*. Second edition. Oxford: Oxford University Press.

Zavitukhina, M.P. and Barkova, L.L. 1978 *Frozen Tombs: the culture and art of the ancient tribes of Siberia*. London: British Museum.

Zhang, Z.-P. 1985 The social structure reflected in the Yuanjunmiao cemetery. *Journal of Anthropological Archaeology* 4: 19–33.

Zimmerman, L.J. 1989 Made radical by my own: an archaeologist learns to accept reburial. In R. Layton (ed.) *Conflict in the Archaeology of Living Traditions*. London: Unwin Hyman, 60–7.

Zimmerman, L.J. 1992 Archaeology, reburial, and the tactics of a discipline's self-delusion. *American Indian Culture and Research Journal* 16: 37–56.

Zimmerman, L.J. 1996 Sharing control of the past. In K.D. Vitelli (ed.) *Archaeological Ethics*. Walnut Creek: Altamira Press, 214–20.

INDEX